INTEGRATING HEALTH PROMOTION AND MENTAL HEALTH

INTEGRATING HEALTH PROMOTION AND MENTAL HEALTH

AN INTRODUCTION TO POLICIES, PRINCIPLES, AND PRACTICES

VIKKI L. VANDIVER

OXFORD
UNIVERSITY PRESS
2009

OXFORD
UNIVERSITY PRESS

Oxford University Press, Inc., publishes works that further
Oxford University's objective of excellence
in research, scholarship, and education.

Oxford New York
Auckland Cape Town Dar es Salaam Hong Kong Karachi
Kuala Lumpur Madrid Melbourne Mexico City Nairobi
New Delhi Shanghai Taipei Toronto

With offices in
Argentina Austria Brazil Chile Czech Republic France Greece
Guatemala Hungary Italy Japan Poland Portugal Singapore
South Korea Switzerland Thailand Turkey Ukraine Vietnam

Published by Oxford University Press, Inc.
198 Madison Avenue, New York, New York 10016
www.oup.com

Oxford is a registered trademark of Oxford University Press

Library of Congress Cataloging-in-Publication Data
Vandiver, Vikki, 1956-
Integrating health promotion and mental health : an introduction to policies,
principles, and practices / Vikki Vandiver.
p. ; cm.
Includes bibliographical references and index.
ISBN 978-0-19-516772-6
1. Mental health services. 2. Health policy.
3. Health promotion. I. Title.
[DNLM: 1. Mental Health Services. 2. Health Policy. 3. Health Promotion.
WM 30 I604 2009]
RA790.V343 2009
362.1—dc22
2008018025

9 8 7 6 5 4 3 2 1
Printed in the United States of America
on acid-free paper

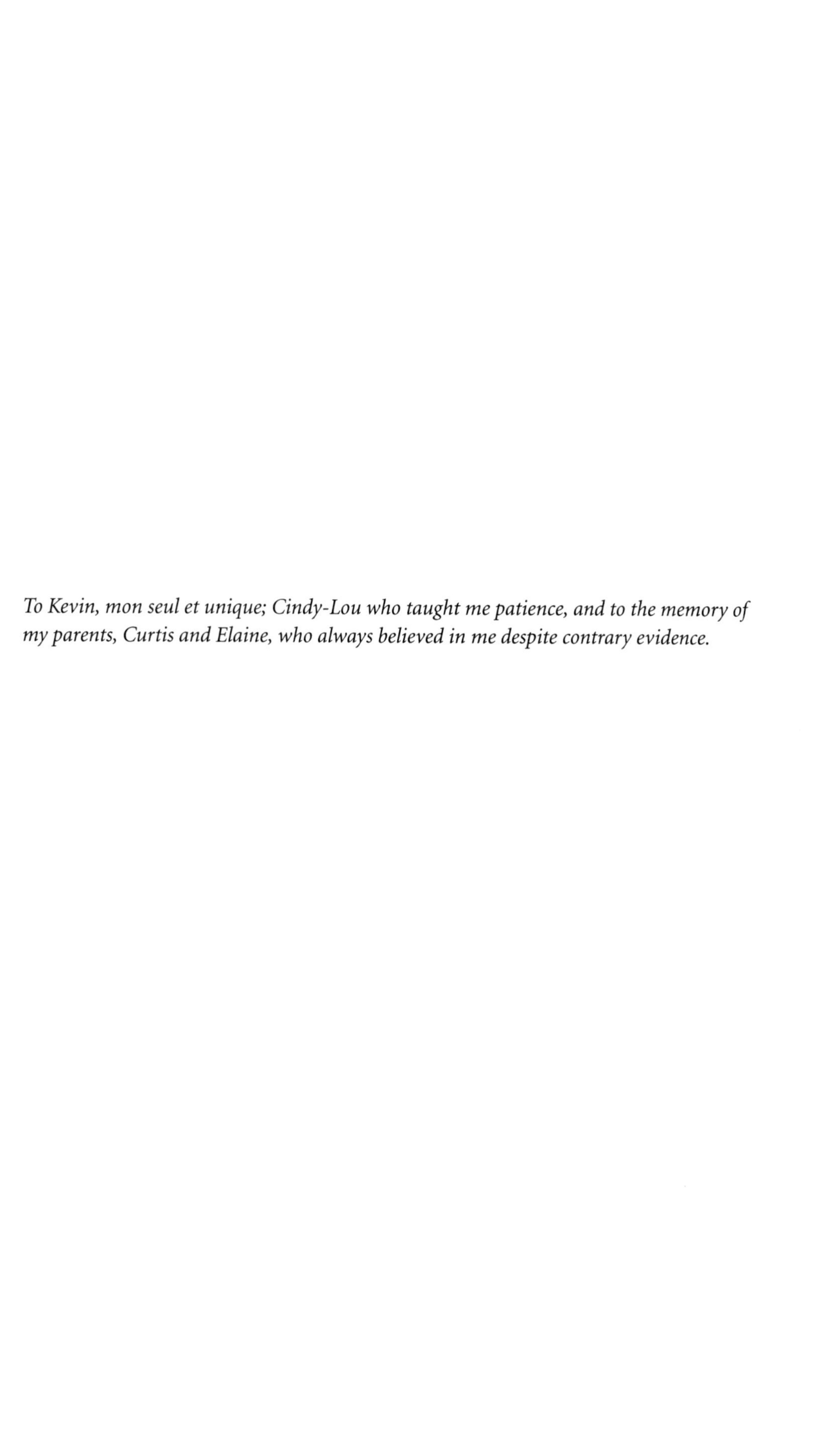

To Kevin, mon seul et unique; Cindy-Lou who taught me patience, and to the memory of my parents, Curtis and Elaine, who always believed in me despite contrary evidence.

Contents

Preface

We just want what everyone else wants ... we want to pursue our wellness as much as you do. We are more than our illness and want to be recognized for who we are. We just need extra help.

—*JVS, consumer from NAMI focus group*

If you have ever been asked by a client, family member, student, or policy maker, if there is more to treatment for mental illness than just symptom reduction, this book is for you. This question first emerges from the idea that the pursuit of health is a common, human goal, intrinsic to all individuals in all societies. This is not a new phenomenon. However, there are certain groups who suffer greatly from the dual challenge of physical illness and mental health conditions. In their case, health has been less of a goal and more of a byproduct following treatment for distressing symptoms. Up to this point, most health and mental health practice operated under the assumption that patient health is achieved primarily through the treatment of a specific illness and the elimination of symptoms. Minimal thought was given to notions of client and family wellness, choice, recovery, empowerment and quality of life—all concepts that are known to influence health status. However, there is a paradigm shift occurring in the field of mental health policy and practice, actually in all of health practice. This shift is toward a more integrative approach to mental health care in which health and wellness are increasingly considered a desirable core clinical goal, community outcome and policy strategy. This approach has a name and it is called *Health Promotion.* While health promotion is not a new concept, the idea of formally pairing it with mental health treatment is. The primary goal of this book is to illustrate how the field of health promotion can be mainstreamed into all aspects of community mental health care, including policy, practice, research, evaluation, and organizational structure. It contains an array of clinical cases, historical analyses, assessment models, evidence-based interventions and evaluation tools, and strategies for administrative and policy reform.

The purpose of this book is to help practitioners, students, administrators and policy makers from a variety of disciplines—public health, social work, nursing, health psychology, public psychiatry, psychiatric rehabilitation, health care administration, and health policy—work effectively with and on behalf of individuals who present with co-occurring health and mental health conditions, their families, and community and policy makers. Effective practice, in this sense, means integrating health promotion into mental health practice at three levels: policy, clinical and community level.

At its broadest level, the integration of health promotion and mental health can be seen in policy reports which include the *New Freedom Commission Report on Mental Health- Achieving the Promise: Transforming Mental Health Care in America* (2003) www.mentalhealthcommission.gov and its companion report; *The Federal Health Action Agenda* (2005) www.samhsa.gov. and in lead articles in respected journals like *Psychiatric Rehabilitation*—Special Issues: *Health Promotion* (Spring, 2006, Vol.29, 4).

David Satcher, former Surgeon General for the U.S. Public Health Service, boldly challenged "mental health systems to flow in the mainstream of health." (Preface, 1999; U.S. Department of Health and Human Services) and to "confront the attitudes, fear and misunderstanding that remain as barriers." In the seminal document entitled *Mental Health: A Report of the Surgeon General* (1999; U.S. Department of Health and Human Services), he asserts that we know more about treatment for mental illness than we know how to promote mental health. He calls for societal resolve to address issues of stigma and hopelessness and to promote opportunities for recovery. As we fast forward nearly a decade later, another Surgeon General's report (i.e., Richard Carmona) echoes this same call with a report entitled *A Call to Action to Improve the Health and Wellness of Persons with Disabilities.* (http://www.surgeongeneral.gov// library/disabilities).

At the clinical and community level, health promotion recognizes and incorporates cross-cutting linkages among members of various populations and community groups. Israel and colleagues (1994) point out that health promotion has a uniquely empowering orientation that enables individuals with mental health conditions and communities to increase their control and choice about decisions affecting personal and societal wellness. All three of these levels of health promotion strategies parallel recent initiatives among mental health consumer and family groups who, in their own right, have taken up the call for mental health reform, part of which looks at what health and wellness means to individuals, families and communities and working forward from that understanding.

In support of this paradigm shift, this book has several unique features: person-first language, focus group material, and extensive figures and tables.

Person-first language. When referring to individuals with mental health conditions, the language used in this book adheres as closely as possible to the use of person-centered language, or person-first, as endorsed by the psychiatric rehabilitation and disability literature (www.iapsrs.org). This means that the reader will see the following terms used interchangeably: consumer, client, patient, individual. With a mental health condition or person with a diagnosis of schizophrenia. The choice of term is determined more by the context of the discussion rather than any allegiance to a particular label or politically correct term. Similarly, when referring to mental health workers, the following terms will be used interchangeably: provider, prescriber, clinician, case manager, and staff.

Focus group material. Each chapter begins with a quote derived from either a mental health consumer or a family member who participated in focus groups specifically designed to provide input for this book. Similarly, at the end of each chapter, the reader will find a summary of qualitative data taken from these focus groups. Information is presented both in direct quotes and in categorical themes and subsequently ranked in priority as determined by the participants. Questions were matched with the topic of each chapter of this book and were solicited for the purpose of helping guide content development. Interpretation of this information on the part of the author is kept to a minimum. Instead the reader is encouraged to draw his or her own conclusions.

The focus group section at the end of each chapter represents the end result of a research project sponsored by the Multnomah County National Alliance of Mentally Ill—Portland chapter and Portland State University—School of Social Work. Informed consent was obtained for all participants; the project was reviewed and received approval through the Institutional Review Board (IRB). The idea for consumer and family input for this book emerged from the recognition that these groups are seeking more participation and say-so in the design and delivery of mental health treatment services. Today, more than ever before, mental health clients and their families are better informed of their political, civil and clinical rights, medical options and effective treatment interventions. One of the goals of this portion of the book was to increase public and mental health provider awareness of the issues and concerns from the perspective of consumers and family members, thus the title for each section: "In Our Own Words . . ."

Figures and tables. The reader is encouraged to refer to the many figures and tables provided in each chapter. These are designed to provide a heuristic overview of the organization and concepts described in each chapter. Although some chapters are free standing (e.g., Chapter 9, Health Promotion Strategies for Women with Co-Morbid Health and Mental Health Conditions), others are designed to link with the previous chapter in terms of conceptual and descriptive content. For example, Chapter 5 (Principles, Policies and Programs) introduces the reader to key health promotion principles which are, in turn, used in subsequent chapters. The idea is that health promotion should be a seamless concept that can be cross-listed across multiple domains and woven into all aspects of mental health work—and the task of each chapter is to visually illustrate these ideas and concepts.

■ Structure and Content

This book reflects the belief that health promotion is a philosophy, practice and an approach that is compatible with all aspects of community mental health care, which includes treatment, administration, and policy development. The following section describes the structure and content of each section and chapter. The book is divided into five parts: Part I, *Fundamental Concepts;* Part II, *Theory, Principles and Policies;*

Part III, *Integration and Application;* Part IV, *Special Populations;* and Part V, *Organizational Leadership, Readiness and Cultural Competence.* One structural point worth noting is that readers will notice that most chapters have a section on principles. Depending on the topic or the design of each chapter, principles are used throughout this book as a way to provide a conceptual anchor to the methods and strategies of the approaches described. It is this author's belief that any approach that makes a human connection be driven and shaped by principle rather than personal ideology.

Part I—Fundamental Concepts. This section provides the groundwork for understanding why mental health reform is necessary and provides a review of the concept of health promotion and need for evidence based research for health promotion practice.

- Chapter 1—*Pursuing Wellness through Mental Health System Reform* explores the need for mental health system reform based on the viewpoints of five stakeholder groups (e.g., mental health consumers and family members, mental health clinicians, administrators and policy makers). The chapter concludes with strategies for mental health reform using health promotion strategies.
- Chapter 2—*Health Promotion* provides an in-depth discussion of the field of health promotion including various definitions of health promotion, differences between prevention and health promotion, early principles, contemporary approaches, objectives, funding, limitations, and critical issues for implementing health promotion; lest we not get too discouraged, a final section is added on why things will get better.
- Chapter 3—*Evidence-based Mental Health for Health Promotion Practice* is an overview of the concepts of evidence-based practice (ebp) beginning with an discussion on the various definitions of "evidence" with examples ranging from evidence-based medicine to general definitions that describe ebp as process to integrative; two core principles of ebp and related strategies are discussed; namely assessment driven intervention and right to informed and effective treatment. An extensive aspect of the chapter is devoted to describing various models and methods that undergird ebp, including systematic reviews, randomized controlled trials, practice guidelines, resources. A final review is given to the role that state and national policies play in enforcing ebp; strengths and limitations for health promotion are discussed with a concluding section on the challenges of ebp and health promotion.

Part II—Theory, Principles and Policies. This section provides an in-depth analysis of health promotion from the perspective of linking mental health theories to health promotion practice, reviewing core health promotion principles and their influence on mental health policies and programs.

- Chapter 4—*Health Promotion and Theories for Mental Health Practice* examines the role of mental health theory and how to select the appropriate theory for health promotion practice; theory and conceptual framework are defined using three examples: conceptual (e.g., recovery model), perspectives (e.g., strengths) and explanatory theory (e.g., stages of change). A lengthy discussion is given to various change theories (individual—health beliefs model to community—community empowerment theory) and their relationship to health promotion practice

- Chapter 5—*Connecting Health Promotion Principles to Mental Health Policies and Programs* is the chapter with the most extensive review of health promotion principles and their relationship to shaping mental health policies and programs. At the beginning of the chapter, principles are linked to policy formation which is followed by a review of nine health promotion principles and a history of public mental health and health promotion policies for the last fifty years. The final section provides the reader with five strategies for integrating health promotion principles into mental health policies and concludes with ideas for conducting health promotion policy advocacy.

Part III—Integration and Application. This section emphasizes various methods for pursuing wellness. Using practical terms, the chapters describe the linkage of assessment to intervention to evaluation using health promotion strategies with mental health interventions—all of which are guided by core health promotion principles, particularly the concept of empowerment.

- Chapter 6—*Using Health Promotion Principles to Guide Clinical and Community Based Mental Health Assessment* picks up on the principles described in Chapter 5 and links them to the assessment process. This chapter begins with an overview of assessment—what it is, how it is defined, what makes for an evidence-based assessment, and what are the different kinds of assessments—from individual to community oriented assessments. A more detailed discussion is provided on the rationale for using health promotion principles, such as multiple methods and feedback for selecting assessment models; six health promotion principles, are described and illustrated with corresponding assessment models, including goal assessment using stages of change, health beliefs model, and others.
- Chapter 7—*Integrating Health Promotion Strategies into Traditional Mental Health Interventions* describes the application of evidence-based interventions at three levels—intrapersonal, interpersonal and intergroup; these interventions reflect commonly recognized evidence-based mental health interventions such as illness management and recovery and family psychoeducation. These standard evidence-based mental health interventions are paired with corresponding health promotion strategies (e.g., like Wellness Recovery Action Plan and Coaching) under the umbrellas of an empowerment based philosophy.
- Chapter 8—*Evaluating and Measuring Health Promotion Strategies for Mental Health Interventions* overviews standard evaluation procedures necessary for evaluating health promotion efforts. Beginning with a review of evaluation approaches (e.g., from qualitative to experimental designs), the reader is guided through a series of topics on measurement and design issues (e.g., snap shot

measurement), challenges of health promotion measurement (e.g., from multiple [mis]understandings to multiple perspectives), measures for health promotion strategies (e.g., adherence determinants questionnaire to empowerment evaluation), using examples carried over from chapter 7 and concluding with examples of recommendations for evaluation (e.g., culturally competent evaluation).

Part IV—Special Populations. Even within mental health populations, there are co-populations that seem to warrant even closer attention due to the complexity of health and mental health conditions or issues associated with developmental stage. This section reviews two such population groups: women with co-existing medical and mental health conditions and children diagnosed with a combination of health and mental health conditions and their family members.

- Chapter 9—*Health Promotion Strategies for Women with Co-Morbid Health and Mental Health Conditions* begins with an overview of the terms morbidity and co-morbidity followed by discussion of four health related concerns: psychosocial/personal history, medication induced weight gain, pregnancy, and substance use. A final section identifies health promotion strategies for these conditions which range from health and family planning classes to fitness programs and concludes with barriers and recommendations for integrating health promotion strategies into mental health services.
- Chapter 10—*Health Promotion Strategies for Mental Health Needs of Children and Families* explores key clinical and diagnostic categories associated with children who have mental health and health needs. These categories range from anxiety disorders due to a general medical condition to health related disorders such as anorexia nervosa. The chapter provides a review of ecological systems theory, multiple assessment measures for client and family functioning, and concludes with five evidence-based health promotion strategies (e.g., medical family therapy, educational self-management, psychoeducation, family therapy, and community visitation program) for use with family, children, and community.

Part V—Organizational Leadership, Readiness and Cultural Competence. Our final chapter ends where the first chapter began, by examining the role of administrators as stakeholders and the important role they play in setting the stage for mental health reform using health promotion strategies. In this final chapter, mental health administrators are identified as key stakeholders who can make or break the successful mainstreaming, or integration, of health promotion into community mental health organizations. The success of any new community mental health service initiative, like health promotion, is as much dependent on the leadership, their level of cultural competence and organizational readiness as it is workforce preparedness. In this respect, this chapter is dedicated to all the current students, administrators and future leaders in the field of health promotion and mental health who wish to make a difference in the lives of their clients, families, and communities, by creating health enhancing policies and organizations—may your own health and wellness be promoted by your bold efforts.

- Chapter 11—*Moving Health Promotion Forward: Culturally Competent Leadership, Strategic Planning and Organizational Readiness* is our final chapter and concludes with a review of mental health and health promotion from the time frame of yesterday, today, and tomorrow. Extensive discussion is given to the role of culturally competent leadership, vision, strategic planning, action plans, and reasons for organizations to move forward (or not). Borrowing from the clinical world of motivational readiness, a final challenge is issued to leaders regarding their organizations readiness to change to a health promotion model of care.

Acknowledgments

True to the spirit of health promotion, my own level of health was greatly promoted by the following life support teams: my husband, Kevin, whose steady support, endless humor and gourmet cooking ensured the completion of this book and my sanity; Al Roberts (Rutgers University), mentor supreme, who believed in my ideas before I even knew I had any, and the amazing editorial team of Oxford University Press, Joan Bossert, Maura Roessner, Mallory Jensen, and Helen Mules, whose patience, professionalism, and long-term commitment to their authors rank as the most pleasant publishing experience ever known. Special thanks go to the hardworking reviewers, whose suggestions were precise, detailed, and enormously helpful. Other stellar supports include the following graduate students who helped with interviews, cases, and library searches: Kathy Jesenik, Theresa Vasolli, Robert Colpean, Sarah White, and Kathy Spofford. Special thanks to Ginny Gay and Lesly Verduin for preparing tables, figures, and references, and John Holmes, Executive Director, National Alliance for Mental Illness/Multnomah County, for his support in helping coordinate consumer and family member focus groups. Heartfelt appreciation goes to my horse-women friends, Crystal, Karen, Terre, Rebecca, Leah, Claudia, Emily, and Kirsten, who continually reminded me that good writing always followed good riding . . . and they were right. Finally, this book is a tribute to the many clients and family members I have known over the last thirty years. In particular, appreciation is extended to the consumers and family members who participated in the focus groups. In addition to providing suggestions for the content of this book, their experiences, wisdom, and stories allowed me to understand the power of relationships, dignity, and resilience, and what promoting health is really about. For without them, this book would never have happened. This book is dedicated to their achievements.

FOREWORD

In the surgeon general's report on mental health which we released in December 1999, mental health was defined as:

> The successful performance of mental function, resulting in productive activities, fulfilling relationships with others, and the ability to adapt to change and to successfully cope with adversity.

The major findings of the first ever surgeon general's report on mental health were that (1) mental disorders are common—mental health is critical to overall health and well being; (2) mental disorders are disabling, in fact, mental disorders are second only to cardiovascular disease as a cause of disability-adjusted life years.

The good news in our report was that mental disorders are treatable and that 80–90 percent of the time we have the ability to return people with mental disorders to productive lives and positive relationships with the appropriate range of therapy. The bad news in the report was that fewer than half of persons who suffer from mental disorders each year seek treatment and less than one-third of children receive the treatment that they need. According to our assessment of the barriers to access, mental health care stigma was a major factor for individuals, families, and policy makers. Perhaps what is clear from our report on mental health is that we know more about mental disorders and how to treat them than we know about mental health and how to promote it; therefore this book on the integration of health promotion and mental health is long overdue.

Before becoming surgeon general in 1998 I served for almost five years as director of the Centers for Disease Control and Prevention (CDC). It became clear to me early in my tenure that even though the CDC was the nation's prevention agency, there was no program of mental health promotion or mental illness prevention. So we appointed the first associate director for behavioral science, which led to the CDC-wide coming together of behavioral scientists to begin to deal with the mental health aspects of programs in chronic and infectious diseases. However, until this day there is still no designated program for mental health promotion.

It is clearly time to focus more attention on mental health and how to promote it, and the role of mental health promotion in dealing with an ever increasing challenge of mental disorders in our environment. While biology plays a significant role in mental disorders, as with other health problems, it is ultimately the interaction between environment and biology that determines the magnitude and nature of mental health problems. In this book, Vandiver has thoroughly examined the components of mental health and health promotion that need to be brought together in a system of healthcare that is today clearly missing. Not only does she thoroughly examine health promotion in mental health, but also the role of leadership, the role of culture, and, in general, the role of community.

David Satcher, M.D., Ph.D.
Director, Center of Excellence on Health Disparities and
The Satcher Health Leadership Institute
Poussaint-Satcher-Cosby Chair in Mental Health
Morehouse School of Medicine
16th Surgeon General of the United States

PART I

FUNDAMENTAL CONCEPTS

1. Pursuing Wellness Through Mental Health Systems Reform

The public mental health system does not address health even though we are trying to keep ourselves healthy. We want to pursue wellness just like you—we just need more help.

—*J.V.S., consumer*

■ Chapter Overview

The pursuit of individual wellness and the responsibility of caring for individuals with mental health conditions and their families has been an aspect of every society for millennia. For just as long, societies have struggled to get it right—resulting in various levels of policies, systems, and interventions ranging from publicly shackling mentally ill people in stocks to the creation of nationally recognized consumer advocacy organizations. Currently, mental health systems in countries across the industrialized world are in transition—some in response to geopolitical forces, others in response to declining health care systems, and yet others through enlightened leadership and policy initiatives. Despite the various reasons for transition, most governments echo the same message: mental health systems are in need of reform to reflect contemporary approaches of care that support the pursuit of individual, community, and societal health and wellness; promote the concepts of recovery and hope; and provide sustainable outcomes. Health promotion is one such approach and the focus of this book.

The first section of this chapter begins the discussion of health promotion by identifying national and international initiatives that call for mental health system reform using public health approaches: namely health promotion. The next section introduces the reader to key issues in the mental health field as viewed through the eyes of five key stakeholder groups—namely clients, clients' family members, clinicians, administrators, and policy makers—all of whom are proving to be the driving force behind mental health system reform. The remainder of the chapter describes four health promotion strategies useful for addressing stakeholder concerns: (1) a multidimensional health promotion framework, (2) a philosophical shift, (3) an integrated practice model, and (4) a policy level call for reform. Last, this chapter (as well as subsequent chapters) concludes with a section entitled "In Our Own Words," which is a summary description of qualitative information obtained from consumer and family focus-group interviews on a topic derived from the focus of each chapter. For this chapter, participants discuss the following focus group statement: "Describe your experiences with the mental health system when you have a health problem."

Learning Objectives

When you have finished reading this chapter, you should be able to:

1. Discuss concerns of five stakeholder groups based on their experiences with the mental health care delivery system
2. Describe four strategies for mental health reform based on health promotion concepts
3. Identify core themes expressed through consumer and family focus groups when asked to describe their experiences with the mental health system when they had a health problem.

■ Introduction

Over the last decade, the mental health care system in the United States has been under scrutiny by prominent governmental agencies, policy institutes, and research centers. Three recently published federal reports [*Transforming Mental Health Care in America: The Federal Action Agenda* (2005), *Achieving the Promise: Transforming Mental Health Care in America* (2003), and *A Call to Action to Improve the Health and Wellness of Persons with Disabilities—Surgeon General's Report* (2005)] drew similar conclusions: the mental health system, in general, is fragmented, leaving many vulnerable persons to fend for themselves in bureaucracies characterized as overburdened, unresponsive, provider-driven, inaccessible, punitive, consumer- and family-unfriendly, and plagued by treatment approaches that are outdated and deficit-oriented, consisting mostly of symptom management and accepting of long-term disability (Substance Abuse and Mental Health Services Administration, 2005; New Freedom Commission on Mental Health, 2003; U.S. Department of Health and Human Services, 2005).

Despite this grim appraisal of the U.S. mental health system, encouragement is found in recent initiatives of the World Health Organization (WHO, 2004a; WHO, 2004b), World Federation for Mental Health (2007), and Healthy People 2010 (U.S. Department of Health & Human Services, 2000). Together, these organizations call for the inclusion of public health strategies such as health promotion to guide mental health system reform and redesign.

But what is health promotion and why should it be a part of mental health system reform? Public health literature defines "health promotion" as any planned combination of educational, political, regulatory, and or organizational approaches that supports the actions and conditions of living conducive to the health of individuals, groups, and communities (Green & Kreuter, 1999). A more detailed definition and description is discussed in Chapter 2. However, what makes health promotion such a promising public health strategy to guide mental health system reform is the focus placed on the concepts of wellness, recovery, hope, and the inclusion of multiple perspectives from diverse groups (e.g., individuals, families, providers, and communities). In other words, those who have "been there" or have experienced the system in a variety of ways are considered the best voices to guide system change. As one may imagine, there is much diversity of perspectives among these groups about what the issues are, how a mental health system should be reformed, what it should look like, who should set the agenda, and how it will be paid for. Although gathering these diverse perspectives may prove the to be most challenging first step in planning for mental health system reform, it clearly is the most informative. A core health promotion principle is that system change occurs most successfully when it is informed and guided by those most affected—the stakeholders. Let's see what they say.

■ Stakeholders for Mental Health Reform

In this section, the reader is introduced to key issues in the mental health field as viewed through the eyes of five key stakeholder groups: clients and family members, clinicians, administrators, and policy makers—all of whom are proving to be the driving force behind mental health system reform. For purposes of our discussion, "stakeholders" are defined as "people who are affected by or can affect the activities of the system" (Lewis, Goodman, & Fandt, 2004, p.79). These stakeholders, despite their diverse perspectives, do share common ground on one view: that the current mental health treatment system is in need of change from a deficits model of care to one of wellness and recovery and that the current approach of separate services for health, mental health, and substance use is no longer feasible or desirable.

Increasingly, *mental health consumers and their families* are requesting services that are more culturally compatible, more user-friendly, and incorporate broader and more holistic approaches to care that embrace wellness, partnership, quality of life, and recovery. *Clinicians* are experiencing an unprecedented increase in complex psychiatric cases in which serious co-occurring physical, mental, and substance use conditions challenge the effectiveness of traditional, office-based approaches to mental health care. *Administrators* of mental health agencies face an array of obstacles related to the human and economic costs associated with trying to coordinate integrated care in a health and mental health care system that is itself considerably fragmented and lacks parity between mental health conditions and physical health conditions. *Mental health policy makers* are frequently scanning national and international epidemiologic reports in search of scientifically supported population health trends data that can be used to advocate for reform. Taken together, the experiences and perspectives of each of these stakeholders is central to informing a new vision for mental health system reform using health promotion strategies. Let's now look more closely at the experiences of each of these stakeholder groups.

■ Stakeholder Experiences

Consumers and Family Members as Stakeholders

Consumers—also referred to as clients, patients, survivors, and/or users of mental health services—represent the primary stakeholders in that they are the target audience or focus of services. Regardless of the terms, mental health consumers are the reason services exist in the first place. Yet because families can be intimately involved in mental health services, they too are coupled with the "identified" consumer. Involvement of family members in mental health settings will vary according to agency policy, structure, and client–family member relationship. Although substantial documentation exists regarding the distinct issues of consumers separate from family members, our discussion focuses on their shared experiences. Research has identified key areas of concern expressed by both consumers of mental health services and their family members: stigma, health-related quality of life, provider respect and competence, and organizational cultural competence.

Stigma. Stigma is described as a cluster of negative attitudes and prejudicial beliefs (World Health Organization, 2001), is a pervasive reality for people with mental illness and their families and is a leading factor in discouraging both from getting the services they need (Warner, 2005). Just the perception of stigma by people with mental illness is associated with enduring negative effects on self-esteem, well-being, mental status and income.

For consumers and family members, a shared concern regarding the mental health system is feeling fearful of a negative evaluation or criticism (e.g., stigma) by providers. Research reports that consumers often feel like outcasts in society because of the symptoms of their mental illness, and this leads to hesitancy or unwillingness to access physical or mental health care (Magana, Ramirez, Garcia, Hernandez & Cortez, 2007; Angermeyer, 2003). Consequently they are less likely to receive needed treatment, including social interventions like peer support groups, psychosocial rehabilitation services, and health interventions like medication education groups.

Similarly, family members report difficulties with accessing mental health services, either on behalf of their family member who has a mental illness or because of their own need, such as respite from the freedom of care giving for a parent, child, or sibling with a mental illness. Some parents, for example, report having been forced to relinquish custody to obtain needed mental health services for their children (SAMHSA, 2005). Others describe experiences in which they perceive mental health workers as blaming them for family problems and refuse to deal with their grief issues (New Freedom Commission on Mental Health, 2003).

Stigma also plays a role in the underutilization of mental health services by consumers and family members from ethnic communities. Corin (1994) points out that recent immigrants are often reluctant to use mainstream health, mental health, or social services due to stigma-related concerns. These include feelings of personal shame about mental illness and social embarrassment for one's family or community.

Health-Related Quality of Life. When consumers receiving mental health services are prescribed medications, many express concerns about their quality of life in relation to weight gain and other side effects of medication. For our discussion, quality of life is defined as "an individual's perception of his/her position in life in the context of the culture and value systems in which he/she lives, and in relation to his/her goals, expectations, standards and concerns" (WHO, 2004a; p.21). Allison and colleagues (1999) found that weight gain due to psychiatric medication was related to poorer quality of life as well as reduced well-being and vitality for individuals diagnosed with schizophrenia.

Provider Respect and Organizational Cultural Competence. An additional concern identified by consumers and family members has to do with the cultural competence of providers and organizations. Consumers and family members who present from ethnically diverse communities are being referred to mainstream mental health settings by health care and social services providers. However, many of the available services are perceived as inadequate or inappropriate.

Consumers from ethnically diverse communities express concern that mainstream mental health providers do not understand their community or respect their use of traditional methods of treatment and thus may not fully disclose to providers the various methods of self-treatment they are using. These methods may involve the use of potions, applications of poultices, and or consultations with a spiritual healer (Spector, 2000)—none of which is reimbursable under most insurance plans or federal and state programs.

Family members often play a dominant role in health-seeking behaviors and compliance with treatment. Despite providing information and playing a pivotal role in guiding their ill family members' health care decisions, family members describe feeling disrespected when providers exclude them from "sessions" that involve the family member who has the mental illness (Vandiver, Jordan, Keopraseuth, & Yu, 1995).

Organizational cultural competence is just as important as provider respect and competence. The following example shows why. In one outpatient psychosocial rehabilitation program specifically designed for refugees diagnosed with trauma-related mental health conditions, six women clients who had recently immigrated from Somalia politely told the staff they would not participate in an annual fund-raising meal-preparation activity because it was held in the kitchen of the neighborhood church. At first, staff thought the clients were being "resistant" to the treatment program. After a group meeting in which the issue was discussed, the women explained that their Muslim tradition did not permit women to enter a religious center. This cultural prohibition had not been considered by staff; once they understood this important sociocultural fact, the meal-preparation activity was moved to a different location and the women were able to be involved in all aspects of subsequent community-building activities.

Consumers and families from non-English-speaking communities express difficulty with mental health organizations that rely heavily on English-only versions of health care information. Since a great deal of health and mental health information is organized around the assumption of literacy in the English language, some non-English-speaking clients and family members express concern that they cannot participate or even comprehend important treatment information presented in English-only pamphlets, manuals, or—worse—prescription directions (Institute of Medicine, 2002).

Each of these examples illustrates the shared concerns that consumers and family members have when it comes to their experiences with the mental health system. As stakeholders in mental health system reform, consumers and family members are calling for a new system of mental health care that is holistic in approach and embraces notions of health, wellness and cultural competence. Let's now turn to another key stakeholder group who has a vested interest in mental health system reform.

Clinicians as Stakeholders

Mental health clinicians, or providers, represent a second group of stakeholders in the mental health service system. As the designated frontline providers of mental health care, they are responsible for delivering and coordinating a wide range of services for the diverse needs of their mental health clients. In the last decade, clinicians have raised concerns about the increasing severity of symptoms and complexity of their client's health and mental health problems. They describe clinical scenarios in which clients present to hospital emergency departments and public mental health clinics with serious health problems (e.g., untreated hypertension) combined with psychiatric conditions (e.g., depression) mixed with substance abuse issues. If clients even manage to engage in treatment services, given their compromised health and mental health status, clinicians find that they must then address issues related to medication nonadherence, which is understandable given the variety of severe side effects (e.g., weight gain) of most psychiatric medications. Clinicians often find themselves scrambling to piece together treatment plans *for* their clients that incorporate numerous health and mental health providers from various agencies with varying levels of expertise or understanding about complicated mental health and health conditions. These efforts at multilevel triaging may be both daunting and frustrating to clinicians trained in traditional psychodynamic methods, who are more familiar with practices that are office-based and delivered within a 50-minute hour.

This professional frustration is further exacerbated when agency policies do not consider health issues to be within the purview of mental health clinicians' work expectations and thus do not support such outreach efforts. A brief examination of the literature highlights the extent of disconnect between agency policy and the clinical reality for clinicians. Specifically, we'll look at two issues that clinicians identify as the most challenging part of their work. These are treating co-morbid conditions (e.g., medical condition combined with psychiatric condition) and monitoring medication adherence complicated by side effects (e.g., sexual dysfunction and weight gain).

Co-morbid Conditions. For clinicians working in public mental health settings, schizophrenia and depression represent two of the more persistent mental health conditions that bring clients and their families in for treatment. These diagnoses also represent two diagnostic categories with high rates of co-occurring disorders (e.g., substance abuse and mental health condition) and comorbid health conditions (e.g., hypertension and depression). Before treatment begins, clinicians must first provide a primary diagnosis using the *Diagnostic and Statistical Manual of Mental Disorders*—IV-TR; or DSM for short (APA, 2000).

The DSM lists schizophrenia under psychotic disorders and depression under mood disorders. The diagnosis of schizophrenia is made if the symptoms of delusions, hallucinations, disorganized speech, and/or disorganized behavior are present for at least 6 months. The diagnosis of depression is more complicated, depending on the type of depression, but it may be considered if the person's mood is depressed, elevated, expansive, or irritable during a particular time period, such as 4 days (hypomanic), 1 week (manic), 2 weeks (major depressive), or every day for at least 1 week (mixed episode), or 2 years with more depressed days than nondepressed days (dysthymia) (APA, 2000). Both conditions have complex health-related issues.

For individuals diagnosed with schizophrenia, poor physical health seems to be related to poorer mental health. In a survey of 719 persons diagnosed with schizophrenia, Dixon and colleagues (1999) found that individuals who had a greater number of medical problems were at higher risk for increased depression, psychotic episodes, and suicide attempts. In a Veterans Administration study of nearly 40,000 individuals diagnosed with schizophrenia, researchers found significantly higher rates of diabetes among those under age 40 if they were taking one of the newer drugs. This emerging research suggests that medications may create even greater side effects than originally intended to alleviate (Dixon et al., 1999).

For individuals diagnosed with depression, research in the last decade has consistently shown that depressed people are more vulnerable to coronary artery disease, ischemia (lowered blood supply to the heart muscle), and coronary events—heart attacks or cardiac arrest (Murray & Lopez, 1996). These associations hold even after many other risk factors for heart disease are accounted for, including age, gender, tobacco use, cholesterol levels, blood pressure, weight–height ratio, and other chronic illnesses (Rugulies, 2002). Meta-analyses of 11 studies covering more than 36,000 participants reveal clinical profiles of at risk groups. For example, men in their fifties with high levels of depression and anxiety were over three times more likely than the general population to have a fatal stroke during the next 14 years. In a 6-year study of 5000 people of age 65 and above, those who had frequent depressive symptoms were 40% more likely to develop coronary artery disease and 60% more likely to die. The impact of depression is exponential. That is, for every 5% increase in the score on a standard rating scale for depression, the risk of developing coronary artery disease within 6 years rose by 13% and the risk for dying by 11% (Sadock & Sadock, 2007).

Medication Adherence and Side Effects. For clients with a diagnosis of a major mental disorder, such as schizophrenia or depression, multiple treatment approaches almost consistently involve the use of medications. Research has consistently shown that medication adherence, which refers to a willingness to follow a medication plan, is influenced by two critical variables: clients' subjective reports of how the medication made them feel and the disabling side effects—both of which may contribute to medication refusal or nonadherence (Sadock & Sadock, 2007; Bentley & Walsh, 2001).

Clinicians may find themselves conflicted with the practice of encouraging medication adherence while at the same time observing the negative side effects of certain medications. For example, the known side effects of the older or conventional medications (e.g., haldol and thorazine) included constipation, dry mouth, blurred vision, and severe movement disorders, such as tardive dyskinesia. It is hard to say to a person with a mental illness who adheres to medical treatment but has severely trembling arms, hands, and legs "Aren't you glad you're on your meds?" The newer medications are also problematic if not more so. In particular, two notable side effects account for most of medication discontinuation: sexual dysfunction and weight gain.

In terms of sexual dysfunction, medication side effects have been shown to produce the following physiologic changes: rise in the level of the hormone prolactin, which can cause breast development in men, disturbances of the menstrual cycle and inappropriate production of breast milk in women as well as a dramatic decrease in sex drive for both men and women (Perese & Perese, 2003; Sadock & Sadock, 2007). In terms of weight gain, the new or novel antipsychotic medications—such as clozapine, risperidone, olanzapine and quetipine—have been implicated as causes of side effects, with the most far-reaching biopsychosocial implications. For example, clients taking clozapine, olanzapine, or risperidone may put on as much as a pound a week for the first 2 months—the equivalent of consuming 500 extra calories a day, but without the enjoyment or nutrition of eating food. For more than half the people who continue to take psychiatric medications, obesity is inevitable, which is conservatively defined as 20% or more above the healthy weight range.

The problem is not simply a matter of gaining a few pounds or even several. Being overweight, and especially if one is obese, carries other health consequences, including diabetes, arthritis, high blood pressure, coronary artery disease, and stroke (Vania et al., 2002; Kramer, 2002). The research is quite clear: these conditions further the likelihood of a shorter life span, with even more distress and discomfort.

As the above discussion highlights, more than ever before, clinicians are called upon to understand and address their clients' complex health and mental health conditions regardless of their agencies' willingness to let them do so. As stakeholders in mental health system reform, mental health clinicians recognize that for their clients to become well and treatment to be effective, there must first be a shift in the way they define, appraise, and treat their clients' problems—moving from a primary focus on illness to incorporating a focus on health and wellness. Administrators of mental health systems also face challenges to the tradition of doing business as usual. Let's review their experiences with the mental health system.

Administrators as Stakeholders

Mental health administrators represent a fourth group of stakeholders. Their role is immense. They are responsible for the structural and fiscal health of their organizations, without which there would be no mental health services. Key concerns expressed by mental health administrators are the human and economic costs associated with a fragmented mental health system.

Like our clinician stakeholders, mental health administrators are recognizing the human and economic costs of treating individuals who require care in both the physical health and mental health care systems (New Freedom Commission on Mental Health, 2003). The human cost refers to clients who are vulnerable, experience poverty, and do not feel welcome in either care settings. Economic cost refers to cost upswings and cost-containment strategies associated with clients who require a combination of medical (i.e., primary care or emergency room) and mental health services. Although each of these costs can be significant in its own right, the real issue is not as simple as whether clients need both medical and psychiatric services—they often do, but the issue is whether the two systems can be better coordinated and welcoming and at what cost. It is this systems dilemma—fragmented care and its associated human and economic costs—that mental health administrators acknowledge as a pressing concern in their ability to cost-effectively manage their agencies. The intricacies of these costs are described below.

Human Costs. Increasingly, mental health administrators recognize that untreated mental illness will send numerous individuals in search of more expensive medical care many years before they would naturally need it. In a study by Miller and Martinez (2003), individuals with a psychiatric diagnosis (e.g., posttraumatic stress disorder, substance abuse, or schizophrenia) report having been turned away at some point from primary care clinics. When they were treated, they reported feeling a general lack of respect along with the implication that their medical problems were psychiatric in origin.

Over time, these kinds of frustrating experiences affected the person's willingness to seek medical care. In a study of 220 individuals diagnosed with severe mental illness and receiving Medicaid, Berren and colleagues (1999) found higher rates of emergency room visits for them than for those without mental illness. These individuals sought treatment at a later time, when emergency services were needed, or they used the emergency room as their point of entry into the health care system.

Even when clients with mental illness are able to access early care, a different set of challenges occur through the use of multiple systems over time. Fleishman (2003) provides a unique perspective on the human costs of receiving multiagency care for mental illness. He makes the point that the benefits of early treatment for symptom management (e.g., medication) actually increase the lifetime costs associated with maintaining that stability over time.

> Drug therapy for schizophrenia has complex effects on the global burden of disease. Currently, the savings attributable to drug therapy results from the reduction in direct hospitalization costs. However, people with schizophrenia are now living longer because of decreased suicide rates and better psychiatric care and many will continue to live in economic dependency. As a result, they will

> incur the increased costs of medical illnesses associated with advancing age, such as heart disease, diabetes, chronic obstructive pulmonary disease, osteoporosis and arthritis. Given the high costs of atypical antipsychotic medications, it appears to be safe to say that even if some people who have chronic schizophrenia improve sufficiently to be less than totally disabled, many will continue to be dependent on public subsidies because they cannot afford the medication that produced the improvement (p.143).

Overall, mental health administrators recognize a flaw in their systems when, more often that not, individuals with mental illness and physical conditions seek the most expensive kinds of services, such as emergency departments, because existing community services are perceived as unfriendly and less accessible.

Economic Costs. All mental health administrators are required to practice some form of fiscal accountability. Different health systems have different mechanisms, but most rely on data sources such as client service utilization patterns to determine the appropriate cost-containment strategies. Cost containment is one mechanism that is used to monitor and control health care costs (Vandiver, 2007). It is also cited as the most controversial aspect of an administrator's responsibilities. Also known as capitated care, the term *cost containment* refers to a fiscal arrangement in which the distribution of mental health services is restricted to a capitated budget. In other words, those services are managed, thus "managed care." Supported by early research, managed care was found to have achieved cost savings as much as 30% to 40% through the cost-control strategy of substituting less expensive outpatient care for inpatient care (Zuvekas, Rupp, & Norquist, 2007). Armed with these data, mental health administrators adopted service rationing measures; that is, providing only the most necessary services. In practice, service rationing may have assured fiscal solvency, but it created ethical dilemmas in sometimes discouraging clients from seeking needed hospital care.

For mental health clients who need access to both physical health and mental health services, mental health administrators recognized that cost-containment practices could interfere with client's ability to access care in either setting. When clients do access care, usually through separate systems that have little to do with each other, costs may be so prohibitive that they may not receive adequate care in either area.

Children with mental health conditions represent one client group that is sensitive to fragmented service systems and cost-containment practices. As a group, these children have multiple needs across multiple service providers and tend to use the more expensive forms of care. For example, children diagnosed with depression were more likely to use emergency and ambulatory care services and to have higher expenditures associated with almost every type of service than children without depression. Whereas children diagnosed with attention-deficit hyperactivity disorder (ADHD) have been found to use more medical services, with associated costs approximately twice those of other children; they have significantly more pharmacy fills and mental health and primary care visits, with costs comparable to those associated with asthma (Sadock

& Sadock, 2007). When a child uses such expensive emergency and medical services, his or her insurance or benefits plan may be quickly exhausted, thereby eliminating coverage for mental health services that could have been used for stabilization and ongoing care. The fragmentation of services comes into play when administrators of both health and mental health agencies attempt to bill for the services incurred by the client, often the same service (e.g., assessment/evaluation). It is this duplicate service that is denied by the insurer, and the whole process starts over again, with the child and family making a crisis trip to the emergency room because they cannot be seen in outpatient services, having reached the maximum amount of care allowable under the agencies' or insurer's capitated amount. For the mental health administrator, the fiscal issues are obvious; the economic solutions are more elusive. Let's now turn to a review of our final stakeholder: the policy maker.

Policy Makers as Stakeholders

Mental health policy makers represent a fifth group of stakeholders who have an investment in mental health system reform. Mental health policy is defined as "an organized set of values, principles, and objectives for improving mental health and reducing the burden of mental disorders in a population" (WHO, 2004b, p. 49). Public mental health policy has been shaped as much by historical and scientific developments of our understanding of mental illness as by the efforts of policy makers and or politicians working on behalf of individuals, families, and communities that have experienced mental illness at first hand (Mechanic, 2001). Some of the most progressive mental health policies to date have come about because these same policy makers have considered themselves stakeholders in the success of mental health initiatives as guided by their respective constituients and communities. For example, *Building on Strengths* (Ministry of Health, 2002; www.moh.govt.nz) is a national policy initiative spearheaded by the Ministry of Health of New Zealand in coordination with local, state, and governmental entities. Its aim is to provide guidance and education to health and mental health sector providers on what they can do to contribute to the positive mental health and well-being of New Zealanders. However, these progressive kinds of policy initiatives come with a sizable degree of background evidence for need and effectiveness. One key concern voiced by state policy makers is not knowing what the evidence or science or level of effectiveness is behind mental health proposals that their constitutients, voters, and or interest groups present to them.

Evidence and Economic Data. Most policy makers feel that in order to advocate for mental health reform, it is critical to be able to access accurate and sophisticated sources of health information and to understand the level of effectiveness a particular policy will have in terms of the larger population. To paraphrase a popular film caption: "Show me the evidence!" Yet most policy makers acknowledge that they do not have the time or even the training to sleuth through scientific journals to gather evidence and information that would support their constituents' concerns.

As stakeholders, mental health policy makers are in the unique position of speaking in dual voices, to their constituents (consumers, families, providers, and administrators) on the one hand and governmental entities on the other. The success of mental health reform initiatives is often contingent upon policy makers' abilities to authentically persuade legislative budget groups of the need of specific areas of reform. And in the age of political showdowns, of "Show me the evidence and I'll show you some money," mental health policy makers are indeed critical stakeholders for mental health policy reform.

Strategies for Mental Health Reform: The Tenets of Health Promotion

So far, this chapter has identified five primary groups or stakeholders—consumers and family members, clinicians, administrators, and policy makers—who have described in various ways their concerns, experiences, and needs relative to mental health and health systems. These are summarized as, respectively, stigma, health-related quality of life, provider and agency cultural competence, co-morbid health conditions, medication adherence and side effects, human and economic costs of fragmented systems, and need for reliable scientific and economic data for policy development. These issues give rise to four strategies, which are based on health promotion concepts and practices. They are (1) the use of the multidimensional health promotion framework for optimal health, (2) a philosophical shift from an orientation based on illness and deficits to one of health and wellness, (3) an integrated practice model—where health and mental health are seen as a mutual goal, and (4) a policy-level call for reform.

Let's return to our definition of health promotion and illustrate how these strategies are a natural fit within the definition. Health promotion is defined as any planned approach that can be educational (e.g., philosophical shift), political (i.e., policy reform), or organizational (i.e., integrated practice model) and supports the actions and conditions of living conducive to the health of individuals, groups, and communities (e.g., a multidimensional health promotion framework). These strategies are illustrated in Figure 1.1.

Multidimensional Health Promotion Framework

Based on the concerns that consumers and families have identified, successful mental health system reform begins with addressing the issues of stigma, health-related quality of life, and provider and agency cultural competence. One way to accomplish this task is for providers, consumers, and family members to work together to create user-friendly, holistic approaches of care that embrace notions of wellness, partnership, quality of life, and recovery. O'Donnel (1989) understood the importance of this alliance when he developed a multidimensional, health promotion framework using five concepts considered necessary for wellness, holistic care, and optimal health. These concepts are emotional, social, physical, intellectual, and spiritual (p. 5). O'Donnel (1989) describes

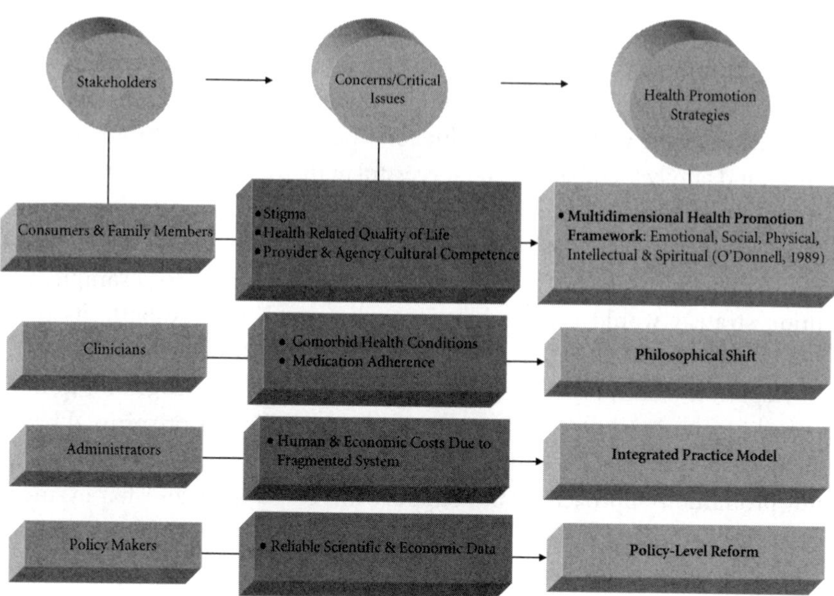

FIGURE 1.1. Conceptual model for mental health reform using health promotion strategies to address stakeholder concerns.

these health promotion aspects accordingly. The *emotional* aspect refers to the caring for emotional crises and the management of stress. For example, a health promotion strategy would identify areas/aspects of consumers' and family members' lives that are meaningful and emotionally supportive (e.g., close relationship with partner or friends at school or work) and to identify comfort strategies that can be put in place during times of distress—like phone outreach.

The *social* aspect refers to communities, neighbors, families, and friends. For example, a health promotion strategy would be to encourage consumers and family members to explore naturally existing social support systems or connections (e.g., bingo group, church family, or coffee group) that can be accessed on a regular basis—not just during times of illness. Ideally, these supportive connections are separate from the formal mental health system. The mental health care provider seeking to support the coordination of these connections will need to be prepared to consult with all levels of familial and social support: nuclear, extended, adopted, and possible foster families as well as friends, acquaintances, and community people—such as pastors and landlords.

The *physical* aspect refers to fitness, nutrition, medical self-care, and control of substance abuse. For example, a health promotion strategy would be to develop a personal wellness plan that incorporates physical activities, health education, nutrition, and fun. A wellness-oriented approach to physical care can promote treatment adherence through an awareness of the benefits and liabilities of certain health and lifestyle practices (e.g., nutrition, exercise, and medication use).

The *intellectual* aspect refers to education, achievement, and career development. For example, a health promotion strategy would be to develop agency and community-wide public service announcements (a common public health approach) that showcase the successes of people with mental health conditions. By working together, providers, consumers, and family members can be successful in their efforts to combat professional and community stigma, enhance provider and organizational competence; and illustrate the vital role that recovery plays in the lives of consumers and their family members.

Finally, the *spiritual* aspect refers to love, hope, and charity. For example, a health promotion strategy would explore belief systems which include faith, its meaning, associated religious or spiritual practices and impact on well-being and coping. Part of being a respectful, culturally competent clinician is to acknowledge and honor consumers and family members belief systems given that religious or spiritual beliefs are often associated with mature and active coping methods (Sadock & Sadock, 2007). A health promotion approach would support the consumer's and family members' choice of spiritual guide.

While seemingly simplistic in its design, the multidimensional health promotion framework offers providers a whole new approach to conversing with consumers and families. If used as part of the initial intake or assessment, critical information can be exchanged about what is meaningful and working well in the lives of consumers and family members. The multidimensional framework offers a radical departure from most assessment methods that tend to be deficits and problem oriented. This holistic approach to recognizing the mind/body/spiritual/social connection ensures a more comprehensive approach to health and mental health care and is essential for understanding what is valued by consumers and their family members.

Philosophical Shift

Based on clinician concerns about their ability to respond effectively to the increase in complex health issues and medication-related side effects that their clients are presenting, successful mental health system reform can begin right at home—starting with a philosophical shift in how clinicians (re)define the focus of their work. For example, Anthony (2000) and colleagues describe how, in the past, mental health treatment was based on the belief that people with mental illness did not recover, that the course of the illness was essentially deteriorative, particularly without medication, and that the prognosis was poor at best. The practitioner's orientation was based on a deficits model, and treatment services were provider-driven rather than consumer-driven. Further, most mental health clinicians have not been trained to recognize health conditions despite high rates of co-morbid health conditions in psychiatric populations. Fortunately, practitioners are now beginning to participate in a philosophical shift away from a primary focus on a deficits model of assessment and practice to one that is strengths-based, wellness-oriented, and recovery-focused—or in other words, a health-promoting focus that embraces the concepts of health and mental health.

Cognitive theorists tell us that how we appraise or define a situation determines the course of action we choose and or how we respond. That is, how we define the problem influences the solutions we seek. Let's look at some of the various definitions of the term *mental illness* from three perspectives: legal, professional, and individual/ personal.

- Legal: "Mental illness is determined by a state statute: an illness which so lessons the capacity of the person to use self-control, judgment, and discretion in the conduct of his affairs and social relations as to make it necessary or advisable for him to be under treatment, care, supervision, guidance or control." (North Carolina Gen. Stat. (1991) 122C-3(21) (Weiner & Wettstein, 1993, p. 48)
- Professional: "Mental illness collectively refers to all diagnosable mental disorders–which are in turn defined as health conditions that are characterized by alterations in thinking, mood or behavior or some combination—which are associated with distress or impaired functioning, disability, pain or death." (Healthy People 2010; U.S.Department of Health and Human Services, 2000)
- Focus Group Participant: "Mental illness is the fear of being out of control and nobody will listen." (In Our Own Words: Focus Group Participant, 2005)

In most academic training programs and some agency staff development workshops, the topic of mental illness is usually covered in terms of individualistic diagnostic categories (sometimes referred to as "labels"), level of functioning (or lack thereof), symptom expression and management, needs, biological treatment, hospital treatment history, risk factors, and disability—all of which are absolutely necessary kinds of information to have in order to understand the pain and distress experienced by a person. However, this focus is mostly on what is not working with a person. In some settings, the person may actually be defined by his or her diagnosis (e.g., "Sandy the schizophrenic"). While part of the emphasis on the deficits model of assessment and practice can be attributed to the insurance industry, which requires "medical necessity as determined by a diagnosis and active symptoms" in order to pay for services, clinicians still share some responsibility in limiting the assessment process to these narrow categories.

If practitioners are to shift their practice philosophy from a focus on a deficits orientation to incorporate a wellness orientation, let's first begin with shifting the language of assessment from mental "illness" to mental "health." Using the same categories of legal, professional, and individual definitions, let's review how mental "health" is defined.

- Legal: It is worth mentioning that there is no "legal" definition of mental health.
- Professional: "Mental health is both an outcome and a state of being which has numerous dimensions: self-esteem, realization of one's potential, the ability to maintain fulfilling, meaningful relationships and psychological well-being; it is not a statistical norm but a goal toward which to strive." (Horwitz & Scheid, 1999, p. 2)

- Individual: "Mental health involves feelings and beliefs; a feeling that one can control and influence their life experiences; a belief that one has the right as an individual who is worthy; involves understanding and accepting that psychological and or emotional problems can occur in ourselves and others and that this is normal for most people at some state of their lives." (Society of Health Education and Promotion Specialists, 1997, p. 4)

While both terms, *mental illness* and *mental health*, are necessary in clinical work, each carries its own set of assumptions and actions. DiNitto (2000) notes that "mental health professionals have long debated the best way to apply these terms, although it is generally agreed that these concepts exist as two ends of a continuum" (p. 324). Taken more broadly, most societies see these concepts as interrelated and would not even attempt to separate them into distinct categories. Nor do many societies have the mind–body dualism that western societies have when it comes to defining these terms.

The objective of presenting the distinctions in the definitions of mental health and mental illness is to illustrate how the profession is being pushed to pay more attention to the more positive definitions of mental health; yet most clinical practice is still focused on the illness orientation. This is not to say that all it takes is a change of mind on the part of the clinician to make all those complex issues go away. Rather, the emphasis is on encouraging clinicians to see their clients in a broader light, in which health and mental health become the focus of the assessment and the goals of treatment rather than a by-product of symptom remission. A true philosophical shift will have occurred when clinicians are able to draw their professional philosophies from both definitions. The importance of possessing this dual perspective is captured in the poignant comments made to this author by the mother of an adult son diagnosed with schizophrenia. See Box 1.1—Of Mother and Son: "We Need to Know."

Integrated Treatment Services

Administrators of mental health agencies face an array of obstacles related to the human and economic costs associated with trying to coordinate care in a fragmented health and mental health care system. Numerous governmental (Department of Health and Human Services) and nongovernmental organizations (World Health Organization) have all produced consensus reports that essentially recommend a common strategy to address this fragmentation: *integrated treatment services*—also referred to as *integrated practice model*. Integrated care is now seen as a priority for individuals with severe and persistent mental illness. The term *integrated* originally emphasized the relationship between models of treatment for mental illness and addictions in a residential setting. However, during the last decade, integrated treatment has evolved to refer to "any mechanism by which treatment interventions for co-occurring disorders are combined within the context of a primary treatment relationship or service setting; this means the coordinating of substance abuse, mental health and health treatment systems in a manner in which the client is treated as a whole person,

Box 1.1. *Of Mother and Son: We Need to Know*

Several years ago I was invited to speak at the annual conference of the Schizophrenia Society of Nova Scotia held in Halifax, Nova Scotia, Canada. I was a newly minted doctoral graduate from a public health program in the United States and was excited about sharing my new-found brilliance on the topic of health promotion. The organization was a family advocacy group, similar to the U.S. National Alliance of the Mentally Ill. Audience members were a collection of family members, consumers, and professionals. My talk was titled "Finding Common Ground in Diverse Settings: Strengths-Based Case Management,"—a fairly radical notion, I thought at the time. At the end of my lecture, audience members applauded politely and I was sure I had swooned them with my lilting southern accent and brilliant notions about how to focus on the good and healthy parts of clients—as opposed to the typical problem-oriented focus so typical of mental health practices of the 1980s and 1990s. At the back of the room, a woman stood up, thanked me for coming to the meeting, and then, speaking in a soft voice, taught me an important lesson. Her words were brief and heartfelt. "I am the mother of a son diagnosed with schizophrenia. I agree with part of what you say . . . we must remember the healthy parts of our family members who are ill with this dreadful disease. However, as family members, that's all we have to hold onto . . . tiny glimpses of their strengths, and it doesn't always help. We need to *know* what's wrong, we need to know what's not working, and, when possible, why things are the way they are. So you can say all you want about being focused on the strengths of people, but if we don't know what's wrong, how can we help them make it right? So please, miss, don't forget to do both. We need the hard information . . . and so do they." Clearly, she gave the author information she needed to know too.

Source: Presentation delivered at Ninth Annual Provincial Conference on Schizophrenia. Sponsored by Schizophrenia Society of Nova Scotia, Halifax, Nova Scotia, Canada, 1996.

not just a diagnostic category" (DHHS, 2005, p. 12). In other words, an integrated practice model will support the delivery of specialized assessment and treatment wherever the client enters the treatment system, link the individual to appropriate referrals when a provider or agency does not have in-house expertise, and promote the cross-training of all counselors and staff to develop competencies to treat individuals with co-occurring mental health and health conditions as well as work as interdisciplinary teams both internal and external to the agency.

The focus on an integrated practice model can be a combination of attention to co-occurring disorders (e.g., substance use and mental illness), comorbid conditions (e.g., schizophrenia, HIV, and diabetes), family, employment, and health care. The types of interventions offered in an integrated service model will comprise an array of evidence-based interventions including cognitive-behavioral therapy, motivational interviewing, contingency management, mutual self-help groups, psychoeducation, and family support. Research on services for clients with severe mental illness over the last decade has found that integrated treatment models that provided services on site and for at least 18 months resulted in significant reductions in substance abuse, relapse, and hospital use (DHHS, 2005, p. 13)—all of which address administrators' concerns over the human and economic costs of a fragmented system of care.

Administrators who are invested in mental health system reform need not look far for examples. Miller and colleagues (2003) describe an integrated treatment system of care involving primary care for veterans with major psychiatric disorders. Like mental health clinics, the primary care clinic offered treatment for patients with co-occurring disorders—which in this case involved medical patients who also had serious mental illnesses. Although the initial focus was different—medical versus psychiatric, the program design was similar. The Veterans Administration integrated treatment model had the following components: on-site primary medical care, medical case management, and active collaboration and communication between primary medical care and mental health providers.

Policy-Level Call for Reform

Mental health policy makers frequently scan international and national reports for population data trends that can be used to advocate for specific policy reform. The most reliable source of population-based health information is generally derived from a field of public health research known as epidemiology, defined as "the study of the distribution and determinants of health-related conditions or events in defined populations and application of this study to control health problems" (Green & Kreuter, 2005; p. 86). Policy makers can reliably determine from epidemiologic data if there are trends, or patterns, in particular mental health and health conditions that impact their communities, which, in turn, can guide policy development for resource allocation and or reform.

Mental health policy makers find epidemiologic data informative because they describe the health status of populations (perhaps even of constitutients or voters) and can be used to track global trends in illness rather than individual cases. Standard measures to track health status are usually incidence and prevalence. *Incidence* refers to a measure of the frequency of occurrence of a health problem in a population based on the number of new cases over a given period of time—usually a year. *Prevalence* refers to a measure of the extent of a health problem in a population based on the number of cases (old and new) existing in the population at a given time (Green & Kreuter, 2005).

For example, state mental health policy makers may be asked by local public health officials to fund more homeless shelters for individuals with mental illness and human immunodeficiency virus (HIV) infection. Policy makers would then turn to data reports derived from epidemiologic research to determine the need for this service based on the incidence of new cases of HIV among homeless individuals with mental illness compared to the existing number of cases of people already being served. If the incidence of new HIV cases exceeds an already established low prevalence rate, then a case can be made for designing policies that can jump start funding for the development of new resources.

Three seminal sources of epidemiologic data reports that mental health policy makers may turn to are the *World Health Report* 2001 (2001), *Healthy People* 2010 (2001) and the Institute of Medicine Report—The *Future of the Public's Health in the 21st Century* (2003). For example, epidemiologic research has shown that mental illness occurs in all regions of the world and is considered an immense public health burden of disability (WHO, 2001). Epidemiologic data from the *World Health Report* identify the top 10 global health risks in terms of the amount of disease, disability, and death. Many are directly related to mental health. These are unsafe sex, high blood pressure, tobacco consumption, alcohol consumption, high cholesterol, and obesity. The report's admonition is that even with modest changes in health behaviors, risk levels may net major benefits in the health of peoples and costs to countries (WHO, 2001).

A second document, *Healthy People* 2010, notes that in established market economies, such as that of the United States, mental illness is on par with heart disease and cancer as a cause of disability (U.S. Department of Health and Human Services, 2000). Further, approximately 40 million people aged 18 to 64 years, or 22% of the U.S. population, had a diagnosis of mental disorder, and suicide was found to occur most frequently as a consequence of a mental disorder.

A third document, the Institute of Medicine Report *The Future of the Public's Health in the* 21st *Century* (IOM, 2003), found that America is far from achieving its goal of good health for all, despite 20 years of health initiatives. The report lists 20 areas of continuing priority focus and, like the WHO report, includes many that are directly related to mental health. These are care coordination, diabetes, hypertension, ischemic heart disease, major depression, medication management, pregnancy and childbirth, self-management and health literacy, severe and persistent mental illness, stroke, tobacco-dependence treatment in adults, and obesity.

In combination, these reports call for much public mental health policy reform. Their recommendations are based on health promotion principles and practices. These include:

- Do more than just manage symptoms and actually help consumers move into recovery with housing and employment assistance.
- Challenge the stigma of mental illness whenever and wherever possible so people can seek treatment and can function without shame in society.
- Increase awareness of cultural diversity for practitioners.
- Improve sensitivity to the unique behavioral health care needs of both children and older adults.
- Implement evidence-based treatments that traditionally take way too long to get from researchers to the field.

- Become more responsive to co-occurring disorders, since substance abuse and mental health problems are extremely prevalent.
- Detect problems and intervene as early as possible.

The information contained in these documents clearly indicates a key trend in mental health that is supported by epidemiologic evidence: a continuing rise in co-morbid physical health and mental health conditions. If mental health system reform is to occur, policy makers recognize that they need to be brought on board with the latest in scientific knowledge on evidence-based mental health practices. One way is to use epidemiologic data as a source of scientific data to spotlight trends in the presence of disability, the plight of the individuals, families, and communities affected by these trends and the lack of appropriate resources to address the residual issues brought on by these trends (e.g., poverty and homelessness).

■ Conclusion

One of the goals of mental health system reform is to enhance the growth of competencies in both individual and social systems. It is anticipated that the mental health care system's current treatment orientation of pathology and disease will be replaced by an orientation toward wellness, recovery, and hope using a health promotion framework. This shift will require a change in philosophy and priorities of mental health care systems and an even greater change in the roles and relationships of mental health care providers, consumers, family members, policy makers, and members of the general community. As the systems shift their focus from illness to wellness, consumers and their families simply must become collaborative partners in the mutual effort to become healthy in the face of mental illness.

After all these decades of a disease-oriented approach, which has had variable results in controlling symptoms, it seems that now is the time to approach mental health system reform using the wellness-oriented approach known as health promotion. True to the expressed desires of the various stakeholders—consumers and family members, providers, administrators, and policy makers—a genuinely integrated system of care will incorporate the very best of what is known about quality mental health care and blend it with what is known about quality health care. As stated at the beginning of this chapter, societies have had the responsibility for millennia to care for individuals with mental illness, regardless of how it was defined. Let's make sure that that responsibility is carried out with the concerns of the stakeholders in mind and that strategies reflect a health promotion framework. This framework must be multidimensional, wellness-oriented, integrated with multiple systems, and be supported by policy that makes a real difference in the lives of the stakeholders and their communities.

As Confucius says, " The fully integrated person (*jun zi*) is calm and at ease, the fragmented person is always stressed (sad, worried, anxious, sorrowful, distressed" (Cleary, 1991, p. 33). Our challenge is to help both individual and system move from the experience of fragmentation to one of calm and at ease—what is also referred to as wellness. The remaining chapters explore the various ways in which mental health and health promotion work together to facilitate the pursuit of wellness.

In Our Own Words . . . Family and Consumer Perspectives on Mental Health Treatment Services: Focus Group Feedback

Topic: Integration of Health and Mental Health Care—Part 1

Summary

As this chapter illustrates, current mental health delivery systems are poised to make systemwide changes, with particular emphasis on the integration of health and mental health care. Staying with this theme, consumers and family members were asked to comment on their experiences with the mental health system when they had a health concern. As noted below, both groups experienced positive and negative aspects of the mental health system when a health need arose. Family members were quick to praise the good efforts of providers who offer education on medication but were critical of the lack of consistent providers and treatment for health conditions and the crisis orientation of existing care. Similarly, consumers considered lack of integrated care, stigma, and limited treatment to be serious concerns.

What Can We Learn?

Based on these perspectives, systemwide mental health reform initiatives can continue to support client and family health education efforts, encourage providers to work together for optimal integrated care, and reduce the crisis orientation of services.

The following sections details the results of the focus group meeting as reported by family members and consumers.

Focus Group Statement: *"Describe your experiences with the mental health system when you have a health problem."*

Family Perspectives

Core Themes	Summary of Experiences	Comments
(Ranked in order of priority)		
First. Education	Good efforts at client and family education about physical effects of nicotine and substance abuse with meds.	"Mental health caseworkers and doctors have been helpful at educating me and my son on the effects of mixing substances and how smoking and nicotine effect medication." (L., *parent*)

(continued)

Focus Group Statement: *"Describe your experiences with the mental health system when you have a health problem."* *(continued)*

Second—Lack of Integrated Care	Multiple providers leads to fragmented care.	"My daughter has two different doctors and when first diagnosed with a mental illness, no physical exam was given for a well-rounded diagnosis and care." (M., *parent*)
Third—Crisis Services	Mental health services are too crisis oriented.	"Treatment is often offered as a band aid approach, applied only after a crisis and often after repeated requests by family; and even after that, family are not even listened too." (M., *parent*)

Consumer Perspectives

Core Themes	Summary of Experiences	Comments
(Ranked in order of priority)		
First—Lack of Integrated Care	Mental health system does not address health issues.	"My psychiatrists have never asked what medications I am taking for physical problems; my case manager has never asked me about my physical health. The public mental health system does not address health even though we are trying to keep ourselves healthy. We want to pursue wellness just like you—we just need more help." (J.V.S., *consumer*)
Second—Stigma	Stigma about having a mental health problem exists even in mental health clinics.	"I feel more like a label or a number than a person with complex needs—especially when my worker sees my mental illness above my physical illness." (R., *consumer*)
Third—Treatment Limited	Treatment options are limited.	"Although my clinic used to offer a health class, most of my experiences with mental health treatment are primarily focused on psychiatric medications and behavior in groups. Most frequent advice was that I should socialize more." (J., *consumer*)

2. Health Promotion

When I go to the emergency room for medical care, they turn my case over to the social worker when they learn I take psychiatric meds for depression—and then don't get around to treating my heart problems; it's as if we are not supposed to have medical needs.

—*J.V.S., consumer*

■ Chapter Overview

Health promotion is a field born out of an international movement calling for fundamental change in the way societies achieve and maintain health for all people, particularly those with mental health conditions (WHO, 2004a). Considered the "new public health," health promotion reflects this movement and is considered an emerging field of action and advocacy designed to address the full range of modifiable and interactive determinants of health (Baum, 1998). This chapter begins with an overview of the various definitions and applications of the term *health promotion*. This is followed by a review of key public health concepts: prevention and promotion, risk and protective factors, and their relationship with determinants of health. The remainder of the chapter provides a chronological history of health promotion up to present day, reviews the numerous ways in which health promotion is integrated into mental health services and policies, outlines limitations, and identifies critical issues for the field. Last, the chapter concludes with a section entitled "In Our Own Words," a summary of focus group comments from consumers and family members on the topic of integration of health and mental health care. For this chapter, participants discuss the following focus group statement: "Describe your experiences with the health system when you have a mental health problem or need."

Learning Objectives

When you have finished reading this chapter, you should be able to:

1. Describe the multiple definitions and activities that encompass the field of health promotion
2. Discuss the differences between health promotion and prevention including risk and protective factors
3. Describe the history of health promotion efforts and the numerous limitations and barriers to incorporating this approach into the field of mental health practice

4. Identify core themes and concerns expressed through consumer and family members when asked to describe their experiences with the health system when they had a mental health problem.

Introduction

Public health philosophy rests on the notion that the concepts of health and mental health exist on a continuum and that public health models (e.g., health promotion and prevention) attempt to do the greatest good for the greatest number of people (Denning, 2000). From these perspectives, it is health promotion that emerges as the most universal practice model. But what is health promotion? As noted in the previous chapter, health promotion is defined as any planned combination of educational, political, regulatory, or organizational approach that supports actions and conditions of living conducive to the health of individuals, groups, or communities (Green & Kreuter, 1999). In essence, health promotion promotes action strategies that help individuals and communities build healthy public policy, create supportive environments, strengthen community action, and build people's capacity to manage their health and mental health through lifestyle awareness (WHO, 1986). As suggested in the previous chapter, in this millennium, it is anticipated that the mental health care system's current treatment orientation toward illness, pathology, disease, and risk will be modified to incorporate an orientation toward health, wellness and recovery—the heart of health promotion.

Defining Health Promotion

Health promotion is a term with a wide range of definitions that have numerous applications. Its focus ranges from micro applications, such as individual awareness, to macro applications, such as global risk reduction. Let's look at some of the various definitions and applications of health promotion as seen in the literature:

- *Individual:* At the individual level, health promotion is defined as "the art and science of helping people change their lifestyle to move toward a state of optimal health. Lifestyle change can be facilitated through a combination of health promotion efforts to enhance awareness, change behavior, and create environments that support good health practices. Of the three, supportive environments will probably have the greatest impact on producing lasting change." (O'Donnell, 1989, p. 5)
- *Outcome:* As an outcome, health promotion is "a process directed toward achieving a goal or outcome. Although specific outcomes will differ, they nearly always involve improvement in quality of life and individual change." (Mittlemark, 1999, p. 6)
- *Educational:* As an educational approach, health promotion is "any educational activity which promotes health related learning—i.e., some relatively permanent

change in an individual's capabilities or dispositions. It may produce changes in belief or attitude and facilitate the acquisition of skills; or it may generate changes in behavior and lifestyle." (Green & Kreuter, 2005, p. 114)

- *Activity:* As an activity, health promotion can be "any set of specific activities directed at particular goals, with a strong focus on the rational management of the population's health. Much emphasis is placed in the health promotion literature upon planning and coordination, assessing needs, consultation with the appropriate individuals and groups, piloting and evaluating programs." (Lupton, 1995, p. 51)
- *General Philosophy:* As a general philosophy, health promotion is "based on the belief that individuals should be allowed to uncover their true state of health, to reveal their moral standing and indeed shape their true selves by strategies of personal management and social empowerment." (WHO, 2004a)
- *Strategy:* Considered a strategy, "mental health promotion activities imply the creation of individual, social and environmental conditions that enable optimal psychological and psychophysiological development; such initiatives involve individuals in the process of achieving positive mental health, enhancing quality of life and is an enabling process, done by, with and for people." (Hosman & Jane-Llopis, 1999, in WHO, 2004a, p. 16)
- *Environmental:* As an environmental approach, health promotion is "the combination of educational and environmental supports for actions and conditions of living conducive to health." (Green & Kreuter, 1991, p. 4)
- *Human Rights:* Considered a human rights value, "mental health promotion refers to positive mental health, considers mental health as a resource, as a value on its own and as a basic human right essential to social and economic development." (WHO, 2004, p. 16).
- *Political:* Tied to health policy, health promotion is "a process of enabling people to exert control over the determinants of health and thereby improve their health; it does so through the actions of building healthy public policy, creating supportive environments, strengthening community action, developing personal skills and reorienting health services." (Ottawa Charter of 1986, WHO, 1986, in Mittlemark, 1999, p. 6)
- *Global:* As a macro approach to global issues, "key commitments of health promotion globally are to make the promotion of health central to the global development agenda, a core responsibility for all of government, a key focus of communities and civil society and make the promotion of health a requirement for good corporate practice; health promotion works to enable people to increase control over their health and its determinants by developing personal skills, embracing community action, and fostering appropriate public policies, health services and supportive environments; health promotion is currently guiding global, national and community health policies to reduce health risks." (Bangkok Charter of 2005 for Health Promotion, WHO, 2005a, p. 1; WHO, 2005b, p. 1)

■ Health Promotion and Prevention

Although the focus of this book is on integrating health promotion into mental health practice, a question bound to arise is "What about prevention?" In deference to the other half of this important public health duo (health promotion and disease prevention), this section describes the key concepts of prevention, including a discussion on risk and protective factors, determinants of mental health, and their relationship to health promotion.

What's the Difference Between Health Promotion and Disease Prevention?

Although the terms *health promotion* and *disease prevention* are often used interchangeably, conceptually they are distinguishable. The distinction lies in their targeted outcomes (WHO, 2004b). Health promotion is a much broader concept than disease prevention. Specifically, health promotion differs from disease prevention in that disease prevention starts with a particular target condition (e.g., depression related to hyperthyroidism) and works back through a causal pathway to preventive actions that can reduce the risk of the disease (e.g., low-fat diet and exercise). Health promotion, on the other hand, is directed at facilitating and improving people's general well-being. It aims to "promote positive mental health by increasing psychological well-being, competence and resilience and by creating supportive living conditions and environments" (WHO, 2004b, p. 17). Health promotion is not diagnosis-specific, as is typical in prevention efforts. It transcends specific medical concerns and embraces less defined concepts of wellness, personal growth, social betterment, and community enhancement. Prevention and promotion elements are often present in the same programs and strategies, involving similar activities and producing different but complimentary outcomes (WHO, 2004a; WHO, 2004b).

What Is Prevention?

The public health definition of prevention as applied to mental disorders is as follows: "Mental disorder prevention aims at reducing incidence, prevalence, recurrence of mental disorders, the time spent with symptoms, or the risk condition for a mental illness, preventing or delaying recurrences and also decreasing the impact of illness in the affected person, their families and the society" (IOM, 1994, p. 17). Prevention is typically about actions that eliminate or minimize conditions known to contribute or cause different diseases (Dhooper, 1997), such as salt intake for hypertension or stress in brief reactive psychosis.

Levels of Prevention

Prevention can occur at various levels. The *Institute of Medicine Report* (1994) describes the distinctions between three classic public health prevention levels for physical illness: primary, secondary, and tertiary.

Primary Prevention. *Primary prevention* refers to steps directed to susceptible persons before they have developed a disease (Roberts & Yeager, 2004). Primary prevention itself has three levels: *universal, selective,* and *indicated.*

Universal prevention refers to interventions that target an entire population, such as the population in a state or province, city, community, and or the population overall. As such, universal prevention focuses on a population group that has not been identified on the basis of increased risk. An example of universal prevention of tooth decay is the fluoridation of drinking water.

Selective prevention targets individuals or subgroups of the population whose risk of developing a physical or mental condition is significantly higher than average, as evidenced by biological, psychological, or social risk factors (WHO, 2004b, p. 17). Selective prevention is illustrated by steps targeting racial and ethnic minority groups who bear a disproportionately high burden of mental and physical disability because they receive less care and a poorer quality of care (U.S. Public Health Service Office of the Surgeon General, 2001; IOM, 2000).

Indicated primary prevention "targets high risk people who are identified as having minimal but detectable signs or symptoms foreshadowing mental disorder or biological markers indicating predisposition for mental disorder but who do not meet diagnostic criteria for disorder at that time" (WHO, 2004, p. 17). There are many examples of the need for this type of primary prevention, such as daughters who bear a familial genetic risk of developing bipolar disorder due to parents having a history of affective disorders or a family history of any number of conditions from hypertension to colon cancer.

Secondary Prevention. *Secondary prevention* refers to efforts to lower the rate of established cases of a mental or physical disorder in the population (prevalence) using early detection and treatment of diagnosable diseases (WHO, 2004b, p. 17). An example of a secondary prevention measure used in public mental health settings is blood work performed to screen for agranulocytosis, a potentially fatal blood condition that can occur in association with certain psychiatric medications, such as clozapine.

Tertiary Prevention. *Tertiary prevention* refers to interventions that reduce disability, enhance rehabilitation, and prevent relapses and recurrences of an illness (WHO, 2004b, p. 17). It is clearly focused on people who already have a physical or mental health condition. An example is a person diagnosed with schizophrenia who participates in a psychosocial day program designed to decrease or prevent social isolation and facilitate the development of social skills.

The Role of Risk and Protective Factors

Prevention efforts are designed to reduce risks associated with a person's physical or mental health condition, while health promotion is designed to facilitate that which protects a person from the condition. These are known as risk factors and protective factors. The model comprising risk and protective factors has a long-standing history in public health and has more recently been applied to social problems, such as substance abuse, delinquency, and violence (Hawkins, Catalano, & Arthur, 2002).

Risk factors are typically associated with prevention efforts. The term *risk factors* refer to factors that increase the probability of developing a disease, health condition, or social problem. Risk factors may be associated with the increased probability of early onset, greater severity, and longer duration of major health and mental health problems (Dhooper, 1997). Mental health risk factors are usually a combination of social, environmental (community or neighborhood), economic, individual, and family characteristics. Examples include hunger and poor nutrition, poverty, discrimination and racism, lack of adequate and safe housing, substance abuse, unemployment or underemployment, lack of access to health care or medications, exposure to trauma, such as war, violence, intimate partner violence, and family genetics (Green & Kreuter, 2005; WHO, 2004b).

Prevention interventions work by focusing on reducing risk factors associated with mental illness. For example, the primary expression of conduct disorder and substance abuse among juveniles is running away from home, where the runaway is nine times more likely to do drugs and alcohol than the juvenile who does not run away (Tripodi, Springer, & Corcoran, 2007). Substance abuse prevention, then, would do well to focus on the youth and family at the time of the first incident of running away from home; a family or school-based approach would be appropriate here to support the family given findings suggesting that family discipline (actually defined by the likelihood of getting caught for transgressions) and school failure are predictive of actually running away. See Chapter 10 for a discussion on children and conduct disorder.

Protective factors are typically associated with health promotion approaches and refer to variables that improve people's resistance to risk factors and disorders and helps protect the person from the onset of the condition or problem. Research finds that protective factors, like risk factors, are distributed across individuals and family, environmental (community), and social groups. Individual protective factors are embedded in features of positive mental health, such as self-esteem, emotional resilience, positive thinking, problem solving and social skills, stress management skills, and feelings of mastery or self-efficacy (WHO, 2004b). Examples of family protective factors include shared meals; environmental or community protective factors includes safe housing; and social protective factors involve participation in community organizations or activities. Health promotion interventions work by focusing on enhancing protective factors associated with health, mental health, wellness, and quality of life. For example, wellness education is one health promotion intervention that focuses on exercise and diet as protective factors against obesity.

In summary, we are considering prevention chiefly as that which attempts to alleviate risk factors, while health promotion attempts to develop and enhance protective factors. It is these distinctions in these two concepts that serve as the foundation for this book.

Prevention Meets Health Promotion: The Interface of Risk and Protective Factors

Traditional approaches to treating mental illness have been to first assess for symptoms (e.g., presence of hallucinations for at least 6 months—schizophrenia), then to identify risk factors (e.g., substance abuse), and finally to provide a prevention-focused intervention (e.g., a drug-free living program) to address those risk factors. These steps are followed by a program evaluation to determine if an impact has occurred. A health promotion approach would, in contrast, assess mental health (e.g., well-being), identify protective factors (e.g., supportive family), and then provide a health promotion intervention (e.g., family psychoeducation) to enhance the protective factors.

For example, it is established that substance abuse is a risk factor and has an adverse impact on mental health symptoms for individuals diagnosed with schizophrenia (Netski, Welsh, & Meyer, 2003).The traditional approach would be to provide a program like drug-free living, which is evaluated to determine if there is a reduced rate of substance use and lessening of the severity or number of mental health symptoms for a group of clients. The traditional approaches tend to focus on the illness aspects of the individual, with a target being to reduce or eliminate certain "harmful" activities. Human nature being what it is, this usually means that when one thing is removed (e.g., smoking three packs of cigarettes a day), it is often recalled at a higher cost (e.g., overeating). For example, we know this from data related to weight-loss programs whose clients often gain more weight after "relapse." Isaac Asimov (1920–1992) understood this paradox when he said "the first law of dietetics seems to be: if it tastes good, its bad for you."

A contemporary approach for mental health treatment would be to identify protective factors, provide a health promotion program to support those protective factors, and then evaluate the impact on mental health. For example, a protective factor in mental health is a supportive family. A health promotion approach would be to involve the family in a psychoeducation program that emphasizes social interaction (e.g., family activities) and then evaluate outcomes and the extent to which there are increased involvements in family life and social life. This approach has the advantage of giving the family and client something to work with and develop, instead of taking something away (e.g., placing client in residential facility or independent living arrangement away from family).

While it may seem confusing at first, health promotion does have prevention components. For example, health promotion programs that offer family psychoeducation can also include prevention materials targeting family conflict as a risk factor. Research in the mental health field has suggested that the interplay between risk and protective factors is associated with good health and mental health outcomes (Ingram & Price, 2000). One way to illustrate this benefit can be seen in Figure 2.1. In the case study illustrated in this figure, the client's situation is assessed using both a prevention and health promotion oriented assessment. As the case illustrates, typical prevention approaches to assessment begin with a focus on mental illness, followed by an assessment for symptoms, which in turn, lead to identifying risk factors that then provide guidance for determining a prevention intervention. When health promotion approaches are included, the focus on mental health is followed by an assessment for well-being, which, in turn, leads to identifying protective factors that then provide guidance for determining health promotion interventions. Taken together, both approaches yield critical information in our understanding of the client, his perception of events, and the concerns and needs of his family.

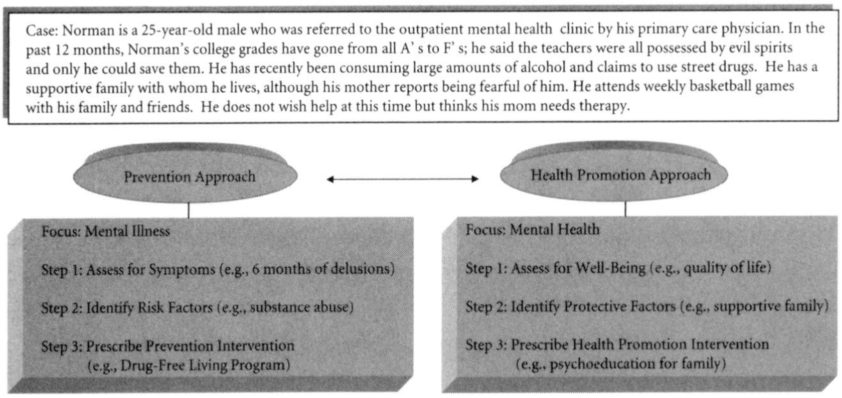

Case: Norman is a 25-year-old male who was referred to the outpatient mental health clinic by his primary care physician. In the past 12 months, Norman's college grades have gone from all A's to F's; he said the teachers were all possessed by evil spirits and only he could save them. He has recently been consuming large amounts of alcohol and claims to use street drugs. He has a supportive family with whom he lives, although his mother reports being fearful of him. He attends weekly basketball games with his family and friends. He does not wish help at this time but thinks his mom needs therapy.

Prevention Approach ↔ Health Promotion Approach

Focus: Mental Illness

Step 1: Assess for Symptoms (e.g., 6 months of delusions)

Step 2: Identify Risk Factors (e.g., substance abuse)

Step 3: Prescribe Prevention Intervention (e.g., Drug-Free Living Program)

Focus: Mental Health

Step 1: Assess for Well-Being (e.g., quality of life)

Step 2: Identify Protective Factors (e.g., supportive family)

Step 3: Prescribe Health Promotion Intervention (e.g., psychoeducation for family)

FIGURE 2.1. The interface of prevention and health promotion in mental health practice: Steps for incorporating risk and protective factors in the assessment process.

The combination of both approaches, however, is not without its detractors. Critics of the prevention/risk factor approach argue that it has too much of a health problem or disease/deficits orientation rather than the health and wellness orientation typically associated with health promotion and protective factors. Green and Kreuter (2005) argue that this is a needless criticism as it is unnecessary to construe risk-factor information as negative in tone. Their position is that the positiveness of a mental health education program continues to be a manifestation of the method and sensitivity with which the program is planned and delivered, not of the data and information used to justify the importance of the problem that the program is trying to mitigate.

In essence, clients would benefit from both approaches—health promotion in particular. From a funding perspective, the WHO (2004b) makes the argument that there is already sufficient evidence-based knowledge on risk and protective factors to warrant governmental and nongovernmental organizations' (NGOs) investments in the the development, dissemination, and implementation of evidence-based health promotion programs and policies. In particular, health promotion interventions that target protective factors and include individual, family, social, and economic groups, will be cost-effective, which in turn should be attractive to policy makers and other stakeholders. In fact, O'Donnell (2003) makes the argument that health promotion activities have already shown evidence of reducing the burden of health care costs.

■ Determinants of Health and Mental Health

Beyond risk and protective factors, what determines our health and mental health status? Research suggests that there are multiple "determinants" or influences that are known to promote physical health and mental health as well as to prevent or reduce the risks of mental illness (Green & Kreuter, 2005). These influences, also known as "determinants of health," include broad classes of factors (e.g., individual, family, social, economic, environmental, economic, and political) that are considered powerful forces in shaping behavioral and environmental risk factors. One method for organizing these health influences is through a public health framework known as the "determinants of health." This framework is typically constructed using information from extensive epidemiologic reviews of health and mental health conditions. The framework is often used to assist policy makers and researchers in their efforts to prioritize activities related to the development of health and mental health programs development and their funding.

One useful example of a determinants of health framework is provided by the World Health Organization (WHO, 2004a,b). Understanding the determinants of health and mental health begins with an examination of two levels:

micro level, which considers individual and family determinants and the *macro level*, which considers social, environmental, economic, and political determinants. Each of these categories of determinants may then be examined from our understanding of empirically supported risk and protective factors. For example, research suggests that micro-level determinants (e.g., individual and family) may have their strongest impact on mental health at sensitive or vulnerable periods along the lifespan and even have impact across generations. Risk factors such as child abuse and depression among young mothers have been shown to influence the mental health of their young children (Goodman & Gottlieb, 2002; Hammen & Brennan, 2003). In contrast, protective factors such as secure attachment, family social support, maternal warmth, and home learning environment have been shown to help promote family quality of life and guard against depression and anxiety in later life (Corcoran & Roberts, 2005; IOM, 2001).

Similarly, research has found that macro-level determinants (e.g., social, environmental, economic, and political) may have their strongest impact on the health and stability of the larger community. Although not mutually exclusive, a variety of risk factors and risk conditions (characteristics of the physical environment) have been linked to increased levels of psychiatric symptomatology and morbidity and barriers to participation in society (Ministry of Health, 2003). Similarly, research identifies a number of protective factors that are associated with broad-based social and environmental stability and health. A list of micro- and macro-level health determinants, risk, and protective factors is given in Figure 2.2.

Health Promotion: From Past to Present (1800 to 2000)

The philosophy and practice of health promotion is actually nothing new; it has been with us for many centuries, as illustrated in the following section.

- *In the beginning*. Health promotion is evidenced in the writings of western civilization's great philosophers, who drew close connections between body, mind, and soul and the proposed remedies for human ills (Catford, 2004).

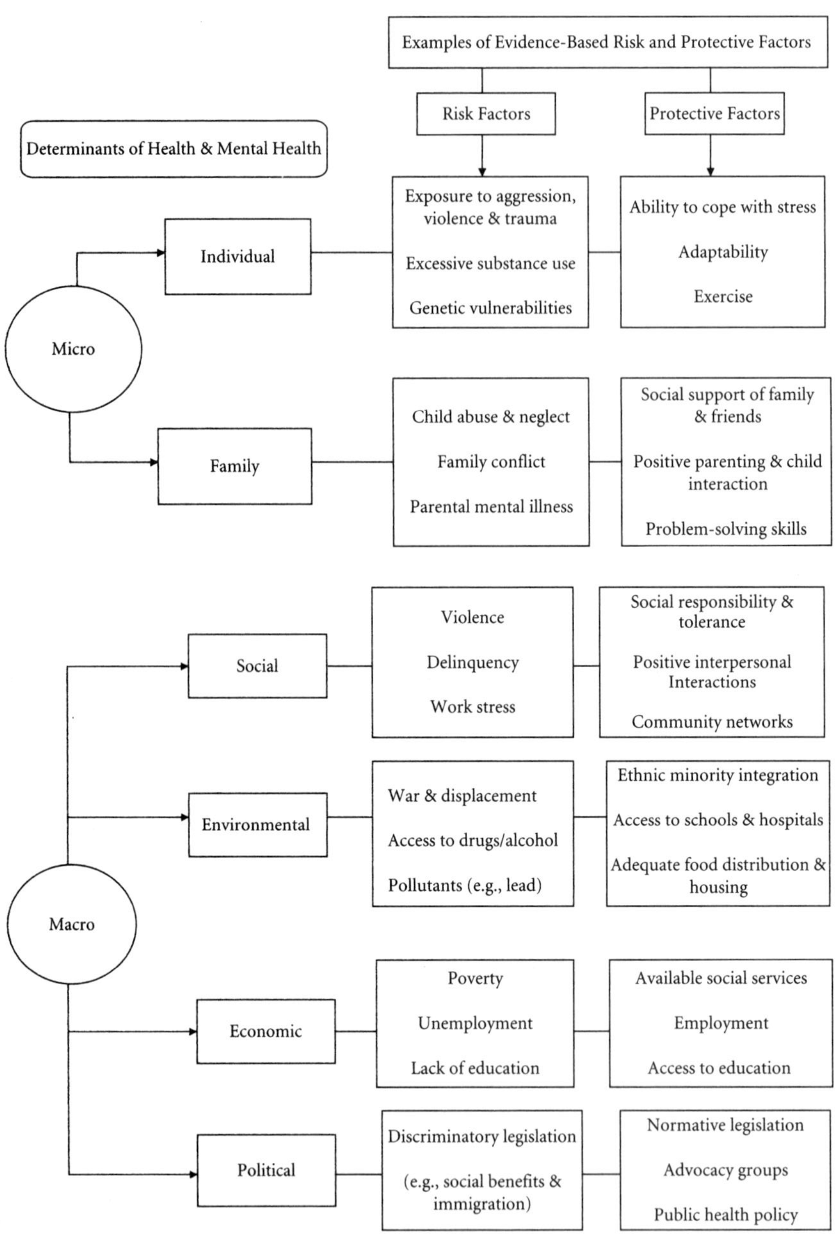

FIGURE 2.2. Determinants of health-mental health in relationship to evidence-based risk and protective factors. Adapted from World Health Organization, 2005.

Juvenal (ca. 60–130 A.D.) wrote: *Mens sana in corpore sano*, also known as "A sound mind in a sound body." Historically, early health promotion efforts were based on the notion that "The health of the soul and the vitality of the mind had a direct effect on the state of the body; evidence of effectiveness was [found] by virtue of observation." (Catford, 2004, p. 3). Hammurabi, a famous ruler of

Babylonia some two thousand years before Christ, established a community code of health care for the "protection of widows, orphans and the weak" (Trattner, 1999, p. 1). Even medieval hospitals, often attached to monasteries, recognized that their job was to promote the health not only of the sick poor but also of "wayfarers, pilgrims, orphans" by providing housing, food and an array of services (Trattner, 1999, p. 5).

- 1800s—In 1883, Jane Addams opened the country's first well-baby clinic in Chicago with the assistance of the first woman to graduate from the Johns Hopkins Medical School. Social workers established the first neighborhood health center, called the Cincinnati Social Experiment, in Ohio. The emphasis was on neighborhood and environmental health. It advanced a notion that was radical for the nineteenth century—that illness and disease may not be the result of race, nationality, or "bad blood" but rather the outcome of risk factors or the filthy environment and lack of reliable (if any) sanitation services almost anywhere (Dhooper, 1997, p. 316). This view of the situation as advanced by Addams became known as the "urban ideal" or "environmental ideal" (Trattner, 1999). Addams, in fact, received considerable national attention for her efforts to improve sanitation in her ward and became the first "garbage inspector" for her neighborhood in 1895 (Davis, 1973). Seeing the environment as a determinant of health was radical for those times, and yet its truth is so apparent that it is common knowledge today.
- 1940s to 1960s—For most of the early twentieth century, not much thought was given to health other than to think that it occurred through the financing and development of education programs. Health promotion was a remote notion, seldom translated into policy; it existed mostly within the confines of health education and fitness programs. The role of the environment was further accepted as a determinant of mental health, as seen by the studies of urban density and mental illness. The two classic studies of this were the Midtown Manhattan Study and the Chicago Study (Starr, 1982). Aside from the acceptance of the general notion of environmental determinants, not much happened during this period.
- 1970s—During the 1970s, health care in the United States focused on tackling preventable diseases (e.g., heart disease and some cancers) and risk behaviors (e.g., tobacco and poor nutrition) primarily through funding information and simple education efforts. The first effort to rethink this approach occurred at the behest of the World Health Organization in 1978 (WHO, 1978), which recognized that health improvements would not occur just by financing health services. At a meeting in Kazak of the former Soviet Union, the Declaration of Alma Ata adopted primary health care as the principal mechanism for health care delivery. This represented a shift in power from providers of health services (e.g., doctors, nurses, and hospital administrators) to consumers of these services and the wider community that pays for them, either directly or through insurance benefits or taxes. The focus shifted to health education and disease prevention. Following the WHO initiative, the Surgeon General's Report on Health Promotion and Disease

Prevention, *Healthy People* (U.S. Department of Health, Education and Welfare, 1979) sparked what has come to be known as the second public health revolution, in which health promotion was central. Paralleling the Surgeon General's Report was the landmark 1974 Canadian initiative, referred to as the 1974 LaLonde Report, entitled *A New Perspective on the Health of Canadians* (Lalonde, 1974). This report signaled the beginning of putting health promotion in the public spotlight (Green & Kreuter, 1999; p. 10). In 1975, U.S. Public Law 94–317 gave policy support to health promotion in the form of the Health Information and Health Promotion Act and the creation of the federal Office of Disease Prevention and Health Promotion (Trattner, 1999).

- 1980s—A number of policy and practice shifts occurred in the 1980s. The practice of professional health promotion gained its first international recognition and framework with the development with the Ottawa Charter for Health Promotion in 1986 (WHO, 1986). This document was the first of its kind to codify public health policy. That same year, the first significant document on health promotion to be published, *Concepts and Principles of Health Promotion*, gave the five principles discussed below. Also, in 1986, the first international journal on health promotion was established, a quarterly journal published by Oxford University Press. In 1988, a second conference began the discussion on developing partnerships with corporations, business, and community groups within the framework of public health policy. The term *health promotion* then superseded the term *health education*. The former became the preferable term, since it was thought that *health education* continued to imply individualistic approaches to the enhancement of health status and the notion of the passive individual requiring "facts" to defeat ignorance. This resulted in a shift from focusing on personal skills to supportive environments, community action, and health services (Green & Kreuter, 1991). The WHO prepared a global strategy report called *Health For All in the Year* 2000 (WHO, 1983), which became the driving force for comprehensive health development for the next 20 years.
- 1990s—During the 1990s, the emerging model of health promotion placed increasing emphasis on the importance of working closely with multiple sectors in order to achieve change in the upstream determinants of health. This approach stems from the recognition of the limitations of a reliance on educational approaches focused on individual behavior change to improve health. The core value of health promotion became that of reaching people through the sectors and settings where they lived and gathered (e.g., schools, neighborhoods, health care settings, workplaces, religious congregations). In this sense, contemporary health promotion theory and practice has shifted to one that advocates influence through engagement and partnership building (Dixon, Sindall, & Banwell, 2004). Professional meetings continued to be instrumental in developing a worldwide approach to health promotion. New themes emerged that emphasized building intersectional alliances and promoting partnerships in health, including the private sector, media, and the communication and

pharmaceutical industries. A seminal document used to raise public and policy makers' awareness of the need for mental health with a health promotion perspective was the U.S. Department of Health and Human Services (HHS) report, submitted by David Satcher, M.D., entitled *Mental Health: A Report of the Surgeon General* (1999). This report, the first produced in nearly 20 years on mental health, reviewed scientific advances in our understanding of mental health and mental illness and provided the impetus for health promotion efforts in addressing gross disparities in health and mental health practices for vulnerable populations (Department of Health & Human Services, 1999).

- 2000s—Health promotion now moved to include social determinants, tool kits, and new theories, such as the social development model of risk and protective factors (Hawkins, Catalano, & Arthur, 2002). Leadership development (discussed at length in Chapter 11), coupled with a focus on social determinants of health, seemed to be the key ingredients for the continued growth of health promotion. The current goal of health promotion is to respond to massive social changes that impact health, mental health, welfare, and the environment. The newest global effort toward this goal is found in the Bangkok Charter for Health Promotion (2005) initiative. Sponsored by participants in the Sixth Global Conference on Health Promotion and cohosted by the World Health Organization and the Ministry of Public Health of Thailand, this charter calls for policy coherence, investment, and partnering across governments, international organizations, civil society, and the private sector to work toward four key commitments, as listed earlier in this chapter (WHO, 2005).

Early Principles of Health Promotion

Catford (2004) describes the early principles of health promotion as reported in *Concepts and Principles of Health Promotion*, the first official document on health promotion developed by the World Health Organization (WHO, 1986). These early principles set the standard for which contemporary health promotion principles owe their origins.

- *Principle of Personal Empowerment: Health promotion involves the population as a whole in the context of everyday life, rather than focusing on people at risk for specific diseases.* This principle supports the notion that people must and are able to take control over their health as part of everyday life. This may be accomplished through spontaneous and/or organized action for health. In order to do this, people need complete and continuing access to information about health and mental health and how health and mental health might be sought by the entire population using all dissemination methods possible.
- *Principle of Determinants of Health: Health promotion is directed towards action on the determinants or causes of health.* This principle recognizes that a diversity of conditions influence or determines health, and consequently that health

promotion efforts require the close cooperation of multiple sectors that go beyond health services. Government—at the local, state, provincial, and national levels—has a distinct responsibility to ensure that the total environment, which is beyond the control of individuals and groups, is conducive to health (e.g., sanitation, physical education, and vaccinations).

- *Principle of Complementary Interventions: Health promotion combines diverse but complementary methods or approaches.* This principle highlights the multiple means whereby health promotion efforts may be used to campaign against health hazards in order to promote health. Examples include education, communication, legislation, fiscal measures, organizational change, community development, and spontaneous local activities.
- *Principle of Public Participation: Health promotion aims particularly at effective and concrete participation.* This principle stresses the importance of developing decision-making and problem-definition skills at the individual and collective levels. In essence, this is the notion that civic involvement is the most effective means of promoting health, in contrast to being told what is "good for you." This principle eliminates the notion of "substituted judgment," where a physician determines what is best.
- *Principle of Primary Health Care: Health promotion is an activity conducted in the health and human service fields of practice and is not just a medical service.* This principle highlights the important role of health professionals, particularly those in primary health care, in nurturing and enabling health promotion activities to occur through education and advocacy. This principle recognizes that medical services are appropriate for intervening and ameliorating a physical or mental health condition. Health promotion, in contrast, involves an array of health care professionals, from nurses, social workers, educators, physical and occupational therapists, and many other in allied health care.

While these principles were initially considered radical at the time they were first presented in 1986, they are now recognized as mainstream responsibilities. A more contemporary list of principles is discussed in Chapter 6.

■ Health Promotion Today

This section reviews the many facets and arenas of health promotion seen in contemporary society. Remember, the Ottawa Charter is over 20 years old and a lot has changed in health promotion during this time.

As suggested so far, the term *health promotion* is generally used to describe specific activities directed at particular goals, with a strong focus on the "rational management of both individuals and a population's healt h." Much emphasis is placed in the health promotion literature upon planning and coordination, assessing needs, consultation with the appropriate individuals and groups, as well as piloting and evaluating programs (Lupton, 1995, p. 51). These activities are fairly linear and reflect the process of effective health promotion.

As for health promotion for mental health conditions, interventions vary in scope and include strategies to promote the mental well-being of those who are not currently at risk (similar to prevention), those who are at increased risk, and those who are suffering or recovering from mental health problems (Hermann, Saxena, & Moodie, 2004). This would include the general population, persons with genetic vulnerabilities, persons with current mental illness—treated and untreated alike, and those with mental health conditions who no longer require or participate in treatment.

Activities of Health Promotion in a Mental Health Setting or Program

Health promotion programs for community mental health may look similar to programs in hospital settings offering active wellness programs. Understanding health promotion for mental health settings is enhanced by considering five categories of wellness-focused health promotion programs. These categories include the following: (1) client and family education, which focuses on such topics as living with depression, managing a family member with mental illness, or dealing with advanced directives in the event of an episode of mental illness; (2) behavior change for smoking cessation, weight control, and stress management, which is particularly predictive of a number of mental health conditions; (3) going hand in hand with behavior change are wellness and lifestyle programs involving aerobic exercises, walking, healthy eating, and socializing at community events; (4) medical self-care programs that provide knowledge about health providers, local availability, one's own medical status—for example, diabetes management; and (5) workplace-related activities programs for wellness in the workplace in order to have healthy workers who are productive (Mittlemark, 1999; Dibble, 2003; Green & Kreuter, 1999).

Location of Health Promotion Activities in Mental Health

Health promotion activities are hardly confined to the mental health clinic setting. Health promotion activities can be offered not only at the mental health clinic or program locations but also at community centers, schools, fairs, churches, libraries, recreational sites like parks, and places of business such as pharmacies or beauty parlors offering blood pressure screening or depression assessment.

Green and Kreuter (2005) suggest that the community is the proper center of gravity for health promotion. *Community* is broadly defined as either a geographical community (e.g., neighborhood) or identity community (e.g., consumer community). Specifically, the consumer community would include those individuals who receive or participate in mental health services. Health promotion activities would be targeted to their identified needs within a particular geographic area.

Who Can Do "Health Promotion" in a Mental Health Setting?

Health promotion is considered an interdisciplinary field; therefore no one discipline has a monopoly on the opportunities to conduct health promotion activities. Since many mental health consumers' central point of contact in the geographic community is a community mental health center, all staff in this setting have an opportunity to affect basic health and mental health care for this population. Within one mental health setting, social workers may take the lead as health promotion educators and community advocates, since their training is geared toward issues of social justice and advocacy. In the same setting, registered nurses or nurse practitioners may assess and coordinate health care, developing educational and health promotion opportunities specific to this population—such as working with the consumer on techniques for the management for diabetes (Miller & Martinez, 2003). Research by Miller and Martinez (2003) found that when nurse case managers were responsible for overseeing consumers' physical health, other staff/case managers had more time to spend on treatment consistent with their education and training. Secondary findings revealed that this type of personnel structure improved job satisfaction and that consumers' health care improved in terms of quality, efficiency, access, continuity, and follow-up. Mental health case managers can be involved in coaching on-site workplace wellness skills, such as reminding consumer employees about the need for breaks and bringing healthy foods for lunch. Mental health consumers are equally qualified to provide peer-based health promotion activities using peer helper strategies. Examples would include a peer-run socialization program or peer-facilitated self-help groups.

In school settings, school counselors have a unique opportunity to work with students and teachers to incorporate mental wellness topics into curriculums. The National Alliance for the Mentally Ill (NAMI) has a new program that is bringing mental health awareness programs onto college campuses. Such programs, called NAMI Campus-Based Affiliates, may be coordinated by students themselves through student associations and student health services or by consumers from mental health agencies. Their purpose is to educate the campus community about mental illnesses and early intervention, provide support for students with mental illnesses, and to reach out to family members and friends of students living with mental illnesses (Hollingworth, 2006). Psychiatrists are uniquely qualified to support health promotion activities, given their medical training and specialty in community psychiatry. Primary care physicians in preventive medicine see a number of patients with multiple health and mental health issues and are now encouraged to take a lead in health promoting activities that address preventable deaths, including such factors as tobacco use, diet, physical exercise and general activity levels, and the abuse of alcohol. As Dibble (2003) points out, physicians are in a unique position to assist patients in behavior change through four main roles: (1) health promotion researcher, (2) educator-communicator, (3) systems manager, and (4) health promotion advocate. As health promotion researchers, physicians can provide consumers with the latest in research findings (e.g., evidence-based practice guidelines) to support health plan efforts. As an educator-communicator, the physician can actively discuss options of health interventions with clients and family members and even act as community speakers at mental health events. Physicians also act as change agents for mental health organizations. For example, physicians can monitor wait lists and triage procedures to ensure timely access to care for mental health clients. Last, physicians are in a key position to influence agency culture by advocating a health promotion philosophy as well as related strategies and interventions.

As this discussion illustrates, health promotion is really about a philosophy, not the discipline or degree, and can be done with one person at a time and with groups of people regardless of the professional discipline. This does not preclude the importance of training, but it does suggest that health promotion is an activity that can be experienced by a variety of individuals, community members and political groups. As one client said at our focus group meeting: "Healing is a social process and we need each other." At the Boston Center for Psychiatric Rehabilitation, an entire team of multi-trained professionals, consumers, and volunteers provide core activities that are all about health promotion. Topics are presented as courses and students/clients enroll in a variety of classes ranging from Mindfulness to Physical Fitness to Sexuality to Computer 101. This program is discussed further in Chapters 8 and 9.

Health Promotion Advocates/Health Promoters

A health promotion advocate, also known as a health promoter, can be anyone who works to prevent disease and help individuals or groups to maintain good health (Evans & Degutis, 2003). Such persons may work in a variety of settings, including local departments of physical health and mental health, community health, and mental health centers and clinics, academic institutions as well as in the role of practitioners in the community and in work and school environments.

Health advocates or health promoters may be employed as outreach workers, educators, clinical practitioners, administrators, and policy makers (Evans & Degutis, 2003). Health promotion advocates emphasize the delivery of broad-based mental health services to the general population—not just to the individuals with a health or mental health condition. These services emphasize education and interventions that aid people who have either already developed mental illnesses or those who may be at risk for developing a mental illness (p. 2). By way of example, in one rural community in eastern Oregon, Spanish-speaking outreach workers affiliated with the local mental health authority act as formal and informal health promoters for homebound Latina mothers whose husbands are employed as migrant workers in the local orchards. Common complaints expressed by these women are depression, isolation, and domestic violence—all serious issues that would not receive attention through local mental health clinics were it not for the trusted role that health promoters play with these women.

Goals of Health Promotion

The goals of health promotion are diverse and easily applied in mental health settings. Broadly stated, health promotion has the following goals: "lifting the health status of people, improving their quality of life and providing cost-effective solutions to health and mental health problems" (WHO, 2000, p. 3). Specifically, health promotion has four targets goals: *individual well-being*, *cost-effectiveness*, *social equity*, and *sustainability*.

At the *individual* level, the goals of health promotion include short circuiting illness, improve quality of life through change or development of health-related behavior and conditions of living, increasing an individual's emotional and psychological well-being, and supporting the ability to deal with life's adversities (Green & Kreuter, 1991, p.22).

At the *economic* level, the goal of health promotion is to provide cost-effective solutions for mental health and health conditions while developing performance indicators based on specified objectives. For example, educating a client who has diabetes on how to test for blood sugar daily will, in the long run, avert unnecessary trips to the emergency department due to hypoglycemia and fainting. The performance indicator is a reduction of trips to the emergency department after the diabetes educational component has been introduced into the treatment plan.

At the *social* level, a health promotion goal is to reduce inequities in the way physical health and mental health care are accessed. For example, a major goal of *Healthy People* 2010 is to eliminate health disparities (U.S. Department of Health and Human Services, 2000). Thus, any effort to promote health among mental health populations must be to "reduce the multilevel disparities that people experience by working with communities to develop health enhancing environments" (p. 51). Finally, the goal of any health promotion program is to ensure that positive results are *sustained* over time, which includes healthful living patterns and behavioral and environmental changes induced by the program or intervention.

Health Promotion Objectives. To achieve these health promotion goals, we can borrow from the fields of public health and social work. Dhooper (1997) summarizes seven objectives that can be used to accomplish health promotion goals. These are:

- Ensure the provision of psychosocial services for individuals and families.
- Provide information and knowledge about community service networks to consumers and health care providers.
- Collaborate with professionals from other disciplines in delivering comprehensive care.
- Promote universal and humanistic values within the health care system, such as the social work value of self-determination.
- Facilitate consumer participation in the planning and evaluation of services.
- Discover systemic factors that prevent access or discourage use of services.
- Document social conditions that interfere with the attainment of health and working for policy and program changes to address those conditions (p. 210).

Strategies

The goals and objectives of health promotion can be achieved by using two organizing activities directed toward individuals or groups and the community.

At *the individual or group level,* mental health clinicians using health promotion strategies can provide relevant information, clarify misinformation, offer advice, provide and invite feedback, develop an action plan and prepare and establish objectives for goal completion.

Dhooper (1997) recommends four key strategies when choosing an educational health promotion activity for individuals and groups in mental health settings. These are as follows: (1) Strive for a match between the educational strategy and the characteristics of the system (individual, group or community), which include composition, culture, and demographics. (2) Remember that different people learn in different ways and to organize educational groups using a mix of methods. Examples include the didactic method—sharing information and ideas; the discussion method—which allows for more interaction between worker and client system; the visual method—which uses graphs, diagrams, pictures, and films; and the action method—which emphasizes learning through experiencing, role modeling, and coaching. (3) Be sensitive to individual/group characteristics such as intelligence, verbal and comprehension ability, and cultural qualities. and (4) Carefully select the context of the educational activity in which to maximize success—i.e., selecting a comfortable setting and materials that embrace normal health approaches rather than mental health symptomatology (pp. 229–230).

An example of a consumer-driven health promotion activity offered for individuals in a group setting is illustrated below.

Case Example. A case management team at the local community mental health clinic was asked by members of the women's support group to provide a "class" on tai chi. One of the team members has just read a research study on the health benefits of tai chi and consulted with the local YMCA to recruit volunteers. In coordination with members of the women's support group, a case manager from the team contacted a tai chi instructor, who agreed to provide a free session once a week at the local YMCA. The beauty of this effort was that the women clients were now able to go to a regular community program rather than having all their services provided at the mental health clinic.

At *the community level*, organizing or advocating for health promotion activities for mental health services requires skills that are similar to individual and group work. In contrast, at the community level there is more of an emphasis on community building, such as facilitating civic participation and volunteerism. Dhooper (1997) recommends four strategies for organizing community level health promotion activities for mental health: (1) use existing resources in the community and the mental health agency, (2) target specific groups and populations for intensive education and use multi-pronged, audience-appropriate educational strategies, (3) create a package of appropriate strategies by targeting one's own agency resources, and (4) utilize the local mass media as a special resource for disseminating information. There is interest in the community development approach to health promotion with the intended outcome of the ability to recognize, use, and increase the capacities and resources within the community—as opposed to depending on a significant infusion of resources from outside the community (pp. 229–230).

Case Example. Members of a consumer-run art class hosted by a neighborhood-based mental health center decided to take their art class to another level by holding an art exhibit. There were two reasons for this: first, in order to raise awareness of mental illness, and second, to obtain needed funds to rent a studio to do their artwork. Through the use of media blitzes, lectures to community and professional groups, and neighborhood flyer announcements, and food/music/show space donations by local businesses, an art show and fund raiser was held at the local Masonic temple. Portions of the proceeds went back to the artist themselves and the remainder was dedicated to a fund for supplies and studio rental space. At the time of this publication, the artists as consumers are part of a very active art community in an urban northwest city.

Integrating Health Promotion into Mental Health Services and Policies

Services. Planning community-based health promotion activities for mental health services requires a dual approach that provides for activities that help modify existing health concerns and the circumstances and environments that support those behaviors. Dhooper (1997) suggests that these activities include communitywide health education, wellness interventions, and efforts to change laws and regulations in areas that create barriers to health. For example, planning for a mental health agencies health promotion program would involve deciding on "what," "where," and "how" activities are implemented. Individuals who participate in these programs are encouraged to examine their health-related behaviors and readiness to alter or change those behaviors that may be a barrier to wellness. Additionally, the community will need to have a reinforcing atmosphere.

One seminal health promotion planning model is the PRECEDE-PROCEED model presented by Green and Kreuter (2005). PRECEDE stands for *p*redisposing, *r*einforcing and *e*nabling *c*onstructs in *e*ducational/ecological *d*iagnosis and *e*valuation (p. 9). PROCEED stands for *p*olicy, *r*egulatory, and *o*rganizational *c*onstructs in *e*ducational and *e*nvironmental *d*evelopment (p. 9). Although quite extensive, this planning model has much to offer mental health programs who wish to conduct a comprehensive analysis or diagnosis of program conditions followed by an analysis of implementation and evaluation factors. Briefly, the model has eight phases: (1), social assessment (e.g., quality of life using social indicators); (2), epidemiologic assessment (e.g., genetics, behavior, environment and health); (3), educational and ecological assessment (e.g., predisposing factors, knowledge, reinforcing factors, attitudes and enabling factors, accessibility); and (4), administrative and policy assessment and intervention alignment (e.g., health education and policy regulation and organization).

After the assessment and diagnosis phases of analysis, the program planner would review implementation strategies as follows: (5), implementation; followed by (6), process evaluation, which begins as soon as the program starts and describes how the intervention was implemented; (7), an impact evaluation, which is conducted during the implementation, such as monitoring the fidelity of the implementation of the strategies; and finally (8), outcome evaluation which assesses the change on critical variables from before to after the program, including follow-ups. This model has been well received in public health circles for years and remains one of the standard models for health promotion program planners (Green & Kreuter, 2005). For a more detailed review of this model, see Green and Kreuter, *Health Program Planning*, 2005—listed in the references.

Policies. Integrating health promotion into a national mental health strategy is an important goal. Ganikso (1994) identified four roles that a national health promotion program should take. It should (1) provide knowledge, information, and communication strategies; (2) produce educational strategies, messages, and materials, (3) energize, through sponsorship of market research, educational models development and demonstration programs, and 4) serve as a catalyst by stepping forward as the consensus builder and coordinator of a national strategy. The Ministry of Health of New Zealand (2002) provides a good example of how to integrate health promotion principles into mental health policy initiatives through their national program entitled "Building on Strengths." See http://moh.govt.nz.

Funding for Health Promotion in Mental Health Settings

Funding for health promotion programs and activities is typically different from agency to agency, state to state, and country to country. In the United States, most public health departments receive minimal local, state, and federal funds for health promotion activities. Mental health settings receive even less. Consequently, mental health programs that wish to provide health promotion activities as part of mainstream services typically have to be creative in the way they access funds, such as the art exhibit example mentioned above. Short of public policy that actually provides funding for health promotion activities, most programs are funded through a combination of state and federal grants, government contracts, fund raising, and foundation support. Some state and federal grants require the applicant to match the government grant. Formula grants are funding that are distributed to a class of entitled agencies, such as a mental health department or university, that have met the conditions governing entitlement and are commonly weighted according to population and determination of need. Project grants are awarded on a competitive basis and based on a proposal that identifies need and plan for what would be done with the funding. Examples of health promotion projects that have received federal funding are the Center for Psychiatric Rehabilitation in Boston, Massachusetts. The center is jointly funded by National Institute on Disability and Rehabilitation Research and the Center for Mental Health Services, of the Substance Abuse and Mental Health Services Administration (SAMHSA), which is under the federal Health and Human Services. For more information about this program, see the website www.uspra.org.

Another source of revenue is foundation funding associated with health promotion and mental health, which might include community trusts, such as the Meyer Memorial Trust in Oregon, and special purpose foundations, such as Robert Wood

Johnson Foundation, which focus on health issues, and the Ford Foundation, which has a program on promoting healthy sexuality. The advantage of foundation support is that these organizations are likely to fund demonstration projects more readily than ongoing projects. This has important relevance for mental health settings that wish to introduce new methods of health promotion activities, such as wellness classes, that may not be considered evidence-based practice approaches or funded by Medicaid or private insurance but are requested by consumers, families, and staff.

Fund raising is a fairly new phenomenon for mental health agencies, which have typically depended on local, state, and federal revenues. In the United States, recent governmental funding streams for mental health have been reduced or redirected to military campaigns, law enforcement, and corrections. As a consequence, new funding strategies are needed. Mental health agencies are now participating in fund raising events in order to support new health promotion initiatives. Examples include community art shows, wine tastings, auctions, and donor development. Moreover, fund raising may be a successful way to highlight the need for health and wellness programs that counter public stigma regarding mental illness. The other benefit is that fund raising tends to be local and may therefore establish more partnerships in the efforts of building community health. This is, of course, one of the essential elements of health promotion.

■ Limitations of Health Promotion

Despite the potential benefits of integrating health promotion into mental health practice settings, there are limitations. These can be summarized as natural resistance, personal blame, shame, and conflicting messages. These issues are also addressed in Chapter 11.

Natural Resistance

It is likely that every mental health clinician has at one time or another uttered the words, "My client just won't change; he or she just seems so unmotivated." Lupton (1995) sees reluctance to change, also referred to as "resistance" as a normal reaction when individuals feel forced to accept knowledge that is deemed "appropriate" by others or when they are engage in behavior change that feels either unnatural and conflicted with their emotional state. When health promotion strategies conflict with a client's self-image, the result can be a certain dissonance or sense of uneasiness that leads to resistance at the personal level and possibly at the organizational level (see Lupton, p. 134). It is a natural human desire to want things to be different in terms of antecedents and consequences; it is also natural to not really want to change one's behavior. For example, a lonely person may want more friends but may be "resistant" or reluctant to changing the self-imposed social isolation or learn the personal skills for assertion or communication. Given that this dilemma is a common human experience, it becomes easier to see why persons with mental health problems would be similarly reluctant to change.

Studies have shown the paradoxical attitude people have to health promotion strategies, both accepting the orthodoxies and rejecting them as too difficult to apply to their own lives (Lupton, p. 140). Klein (1998) argues that, ironically, the "health promotion discussion around the prohibition of alcohol or smoking may thus serve to underline their meanings, paradoxically promoting these actions rather than discouraging them. The more an entity represses, the more they incite. The more a behavior is discussed, overtly prohibited, denounced as evil, sinful or health damaging, the more pleasurable it becomes. Censorship thus fosters its use" (p. 154).

Personal Blame

Given the emphasis that health promotion has on lifestyle, many of the essential elements of health promotion are directed toward the regulation of individual consumption. One's lifestyle may be pathologized as a source of ill-health resulting from the culmination of a variety of specific and discrete risky behaviors. Examples of such behaviors include excessive use of alcohol and tobacco, which are considered direct threats to one's health and contrary to the interests of public health. Other lifestyle risk factors are being overweight or obese and consuming a poor diet including too much fat, salt, and sugar. Risk also stems from limited exercise patterns, unsafe sexual activity, insufficient sleep, and the misuse of medications. Lupton (1995) notes that individuals or social groups who are considered to have a "problem" in one or more of these areas are represented in health promotion discussions as weak and easily susceptible to external pressures and in need of a higher level of rationality (p. 150). What this interpretation suggests is that these risk behaviors are removed from the social meaning they have for individuals and the context in which they occur. Even the uses of dire warnings about alcohol have little effect in settings where the social exchange benefit is greater than the social prohibition, as exemplified by traditional beer festivals in local communities.

Shame

As Lupton (1995) argues, some efforts at health promotion may serve to restigmatize people by focusing on individual responsibility to change what has been deemed "dangerous" or risky. And when they don't, they are viewed within the moral judgments of their providers, or at least from the perspective of the consumer. Health promotion has been criticized as serving as an apparatus of moral regulation, serving to draw distinctions between civilized and uncivilized behaviors, and to privilege a version of subjectivity that incorporates rationality; it has also been scorned as if it promotes notions of the human body that is separate from the mind, free will and personal responsibility, and needful of careful management and control to represent certain social groups as uncontrolled and thus the threatening (Lupton, 1995). What we "profess as truth" may have no place in the clients' daily lives.

Conflicting Messages

In terms of philosophy, Beatie (1991, in Lupton, p. 52), sees health promotion activities as directed by conflicting political perspectives that are split between paternalist versus participatory, and individualistic versus collective. In terms of alcohol use, most health promotion literature tends to emphasize the negative effects of alcohol, concentrating on excessive use without acknowledging the research indicating that moderate alcohol consumption appears beneficial for protecting against heart disease and stroke (Beatie, 1991; National Institute on Alcohol Abuse and Alcoholism, 2000). Similarly, there are a number of epidemiologic studies suggesting that the nicotine in cigarettes may not be as harmful as previously thought and may actually be helpful in small doses (IOM, 2001a). In the United States, most politicians have supported the zero tolerance policy on marijuana use despite evidence from the Institute of Medicine Reports (1999; 2000a) concluding that marijuana use has moderate medicinal benefits. Such studies have tended to be downplayed in the medical and public health literature, and funding is generally not forthcoming from national funding bodies to follow up these findings because of the stigmatization around cigarettes and marijuana and the current obsession with their side effects (Lupton, 1995, p. 150). And every politician fears being criticized as being "soft on drugs."

Lack of Protocols

Empiric data from the Institute of Medicine's report *Promoting Health* (2000c), show effective health promoting social and behavioral interventions. Despite these, Dibble (2003) comments that health promotion practice protocols have been slow to disseminate and implement due to the confusing science base. Some providers receive confusing guidelines and decide not to implement them because of the modest health promotion research. Given the move toward evidence-based practice protocols, clinicians may be less inclined to include an approach that cannot be linked to an evidence-based practice protocol and particular outcomes.

■ Critical Issues for the Field of Health Promotion

If health promotion is to assume a more active role in mental health care, it must first examine critical concerns which include (1) barriers and limited standing as a viable and integral dimension of mental health care and (2) lack of political will. Dibble (2003) provides an extensive literature review on why health promotion has not been integrated into preventive medicine. Many of the same factors that contribute to the barriers in preventive medicine also apply to mental health. These barriers are presented in the following three categories: *systems*, *clinician-office*, and *patient*.

Systems barriers make up a long list, including (1) the lack of health promotion and prevention accountability to direct multiple partners within a wide political arena to deliver complex interventions; (2) competing commercial or corporate forces; (3) the medical tradition of serving urgency or crisis before severity; (4) patient mobility; (5) difficulties formulating guidelines to evaluate progress of long-term behavioral interventions; (6) lack of established or accessible information centers (e.g., evidence-based practice); (7) inadequate resources, including communication technologies to train supportive mental health teams and establish and maintain integrated service delivery systems; and (8) insufficient insurance or reimbursement for services, which may be perceived as expensive to purchasers looking for short-term cost effectiveness rather than long-term savings. Other systems reasons cited are related to inadequate training in academic programs, poor visibility of health promotion programs in academic settings and poor funding for faculty development related to health promotion training. While this list is not exhaustive, the number of barriers mentioned here makes the point.

Clinician-office barriers are like the systems barriers, numerous. Examples include patient/client population, high patient/client case loads, time pressures to see clients and do the paperwork, low patient expectations, conflicting practice guidelines, inadequate training and confidence to identify when health promotion services are needed and who needs them, lack of team-oriented practice approach, community referral resources, patient education materials, skepticism about patients motivation to modify risk behaviors, insufficient reimbursement limit ability to deliver health promotion services (Dibble, 2003). And the list goes on.

Patient barriers, not surprisingly, are also numerous. Examples include costs, motivation, social values, lack of time, insufficient knowledge and experiences connecting illness and behavioral risk factors, lack of meaningful, customized patient education, and inaccessible services because of language, cultural barriers, and lack of transportation. This list is also not exhaustive. For an extensive citation of each barrier, the reader is referred to the original publications by Dibble (2003).

Limited Standing and Lack of Political Will

O'Donnell (2003) identifies two reasons for the limited standing, or shall we say, limited recognition of health promotion efforts. While not nearly as extensive as the other barriers, these are probably more enormous in size and resistant to change. The three examples are (1) a lack of presidential/political support, (2) failure of health or mental health advocacy organizations to adopt the health promotion issue, and (3) changed legislative environments, which may focus on international policy or economy and war at the expense of domestic policies and programs. These impediments, unfortunately, are not restricted to the federal government but seem to include most state, provincial, county, and municipal jurisdictions as well.

O'Donnell (2003) argues that "the only way a major shift in federal government policy occurs rapidly is through significant financial contributions from lobbying groups or strong political and presidential support." (p. iv). This, too, applies to state and local jurisdictions. In the case of health promotion, the current federal administration of the United States has no national health policy legislation that incorporates the concept of health promotion like we see in the Canadian Charter of Ottawa (1986), the Bangkok Charter for Health Promotion (2005), and the New Zealand Building on Strengths Initiative (2003). As mentioned in Chapter 1, there are however, key documents that have called for a health promotion approach to be included in mental health reform efforts—none of which is funded or has the teeth of legislation behind it. Ironically, the key program that could guide national policy efforts and potential legislation, the Centers for Disease Control and Prevention (CDC) has had its own budget drastically cut to the tune of $6.6 billion for 2004, with 20% of those cuts in programs to address nutrition, physical activity and obesity—all issues of great health significance for many individuals with mental illness. Obesity, for example, accounts for 27 cents of every dollar of health care cost, so effective programs promise considerable savings, or resources that may be allocated to other programs, such as health promotion.

At the administrative level, the Department of Health and Human Services (DHHS) declined to endorse legislation that would have supported efforts to embed health promotion research and programs into mainstream services. For example, Health Promotion FIRST (Funding Integrated Research, Synthesis, and Training) was legislation designed to direct the DHHS to formulate strategic plans to accomplish the following five objectives: (1) develop the basic and applied science of health promotion, (2) integrate health promotion concepts into all aspects of society, (3) create new programs in workplace health promotion research, (4) make existing research funds available to a wider range of organizations, and (5) increase funding to existing federal health promotion efforts. DHHS believed they already had the authority to perform these functions; they felt that they were making good progress in other areas and therefore declined to support the legislation.

A second setback for health promotion has been the failure of any of the established health or mental health advocacy organizations (e.g., the National Alliance for Mental Illness) to adopt health promotion as a cause. Unlike the American Cancer Society, which is disease-specific, health promotion has no distinct illness, disease, or celebrity to advocate for its visibility. The best example of this can be seen in the different funding efforts for prevention over health promotion. While the CDC have been most routinely recognized as the public face of health promotion, "it serves poor people, community health departments, and foreign populations experiencing epidemics. These are groups that have scarce resources—least of all advocacy or lobbying abilities" (O'Donnell, 2003, p. v).

By way of comparison, "Research! America," a not-for-profit, membership-supported public education and advocacy alliance group, has been successful in engaging the public and research community through its Prevention Research Initiative, a campaign to increase public and federal support for prevention research. In 2003, working closely with the Senate Appropriations Committee, they successfully lobbied to have an amendment passed to increase prevention funding to the National Institutes of Health by 9% and to restore part of the 2004 budget of the CDC to the 2003 level.

Research! America has the advantage of having a strong membership base consisting of research organizations, trade associations, and other organizations that together receive billions of dollars in research grants from National Institutes of

Health. The health promotion field does not have the money to support even modest financial contributions or lobbying efforts. At this point it seems that health promotion is dependent on the political will of key legislators or advocacy organizations to help disseminate its message.

Why It Will Get Better

Despite all these gloomy reasons for the stagnation of health promotion activities, there is reason to be hopeful. New legislation on health promotion is being drafted. In the United States, the scientific community—including the National Institutes of Health, Center for Substance Abuse and Prevention, and academic centers—is gaining a fresh perspective on the field of health promotion. There are also efforts at the federal and state levels to enact legislation to establish parity between health and mental health systems, although individual states, like Ohio and Minnesota, have done far more than is seen at the federal level. Part of this has been encouraged by consumer and family groups wanting a different experience from conventional health and mental health services. There is also increasing scientific knowledge of the interplay of individual, social, and environmental circumstances as related to health, mental health, and wellness. At the international level, influential groups like the International Union for Health Promotion and Education and the World Health Organization are staging successful congresses at which policy heads of state are keynote speakers.

Are We Ready for the Challenge?

Not everyone will want to engage in health-enhancing and health promoting activities at all times. If people or a community do not recognize a need for change or have no investment in different outcomes, they will not respond accordingly. Therefore any health promotion intervention will be successful only if the individual, group, or community is ready to change. Rissel and Bracht (1999, p.68) refer to this level of readiness as issue awareness. While a guiding goal of health promotion is to enable people to gain greater control over the determinants of their own health, Green and Kreuter (1991) point out that this may be an ineffective goal given that not all individuals are or can be responsible for their own health matters. For example, most cigarette smokers want to quit but simply are too addicted to nicotine to do so, and most believe that primary care providers should help.

Evans and Degutis (2003) make the point that advocacy for mental health promotion is often much harder than advocacy for other health-related issues, especially treatments (e.g., chemotherapy) and cures (e.g., vaccines). The continuing challenge for health promotion advocates in the field of mental health can be summed up in these points:

- It takes a long time to see the results of health promotion efforts.
- Because of multiple factors, it is difficult to scientifically demonstrate that a particular health promotion intervention impacts individual and community well-being.

- It is also much harder to identify advocates who are "beneficiaries" of health promotion than it is to find advocates who are patients with particular diseases. In other words, it is much easier for funders, insurers and policy makers to conceptualize the lives saved by curing disease than to picture the lives saved by preventing disease and promoting a good lifestyle after disease.

Conclusion

Integrating health promotion into mainstream and conventional mental health service systems is a respectable goal and one that is clearly long overdue. Health promotion is a natural partner with mental health care owing to its three-tiered approach—individual, community and policy.

At the individual level, strategies deal with both the intrapersonal and interpersonal dimensions of human behavior. At the community level, strategies have been built on ideas from community organizations, advocacy, and an ecologic approach to problem solving. All which should be tailor-made for the particular physical and mental health risks of the community. At the policy level, although there has been a neglect of legislation to infuse health promotion into mainstream mental health care policy mandates, politicians are becoming increasingly educated about the benefits of health and mental health parity.

As a field, health promotion has matured from its early emphasis on simple education and information to responding to massive social change that impacts health, mental health, welfare, and the environment (Catford, 2004). As a philosophy, it is a notion that supports clients as they set their own course for achieving health and mental health and for having communities determine what is healthy and helping them get there. Further, the philosophy of health promotion mirrors what many consumer groups are advocating for today: health and wellness should be recognized as starting at the individual level and moving to family, community, and the political arena (New Freedom Commission, 2003).

A final thought comes by way of the Scottish Health Education Authority (1997), which has reviewed a number of mental health promotion interventions. Part of their conclusion reminds us that it is important to ensure that any initiative aiming to enhance mental health through health promotion efforts should not impose on people without their consent. The report cautions that steps should be taken to ensure empowerment-based practice, which works with people and involves them in the whole process. This means understanding and respecting the way people feel, think, and act. Subjective experience has a legitimate and crucial place in contributing to the understanding of mental health and informing the development of services. Without consideration of these individual proclivities, most efforts will just be "full of sound and fury, signifying nothing" (Shakespeare, 1603).

In Our Own Words . . . Family and Consumer Perspectives on Mental Health Treatment Services: Focus Group Feedback

Topic: Integration of Health and Mental Health Care—Part 2

Summary

As this chapter illustrates, health promotion is a field of public health practice that emphasizes action and advocacy as a means to support and influence the determinants of health for individuals, communities, and public policy. Central to this approach is how health and mental health systems interface when it comes to promoting the health of individuals with mental health conditions. Staying with this theme, family members and consumers were asked to comment on their experiences with the health system when they had a mental health concern. As noted below, family members and consumers both ranked staff/provider training or education as the most important concern they had when mental health needs brought them into health care settings.

What Can We Learn?

Based on these perspectives, health and mental health care systems would benefit from cross training staff to recognize, treat, and/or to collaboratively refer out clinical cases in which comorbid health and mental health conditions are present—all in a respectful manner. The following section details results of the focus group meeting as reported by family members and consumers.

Focus Group Statement: "*Describe your experiences with the health system when you have a Mental health problem or need.*"

Family Perspectives

Core Themes	Summary of Experiences	Comments
(Ranked in terms of priority)		
First— Education	Health professionals need to be educated about mental illness.	"I feel that I have to constantly educate health professionals about mental illness since I am the keeper of the medical records and our primary care doctors seem afraid to have mentally ill people in treatment." (M., *parent*)

(continued)

Focus Group Statement: " *Describe your experiences with the health system when you have a Mental health problem or need.*" *(continued)*		
Second—Communication	County clinics and public sector mental health clinics do not communicate consistently with each other.	"My daughter found a primary care doctor willing to coordinate services but not the mental health caseworkers. This resulted in medication errors because the files were not jointly reviewed." (L., *parent*)
Third—Legal	Legal action is arbitrarily used as a treatment issue.	"Before my son turned 18, I was threatened with custody issues if I didn't comply with his treatment plan. When he turned 18, the doctors would not talk to me because he was considered an adult." (J., *parent*)

Consumer Perspectives

Core Themes	***Summary of Experiences***	**Comments**
(Ranked in terms of priority)		
First—Training and Education	Hospital staff don't seem to be trained to deal with a mentally ill person who also needs first aid.	"When I go to the emergency room for medical care—like heart palpitations—they turn my case over to the social worker when they learn I take psychiatric meds for depression—and then don't get around to treating my heart problems; its as if we are not supposed to have medical needs." (J.V.S., *consumer*)

3. Evidence-Based Mental Health for Health Promotion Practice

Treatment should include all areas of a person's life—school, home and community; attention should be on modifying behaviors that contribute to the mentally ill person being and not being successful in his or her environment.

—*S., sibling*

■ Chapter Overview

Evidence-based practice (EBP) is an aspect of health promotion that describes a process of using the best available scientific evidence to answer the question: What seems to works best? This chapter provides a snapshot of contemporary definitions, principles, topics, issues, and strategies encountered in the process of selecting efficacious mental health and health promotion interventions for complex clinical problems.

The chapter begins by examining evidence-based practice (EBP) from four perspectives—those of researchers, administrators, health promotion advocates, and policy makers. Next, descriptions are provided of various categories, definitions, principles, strategies and goals of EBP that shape the application of EBP for health promotion activities. The remainder of the chapter reviews the various means of establishing criteria for "levels" of evidence, followed by discussion on research methods, practice guidelines, resources, and policies. It concludes with a review of the strengths, limitations, challenges, and future recommendations for integrating EBP into health promotion efforts. The chapter concludes with a section entitled "In Our Own Words," a summary of consumer and focus group perspectives on the topic of EBP. For this chapter, participants responded to the following question: "What do you think makes for effective treatment?"

Learning Objectives

When you have finished reading this chapter, you should be able to:

1. Describe EBP issues identified by researchers, administrators, advocates and policy makers
2. Define, describe, and distinguish broad categories of EBP.
3. Understand what constitutes "evidence" through a review of research methods, guidelines, and resources.

4. Describe state and federal policies that are driving the use of EBP and the strengths, limitations, challenges, and future of applying EBP in the field of health promotion.
5. Identify core themes and concerns expressed by consumer and family focus group members when asked to describe what they considered to be effective treatment.

■ Introduction

Chapter 2 provided an overview of the field of health promotion and its many facets. While the purview of EBP has been dominant in the field of medicine and, more recently, mental health, little is known about what constitutes evidence-based (EB) health promotion practice (WHO, 2004a). This dearth of EB health promotion knowledge may be changed in the same way that EB mental health interventions are slowly entering practice circles—awareness, research, education, policy, and training—not to mention funding.

As mentioned in Chapters 1 and 2, one of the goals of this book is to help facilitate the mainstreaming of the field of health promotion into mental health practice. This chapter begins that process by looking at what the field of mental health is doing from the perspective of research and the use of EBP in clinical practice. From here, let's apply the principles and strategies for evaluating health promotion practice in the same way as in mental health practice. The first step toward that goal is to first understand the different perspectives behind the idea of "What works best?"

■ What Works Best? Four Perspectives

What approaches work best in promoting the mental and physical health of people with severe and persistent mental illness? This single question has inspired an international discussion between researchers, administrators, health promotion advocates, and policy makers (WHO, 2004a,b). Together they are calling for EBP in the fields of health promotion and mental health. "What works" is a relative notion in that we still have many conditions where it appears that single-focused interventions do not work, such as psychotherapy for narcissistic personality disorders and antisocial disorders in adults. Consequently, "what works" is a question reframed into "What works compared to other efforts?" Thus, the question is "What seems to work best?"

Much of the discussion has turned on what constitutes "evidence." Increasingly, there is societal and political pressure for more accountability in spending public or private money on mental health and health promotion activities (WHO, 2004a). Given the limited resources available for mental health services, these groups understand that funds must be targeted at practices based on tested outcomes and known to facilitate improved outcomes. It seems everyone, from researchers to policy makers, all realize there is a need for the best cost-benefit ratio–or, as the saying goes, the best bang for the buck. Let's look at what these groups are saying.

Specifically, *researchers* are often the first to report new information about the impact of innovations for treating illnesses such as schizophrenia and mood disorders through health promotion strategies. There is, however, an apparent disconnect between mental health research, the utilization of EBP interventions and services for persons with severe mental illness (New Freedom Commission on Mental Health, 2003; Solomon & Stanhope, 2006). Part of this disconnect may be related to the traditional way of conducting empirically based research. For example, in evidence based medicine, the randomized controlled trial (RCT) has been considered the "gold standard" and the best strategy for assuring valid conclusions from research. However, RCTs are rather limited in health promotion research. RCTs tend to be used more in mental health where the study of causal influences using individual level interventions is more common. Many health promotion interventions address issues related to the interaction of cultural, social, economic, and political factors (Tang, Ehsani, & McQueen, 2003). Examples include quality of life and well-being as well as whole classes of individuals (e.g., refugees), schools, communities, and populations, all of which do not lend themselves as easily to RCT methods. In other words, a RCT seems a better fit with an individualistic mental health condition addressed by an independent intervention and is uncommon for studies of systems or population health change, which are more the focus of health promotion.

Administrators are demanding greater accountability and positive results, particularly in light of increased knowledge about the efficacy of services and their effectiveness in the community (Solomon & Stanhope, 2006). See Chapter 11 for a detailed discussion of the role and perspectives of administrators.

Health promotion advocates argue that even trying to measure mental health instead of the incidence or prevalence of a mental illness is a challenge. As stated in Chapter 1, the classic phrase "The questions we ask determines the solutions we seek" seems to apply here. In the field of mental health, what we choose to measure will determine the evidence we discover. Health promotion advocates have long argued the point that the "evidence" we use to guide mental health practice is based on clinical definitions of mental *illness* (i.e., diagnosis of a particular mental health condition), not mental *health*. Brown (2002) argues that there is a need to develop indicators of mental health as opposed to illness if we are to be guided by "evidence" that reflects the totality of the individual. He proposes three categories of mental health indicators, *individuals*, *community*, and *quality of life*, each of which are expressly related to health promotion objectives. The mental health of *individuals* can be measured by feelings of safety, feeling in control, trusting unfamiliar others, confiding relationships, and access to social networks. It may also be ascertained from feelings of well-being and the absence of symptoms, as seen with the Health Status and Mental Health Status scale (Ware, Kosinki, & Keller, 1994). This scale is available at www.outcomes-trust.org.

The mental health of *communities* can be measured by access to and use of resources and services, support for parents, opportunities for lifelong learning, affordable housing, cultural life, friendly physical environment and robust local democracy as seen in active citizen participation. *Quality of life* has long been acknowledged as a component of health promotion and can be measured by experience of equity, empowerment, control, involvement, safety, lifelong learning, cultural assets and satisfaction with meeting basic needs, such as food, housing, finances, and social affiliations. Remembering that providers and consumers will likely have differing conceptions of what is important for quality of life, the very notion of trying to quantify quality of life factors will have a range of options due to cultural, gender and individual preferences.

And last, *policy makers* find themselves accountable to the larger public. Policy makers face the need to determine the benefits and cost-effectiveness of evidence-based mental health and health promotion interventions. Accountability is needed in order to warrant the sustainability of governmental and public support. Scientific evidence "can never provide a fully satisfactory answer, and political considerations enter naturally into the decision-making process." (WHO, 2004a, p. 17). Heath promotion policy makers find themselves advocating for both individual and collectivist interventions for social change.

Categories of Evidence-Based Practice

Although there is no uniformly agreed upon definition of EBP, its various categories are described below.

- *Evidence-Based Medicine (EBM).* EBM is the process of systematically finding, appraising, and using contemporaneous research results as the basis for making clinical decisions (Rosenthal, 2006; Sackett *et al.*, 1996). EBP as we know it today actually emerged from the field of EBM whose early origins can be traced back to nineteenth-century France. Shortly after the French Revolution, Napoleon started the Paris Clinic, where physicians did something new and radical: they used a thermometer to take a patient's temperature, and this occurred more than 200 years after the thermometer was first invented. The term *evidence-based medicine* was coined in the 1980s to define the clinical learning strategy developed at McMaster Medical School in Canada in the 1970s.
- *Evidence-Based Health Promotion (EB-HP).* EB-HP is the conscientious, explicit, and judicious use of the most current and best evidence related to the promotion of health. This evidence is used to make decisions about interventions for individuals, communities, and populations that facilitate the maximum possible outcomes in enabling people to increase control over and to improve their health and mental health (Hosman & Jané-Llopis, 2005).

  As a practice, EB-HP has a particular conceptualization about what is informed choice. Specifically, informed choice is facilitated when information about health and mental health is connected with information about how to improve health and mental health (Sackett *et al.*, 1996). For example, telling a client about the risks of consuming alcohol with psychiatric medication is not nearly as effective as having the client weigh the costs and benefits of continuing to drink while taking medications. The client, not the provider, then owns the health choice.

Key elements of effective, EB-HP interventions include actions that support people's ability to adopt and maintain lifestyles that create supportive living conditions for health (Nutbeam, 2000).

- *Evidence-Based Mental Health (EB-MH).* Mental health practice that is evidence-based includes services or interventions that have demonstrated outcomes in multiple research studies and are offered to individuals or consumers with mental illness. Typically, the randomized clinical trial (RCT) is considered the best research method when it comes to building the scientific evidence base on the basis of which mental health treatment decisions are made (Anthony, 2003a, p. 7). RCTs are considered the highest standard because the methods are internally consistent, the results tend to be accurate, and others may replicate the study to validate its persuasiveness. Examples of evidence-based mental health interventions are discussed in Chapter 7.

General Definitions of Evidence-Based Practice

As the following definitions suggest, there are a variety of lenses through which to observe and apply EBP. Let's review six general definitions.

- *Process.* As a process, EBP attempts to use systematic procedures, and to blend current best practice, client preferences (when possible), and clinical expertise, resulting in services that are both individualized and empirically sound (Shlonsky & Gibbs, 2004, p. 137). Other definitions refer to EBP as a process of utilizing a continuum of empiric and nonempiric databases (e.g., research studies, systematic reviews, and practice guidelines) to guide interventions that foster client change (Vandiver, 2002).
- *Intervention.* As an intervention, EBP is the use of treatments for which there is sufficiently persuasive evidence to supports their effectiveness in attaining the desired outcomes (Rosen & Proctor, 2002, p. 745).
- *Approach.* As an approach to clinical practice, EB clinical practice is an approach to decision making in which the clinician uses the best evidence available in consultation with the client to determine which option best suits the client (Muir-Gray, 1997, p. 102).
- *Strategy.* As a strategy, EBP is a way for clinicians and clients to select from the corpus of available evidence the most useful information to apply to a particular client who has sought services (Corcoran & Vandiver, 2004; Thomlison & Corcoran, 2008).
- *Empiric.* As an empirically driven approach, EBP in behavioral health refers to the use of clinical interventions for a specific problem that has been (1) evaluated by well-designed clinical research studies, (2) published in peer-reviewed journals, and (3) consistently found to be effective or efficacious upon consensus review (Rosenthal, 2006, p. 68).

- *Integrative.* As an integrative process, EBP is the blending of best-researched evidence and clinical expertise with patient values (IOM, 2001).

As one can see, EBP is a broad-based concept with multiple layers of definitions. What's common across all of these definitions is that "evidence" is ranked on a continuum from more rigorous (RCTs) to less rigorous (case studies). Clinicians must then be clear about what level of evidence they are using to support a particular intervention.

Principles and Strategies for Applying Evidence-Based Practice

EBP is based on two principles—the principle of assessment-driven intervention and the principle of right to informed and effective treatment—both of which are highly valued strategies of health promotion.

Principle of Assessment-Driven Intervention. When a health promotion and mental health intervention is derived from the EBP literature, treatment effectiveness is likely to be enhanced. For the clinician, there is one overriding principle that directs this process: it states that assessment determines intervention (Vandiver, 2002). EBP methods are only as good as what they are designed to do. The best evidence for a particular problem will be of questionable value if the problem has been incorrectly framed or the diagnosis is incorrect (Rosenthal, 2006). This is why it is so critical to spend quality and quantity time in the front end of the assessment phase, doing a thorough diagnostic review. See Chapter 6 for a detailed discussion on assessment strategies.

Strategies. Now, putting this to practice means utilizing the following strategies: (1) let the assessment be the guide to selecting the appropriate diagnosis, which in turn will lead to the selection of the best EBP intervention;
(2) use information from all three sources (i.e., systematic reviews, practice guidelines, and expert consensus guidelines) as a guide for determining the most appropriate interventions; (3) if no guideline is available for a particular diagnostic category (e.g., schizoaffective disorder), review the professional literature for cutting-edge research or practice articles for implementing evidence-based knowledge into practice settings; and last, (4) remember that EBP serves as a guide and cannot substitute for sound clinical, ethical, and professional judgment that is culturally relevant (Vandiver, 2002).

Principle of the Right to Informed and Effective Treatment. The principle of right to informed and effective treatment is a core principle in many of the helping professions. In other words, consumers and family members have a right to information about effective treatments. Moreover, in clinical areas where EBP exists, they also have a right to access effective services (Thyer, 2007), even though there is no established legal right to effectiveness (Corcoran, 1998).
This ideal right to information about the intervention and alternative interventions is based on the common law of informed consent, which require

informing a client about the procedures, the alternative procedures, and the risks of all procedures (Slobogin, Reisner, & Arti, 2003). The EBP principle of informed consent is founded on the notion that clinical approaches must be based on empiric evidence, applied appropriately to the client and situation and evaluated for effectiveness. This information must be disseminated to clients. Admittedly all this may not happen routinely, but that does not mean it should not happen.

Strategies. An evidence-based treatment plan that rests on the principle of informed and effective interventions will utilize the following seven strategies: (1) a biopsychosocial assessment using standardized instruments; (2) a comprehensive diagnosis using all five axes of the *Diagnostic and Statistical Manual IV-TR* (APA, 2000); (3) selection of a diagnosis-specific, evidence-based guideline derived from a combination of systematic reviews, practice guidelines, or expert consensus guidelines or a combination of all three; (4) delineation of a theoretical base; (5) a specific treatment plan and selection of behavioral descriptions of the planned target of change based on the EBP recommendations and theoretical framework; (6) health promotion intervention using relevant goals and observable description of the planned target of change; (7) and evaluation using repeated administration of outcome measures of the problem and monitoring of client change over the course of treatment (Vandiver, 2002). These strategies are illustrated in Figure 3.1. As indicated, these steps are linear, with the first strategy leading to the second, the second to the third, and so on.

■ Goals of Evidence-Based Practice

There are two key goals for evidenced-based mental health practice. The first is to increase the empiric basis and effectiveness of clinical practice by helping clinicians and client select the most accurate, valid information derived from the best available methods. The second is to help clients realize their own strengths to diminish or alleviate symptoms or states of being that cause discomfort or dysfunctional patterns; this is accomplished through the acquisition of behavioral change strategies (Dziegielweski & Roberts, 2004). Both of these goals reflect a notable shift from earlier practice approaches, which emphasized insight-oriented interventions and cure-focused therapy—neither of which had much empiric support but lots of practitioner adherence.

■ Evidence as a Continuum

The pursuit of the best evidence to apply in mental health practice may be, at its worst, challenging, and at its best, rewarding. At its worst, clinicians can feel bombarded by agency and legislative demands to utilize EBP without an understanding of what it is, why they should use it, or where to obtain the information. The result is that clients may end up receiving the type of intervention that their clinicians were taught to provide in

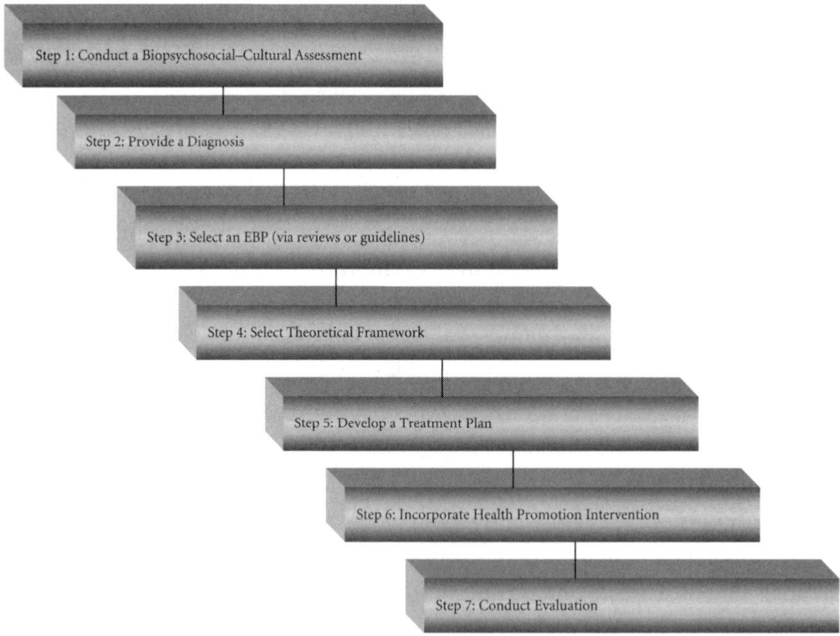

FIGURE 3.1. Steps for formulating an evidence-based treatment plan.

graduate school regardless of the circumstances of client needs. This is not due to negligence but to the fact that understanding the language and methods of EBP is not an easy endeavor. If EBP content is not covered in academic training programs, many clinicians seek to obtain this information in postgraduate continuing education seminars.

At its best, EBP can thwart ineffective, unnecessary, or protracted treatment by endorsing treatment approaches that have demonstrated effectiveness for a particular problem with specific outcomes. As a result, clients and their families get better care, agency costs are reduced, and communities benefit from healthy individuals, as does the economy from productive, taxpaying workers. In between these best and worst scenarios, various levels and quality of evidence can be found. Evidence is generally viewed as existing on a continuum of levels ranging from the most rigorous (e.g., level 1—experimental designs and random controlled trials) to the least rigorous (e.g., level 6—demonstrating poor outcomes).

The following section:

1. Describes the criteria an intervention must possess to be placed on the evidence continuum
2. Describes three different levels of the evidence continuum: the A-B-C model, A-B-C-D model, and levels 1–7
3. Defines the methods used under each level.

■ Levels of Evidence-Based Practice

There are a variety of ways to conceptualize and delineate the levels of persuasiveness in different types of evidence in EBP. Some are defined by an agency; others are defined by state government, professional membership organizations, or federal authorities. One example comes from the Oregon Office of Addiction and Mental Health Services (Oregon Department of Health and Human Services, 2005), which has developed six operational criteria of the attributes a practice or intervention must possess in order to be placed at a certain level on the evidence continuum. The intervention must (1) provide results in a manner that is considered transparent (e.g., peer-reviewed and accessible to the public); (2) be based on empiric research protocols (e.g., randomized controlled trials, quasi-experimental studies, and in some cases less rigorously controlled studies and published in peer-reviewed journals); (3) be standardized such that it can be reliably replicated by others using the detailed descriptions of the essential elements of the intervention provided in manuals or tool kits; (4) produce replicable results, where the research findings emerge from more than one study and more than one group of researchers have found similar positive effects resulting from the practice; (5) verify fidelity to the treatment model or the research that produced the practice by using a fidelity scale that has been shown to be useful in determining if the replicated intervention complies with the essential elements of the original intervention; and last, (6) produce meaningful outcomes—effective interventions must show that they can help consumers to achieve important goals or outcomes related to impairments and or the reduction or elimination of risk factors.

By way of illustration, the evidence-based research on older adults experiencing depression recommends a combination of psychopharmacology and psychosocial treatment interventions (Bartels, Dums, & Oxman, 2002). If a community mental health agency were to provide this level of intervention, it would be considered level 1 (e.g., meeting the requirements of a RCT) and would fulfill the checklist criteria requirements of the state mental health division (see Table 3.1).

TABLE 3.1. *Evidence-Based Intervention: Combination of Psychopharmacology and Psychosocial Treatment for Geriatric Patients Diagnosed with Depression: Checklist Criteria for Compliance with Levels of Evidence.*

Level	Transparency	Research	Standardization	Replication	Fidelity Scale	Meaningful Outcomes
I	Yes	Yes	Yes	Yes	Yes	Yes

Adapted from Bartels, S., Dums, A., & Oxman, T. (2002). Evidence-based practices in geriatric mental health care. *Psychiatric Services*, 53, 1419–1431. Data applied to EBP Criteria Level: Oregon Department of Health and Human Services, Office of Mental Health and Addictions Services, 2005.

Increasingly, different professional groups are attempting to create user-friendly operational frameworks for how to categorize evidence. Three such frameworks are presented here: one from a federal authority, one endorsed by an international organization and the final one an amalgamation of levels composed by the author. The A-B-C level of evidence, used by the Agency for Health Care Research and Quality (IOM, 2001); the A-B-C-D typology, endorsed by the World Health Organization (2004a); and the level of evidence continuum: 1–7 (Roberts & Yeager, 2004; Vandiver, 2004), an amalgam of seven categories or levels generally agreed upon for the field of behavioral health.

A-B-C Level of Evidence. In contrast to Oregon's six levels of evidence, a simpler although more reductionist rating system is recommended by the Agency for Health Care Research and Quality (Institute of Medicine Committee on Quality of Health Care in America, 2001). This system identifies three levels of evidence: A-B-C. A-level evidence is that which comes from randomized, placebo-controlled studies with raters blinded to the study hypotheses and subjects' group membership; some expert opinion can be included. Examples for this level include systematic reviews and meta-analyses of RCTs. B-level evidence is evidence that is from either very large case studies or non-blinded controlled studies; substantial expert opinion can be included. Examples include well designed quasi-experimental (no randomization) and nonexperimental (no control nor randomization). C-level evidence refers to mainly expert opinion with minimal research-based evidence derived from RCTs. Other examples include pilot studies, case series, and case reports (Solomon & Stanhope, 2006; Rosenthal, 2006).

A-B-C-D Strength-of-Evidence Typology. The A-B-C-D typology model, endorsed by the World Health Organization (WHO, 2004a; Tang, Enhansi, & McQueen, 2003) considers three elements of scientific inquiry—falsifiability, predictability, and repeatability—that result in four types of evidence. These are:

- Type A: What works is known, how it works is known, and repeatability is universal.
- Type B: What works is known, how it works is known, but repeatability is limited.
- Type C: What works is known, repeatability is universal, but how it works is not known.
- Type D: What works is known, how it works is not known, and repeatability is also limited (WHO, 2004a, p. 19).

Using this framework, health promotion strives for type B evidence, since most health promotion research operates in an environment where complex cultural, social, economic, and political factors interact and thus rarely lend themselves to produce type A evidence.

Level of Evidence Continuum. While fairly simple, the ABC model and the A-B-C-D model may be too minimalist in that their categories are too wide in scope to sufficiently distinguish the quality of the evidence. Another view is advanced in this book. Evidence can be thought of as existing along a continuum ranging from level 1 (highest level of analysis) to a level 7 (emerging practices, also known as promising practices).

Level 1 refers to evidence that meets the highest level of scientific rigor in terms of the methods used to obtain findings. The methods include two independent randomized controlled trials (RCTs), well designed cohort or case control studies, and/or national consensus panels based on RCTs, or systematic reviews using meta-analysis. *Level 2* is also considered evidence-based; its methods would include only one RCT, research studies showing dramatic effects, or interventions or national consensus panel recommendations based on uncontrolled studies with positive outcomes; no meta-analyses are needed for this level of evidence, as too few results are available to synthesize. *Level 3* represents a lesser degree persuasion of the evidence. At this level of evidence the methods used include uncontrolled trial or observational studies with 10 or more subjects, quasi-experimental designs, descriptive studies, and expert consensus guidelines. *Level 4* represents no rigorous methods to provide convincing evidence of causality, but it does offer some degree of clinical utility. Examples of methods in this level include anecdotal case reports, unsystematic clinical observation (e.g., correlational studies), descriptive reports, case studies, and single-subject designs. All of these methods provide evidence, but evidence that is noticeably less probative than that at the other levels. *Level 5* represents a level on the continuum that offers no evidence but is useful for clinical supervision. Examples include clinical opinion only, noncontrolled studies without comparison groups, no consistently measured outcomes, and that are not research-based. *Level 6* represents a controversial area of non-research-based practice in which interventions used produce demonstrably and consistently poor outcomes for a particular population. An example would be to offer long-term insight-oriented family-of-origin therapy to an individual who was showing signs of psychosis or to offer a similar intervention for a school-phobic child. *Level 7* refers to "emerging (best) practices," (also known as promising practices) in which there is no existing evidence to support the intervention but the intervention is well received by consumers and other stakeholders. The practice may also be in the process of being evaluated but findings have not yet been reported. The phrase "emerging best practices" is defined as "treatments and services that are promising but less thoroughly documented than evidence-based practices" (New Freedom Commission on Mental Health, 2003, p. 68). It is this category where many new research endeavors begin. Most stand-alone health promotion interventions will be classified as meeting the evidence criteria for level 7, emerging best practices, in addition to levels 3, 4, and 5. Table 3.2 provides an overview of this framework.

■ Research Methods: Defining the Methods for the Levels of Evidence-Based Practice

The categorizations of various models of EBP are based on the method from which the evidence is gleaned. The distinction is based on the veracity of the evidence, as determined

TABLE 3.2. *Levels of Evidence Continuum*

	Evidence-Based Practice Continuum						
	Research: Evidence-Based Practice Levels			Non-Research-Based Levels of Evidence			Promising
	LEVEL 1	LEVEL 2	LEVEL 3	LEVEL 4	LEVEL 5	LEVEL 6	LEVEL 7
Description	. Systematic reviews using meta-analyses or . Two randomized controlled clinical trials or . Well-designed cohort or case control studies or . National consensus panels on RCTs	. No meta-analysis but … - one RCT or . Research studies showing dramatic effects of interventions or . National consensus panel recommendations based on controlled studies with positive outcomes	. Quasi-experimental . Uncontrolled trial or observational study with 10 or more subjects . Descriptive studies . Expert Consensus Guidelines	. Anecdotal case reports . Unsystematic clinical observation or . Correlational studies . Descriptive reports . Case studies . Single subject designs	. Clinical opinion only . Noncontrolled studies without comparison groups . No consistently positive measured outcomes . Not research based	. Demonstrates consistently poor outcomes for a particular population	. Emerging Best Practices or Promising Practices

Topic Examples	Adolescent depression & psychopharmacology	Schizophrenia	Women & post partum depression	Treatment resistant clients	Case consultation on school avoidance	Using eye movement desentization response (EMDR) for grieving children	. Recovery for adults with mental illness
Source	Systematic review: Cochrane Library: "Tricyclic drugs for depression in children & adolescents" (Hazell, *et al.*, 2003)	Practice Guidelines for the Treatment of Schizophrenia (*American Journal of Psychiatry*, APA, 1997, Supplement)	Expert Consensus Guidelines: Treatment of Depression in Women: Postpartum depression—A Guide for Patients and Families (Alshuler, *et al.*, 2001)	*Psychiatric Services:* Case Report Column	Practitioner Magazine: *The Family Networker*		. *Psychiatric Rehabilitation Journal* . Boston Center for Psychiatric Hospitalization
Site	www.cochranelibrary.org www.campbellcollaboration.org		www.psychguides.com				www.samhsa.gov

by the rigor of the research methods. There are times, however, when the evidence is a single study and other times when the evidence is from a number of studies that must be synthesized. Synthesizing a number of studies is more difficult than merely hewing the results of a research article or report. Consequently, let's now consider six different research methods: systematic reviews, randomized controlled trials (RCTs), quasi-experimental uncontrolled clinical trials, anecdotal case reports, and single-subject designs (O'Hare, 2005; Thyer, 2007). Each is considered separately, as each is different in terms of the probative value of the evidence.

Systematic reviews (SRs) are considered the ultimate type of research analysis because they are designed to include a number of well-done studies. In SR, a team of independent and unbiased researchers carefully search every published and unpublished report available that deals with a particular clinical question. Some SRs are restricted to RCTs, such as the protocols from the Campbell Collaboration (http://www.campbellcollaboration.org/index.html); others may include reviews of quasi-experimental research reports. Then several variables may be incorporated, such as sample size and representativeness, demographic variables like race, gender and age, the validity of outcome measures, fidelity to treatment manuals or replicable protocols, and so forth. Once the studies are identified a statistical procedure call "meta-analysis" is conducted. Meta-analysis produces an "effect size," such as the effects of an intervention compared to no treatment of some other group or a different intervention. The statistic is nothing more than the means of saying "group A minus the mean of the comparison group divided by the standard deviation of the comparison group." The effect size is a number that is based on a standardized table with scores ranging from −3 to +3, which are easily converted in to percentiles. The percentile essentially illustrates that the percent of the average respondent is better or worse than the average in the comparison group. This procedure may be applied to any quantifiable variable, such as the rigor of the study, or the validity of any variable. As is often the case, this use of meta-analysis illustrates how a variable may have a moderating effect on the outcome of impact studies (O'Hare, 2005; Fischer & Corcoran, 2007a).

There are, of course, times when there are too few studies to integrate or synthesize mathematically. This is illustrated by innovative interventions that have not been around long enough to be studied. The question emerges, then, of how to evaluate the veracity of the evidence from a single study or two. The high-water mark is the RCT, discussed next.

Randomized controlled trials (RCTs). RCTs, also referred to as clinical trials or controlled studies, constitute a type of research design, also called an experimental design, in which participants (subjects/patients) are randomly assigned to a control (no treatment or treatment as usual) condition or to an experimental/treatment condition. The purpose of an RCT is to minimize biases, which may confound the research results, in contrasting the treatment with the control condition. There can be an individual randomized controlled clinical trial, or there may be multisite randomized controlled clinical trials. An individual randomized trial includes large numbers of clients with similar problems assigned to the no-treatment condition, placebo treatment, or a number of alternative, legitimate treatments. Multisite randomized controlled clinical trials use several independent research teams located at multiple centers across the county or countries. When this type of research occurs, the results may be considered individually or as synthesized in a systematic review. In and of itself, a multisite study is more persuasive than a single RCT for at least three reasons: experimenter bias is less likely, regional differences are built into the design by including research participants from around the country, and there are simply more studies that might support each other.

Quasi-experimental. Less rigorous than the RCT are quasi-experimental studies. Quasi-experimental designs are not quite experimental designs, as the research participants are not randomly assigned to different forms of the program. For example, a quasi-experimental design may compare different forms of the program that naturally occur, such as a program evaluation of an Assertive Community Treatment (ACT) Program (an intensive case-management program for individuals with severe mental health conditions) in a rural and an urban setting. Quasi-experimental studies may also use methodologic procedures such as matching or waiting lists to form quasi-control or comparison groups. Conclusions may be tentative at best owing in part to how clients were exposed to differing treatments—which may explain why outcomes differ. Let's consider, for example, the study of an ACT program in rural versus urban settings. Many western states in the United States include "frontier counties" (defined by less than one person per square mile) where the availability, accessibility, and familiarity of mental health programs are considerably different from urban areas, which have more people, more services and less distance between the programs and the people. If a quasi-experimental study of the ACT program found in Randall County—an urban county located in the plains of west Texas—was more effective than one in Denton County—more of a rural county located in mid-Texas—it would be erroneous to conclude that the differences were due to the programs. Why? There are many other competing explanations, such as that people who live in rural settings differ from city dwellers; distance and transportation may also adversely impact the use of services (e.g., a pick-up truck used as a ranch tool versus inexpensive mass transportation), or perhaps even the weather in an area where dust storms, tornadoes, golf-ball-sized hail, flash floods, and cattle stampedes often lead to the closure of highways, and the list goes on. The possible confounding explanation for the differences, then, may be numerous, and we simply cannot make a statement as to cause. We can say that there are differences, to be sure, but we have to speculate what and why before we can adequately use the evidence from quasi-experimental studies. Examples of quasi-experimental designs are offered in Chapter 8.

The results of quasi-experimental studies may be interesting and even encouraging but not persuasive that some intervention actually worked or did not work. And yet the veracity of a quasi-experimental study is more convincing than that of uncontrolled clinical trials.

Uncontrolled Clinical Trials. Uncontrolled clinical trials involve assessing many clients one or more times before providing them with an intervention, but they tend not to include a comparison group. Using pre- and posttest measures, simple inferential statistics are used to evaluate changes in the aggregated level of client functioning. This method is used to test a hypothesis or whether clients were harmed by exposure to a specific treatment. Many confounding factors can interfere with interpretation, such as placebo response and the passage of time.

Single-Subject Designs. Single-subject designs are useful in systematically evaluating the effects of an intervention with just one or two clients. Many EBP procedures start off this way as clinicians seek treatment protocols that show effective treatment approaches for certain conditions—as in psychopharmacology for the treatment of geriatric depression. Clinicians will still need to utilize AB research designs and follow-up, even though it is not possible to make casual inferences regarding treatment effectiveness. Examples of single-subject designs used in health promotion are listed in Chapter 6.

Anecdotal Case Reports. Evidence from case reports is similar to that of single-subject designs, as the results are derived from observing only one or two clients. Anecdotal case reports are considered a valued method of inquiry that often sets the stage for more formal investigation. The "data" tend to be chiefly client or clinician observations that are not based on consistent or accurate assessment tools. A clinician may observe a client's response to a clinical intervention and then write it up in a journal article as a single case report or case study. The limitation of anecdotal case reports is that they are not meant to provide any evidence that would sort out erroneous conclusions from valid ones.

In spite of case reports' lack of rigor, they may be considerably influential. Most clinicians in the mental health field have at least heard of Freud's work with individual clients and the phenomenal impact on cognitive development deriving from Piaget's observations of his three children. As these two examples illustrate, just because a case report lacks rigor does not mean it has no value to mental health practice, since it may suggest either what not to do or what to do.

Unsystematic clinical observations may also include correlational studies. This type of research attempts to determine the association between an intervention and a client problem, progress in treatment, or some potentially moderating variable. Correlational studies, unlike single-subject designs and case studies, typically include a large sample size. They may assist in deriving correct inferences, but they show no causality and must be interpreted cautiously. They can show relationships, such as between alcohol consumption and cirrhosis of the liver, but they can also produce inaccurate causal inferences, which are speculative.

■ Practice Guidelines

Mental health providers can easily access a variety of "guidelines" to help make practice decisions. Although there are a number of practice guidelines in the health and mental health fields (e.g., up to 20,000 in the medical field alone), this section refers to guidelines associated with mental health practice. Practice guidelines have been developed for the treatment of many chronic illnesses, including some mental health conditions. Guidelines are designed to help practitioners make appropriate health care decisions by synthesizing the treatment literature into a usable form and facilitating the transfer of research into practice (Milner & Valenstein, 2002).

There are three kinds of guidelines: *evidence-based research practice guidelines*, *clinical practice guidelines*, and *expert consensus guidelines*. One way to distinguish between the three approaches is to think of research-based practice guidelines as more quantitatively derived and practice guidelines and expert consensus guidelines as more qualitatively derived. These are not pure distinctions, but this does reflect the general differences.

Evidence-Based Practice (EBP) Guidelines. EBP guidelines are a set of systematically compiled, clinically based decision rules that provide recommendations for clinical care based on research findings and the consensus of experienced clinicians with expertise in a practice area (Vandiver, 2002; Rosen & Proctor, 2002). Other terms associated with evidenced-based practice guidelines include *practice protocols, standards, algorithms, options, and preferred practice patterns.* They are designed to help practitioners find, select, and use interventions that are effective for a specific diagnosis (e.g., postpartum depression) and a specific client situation (e.g., 3 months post-pregnancy) (Vandiver, 2002; Roberts & Yeager, 2004). Practice guidelines for mental health were developed using randomized clinical trials, clinical trials (prospective intervention), cohort or longitudinal studies, case-control studies (whereby subjects are identified and information is pursued retrospectively), secondary data analyses (meta-analysis), and literature reviews (qualitative studies, case reports, and textbooks). While they have the advantage of consolidating research evidence into one document, their limitations have been identified, as some are too lengthy, difficult to read, or impractical in content and design.

Clinical Practice Guidelines. Clinical practice guidelines are statements and recommendations for conducting an intervention. One can find clinical practice guidelines in the form of treatment manuals and textbooks (Barlow, 2001). Each of these guidelines is focused on specific mental health populations but includes specific health promotion approaches. Terms associated with practice guidelines include *best practices* and *treatment protocols or standards.* These sources are distinguishable from systematic reviews in that they integrate available evidence through the use of authoritative experience—when practice was guided by authority (Gambrill, 1999).

Best Practices. From an organizational standpoint, EBP uses another term: *best practices.* Best practices is a top-down approach defined as the measurement, bench marking, and identification of processes that result in better outcomes (Kramer & Glazer, 2001).

Best practices differs from EBP, which is individually driven and, as a bottom-up approach, starts with an assessment, moves to a diagnosis, and then proceeds to locate an EBP intervention. Best practices involves an organizational approach to assessing variations in practice from the individual level up through hospital and provider agencies and regions (Glazer, 1998). Organizations, such as the Joint Commission on Accreditation of Healthcare Organizations (JCAHO) have created quality indicators that are driving health care provider systems toward the acquisition of better-quality clinical data for their performance improvement initiatives. Best practices guidelines are one result of these initiatives.

Treatment Protocols or Standards. An example of a treatment protocol is the manual by Leahy and Holland (2000) titled *Treatment Plans and Interventions for Depression and Anxiety Disorders*. Practice guideline reviews are available for eight major mental health disorders: depression, panic disorder with agoraphobia, generalized anxiety disorder, social phobia, posttraumatic stress disorder, specific phobia and obsessive-compulsive disorder, and the related treatment approaches as supported by research. For each of these disorders there is an accompanying treatment plan as well as case examples, weekly activity forms, questionnaires, and checklists. Examples of a health promotion approach would be the use of relaxation techniques for generalized anxiety disorder. The authors provide extensive health promotion examples of cognitive-behavioral techniques that include progressive muscle relaxation, breathing relaxation, thought stopping, and visualization. Each technique is well supported by the available scientific research for that particular disorder and symptoms. The examples are reader-friendly and convenient to use.

Expert Consensus Guidelines. Expert consensus guidelines are derived from a broad-based survey of expert opinion and consist of a compilation of practical treatment recommendations for major mental disorders (McEvoy, Scheifler, & Frances, 1999). Other terms associated with this approach include *treatment manuals* and *protocols*.

The guidelines were developed with an understanding that many controlled research studies do not address the wide variety of clinical issues that practitioners deal with on a daily basis. Although the guidelines are not necessarily empirically derived and are based on a profile of "average" client groups (e.g., schizophrenia, first episode), they offer the advantage of being user-friendly in design, offer primary and secondary intervention recommendations, and provide an educational source for families and consumers. Rosenthal (2004) has speculated that expert consensus guidelines will be replaced by *evidence-based* consensus. This move has been influenced by the realization that expert opinion may have relatively low validity when compared to the scientific evidence of a systematic review.

■ Where to Go for Evidence-Based Practice Resources

Clinicians have access to a variety of resources from which to gather EB information. Table 3.3 illustrates a sampling of selected research resources for health promotion and mental health. For clinicians who wish to focus on level 1, EBP, there are a few seminal resources.

While meta-analyses are excellent sources of systematic reviews, the chief source of systematic reviews is the Cochrane Library. These can be found on the *Cochrane Library's* Cochrane Database of Systematic Reviews. As of 2003, the

TABLE 3.3. ***Selected Resources: Where to Go for Mental Health Research Resources for Use with Health Promotion Practice.***

Category	Source
• Texts	*Evidence-Based Mental Health Practice* (Drake, Merrens, & Lynde, 2005) *Social Work in Mental Health: An Evidence-BasedApproach* (Thyer & Wodarski, 2007) *Evidence-Based Practice Manual* (Roberts & Yeager, 2004)
• Journals	*Journal of Health Promotion, Brief Treatment & Crisis Intervention, Psychiatric Services Evidence-Based Mental Health American Journal of PsychiatryArchives of General Psychiatry Journal of Consulting and Clinical Psychology Research on Social Work Practice Health Promotion International Journal of Evidence-Based Social Work*
• Websites	*Systematic Reviews:* *Cochrane Collaboration* (Mental Health) www.cochranelibrary.com *Campbell Collaboration* (Social Welfare, Education, Criminal Justice) www.campbellcollaboration.org Center for Evidence-Based Medicine www.cebm.net PubMed (National Library of Medicine) www.ncbi.nlm.nih.gov/PubMed Clinical evidence www.clinicalevidence.com Physicians Information and Education Resource (Mental Health) www.acponline.com National Health Society for Reviews and Dissemination www.//york.ac.uk/inst/crd/cnetre.htm Inventory of quality measures for mental health care: www.cqaimh.org/quality.html World Health Organization Report 2002—Reducing risks, promoting healthy life www.who.int/whr/2002/en/ Draft of guidelines for systematic reviews of health promotion research www.vichealth.vic.gov.au/cochrane Global Program on Health Promotion Effectiveness (GPHPE) CDC, Atlanta, GA dvmcqueen@cdc.gov
• Guidelines and Manuals	Expert Consensus Guidelines www.psychguides.gov EBP Practice Guidelines www.guidelines.gov

Cochrane Library has completed 1669 systematic reviews and 1266 protocols or reviews in progress (Doyle, Waters, & Jackson, 2003). While the majority of reviews are in the areas of medicine, nursing, and health procedures, increasingly new reviews are emerging that are specific to health promotion, mental health, and public health. Doyle and colleagues (2003) cited 7 recently completed reviews and 16 others currently under review that reflect health promotion research. Examples of reviews include interventions to modify sexual risk behaviors for preventing HIV infection in men who have sex with men, postnatal parental education for improving family health, brief interventions for excessive drinkers in primary health care settings, self-help and guided self-help for eating disorders, and telephone support for women during pregnancy and the first month postpartum. A random stroll through the Cochran website provides an amazing number of reviews on many different health care problems. A summary is available for free for any of the reviews, although the full review and protocols are sold as a proprietary interest for a reasonable fee.

In the behavioral and social sciences, the Campbell Collaboration provides systematic reviews in the areas of crime and delinquency, education, and social welfare. The resulting available reviews are considerably different between the three areas, with the majority of Campbell reviews in the area of criminal justice. In contrast to Cochrane, Campbell reviews are often free.

Additionally, many journals, such as *Evidence-Based Mental Health, Journal of Health Promotion, Psychiatric Services*, and *Psychological Reviews* are committed to publishing systematic reviews.

Let us return to the example of evidence-based research on geriatric mental health. The following case example illustrates a review of a single research article that provides an extensive systematic review on the most efficacious treatments for older adults with psychiatric problems.

Case Example of Evidence-Based Practice Research Using Information from Level 1

Topic: Geriatric mental health

Population: Older adults who experience mental illness

Source: Bartels, S., Dums, A. & Oxman, T. (2002). Evidence-based practices in geriatric mental health care. *Psychiatric Services*, 53, 1419–1431.

Method: Evidence-based reviews and meta-analyses

Findings: Depression afflicts 10% to 20% of individuals aged 65 and older. The rate is even higher among adults who are socially isolated, have low incomes, and have concomitant health problems. Depression can have a severe adverse impact on the health, quality of life, independence, and longevity of older adults (Phelan, 2003). It also has a dire impact on productivity, but this may be less pertinent to retired older adults. Although depression in older adults can be treated successfully, few receive adequate care. Bartels and colleagues (2002) provide an excellent overview of the empirically validated treatments for the psychiatric problems of older adults. The five most common psychiatric problems associated with older adults are depression, dementia, alcohol abuse, schizophrenia, and anxiety disorders.

Evidence-Based Practice Treatment Recommendations. The key evidence-based treatments for these psychiatric problems are pharmacological, psychosocial, and systemic use of available resources.

Health Promotion Strategy in a Primary Care Setting. For clinicians working in primary care settings who see older adults experiencing late-life depression, EBP research suggests that a collaborative care management program offered through the primary care setting may lead to a better treatment response, remission of depressive symptoms, productive use of antidepressants and psychotherapy, an improved quality of life, and less functional impairment. The key facets of a psychosocial intervention for this program are six to eight sessions of brief structured psychotherapy with a focus on life and functioning domains considered most salient to the client. Essentially, what worked was having a "depression care manager" on staff to coordinate care and conduct the group.

What makes this approach uniquely oriented to health promotion is its holistic approach to care, involving the integration of physical, mental, emotional, and systemic treatment. Figure 3.2 illustrates this case example. Another EB intervention for geriatric populations is offered in Box 3.1.

■ Policy and Evidence-Based Practice

Evidence-based activity is here to stay and with good reason. Increasingly, pubic opinion is that mental health treatment services paid for by local, state/provincial, and/or the federal government ought to be cost-effective, outcome oriented, accessible, and effe ctive. Shifts in state policies toward this end are occurring. The next section explores new developments in policy-driven research initiatives at the state and national levels.

Evidence-Based Practice at the State Level. In the state of Oregon, Senate Bill 267—or the Evidence Based Practice Act—was enacted in 2003. It required five core agencies (the Department of Corrections, Oregon Youth Authority, State Commission on Children and Families, Oregon Criminal Justice System, and Department of Human Services–Mental Health and Addiction Services Unit) to spend a percentage of the state moneys that each agency receives for programs that are evidence-based. The percentages of expenditures increase as EBPs are gradually incorporated into service delivery. The percentages are 25% for the first year, 50% for the second, and 75% within 3 years. Failure to spend state money appropriately on EBP services will result in financial penalties during appropriations for the following year. The programs must be "cost-effective" (meaning that cost savings realized over a reasonable period of time must be greater than costs) and "evidence based" (meaning that a

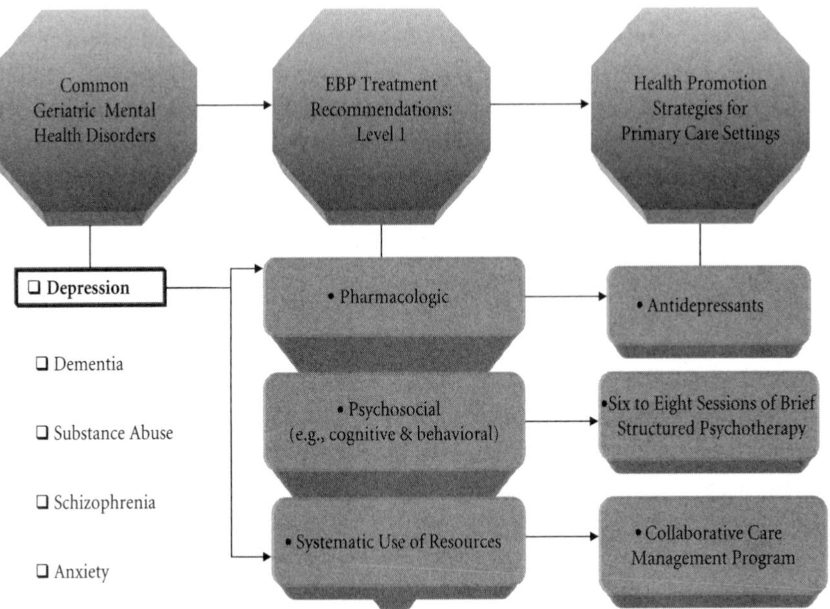

FIGURE 3.2. Common geriatric mental health disorders and depression specific evidence-based practice (EBP) interventions and health promotion strategies. Adapted from Bartels, S., Dums, A., & Oxman, T. (2002). Evidence-based practice in geriatric mental health care. *Psychiatric Services*, *53*, 1419–1431.

Box 3.1. Aging Well in Taiwan

Topic: Aging Mentally Healthy in Taiwan
Goal: Improving the Mental Health of Elderly Populations
Health Promotion Intervention: Exercise Intervention: Tai Chi for Elders
Evidence: Recent cross-sectional studies and controlled trials suggest that exercise, such as aerobic classes that specialize in tai chi, provides both physical and psychological benefits in elderly populations. These benefits include greater life satisfaction, positive mood states and mental well-being, reductions in psychological distress and depressive symptoms, lower blood pressure, and fewer falls. Taiwan offers an example of a culture in which physical exercise, specifically tai chi, is widely practiced by elders.

Source: Li, F. (2001). Enhancing the psychological well being of elderly individuals through T'ai Chi exercise: A latent growth curve analysis. *Structural Equation Modeling*, 8(1), 53–83.

Reprinted from the World Health Organization (2004b) Prevention of Mental Disorders: Effective Interventions and Policy Options—Summary Report. Geneva: WHO, Library Catalogue-in-Publication Data, pp. 34–35.

program must incorporate significant and relevant practices based on scientifically based research). Cost-effectiveness is determined when a program (treatment or intervention program) reduces the propensity of a person to commit crimes and improves his or her mental health, with the result of reducing the likelihood that the person will commit a crime or need emergency mental health services and/or hospitalization.

Evidence-Based Practice at the National Level. In a nationwide survey of state mental health agencies conducted by the National Association of State Mental Health Program Directors Research Institute (NASMHPD; Ganju, 2003), it was found that at least 41 states had implemented at least one EBP (see Figure 3.3).

The most commonly reported EBP was assertive community treatment, followed by supportive employment and integrated treatment for persons with co-occurring mental health and substance abuse disorders, family psychoeducation, self-management, therapeutic foster care, multisystemic therapy for youth, medication algorithm—schizophrenia, medication algorithm—bipolar and other EBPs for adults and youth.

For those states using EBP there were distinctions between having a statewide implementation versus implementation in parts of the state. With the exception of supported employment, states were much more likely to implement the EBP in parts of the state and it is less common to have statewide implementations. See Figure 3.4.

■ Strengths and Limitations of Evidence-Based Practice

There are, needless to say, benefits and burdens of EBP. We shall consider some of the strengths EBP offers and some of its apparent shortcomings.

Strength

Arguments for the use of EBP are strong and convincing. For example, findings reported in the Institute of Medicine Committee on Quality Health Care in America (2001) emphasizes that the cost of not doing the right things or not doing things right is expensive. Moreover, not utilizing EBPs may result in underuse, misuse, or overuse of services, basically as a result of providing ineffective care or services. Within the mental health system, many EBPs have been shown to be very effective in reducing costly hospitalizations. Adding to the importance of EBP, we know that the cost of ineffective care is often borne by other social systems, such as the criminal justice system, juvenile justice, and welfare systems. The point to be stressed is that not implementing EBP may be ultimately a more costly proposition than investing in their implementation.

Another strength of EBP is that it helps clinicians be more effective. The research of Milner and Valenstein (2002) has shown that the following characteristics affect clinicians' acceptance of guidelines: clarity, complexity of treatment recommendations, perceived credibility, and organizational sponsorship. In an effort to make these EBPs

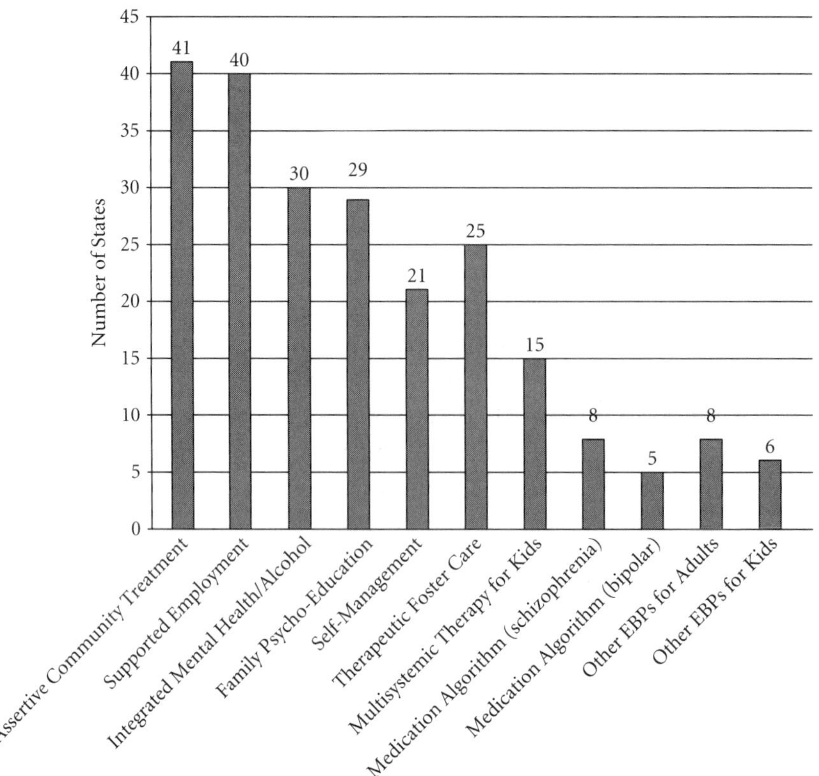

FIGURE 3.3. The number of states implementing evidence-based practices, 2002. Reproduced with permission from Ganju, V. (2003). Implementation of evidence-based practices in state mental health system: Implication for research and effectiveness studies. *Schizophrenia Bulletin,* Vol 29(1), p. 127.

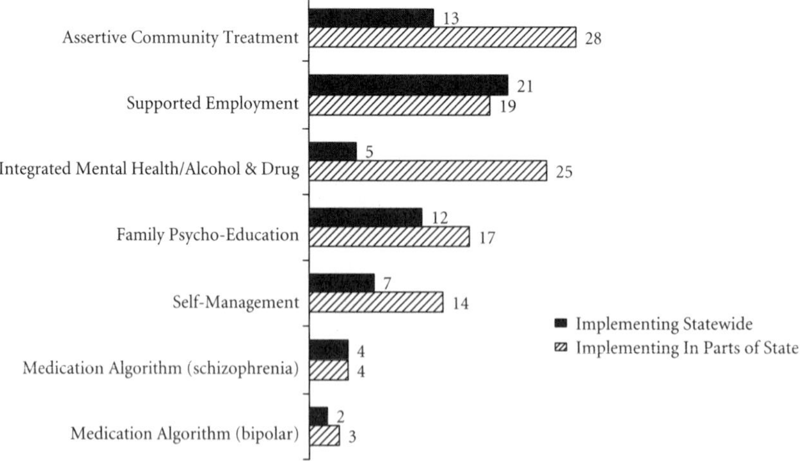

FIGURE 3.4. Partial versus statewide implementation of evidence-based practices. Reproduced with permission from Ganju, V. (2003). Implementation of evidence-based practices in state mental health system: Implications for research and effectiveness studies. *Schizophrenia Bulletin,* Vol 29 (1), p. 127.

more relevant to practitioners, the Substance Abuse and Mental Health Services Administration (SAMHSA), in coordination with the New Hampshire–Dartmouth Research Center has developed "tool kits" that are implementation intervention packages for six of the EBPs. These packages consist of manuals, videotapes, and training modules. As mentioned earlier, the core EBPs are supported employment, illness self-management, family psychoeducation, medications, assertive community treatment, and integrated treatment for persons with co-occurring mental health and substance abuse disorders.

Health promotion, with its emphasis on holistic approaches, supports program initiatives that incorporate system integration. It also has a focus on content and quality—such as supported employment—which is considered an EBP. These efforts cut across traditionally independent service domains, such as vocational rehabilitation, housing, and mental health (Solomon & Stanhope, 2006).

Limitations

The application of evidence-based practice interventions has met with the following barriers: philosophical differences, organizational difficulties, and cultural dissonance. Let's consider each separately.

Philosophical Differences. Critics of EBP argue that the levels of evidence required for EBP are problematic for recovery-oriented services. For example, recovery—which is discussed further in Chapter 7—is an emerging concept within most mental health systems. The concept refers to a complex dynamic involving a sense of control, hope, and self-esteem through which a consumer manages and directs (i.e., "recovers") his or her own life. The recovery concept is still emerging and attempts are being made to operationalize and measure its essential elements and outcomes. Recovery is a goal for consumers receiving services. While most EBPs were developed based on the criterion for "proven" success, recovery did not meet these criteria. Consequently, recovery was not included in the list of EBPs currently supported and in use. As noted by one researcher, "although the evidence is not directly related to "recovery," the outcomes that were used, such as employment, reduced hospitalization, independence in community settings, and improved quality of life, are indicators of recovery. Additionally, they are consistent with a person moving positively over time on a "recovery axis" (Ganju, 2003, p. 128). It has been argued that many of the EBP interventions in use today were developed and researched before the notions of recovery and empowerment was instilled in mental health practices.

Solomon and Stanhope (2006) make an eloquent argument describing the tension between recovery and symptom management approaches to care. For example, in the recovery movement, consumers are reluctant to cede decision-making power about services to the medical community. Consumer groups that are most vocal about their care tend to be those who are well into the course of their recovery. On the other hand, the medical community and some family advocate groups (e.g., the National Alliance for the Mentally Ill) have argued that mental illness is a brain disorder and have actively advocated for EBPs, specifically endorsing ACT, supported employment, and illness-self management. These groups have suggested that focusing on issues of self and empowerment (principles of health promotion) is not useful when clients are experiencing acute psychotic symptoms. The middle road or common ground may be that persons who are very disabled by illness may benefit from EB psychiatric interventions, such as ACT. As the person improves and symptoms subside, he or she will have more control over their treatments and services should address a broad range of their concerns, from dating, banking, shopping, to social supports.

An important point from each of these arguments is to consider the stage of recovery in determining an interventions effectiveness. Programs like ACT may actually be less and less appropriate or needed as time goes on because consumers have less severe symptoms owing to the early and targeted interventions.

Organizational. In a review of the literature on staff dissemination of EBP guidelines, Corrigan and colleagues (2001) note that treatment teams typically fail to use evidence-based practice guidelines. There are at least two explanations for this. Individual service providers lack the necessary knowledge and skills to assimilate these practices, and organizational dynamics undermine the ability of treatment teams to implement the innovative approaches. Two seminal reports on mental health, *The Surgeon General's Report on Mental Health* (U.S. Department of Health & Human Services, 1999) and *The New Freedom Commission Report* (New Freedom Commission on Mental Health, 2003), point out that there is a huge gap between knowledge and practice, between what is known through research and what is implemented in many public health systems across the country. This point is made even more startling by the Institute of Medicine report (2001) concluding that there was, on average, a 15- to 20-year delay between research findings on effectiveness and their translation to routine clinical practice. The challenges for physical and mental health systems are to ensure that EBP's become more readily available and more seamlessly integrated into existing systems of care (Ganju, 2003). In essence, it may be considered a limitation of EBP if they exist but no one seems to use them, although the locus of responsibility for this lies with the provider more than the EBP.

Another limitation is that much of EBP is based on the studies of program structures rather than the interactive process between participants, providers and programs (Anthony, 2003). Much of the research supporting EBP comes from studying program structures (e.g., staffing patterns) in order to differentiate models (e.g., ACT versus standard case management) and their unique effects on clients outcomes (e.g., lowered hospital recidivism). Anthony (2003) argues that these controlled clinical trials of programs have not controlled the processes going on within those programs, which may be indeed where the locus of change actually occurs. Moreover, Ganju (2003) notes three key obstacles to implementing EBP. They include a knowledge gap related to the active ingredients of successful programs, the lack of implementation of innovative programs in mental health systems, and mechanisms that facilitate and catalyze such implementation.

Cultural. If EBP is applied in an uncritical, culturally insensitive way or without a client-centered focus, the results may be not only ineffective but also harmful. Additionally, many of the issues that clients face have not been factored into EBP study protocols. The examples are numerous and include poverty, interpersonal violence, racism, stigma or discrimination—all which may be the very issues that cause or exacerbate mental health problems. Mental health providers must consider the risks and benefits of applying specific interventions to diverse client populations. In other words, not all clients will respond even to effective interventions, even if the literature or an author says they should.

■ Challenges of Evidence-Based Practice

Doyle and colleagues (2003) point out that health promotion interventions differ from clinical interventions in a number of ways. Consequently, meeting the standards for systematic reviews is more challenging. Some of these challenges include recognizing that health promotion interventions include populations rather than primarily individuals, there is context and complexity of the interventions (education programs), and research designs may preclude randomization. They also mention the ability to distinguish between intervention failure and failure to implement the intervention properly, the search strategy required to identify health promotion studies, and the synthesis of results from studies that are often heterogeneous.

Doyle and colleagues (2003) further note that to date empiric aspects of health promotion research have rarely been highlighted in systematic reviews of the research. This is changing with the advent of a global task force, which includes representatives from the International Union for Health Promotion and Education, the World Health Organization, the Global Health Council, the Medical Research Council, Centers for Disease Control and Prevention, Substance Abuse and Mental Health Services Administration, the Carter Center, and the MacFarlane Burnet Institute for Medical Research and Public Health. One goal of the task force is to help reviewers identify interventions that need to be covered by a Cochrane Review.

■ Recommendations for the Future

Many clients, families, and communities have needs that may be beyond the scope of some EBP interventions. Here's where health promotion strategies can help personalize some of the interventions. Health promotion strategies support the notion that outcomes must be "selected and measured in ways that are meaningful and relevant to clients and their families, [that they] consider contextual factors and attitudes about what constitutes success" (Nicholson & Henry, 2003, p. 128). For the typical practitioner, the critical concern is not just the best EBP intervention available but also the one that is most useful for the client's circumstances.

Anthony (2003) recommends that EBP expand its emphasis to study processes within programs. Examples of EBP process studies may include health promotion strategies, such as collaborative goal setting, skills training, developing a person-centered plan, relationship between practitioner and service recipient, providing environmental accommodations, and coaching. He further suggests that investigations of this nature can be made through randomized studies comparing different ways to implement these processes as well as through naturalistic observational studies that more fully incorporate the study design and, data collection process the perspectives of the persons being served (p. 7).

■ Conclusion

If clinicians truly want to provide evidence-based interventions that incorporate a health promotion perspective, it is imperative that they know what is valued by the consumer. The best intervention in the world would be of little value or utility for those who say, "It is not for me" or "I prefer. . . ." For example, if the domains of client interest were excluded from the package of interventions, then the EBP aspect of treatment might be misdirected for this population (Finch-Guthrie, 2000).

The potential benefits of EBP for health promotion are enormous. Health promotion advocates will have access to a broad base of consistent and accurate information about interventions, thereby facilitating decisions for clinical services. By selecting interventions that are demonstrably effective with mental health clients, the likelihood of improving outcomes over the long term will be greatly increased. Moreover, as fewer resources are wasted on efforts that are not effective, more cost-effective practices will be supported in clients pursuit of wellness. Just as Socrates (469–399) proclaimed that "The unexamined life is not worth living," so shall we proclaim that "The unexamined intervention is not worth doing."

In Our Own Words. . . . Family and Consumer Perspectives on Mental Health Treatment Services: Focus Group Feedback

Topic: Evidence-Based Practice

Summary

As this chapter illustrates, evidence based practices are most effective when they are applied in ways that are meaningful, useful and relevant to the lives of clients and their families. Given this understanding, consumers and family members were asked to describe what they thought constituted effective treatment. As noted below, both groups were consistent that the most important aspects of effective treatment were those services that were holistic, therapy specific, educationally oriented and interpersonally strong.

What Can We Learn?

Based on these perspectives, clinicians can support the implementation of certain evidence based practices as long as the overall service package presents a message of hope, caring and individual tailoring based on the clients needs and wishes.

The following section details results of the Focus Group meeting as reported by family members and consumers.

Focus Group Question: "*What do you think makes for effective treatment?*"

Family Perspectives

Core Themes	Summary of Experiences	Comments
(Ranked in order of priority)		
First— Integrated Services	Family members considered mental health treatment *effective* when services were offered as an integrated package that included school, home and community.	"Treatment should include all areas of a person's life—school, home and community; attention should be given to modifying behaviors that contribute to the mentally ill person being and not being successful in his/her environment" (S., *sibling*)
Second— Specific Services	Effectiveness occurred when very specific services happened, which included 1:1 counseling which used an	"One-on-one counseling is very effective. It helps when the provider explains the choice of their methods." (C., *parent*)

(continued)

Focus Group Question: "*What do you think makes for effective treatment?*" *(continued)*		
	interpersonal therapy approach, emphasis on community reintegration,team oriented caseworkers, special health classes, community employment, education and medication monitoring.	
Third— Strengths and Hope	Services considered effective when based on the philosophy of strength and hope	"It is important that caseworkers emphasize hope. We have been told that our family member has a life long illness and will always be on meds. You should never tell someone they will never be ok. Please emphasize strengths, don't just focus on illness." (M., *parent*)

Consumer Perspectives

Core Themes	**Summary of Experiences**	**Comments**
(Ranked in order of priority)		
First— Interpersonal Relationship	The most important aspect of effectiveness was the establishment of a solid relationship between provider and client based on client strengths and therapist use of empathy, listening, support and understanding	"It's important to get to know the client more than just observing them; meet them at their level and believe them—no matter how bizarre their symptoms are, maybe there is a kernel of truth to the story." (J.V.S., *consumer*)
Second— Holistic Interventions	Client should be active participant the use of holistic interventions, such as drama classes, yoga, personal/peer care assistants (PCA's), recreation, dialectical behavior therapy and and 1:1 counseling.	"A home visit by a case manager would have been nice since she never saw the pig sty I was forced to live in. Also ask us: what do you do for recreation?" (R., *consumer*)
Third— Medication Support and Education	Support and education about all prescription medications	"We need staff to really listen to us about how our medications are affecting us; educate us about our medications, help us get the right ones and monitor those we take." (J.V.S., *consumer*)

PART II

THEORY, PRINCIPLES AND POLICIES

4. Mental Health Theory for Health Promotion Practice

Until you can tell me why this is happening, don't tell me how it will end.

—*K., parent*

Chapter Overview

Health promotion is an amalgamation of a number of thoughtful and progressive theories borrowed from the behavioral and social sciences. However, despite health promotion's increasing visibility worldwide and acceptance in political, social, and practice circles, a single, unifying, formal theory does not exist. This chapter begins by describing different approaches for models of practice—conceptual, perspectives, and theory—and how each of these is reflected in distinct approaches to health promotion practice. The next section describes four levels of change theory (individual, interpersonal, organizational, and community) and the corresponding mental health theories applicable to health promotion practices. The remainder of the chapter concludes with a review of the limitations of using traditional mental health theories for health promotion practice, some of which includes lacking a testable framework and cultural competence application for people of color or ethnic populations. Last, this chapter concludes with a section entitled "In Our Own Words," which is a focus group summary of consumers' and family members' comments regarding the following question: "Why Does Mental Illness Happen to People?" In other words, what is their "theory" about mental illness? Such theory is the theme of this chapter.

Learning Objectives

When you have finished reading this chapter, you should be able to:

1. Discuss three approaches to selecting mental health theories for health promotion practice (conceptual model, perspectives, and theory)
2. Describe four levels of change theory (individual, interpersonal, organizational, and co'mmunity) and match these with corresponding health promotion approaches
3. Discuss limitations of applying mental health theory to health promotion practice
4. Identify core themes expressed through consumer and family member focus groups who were asked to describe their own theories about what causes mental illness

Introduction

Mental health clinicians provide services intended to help individuals improve their mental health, reduce risk for relapse, manage the acute and chronic aspects of mental illness, and—using health promotion strategies—improve their well-being and self-sufficiency. However, not all mental health services are equally successful. The services that are most likely to succeed utilize empirically supported interventions guided by theoretical frameworks. While theory alone does not produce effective outcomes or programs, theory-based planning, implementation, and monitoring do.

Mental Health Theory for Health Promotion Practice

Given that the focus of mental health practice is broad and varied, no single theory would be expected to fit all categories of mental health interventions. And just as no single theory fits mental health practice, there is no single theory that dominates health promotion. In fact, most of the theories that health promotion identifies with have been borrowed from the fields of psychology, sociology, biology, community organizing, health economics and management.

How Do You Know When and Which Theory to Use?

Depending on the unit of analysis or target of change (e.g., individuals, groups, organizations or communities) and the topic and type of behavior you are concerned with (one-shot or repetitive behaviors, addictive or habitual behaviors), the goal of applying the correct "theory" is to have a good fit, to be practical and useful (see NIH website for review of theories: http://cancercontrol.cancer.gov/brp/constructs/theory.html). The time to select a theory is after you have completed the full biopsychosocial assessment (see Chapter 6) and looked to the evidence-based literature (e.g., APA guidelines for the treatment of schizophrenia) for empirically supported interventions (e.g., psychoeducation) for that particular diagnosis (e.g., schizophreniform, first episode) or set of circumstances (e.g., family needs for understanding schizophrenia). The steps in this process are discussed in Chapter 3. Examples of evidence-based practice (EBP) interventions are listed in Chapters 6 and 7.

Now that you have established the "when," the next step is to determine "which" theory. In the example above, a clinician might select social cognitive learning theory to support the psychoeducation intervention. There are however, other times when theory selection and application are not so neat or practical—as when there are no practice guidelines available for your client's situation (e.g., schizoaffective disorder) or those that are available are culturally incompatible (e.g., recommending community based psychoeducation classes for Laotian families who have a son or daughter diagnosed with mental illness). The guidelines may suggest the importance of psychoeducation, considered an EBP and discussed in detail in Chapter 7, but the format of the open discussion group used in this approach is inappropriate for many Asian cultures, which see mental illness as bringing shame upon the family and therefore do not talk about it publicly. However, a salient strength of health promotion is that even evidence-based interventions such as psychoeducation may be reframed and renamed in ways that are culturally sensitive—for example, renaming a psychoeducation group "Family Health." In this case, fidelity to the intervention remains, the theory is preserved, and the dignity of the client/consumer and family remain intact.

■ Overview of Theory

In an attempt to appreciate the various theories, models, and perspectives that have influenced the field of health promotion, three different theoretical frameworks and examples are reviewed below. These are the *conceptual model*, *perspectives*, and *theory*. Figure 4.1 illustrates these different ideas.

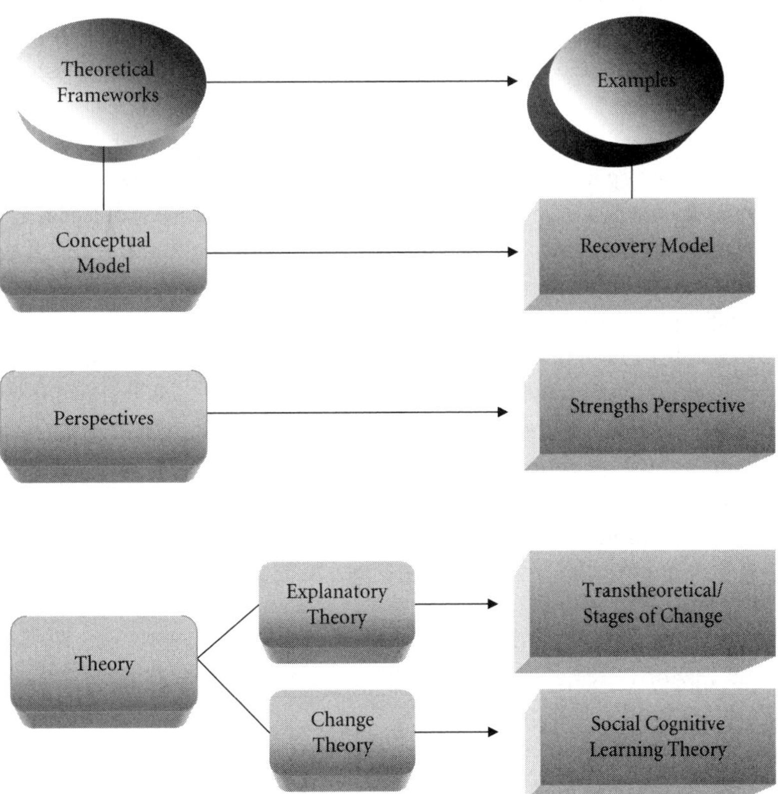

FIGURE 4.1. Three theoretical frameworks and examples used in health promotion practice.

Conceptual Model. A "model" is considered a subclass of a theory and describes what happens during practice in a general way. A conceptual model is characterized by the following:

- Applicability to a wide range of situations
- Structured format, so that certain principles and patterns of activity can be practiced consistently
- Ability to provide a plan for investigation and/or addressing a phenomenon but yet does not attempt to explain the processes underlying learning—rather represents them and provides the vehicle for applying the theories
- Focus on prescribing what to do and promoted because of its practical usefulness, as evidenced by experience or empirically tested effectiveness
- Typically generalized, hypothetical descriptions often based on analogy used to explain or analyze something (Corcoran & Fischer, 2000a)

Example. *The recovery model* is a conceptual model that applies to a wide range of situations and provides a plan for addressing the phenomenon of healing. The concept of recovery is rooted in consumers' experiences and their articulation of what has helped them to heal. The recovery model instills the concept that people can begin to recover not just through individual therapy or medication or self-help but also by learning skills that apply to every aspect of their lives. Only in the last decade, however, has the mental health system acknowledged that people can and do recover from serious psychiatric disability (Anthony, 2000, 2003c).

While there is no consensus on the definition of recovery, it is often described as a process of empowering individuals with hope and self-esteem to find new meaning and purpose in their lives. Recovery does not imply cure but offers a way of learning to work within and beyond the limits of a disability so that a person's desire for friendships, home, family, a satisfying job, access to education, and decent pay may become a reality (Roe, Rudnick, & Gill, 2007).

One example of how this idea goes from concept to reality is illustrated in a program called the Recovery Center, as mentioned in Chapter 1. The goal of this program is to enhance each person's ability to function more successfully and independently in the personally valued roles he or she has chosen and in all environments of life. The Recovery Center provides an opportunity to engage in courses that strengthen the mind-body-spirit connection, which is often disrupted by the experience of mental illness (McHenry, 2000).

Perspectives. When we refer to the "health promotion perspective," we are suggesting a particular way of viewing a mental health issue or situation. The characteristics of such a perspective are as follows:

- Relating health promotion activities to broader categories or activity rather than seeking to explain, describe, or prescribe health promotion activities systematically

- Having less concern with the detailed application or scientific proof of the validity of the intervention

Example. The *strengths perspective* is commonly used in health promotion activities. It seeks to identify, use, build, and reinforce the strengths and abilities that people have in contrast to a deficits or problem-oriented perspective, which focuses on clients' deficiencies and inabilities. This concept is a useful way to view people's experiences across the life cycle and throughout the stages of the helping process (assessment, intervention, and evaluation). It emphasizes people's abilities, beliefs, values, interest, aspirations, accomplishments, and resources (Saleebey, 1997).

Theory. A theory is a set of interrelated concepts, definitions, and propositions that present a systematic view of events or situations. It does so by specifying relations among factors or variables in order to understand, predict, and control events, situations, or behaviors. Concepts are considered the building blocks of theory or the primary elements of theory; variables are operational forms of constructs. They state how a construct is to be measured in a specific situation (Payne, 1997, p. 35).

Theories present an alternative set of prescriptions of practice and are used within the politics of daily practice to offer accountability to managers, politicians, clients, and the public. This accountability is achieved by describing acceptable practice sufficiently to enable health promotion activities to be checked for appropriateness. A theory will also make assumptions about a behavior, health problem, or condition of people or the environment that are logical, consistent with everyday observations, similar to those used in previous successful process examples, and supported by past research in the same or related areas (National Cancer Institute, 2003).

Some of the advantages of using theory to guide the selection of health promotion interventions are to:

- *Promote problem solving*: Theories enrich, inform, and complement practical skills and technologies and enable you to solve problems.
- *Guide research*: Theory directs health promotion research strategies (what to look for), intervention goals (what to achieve), and what might explain outcomes of interventions. In other words, theories help guide the search for modifiable factors like knowledge, attitudes, self-efficacy, social support, and lack of resources.
- *Shape program policy:* Theories help program planners shape the pursuit of answers to what, how, and why. For example, theories help you identify *what* should be monitored, measured, and/or compared in the program evaluation and *what* you need to know before developing or organizing an intervention program. Theories can provide insight into *how* you shape program strategies to reach people and organizations and make an impact on them. Finally, theories can be used to guide the search for reasons *why* people are not following the mental health advice or not caring for themselves in healthy ways.

Example. Theory allows us to do two things: (1) explain behavior and (2) suggest ways to achieve behavior change. *Explanatory theory* focuses on the theory of the problem. This approach helps describe factors influencing behavior or a situation and identify why a problem exists. These theories guide the search for modifiable factors like knowledge, attitudes, self-efficacy, social support, and lack of resources (National Cancer Institute, 2003). An example of an explanatory theory would be the *transtheoretical or stages of change* (Prochaska & DiClemente, 1983) model, where the level of client motivation is said to explain why a problem would continue to exist or be alleviated. *Change theory* focuses on the theory of action. This approach guides the development of health promotion interventions. These theories spell out concepts that can be easily translated into program messages and strategies. They are a point of departure for using theory as the basis for evaluation, and they push you to make explicit your assumptions about how a program should work. In other words, your theory of action will affect your theory of the problem. An example of a change theory would be social (cognitive) learning theory (Bandura, 1977), in which change is activated by the interaction of social, cognitive, and environmental action interventions.

■ Change Theories for Health Promotion Practice

Overall, there are a number of significant theories and models that underpin health promotion practice. These theories can be categorized at four levels: *individual, interpersonal, organizational,* and *community. Individual* level theories are useful to explain health behavior and change by focusing on the individual. Examples include health beliefs model, theory of reasoned action, value expectancy and stages of change. *Interpersonal* level theories focus on the importance of the relationships individuals have with friends, family, and others in their environment (Thompson & Kinne, 1999). Examples include cognitive behavioral theory, social cognitive learning theory, and empowerment theory. *Organizational* level theories focus on interactions in systems or organizations. One example is the chronic care model. *Community* level theories focus on changes in communities through community action. Examples include the community empowerment model, ecologic perspectives and community organization. Let's look at these theories in detail. Figure 4.2 provides an overview of this section.

Individual Change Theories

"Optimal individual health" is the most familiar goal of health promotion activities (O'Donnell, 2003). Individual level theories, with their emphasis on individual characteristics, are based on the assumptions that individual behavior is rational, determined by attitudes and beliefs, and derived largely on perceptions that have been formed as a response to beliefs of what causes disease and whether or not those causes can be overcome. Four theories or models are described that reflect this orientation.

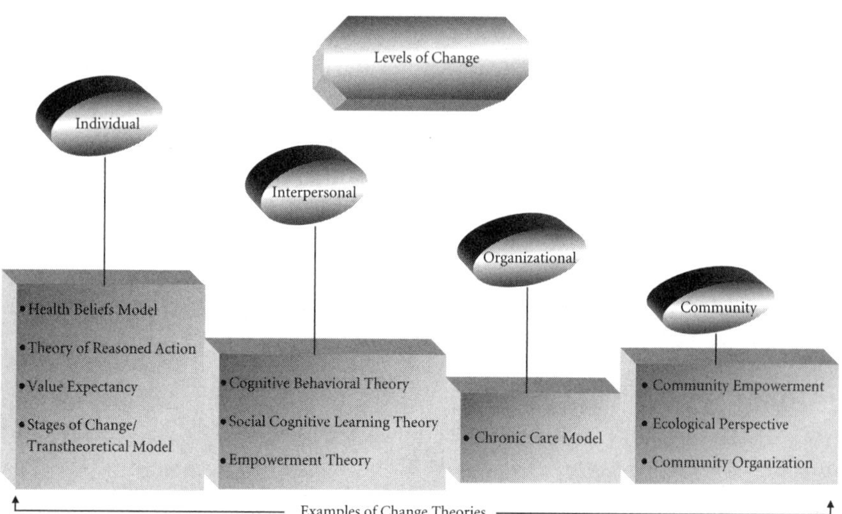

FIGURE 4.2. Four levels of change and examples of change theories for health promotion practice.

Health Belief Model. The Health Belief Model (HBM) attempts to explain and predict health-related behavior from certain belief patterns. The term *belief* is used in the HBM to refer to a conviction that a phenomenon or object is true or real. An example of a mental health–oriented belief statement would be "These medications are bad for me." Originating from cognitive theory, the HBM has been in use for over 50 years. The HBM has been used to understand individuals' perceptions of health and illness. The model can also be used to reflect the viewpoint of the provider and the differences between the provider's viewpoint and the client's belief and expectations (Spector, 2000). The benefit of this model is that it helps providers understand the health perceptions of their clients and for clients to understand themselves in relation to illness, what motivates them to seek care and follow clinical advice (Spector, 2000). The HBM has been used in designing health surveys and interventions and has had specific applications to the following health problems that have mental health implications: HIV/AIDS and sexually transmitted diseases, diabetes, alcohol, dietary behavior, contraceptive practices, sex education, patient adherence to medical regimes, smoking, hypertension, tuberculosis, dental health behavior, exercise and physical activity.

Components. The HBM is composed of five constructs or assumptions: (1) *perceived severity or seriousness*, (2) *perceived susceptibility*, (3) *perceived benefits of action and barriers to action*, (4) *cues to action*, and (5) *self-efficacy* (Spector, 2000; Green & Kreuter, 1999; Frankish, Lovato & Shannon, 1999). These concepts are described below.

- *Severity or seriousness.* People generally express differences in their perception of how serious a problem is. The degree of seriousness is often based on the perceived potential severity of the condition in terms of the amount of difficulty, pain, discomfort, and economic difficulties the condition will cause. For example, a client may perceive that a diagnosis of schizophrenia is "the end of the world and no hope is left," whereas a provider can provide a balanced perspective on treatment, outcomes, and even use examples of famous people who have "recovered" from schizophrenia. A beautifully persuasive example is John Nash, the brilliant economist and Noble Peace Prize recipient.

- *Susceptibility*. People tend to feel that they have varying degrees of susceptibility to certain diseases, conditions, or ailments. For example, a client may know that his or her family history is dotted with family members who have schizophrenia and may therefore be afraid of developing the illness. In this case, the provider can concur with or refute this perception of susceptibility based on known family history, risk factors, or protective factors.
- *Perceived benefits and barriers to action*. Once having assessed the situation, the client must believe that the benefits of the health recommendation outweigh the costs and inconvenience, that it is accessible and within his or her grasp to accomplish. An example is a mental health client who agrees to take medication to reduce anxiety in order to be able to return to work. Conversely, the client may also experience barriers to treatment. He or she may vacillate and delay seeking or using help out of previous negative experience with the health care system or lack of proper documentation. The role of the clinician is to help the client assess the barriers or burdens that must be overcome in order to follow the health recommendations. Factors that influence barriers to care are cost, availability, and time away from work (Spector, 2000; Thompson & Kinne, 1999). An example is an individual who decided not to take medication to reduce debilitating anxiety due to fear of medication costs and time away from work to receive treatment, and in some cases, perceived stigma about taking psychiatric medication.
- *Cues to action*. A cue to action or precipitating force is often necessary for the person to feel the need to take action (Green & Kreuter, 2005). An example of these cues is illustrated with advice from others, mass media campaigns, reminder postcards from case manager or physician, illness of family member or friend, newspaper or magazine article (Spector, 2000). Although difficult to measure, these concepts have practical utility. Green and Kreuter (2005) note that belief in susceptibility and belief in severity could be interpreted as fear of the disease or condition. An example would be a substance-abusing client who is also diagnosed with bipolar disorder and has multiple sexual partners who is identified as being at risk for HIV-AIDS. Green and Kreuter (2005) argue that fear is a powerful motivator and contains the additional dimension of anxiety beyond the belief. The source of the anxiety is the belief in the susceptibility and severity in combination with a sense of powerlessness to do anything about the threat—in this case, acquiring the disease. The authors suggest that this combination of factors produces a flight response which can result in denial or rationalization. Thus,

arousal of fear in health promotion messages may backfire unless the fear-arousing message is accompanied by an immediate action the person can take to alleviate the fear (p. 158). In such circumstances, the immediate action would be for a mental health caseworker to accompany the client for HIV testing.

- *Self-efficacy.* In order for people to succeed at behavioral change, they must feel competent (self-efficacious) to implement change. Rosenstock and colleagues (1988) note that a growing body of literature suggests that self-efficacy helps to account for initiation and maintenance of behavioral change. A key aspect of health promotion is to increase self-efficacy by providing people with information and skills to support identified behavior change.

Theory of Reasoned Action. This theory follows nicely with the fourth stage of the health belief model, in which cues to action are identified. The central tenet of this theory is the concept of behavioral intention. The theory of reasoned action asserts that before action takes place, the formulation of a behavioral intervention must occur. This step is influenced by two aspects: (1) attitudes toward the change behavior and (2) consideration of the perception of social norms favorable to the behavior. Attitudes are influenced both by beliefs concerning the efficacy of action in achieving the expected outcome and by the attitude toward those outcomes. Perception of social norms is influenced by one's own beliefs about others' opinions and their motivation to comply with those opinions (Frankish, Lovato, & Shannon, 1999; Thompson & Kinne, 1999).

Action is influenced by attitudes toward the behavior and by the perception of social norms favorable to the behavior. Behavioral intention is closely tied to existing skills. For example, if a client has experience in resisting drug use, then he or she already has the requisite skills to decline, whereas other clients may not have had the experience of saying "no thank you." Many health promotion programs also include skill-building sections. Skills in this context refer to a person's ability to perform tasks that constitute a health-related behavior (Green & Krueter, 2005).

Components. The central components of this theory are as follows:

- Attitude and facilitating conditions are critical components of behavior change; the individual's internal processes are the primary element of change.
- Applications of the theory of reasoned action in health behavior studies may be found in the literature on dental health, tobacco control, alcohol, drug abuse and HIV intervention and contraceptive practices.

Value Expectancy or Valence Theory. While typically used in prevention and organizational research, expectancy value theories have great application for health promotion practice. Expectancy is the belief that a particular level of effort will be followed by a particular level of performance (Lewis, Goodman, & Fandt, 2004). Valence represents the value or importance of the outcomes to the individual (p. 466). In combination, these two notions form the concept known as *value expectancy*, which refers to the expectations of the future value of taking certain actions in relation to future well-being and health (Huff & Klein, 1999).

Expectancy theories have evolved from research in social psychology and management, which examines the relationships between attitudes, beliefs, and behaviors from behavioral decision theory (see Huff & Klein, 1999, p. 52) The premise of this theory is based on the notion that when clients are presented with carefully crafted learning techniques, attitude changes are produced that are stable, resistant to contrary forces, and likely to be translated into action. Attitude change efforts that employ learning techniques involve careful thinking through of information and the creation of health-oriented values, which are, in turn, reinforced by practice.

Components. Expectancy theories are based on two assumptions: (1) perception is the motivational key to doing something different and (2) positive change is brought about by gentle persuasion. Lewis and colleagues (2004) describe these two assumptionsas follows:

- *Perception influences motivation.* From a management perspective, the expectancy model suggests that motivation to expend effort to do something is determined by three basic individual perceptions: (1) effort will lead to performance, (2) rewards are attached to performance, and (3) outcomes or rewards are valuable to the individual (p. 466). In other words, given choices, individuals chose the option that promises to give them the greatest reward. When you have three choices, you choose the one that provides you with the result you value most and that has the highest probability of getting the result you desire. Another feature of this model is referred to as "instrumentality" or the individual's perception that a specific level of achieved task performance will lead to outcomes or rewards (p. 466). For example, case managers should first determine which goals or rewards clients have under their control and which have the highest valence or value for their clients. Case managers can influence perception and expectancies by encouraging clients to use their own abilities, providing needed resources, and identifying desired goals.
- *Gentle persuasion.* Research has found that persuasion increases with the first few repetitions, but attention and interest decline with further repetitions and that overloading the audience with information impedes persuasion. Information must be presented at reading or comprehension levels that are simple and direct (Lewis, Goodman, & Fandt, 2004). While health threats will produce short-term compliance, positive appeals that are gently presented are recalled better and behavior change is more likely in the longer term. If health threats are involved, a negative approach tends to prompt coping with fear or stress, while a positive approach tends to prompt coping with danger. An example of a health threat is "If you don't stop drinking, you're kidneys will fail, you'll die, and then who will take care of your cats?" Whereas a positive message could be "Your cats seem very important to you. If your health ever declines due to alcohol consumption, what

plans do you have for someone to care for them?" Similarly, health promotion classes with the most persuasive mental health messages are those that tend to provide a clear message, use metaphors, draw explicit conclusions, and present countervailing or opposing viewpoints (Levinton, 1989, in Huff & Klein, p. 52).

Stages of Change/Transtheoretical Model. For many clients who have substance abuse problems, recurrence of use is the rule, not the exception (Mueser, Noorsday, Drake, & Fox, 2002). And although such repetitive use may be more likely than not, it may be perceived as cyclical and does not signal failure or moral decline. While many clients may desire to change, treatment programs often have a "zero tolerance" or "one-stop fits all" approach to treatment, which has shown to be counterproductive for individuals with substance use issues. Research has found that after a return to substance use, clients usually revert to an earlier change stage, not always to maintenance or action but rather to some level of contemplation.

One model for helping clients understand their readiness to change is called the transtheoretical or stages-of-change model. This model emerged from an examination of 18 psychological and behavioral theories about how change occurs. In this sense, the model transcends a variety of theoretical orientations. The stages-of-change model focuses on an individual's readiness to change or attempt to change toward healthy behaviors (Velasquez *et al.*, 2001). The premise of the model is that change is more a process than an outcome, that people move through stages of readiness to change, and that those who make behavioral changes on their own or with professional guidance first move from being unaware or unwilling to do anything about the problem to eventually taking action. The model is respectful of the individual's place in his or her recovery, uses empathy rather than authority and power, and focuses on client strengths and competencies—all of which are synonymous with health promotion approaches. The stages-of-change model is also a welcome shift away from negative, stigma-based labeling such as "drunk" or "addict."

The individual stages of change in this theory are (1) *precontemplation*, (2) *contemplation*, (3) *preparation*, (4) *action*, (5) *maintenance*, and (6) *recurrence*. These are described briefly below.

- *Precontemplation* refers to the stage of change where the client is not yet considering change or is unwilling to change.
- *Contemplation* refers to the stage where the client acknowledges concerns and is considering the possibility of change but is ambivalent and uncertain.
- *Preparation* refers to the stage where the client is committed to and planning to make a change in the near future but is still considering what to do.
- *Action* refers to the stage where the client is actively taking steps to change but has not yet reached a stable state.
- *Maintenance* is where the client has achieved their initial goals such as abstinence and is now working to maintain gains.

- *Recurrence* is where the client has experienced a recurrence of symptoms and must now cope with consequences and decide what to do next (Velasquez *et al.*, 2001).

Interpersonal Change Theories

Interpersonal theories focus on the importance of the relationships individuals have with friends, family, and others in their environment (Thomason & Kinne, 1999). Three theories are reviewed: *cognitive behavioral theory*, *social cognitive learning theory*, and *empowerment theory* or *perspective.*

Cognitive Behavioral Theory. Cognitive theory emphasizes the influence of thoughts—beliefs about the self and the world—on behavior and emotional states. Behavior theory focuses on the environmental conditions or stimuli and reinforcements that omit or elicit, and maintain behaviors. Cognitive-behavioral theory, which incorporates cognitive, behavioral, and social learning components, explains human functioning as the product of reciprocal interactions between personal and environmental variables (Payne, 1997). Sands (2001) suggests that human functioning can be changed by altering cognition, behavior, affect, or interpersonal and social situations. The cognitive-behavioral approach to health promotion is based on the premise that "many people fail to engage new health behaviors not because they *lack* relevant information but more a matter of a lack of the cognitive and behavioral skills necessary to *use* information " (Frankish *et al.*, 1999, p. 55).

Health promotion utilizes two of the core features of behavioral therapy: (1) respondent or classical conditioning and (2) operant conditioning. *Respondent conditioning* is concerned with behavior (anything we do) which responds to (is produced by) a stimulus (a person, situation, event, or thing usually in the environment). Conditioning is the process by which the behavior is learned; that is, it is connected more or less permanently with the stimulus (Payne, 1997).Counterconditioning seeks to associate desirable responses with particular stimuli, in competition with undesirable responses. Counterconditioning techniques used include systematic desensitization, assertiveness training, and extinction techniques.

Operant conditioning is concerned with behavior that operates on the environment and may be used with complex and thought-out behavior; this contrasts with respondent conditioning, which is mainly concerned with learned automatic responses. Operant conditioning focuses on the consequences of behavior. The most common example is the A-B-C model: Something happens, an antecedent event, A, which produces a behavior, B, that tries to deal with the event, and—because of that behavior—consequences, C, arise. Clients manage contingencies that affect the relationships between behavior and consequences by reinforcement and punishment. Reinforcement, whether positive or negative, strengthens behavior; punishment, whether positive or negative, weakens behavior (Vonk & Early, 2002, p. 118).

There are many models of cognitive-behavioral therapy: Beck's cognitive therapy, Meichenbaum's cognitive-behavioral therapy, Ellis's rational emotional therapy.

While they have many differences, all the models share essential elements. Vonk and Early (2000) describe these common elements. For example, each model relies on identifying the content of cognitions, including assumptions, beliefs, expectations, self-talk, and attributions. Using various techniques, the cognitions are examined in order to determine their current effects on the client's emotions and behaviors. Additionally, some models also include exploration of the development of the cognitions in order to promote self-understanding. This is then followed with utilization of techniques that encourage the client to adopt alternative or adaptive cognitions. The replacement cognitions, in turn, produce positive affective and behavioral changes (p. 117).

In cognitive-behavioral theory, the practitioner's role most closely resembles that of supportive teacher or guide (Vonk & Early, 2000). This is very much the essence of the health promotion approach to health behavior change. The clinician teaches the client the relationship among cognitions, affect, behavior, and psychological distress. The practitioner actively facilitates cognitive restructuring—the identification, examination, and alteration of maladaptive thoughts and beliefs. This may be accomplished through the use of assigned tasks like readings or homework assignments. The role of the client is active and he or she is responsible for bringing up topics and sharing thoughts, feelings, and behaviors related to various distressing experiences as well as completing homework and other interactive tasks. Although the practitioner lends methodologic expertise, the client is the ultimate source of information and expertise about his or her own idiosyncratic beliefs and assumptions (p. 117)

Components of Cognitive Behavioral Theory. Sheldon (1995) lists seven components or features of cognitive behavioral assessments.

- Emphasis on visible behavior causing problems or the absence of expected or adaptive behavior
- Attributions by person towards meaning of stimuli
- Present behavior and thoughts and feelings that goes with behavior
- Target sequences of behavior
- Identify controlling situations conditions
- Identify people's labels (or descriptions) but avoid prejudiced attributions and
- Flexibility in listening and guiding client to a clear hypothesis about behavior (p. 127 in Payne, 1997)

Considerable empiric support exists for the use of cognitive–behavioral theory with numerous diagnostic conditions, specific clinical issues, and interventions of health promotion. For example, cognitive-behavioral innovations have been used successfully with people experiencing anxiety disorders, schizophrenia, and depression, childhood disorders such as attention deficit, conduct disorder, mental retardation, and autism. It has also been used in behavioral couples therapy, individuals or couples with sexual dysfunction, parent and family management training, and obesity and eating disorders.

Cognitive-behavioral therapy is the cornerstone of health promotion interventions such as Work Place Health Promotion, as discussed in chapter in Chapter 7.

Social Cognitive Learning Theory. Social cognitive learning theory is a behavioral theory in which observational learning is emphasized and in vivo (real-world) experiences are encouraged. Albert Bandura (1977) formulated social learning theory, which differed from earlier behavioral models by moving away from stimulus-response models to an emphasis on the role of imitation and modeling in learning behavior and on the concept of self-efficacy, a cognitive process pertaining to a person's evaluation of his or her own ability to perform behaviors demanded by a situation.

Components. The core components of social learning theory (SLT) as applicable to health promotion practice include:

- *Reciprocal determinism*
- *Role modeling*

Reciprocal Determinism. SLT is guided by the principle of reciprocal determinism, which refers to the three-way interaction among behavior (e.g., following through with work tasks), external environment (e.g., employment setting), and internal events or cognitions (e.g., sense of self-mastery or competence—"I can do this!"). In other words, the environment affects behavior through the mediation of cognition, and the individual's behavior and cognition, in turn, affect the environment (Frankish *et al.*, 1999, p. 55; Sands, 2001).

Role Modeling. Social learning theory suggests that the learning process is also influenced by observation of, and identification with, others (modeling). For example, a person sees someone performing an action and they learn by copying the example of others around them (Payne, 1997, p. 114). However, according to SLT, one need not perform the behavior oneself to learn it. Observers may learn or acquire new behaviors by watching, listening to, or reading about the models. Observations encompasses the process (what models do and how they perform), and the consequences (rewards or punishments provided to the model or observer) that are perceived to occur. Inferences are made about what can be anticipated (expectancy) and rules that guide the model's behavior (abstract modeling) (Sands, 2001).

Social learning has been used to address target symptoms of anxiety, depression, addiction and obsessive-compulsiveness through behavior shaping, role modeling, role rehearsal, and role playing (Sands, 2001, p. 70). SLT has practical utility for individuals who are working on their own health promotion wellness plans, like the Wellness Action Recovery Plan (WRAP), as described in Chapters 7 and 9.

Empowerment Theory. A critical focus of health promotion practice is empowering people to participate in decisions that affect their lives. *Empowerment* generally refers to the gaining of power by an individual, family, group of persons, or community (Browne & Mills, 2001). It is based on two major assumptions: that all human beings are potentially competent even in extremely challenging situations and, second, that all human beings are subject to various degrees of powerlessness. Empowerment results when persons who belong to a stigmatized group (e.g., individuals with mental illness) are helped to develop and increase their skills in interpersonal influence and the performance of valued social roles (Browne & Mills, 2001). Empowerment is guided by the philosophy that interventions should enhance mental, spiritual, and physical wellness and lead to social justice (Cox & Parsons, 1994).

Concepts. Empowerment theory has three main concepts: *strengths oriented, strives to overcome environmental barriers,* and *promotes individual growth.*

- *Strengths oriented.* Empowerment theory, also known as strengths approach because of its positive approach in helping people and its sensitivity to disempowered groups, considers individual problems as arising not from personal deficits but from the failure of society to meet the needs of all people (Gutiérrez, 1992).
- *Reduces barriers.* Empowerment theories explicitly focus on the structural barriers (e.g., poverty and prolonged powerlessness experienced by oppressed groups) that prevent people from achieving such needs (Robbins *et al.*, 1998).
- *Promotes individual growth.* It is been described as a process that promotes the ability of people to (1) produce and regulate events in their lives, (2) regulate the amount of choice and reduction of uncertainty in day-to-day life, (3) gain control over one's life and or environment by obtaining resources on multiple levels, and (4) achieve personal goals along with the ability to influence others to feel, act, and or behave in ways that further one's own interests (Gutirrez, 1992; Segal *et al.*, 1995).

Components. Clinicians, consumers, and family members can encourage empowerment practice in mental health settings. Components of an empowerment based mental health program include the following:

1. Creation of consumer boards that provide for participatory management
2. The ability of consumers to make independent decisions about the kinds of services they want, need, and are eligible to receive
3. Establish and support communication patterns with case managers and administrators
4. Opportunities for skill and personal development

A number of characteristics of family-focused empowerment practice include:

1. Collaborative relationships between mental health practitioners and family members
2. Capacity building among family members

3. The use of the resources that family members and non-kinship networks provide (Hodges, Burwell & Ortega, 1998).

In essence, then, health promotion practice that uses empowerment strategies in mental health settings will focus on supporting the consumer, family, and mental health practitioner in a manner that conveys mutual respect, uses a nonjudgmental approach, and creates opportunities for collaborative processes to ensure that desired outcomes are reached. See Chapter 7 for further discussion on empowerment based health promotion strategies.

Organizational-Level Change Theory

Organizational theories allow us to look at the interactions of individuals within systems or organizations. The chronic care model is an example of a health promotion approach used in organizations to promote systems interactions.

Chronic Care Model. Increasingly, mental health providers are turning to the field of health promotion for guidance on quality improvement strategies for working with the chronic health and mental health conditions that mental health clients present. The Institute of Medicine's Committee on Quality Health Care in America Report (IOM, 2001), *Crossing the Quality Chasm*, recommends that chronic illnesses, like depression, hypertension, diabetes and heart disease, are the place to start working on improving the quality of care.

One system change model that is gaining acceptance in the mental health field is the chronic care model, a program of the National Coalition on Health Care and Institute for Healthcare Improvement (Wagner, 2002). Although initially tested with patients in primary care settings, this model has significant applications for mental health practice settings. This model is based on the premise that patients must be able to manage their health and treatments and the thousands of decisions that confront them with skill and confidence.

This model works under three assumptions: (1) untreated chronic diseases exacerbate mortality and morbidity in mental health populations, (2) these diseases are becoming increasingly prevalent because of factors involving side effects of medication, poverty, and poor nutrition, and (3) most relevant to health promotion is that, when properly applied to well-informed patients, newer treatments (e.g., physical exercise along with newer atypical neuroleptics) may lead to major reductions in suffering and avoid complications, including disability and even death (Wagner, 2002). The care of most major chronic illnesses has become substantially more effective through recent progress in clinical and behavioral treatments.

The chronic care model is unique at several levels. The model focuses on involving clients and giving practice teams the right systems and tools to proactively manage their client's conditions. The difference between patient education and patient self-management is that the former gives the patient information, the latter gets the patient involved. Conversely, the chronic care model is patient-centered and borrows from the principles of behavior therapy. It is now recognized that behavior modification and lifestyle changes achieve results and clinicians are willing to be participants in their clients' lives. Structurally, the model uses health promotion strategies that involve investing patients in their own care and feedback about what's important to them.

A compelling reason for applying the chronic care model in mental health practice is that clients feel empowered to make changes and improve their health. One perspective is summed up by Lori Stephenson, Director of Quality Improvement for Rocky Mountain HMO (Universal Health Care, Health Partners Medical Group, Rocky Mountain HMO, 2002): "Chronic care is considered an investment. When you think about chronic illness care, programs that take care of people when they are the sickest are the most costly. Whereas rather than spending all your resources when the population is in crisis, proactively treating the chronically ill when their symptoms can be managed will keep people healthier and save resources over time." (p. 27).

Components. There are six components of the chronic care model. Wagner (2002) first categorizes these in two categories: health system and community. Within the health system, there are five components: (1) organization of health care, (2) delivery system design, (3) client self-management, (4) decision support, and (5) clinical information systems. At the community level, we look at resources. In combination, these components are intended to produce productive interactions between an informed client and prepared practitioners. The ultimate goal of these interactions is improved health and mental health outcomes. Figure 4.3 provides a heuristic illustration of this model.

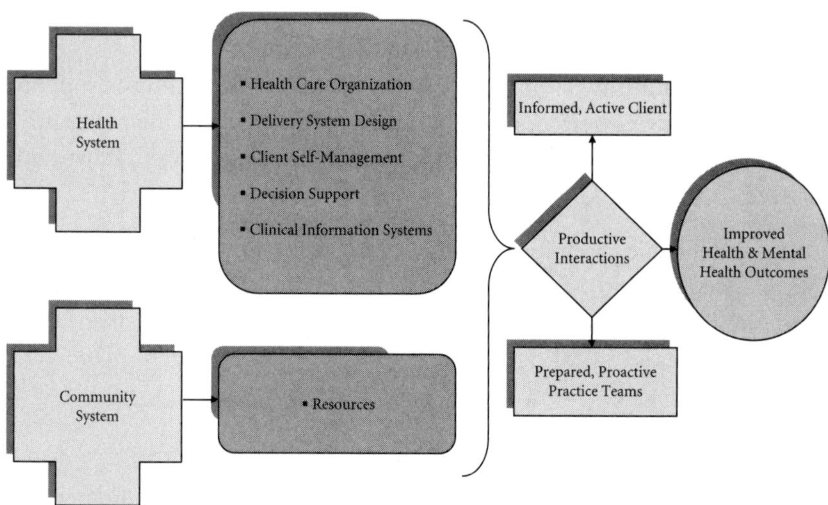

FIGURE 4.3. Chronic care model for health promotion practice. Adapted from Wagner (2002). *The changing face of chronic disease care.* Institute for healthcare improvement, national coalition on healthcare, pp. 2–5. Washington, DC: National coalition on healthcare.

For this section, let's look at the components of both the health system and the community that comprise the chronic care model.

- *Health Care Organization*. Organization of health care refers to the business plan that is in place to support a model like chronic care. Clinician leaders are visible, active members of the team and the commitment to the model is evident across the organization via the visible, active participation of clinician leaders in the delivery of the model.
- *Delivery System Design*. The way the system delivers services is critical in this model and refers to the use of planned group visits by multiple members of the care team. The delivery of services requires proactive, planned visits which incorporate patient goals that help individuals maintain optimal health and allow systems to better manage their time and resources.
- *Client Self-Management Support. Client self-management support* refers to the process of encouraging clients to set goals, identify barriers and challenges and monitor their own conditions. A variety of tools and resources (e.g., calendars) provide patients with visual reminders to manage their health.
- *Decision Support. Decision support* refers to the support that clinicians have for accessing the latest in evidence-based guidelines for care for the chronic conditions that clients present with. Continual educational outreach to clinicians reinforces utilization of these standards. This may involve the use of a specialist support in primary care.
- *Clinical Information Systems. Clinical information systems* refers to the systems ability to harness technology in order to provide clinicians with a comprehensive list of their patients with a specific disease or diseases (e.g., hypothyroidism with depression). Examples of this can be seen in the creation of patient registries which provide clinicians with the information they need to track their patients' health status in order to minimize complications.
- *Resources*. Community resources refers to the variety of community supports (e.g., schools, businesses, community clinics) that bolster the mental health systems efforts to keep individuals with mental illness supported, active and involved (p. 5).

Clearly the chronic care model is quite compatible with the philosophy of health promotion. Given that most chronic conditions are heavily impacted by patient actions, emotions, and lifestyle choices, the movement toward patient involvement in chronic disease management is critical.

Community-Level Change Theory

Although the prevailing emphasis in health promotion for mental health practice is on understanding and changing lifestyle choices and individual health behaviors related to health status, we cannot ignore the association between morbidity (e.g., health) and community factors (e.g., unemployment, isolation, inadequate housing). Recognizing these associations has prompted a focus on community-level change for mental health populations. This is due in part to the growing recognition that behavior is greatly influenced by the community in which people identify with. Community, in this context, is defined as a locale or domain which has the following elements: (1) membership—sense of identity and belonging, (2) shared needs and commitment to meeting them, (3) mutual influence—community members have influence and are influenced by each other, and (4) shared values and norms (Thompson & Kinne, 1999). Further discussion of community is found in Chapter 11.

Community-level change is supported by the conceptual framework of community theory. Proponents of community theory argue that behavioral change is linked to an understanding of the local values, norms, and behavior patterns of a specific community and that this understanding has a significant effect on shaping individual attitudes and behaviors (Thompson & Kinne, 1999, p. 29). In this instance, change is best achieved by changing the standards of acceptable behavior in a community; that is by changing community norms about health-related behavior. Health promotion utilizes three models of community level change: *community empowerment model*, *ecologic perspective*, and *community organization*. Each of these is discussed briefly below.

Community Empowerment Theory. Community empowerment is a concept that is both a process and an outcome and focuses on both individual and community change (Wallerstein & Bernstein, 1994). Community empowerment in mental health is fairly new, but it has a lengthy tradition in public health. Its early historic roots are associated with community psychology, social psychology, feminist theory, the World Health Organization, and the Ottawa Health Promotion Charter mandating community participation, the education philosophy of Brazilian educator Paulo Freire, and the Saul Alinsky traditions of community organizing (Wallerstein & Bernstein, 1994). From these influences, community empowerment involves several themes: a social action process, connectedness to others, critical thinking, the building of personal and social capacity, and the transformation of power relations. This approach is based on the need for a participatory education process. With such a process people are not objects or recipients of political or educational projects but actors in history, able to name their problems and their solutions to transform themselves in the process of changing oppressive circumstances.

The features of an empowered community include opportunities for its members and organizations to:

- Apply their skills and resources in collective efforts to meet their respective needs
- Provide enhanced support for each other
- Address conflicts within the community
- Gain increased influence and control over the quality of life in their community
- Influence decisions and changes in the larger social system
- Emphasize participation, caring, sharing, and responsibility to others
- Conceive of power as an expanding commodity (Israel *et al.*, 1994)

Ecologic perspective. The ecologic perspective uses ecologic concepts from biology as a metaphor in order to describe the reciprocity between persons and their environments. Attention is on the goodness of the fit between an individual or group and the places where they live out their lives (Germain & Gitterman, 1995). The ecologic perspective's emphasis on health, potentiality, and competence highlights human adaptability and problems of living rather than psychopathology.

The ecologic perspective also considers stress and coping. Key to the ecologic approach is the concept of the interaction of the "person-in-environment"—a person is involved in constant interaction with various environmental and social systems (e.g., family, friends, work, politics, religious, educational). The idea is that individual problems may be rooted in maladaptive relationships with other persons, institutions, or communities—problems that may be remediate through community, social, and environmental interventions as well as an individual approach. The social environment presents obstacles and provides resources for change. Sands (2001) notes that the ecologic perspective is applicable to all clients but is particularly germane to understanding and intervening with clients who are severely mentally ill, many of whom are poor, socially isolated, and underserved by the human service system. With its emphasis on competence, mastery, and coping in the context of the natural environment, ecologic theory provides a lens that can be helpful in understanding the situations of these clients and mobilizing the needed community resources and supports (p. 70).

Community Organization. The community organization approach to health promotion in mental health settings is based on the principle of participation. This principle asserts that large-scale behavioral change requires those people heavily affected by a problem to be involved in defining the problem, planning and instituting steps to resolve the problem, and establishing structures to ensure that the desired change is maintained (Thompson & Kinne, 1999, p. 30). The target of change is generally the community itself, and the basic premise is that change is more likely to be successful and permanent when the people it affects are involved in initiating and promoting it (p. 30).

One example of community organization activities are the community walk-a-thons sponsored by National Alliance of the Mentally Ill (NAMI). The purpose of these walks is to awaken public awareness of mental illness. Large-scale advertising and community action campaigns go into these efforts. Despite this emphasis on the community and community organization activities, in practice many community organizing projects pay little attention to norm and value change and seldom measure such change, relying instead on assessing individual change (Thompson & Kinne, 1999, p. 30). Community organization studies have identified two sectors as being important for achieving changes in the community system. These include voluntary and civic groups, such as health-related agencies, and political action groups and other grass roots groups that may be specific to particular communities.

■ Limitations of Mental Health Theories for Health Promotion Practice

Most mental health theories that are applied toward health promotion practice come from the social and behavioral sciences. As such, health promotion cannot at this time claim to have its own theory, and perhaps it does not need to. Because of this, health promotion is often labeled as lacking a conceptual framework or theoretical framework. Because health promotion is such a broad range of allied theoretical and practical approaches, no one theory is applicable—nor should it be. Herein lies the dilemma. Without a testable, empirical framework, health promotion will be limited in its ability to generate empirical support for its interventions. Health promotion practitioners might be able to say something helped a group of people or a community, but the knowledge base will be primarily practical and not contributing to a corpus of a theoretical science.

A second limitation is the lack of cultural competence associated with many of the theoretical approaches described. Most of the theories described in this chapter have not been well tested with communities of color—leaving practitioners to put their own cultural competence twist on the application of these models (U.S. Public Health Service, Office of the Surgeon General, 2001). However, health promotion is a field that does pride itself on its stance on issues of social justice, equity and empowerment—all areas that are particularly relevant to communities of color and vulnerable populations. Still, more effort needs to be given to developing health-oriented change theories and tailor-made interventions that embrace cultural and ethnic differences in all areas, including the pursuit of wellness.

■ Conclusion

The theories discussed in this chapter illustrate the shift from a focus on problems to possibilities with an emphasis on positive, multilevel change. They support a wide variety of health promotion tactics and techniques to address mental health conditions and reflect the need for a synthesis of thought and application. This synthesis takes well-established theories and provides a practical explanation for their utility. The reader can step away from this chapter with an applied knowledge of how to link established theories with health promotion practice. What unites these diverse theories is the common denominator of hope and possibility. As Myles Horton (1990) reminds us, "Nothing good comes from desperation and despair; rather real change comes though hope."

In Our Own Words . . . Family and Consumer Perspectives on Mental Health Treatment Services: Focus Group Feedback

Topic: Theories of Mental Illness

Summary

As Chapter 4 illustrates, our understanding of what causes mental illness is influenced by a variety of theoretical perspectives, individual, interpersonal, organizational, and community. However, when consumers and family members were asked to comment on why mental illness happens to people, their perception was almost unanimously in favor of biological reasons. While both groups acknowledged that environmental and social stressors affect mental illness, biology was, in their opinions, the strongest predictor.

What Can We Learn?

Based on these perspectives, health promotion efforts that embrace a biological understanding of mental illness in addition to other perspectives are an approach that will be appreciated by consumers and family members. The following section details the results of the Focus Group meeting as reported by family and consumers.

Focus Group Question: "*Why does mental illness happen to people?*"

Family Perspectives

Core Themes	Summary of Experiences	Comments
(Ranked in order of priority)		
First—Biological or Chemical	Family members felt that a biological predisposition to mental illness played the strongest role in determining how different people developed different forms of mental illness; brain chemistry can change as environmental stressors increase.	"These disorders still need to be viewed as biological with the understanding that individuals cannot 'will' themselves to get better or 'just get over it' nor can we self-determine any of it. It's like love, brain chemistry can change the way we think about things." (S., *sibling*)

Focus Group Question: *"Why does mental illness happen to people?"* *(continued)*

Second— Environmental Stressors	Environmental stressors, like trauma and abuse, can influence onset of mental illness but won't cause mental illness without a biological predisposition.	"Until you can tell me why this is happening, don't tell me how it will end." (K., *parent*)

Consumer Perspectives

Core Themes	Summary of Experiences	Comments
(Ranked in order of priority)		
First— Biological	Consumer participants all agreed on three core, interrelated reasons why mental illness happens to people: biological, difficulties coping in childhood and environmental stressors such as abuse and trauma.	"The main reason mental illness happens to people is biological mostly but if someone has had a major traumatic event or have to go through an awful pounding over and over again, along with poor coping skills, then they can become mentally ill too. We really aren't born this way!" (J.V.S., *consumer*)

5. Connecting Health Promotion Principles to Mental Health Policies and Programs

Our spirits are broken and we need healing. Consumers need retreats too.

—*J., consumer*

■ Chapter Overview

It is important for any mental health stakeholder to understand how health promotion principles guide the development of mental health policy. This chapter provides the foundation to understand how health promotion principles drive mental health policies, which, in turn, create the programs for mental health clients, families, and the community. Our chapter begins with defining terms such as principles, policies, and programs, followed by a review of nine health promotion policies that reflect individual and community change. Next, there is a discussion of how the different types of policies—from intentional to judicial—influence mental health services and then provide a historical review of key health promotion and mental health policies for the last 200 years. The remainder of the chapter explores international health promotion policy models and reviews five core advocacy strategies describing how to integrate health promotion policies into mental health programs. The chapter concludes with a summary of a focus group discussion held by consumers and family members who responded to the following question: "If you could design a community-based mental health system with all the right services, what would it look like?"

Learning Objectives

When you have finished reading this chapter, you should be able to:

1. Describe nine health promotion principles for individual and community change
2. Understand the key policies that have shaped the mental health and health promotion field for the last 60 years
3. Replicate core strategies for integrating health promotion principles into mental health policies and programs
4. Identify core themes and recommendations expressed through consumer and family focus groups when asked what a mental health system would look like if they could design the services

Introduction

"I know it doesn't make much sense, but it's our policy." If this sounds familiar, it's probably because you have heard this phrase in conversations with a supervisor over why you have to do a particular activity that, for whatever reason, has lost its relevance for you as well as the intended recipient (e.g., like doing a mandatory home visit for a client who doesn't even want to see you or has no interest in what you are offering). So where did this policy come from? What was the initial situation that instituted the need for a policy? What was it about that particular policy that, over time, became less relevant to those who were positioned to uphold it? Usually any kind of mental health policy can be traced back to some discussion between two or more people agency people, administrators in government or federal leaders who are responding to concerns voiced through stakeholders or constituents. What all these avenues have in common is that the origin of policies are typically very much human and very much based on personal beliefs about what is the *right* thing to do or way to be. In other words, policies are created from some standing set of beliefs or principles—be it personal or collective. In this chapter, health promotion principles are presented as a means to encourage their utilization to inform the way mental health policy is developed, and these policies, in turn, determine the kinds of mental health programs that are available for clients, their family members, and the community. A heuristic model for this concept looks like this: Principles → Policies → Programs.

How Principles Influence Policy

Let's begin with a discussion of the term *principle*. It generally refers to a belief in a fundamental truth or doctrine that is used to influence behaviors. Principles also can be viewed as comprehensive rules which furnish a basis or origin for others as well as a way to frame how issues are examined (*Black's Law Dictionary*, 1979, p. 1074). In trying to understand the origin or rationale of a particular policy, one need only look to the underlying principle that first shaped the policy.

Key Principles of Health Promotion

This section reviews nine key health promotion principles that have influenced mental health policies and programs. See Figure 5.1 for a summary of these principles and core characteristics.

Individual- and Community-Level Change Principles. There are two levels of health promotion principles: those that are focused on *individual*-level change and those that promote *community*-level change. *Individual* levels of change relate to values and beliefs that focus on individual growth and relationships. *Community*-level change focuses on broad based community and systems values related to the promotion of health and mental health.

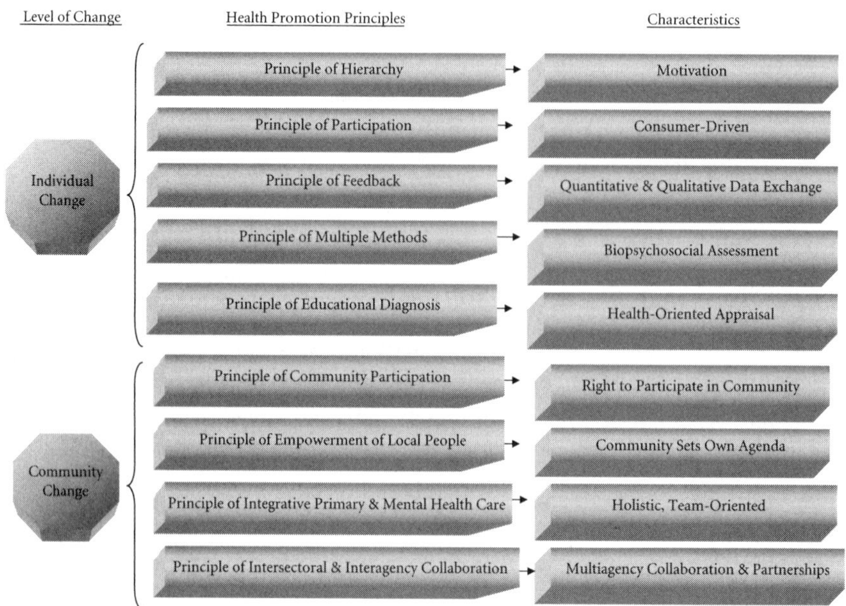

FIGURE 5.1. Health promotion principles for mental health policy: Individual and community levels and characteristics.

Principles of Individual Change

This section reviews five health promotion principles associated with individual change. These are: hierarchy, participation, feedback, multiple methods, and educational diagnosis

Principle of Hierarchy. The principle of hierarchy is founded on the idea that in order to influence human behavior, one must first understand that there is a natural hierarchy or sequence of factors that needs to be addressed prior to an intervention. In other words, if an individual lacks motivation to change at the beginning of treatment, it is inefficient to offer skills training for a behavior that they have no interest in altering. Green and Kreuter (1999) describe this hierarchy as a sequence of factors beginning with *predisposing factors* (e.g., motivation and beliefs), which lead to *enabling factors* (e.g., actual skills training), which result in *reinforcing factors* (e.g., visible results and rewards). For example, a common health promotion intervention used in mental health clinics is the health class, which would include a medication education group. If a case manager believes that his client would benefit from an understanding of the new medications he has been prescribed but the client states that he does not believe taking medications are useful, there is little point in referring him to the medication education group. While some would argue that the client should still be "made to go—just to try it out," this principle would support the notion that without an understanding of hierarchy, no amount of cajoling will result in a good fit for this kind of group experience.

In the best of all worlds, a client would self-express an interest in learning more about his medications (thus meeting the predisposing factor of motivation). An example of the hierarchy principle is illustrated in Box 5.1.

Principle of Participation. The principle of participation rests on the notion that "successful client change will be greater if clients have participated in identifying their own need for change and have selected the method that will enable them to make that change" (Green & Kreuter, 1999, p.457). This principle is based on the assumption that people will be more committed to initiating and upholding behavioral changes if they have participated in the design of their treatment such that it suits their purposes and circumstances, not just those of the providers (Green & Kreuter, 1999, p.15). Specifically, this principle assures that the participants of mental health programs are actively engaged in the planning process, will benefit from the intended program, possess a sense of "ownership" in their treatment, and acknowledge their sense of responsibility for and

Box 5.1. Case Example of Hierarchy Principle: A Lesson (Re)Learned

Most providers have had the experience of getting excited about a group idea and then it not working out so well. Here is one case example that moves from disappointment to delight.

A first-year social work student was assigned a class project of starting a group on the topic of depression at her field practicum agency—a community mental health agency. Advertisements for a new group were posted, the room was reserved, the day came and . . . no shows. Despite mild inquiry by the student regarding consumer interest, group attendance by consumers was nonexistent. The motivation in this case rested with the student intern (and the professor who made the assignment)—not the targeted client population. This same student later asked a group of clients what kind of activities they would like to do as part of their group "therapy." The group suggested a "beading group"—referring to an arts and crafts activity. Once again, advertisements were posted, the room was reserved, a local bead shop donated wire, string, and excess beads, the day came and . . . standing room only. The group became so popular among consumers because of its open style, gentle therapy approach, socialization opportunities, and skill development that it was later taken over by peer consumers.

In review, the student came to understand this very basic principle: there is a hierarchy or sequence of factors that must be understood before an intervention can take place. In this example, it had to do with consumer-driven interest in wellness approaches. By paying attention to motivation and interest levels, the student was able to facilitate a therapeutic activity that addressed motivation, skill development, and rewards. This group was motivated by consumer interest (e.g., predisposing factors), which led to actual skills training of jewelry making (e.g., enabling factors), with the results concluding in an arts and crafts project as a reward (e.g., reinforcing factors).

control over promoting change in their behavior and health status (Huff & Kline, 1999, p. 61). For example, consumer-driven services are an important component in the relationship between provider and consumer—especially for consumers who are actively involved in recovery from mental illness. An example of the principle of participation can be found in literature describing the consumer-driven recovery movement, described further in Chapter 7.

Principle of Feedback. The principle of feedback ensures that individuals have opportunities for direct and immediate feedback on their treatment progress and the effects of the intended change on desired outcomes (Green & Kreuter, 1999, p. 459). This feedback is typically given through information derived from the use of quantitative and qualitative methods. Quantitative measures include the process of monitoring client outcomes and providing data using self-report measures—both of which enable clients to adapt both to the learning process and the behavioral responses at their own pace (Jordon & Franklin, 2003). An example is when providers work with clients using self-report measures to help visually track their progress. One way would be to use a self-anchored rating scale that measured frequency of good conversations with a partner rather than the typical approach of focusing on reductions of poor communication styles. This kind of feedback can provide a different perspective on interactions.

The principle of feedback also applies to agencies. Mental health systems can improve the quality of their services to clients and families by providing legitimate opportunities for feedback and exchange. This form of feedback can be obtained through qualitative methods such as focus groups (Green & Kreuter, 1999). This principle is based on the assumption that when opportunities for feedback are present, there is a greater likelihood that the system of services and policies will be congruent with the needs of consumers and families and will result in high levels of consumer and family satisfaction. To underscore the importance of this principle, the recent report entitled *Achieving the Promise: Transforming Mental Health Care in America* (New Freedom Commission on Mental Health, 2003) found that mental health systems that lack opportunities for feedback limit their chances of making corrections in their approaches while simultaneously increasing their risks of alienating the very individuals they are designed to serve.

Think of mental health agencies you are affiliated with. Is their a format or process by which consumers or family members can provide feedback to agency administrators or board members on a regular, formal basis? If not, there is something you can do. One way to ensure consumer and family feedback to the agency would be to have formal sitting committees, like consumer and or family panels. Another means would be to make sure that the composition of the board of directors had bona fide seats for a consumer and family representative. Another activity is to sponsor a client-written newsletter.

Principle of Multiple Methods. The principle of multiple methods asserts that a variety of methods or interventions are necessary to respond to various levels of assessment and diagnosis. This principle is based on the notion that multiple intervention methods will follow multiple levels of assessment; that is, diagnosis determines or dictates the intervention or action plan. Specifically, Green and Kreuter (1999) recommend that for each of the hierarchal factors listed earlier (i.e., predisposing, enabling, and reinforcing), a different method or intervention must be identified and or provided (p. 458). By adhering to this principle, provider and consumer are both able to engage in a wider variety of resources to support a holistic and wellness-oriented intervention approach. One example of using a multiple method approach is to provide an intervention for each of the Axis I through Axis V diagnoses outlined by the *Diagnostic and Statistical Manual IV- TR* (APA, 2000). For example, when providers/clinicians use the DSM to make a diagnosis on each axis, they also need to provide a corresponding intervention for each diagnosis. We refer to this process as completing a full biopsychosocial assessment (discussed further in Chapter 6). The following case example describes a client who has need of a multiple method approach to services.

> *Case Example:* Bobby is a 45-year-old male who presents to the mental health clinic with complaints of "crippling anxiety." He states that he just panics at the idea of having to go to work and can't understand why no one appreciates his condition. He reports a history of diabetes but has not obtained treatment for this disorder because he cannot find his health cards, explaining that "no one will help me." He tells the clinic staff that if they don't help him, he will just "go home and jump off the neighbors' roof."

Figure 5.2 provides an example of the biopsychosocial assessment, including provisional diagnoses and corresponding multiple-method interventions proposed for "Bobby."

Principle of Educational Diagnosis. The principle of educational diagnosis is based on the notion that an accurate diagnosis, when offered in an educational manner, has the greatest chance of being accepted by both the client and the family. In other words, if the causes of symptoms (i.e., hearing voices) or behaviors can be understood in the context of an illness or health condition (e.g., like having diabetes) rather than a moral lapse or willful abstinence (e.g., "he never was like normal kids"; "always trying to get out of doing things"), client, providers, and caregivers may work in a more respectful and informed partnership.

A thoughtful and accurate assessment and diagnosis can then lead to the appropriate evidence-based treatment approaches, as illustrated in Figure 5.2. This figure lists dialectical behavior therapy as an evidence-based treatment approach for individuals diagnosed with borderline personality disorder. If a clinician adheres to the principle of educational diagnosis, then quite naturally the treatment approaches that follow will combine all elements of a health promotion–oriented appraisal—which includes education, information sharing, training, resource development, and referral.

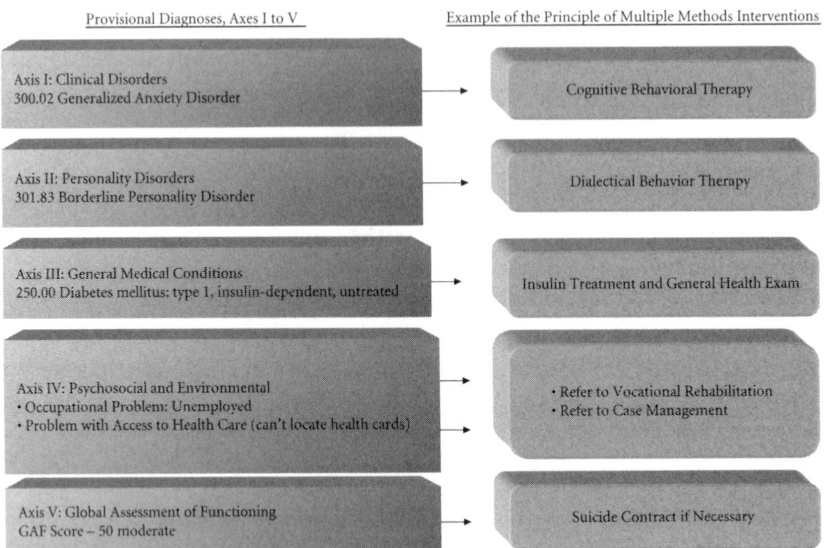

FIGURE 5.2. Example of the principle of multiple methods using DSM diagnostic categories on axes I to V: The case of Bobby.

The principle of educational diagnosis and the corresponding health promotion–oriented interventions is particularly useful for certain ethnic communities where a diagnosis of mental illness for one member of the family would bring shame and ostracism to the larger family from the community (Vandiver *et al.*, 1995). An educational diagnosis can present aspects of the illness in a health-oriented way that is both accurate yet does not reinforce notions of shamefulness to the family.

Principle of Community Change. Applying health promotion principles requires an understanding of communities.

This section reviews health promotion principles that focus on community change. These are: community participation, empowerment of local people, integration of primary and mental health care, and intersectional and interagency collaboration.

Principle of Community Participation. The principle of community participation is based on several assumptions:

1. Community participation is an essential ingredient for effective health promotion practice.
2. Members of communities best understand their own needs and have knowledge and resources vital to the health of the communities' members and citizens and should participate at all levels of public health and mental health policy, program and service development.
3. Community participation strengthens the capacity of community members to act collectively to exert control over the determinants of health.

4. Individuals with mental illnesses have a right to be a part of the active citizenry of their communities in the least restrictive environments possible.

Community or public participation, together with empowerment, has emerged as one of the defining principles in the health promotion movement (Green & Kreuter, 2005; Robertson & Minkler, 1994). So you may well ask: What do we mean by "community?" A "community," in relation to health promotion and the role of participation, may be described as any group of people who are linked by a common identity or ideology (e.g., AIDS community or the mental health community consisting of providers, families, and consumers) or geographical locale (e.g., neighborhood,) and who share formal and informal social networks, support systems, norms, cultural nuances, institutions (e.g., schools or religious congregations) and belief systems (Green & Kreuter, 2005).

The Institute of Medicine report on the future of public health in the twenty-first century (IOM, 2003) describes community as both a *setting* and a *potential partner* in the public health and mental health systems. As a *setting*, it is a place where health is supported or risked given the variability of social connections, economic conditions, and natural environments. Community is also recognized as a *partner* with the public health and mental health systems through its organizations, associations and networks (IOM, 2003). Communities are typically constituted when a group of people form a social unit (e.g., neighborhood association or mental health consumer group) based on common location, interest, identification, culture, and/or common activities (Garvin & Tropman, 1992). Specifically, knowledge about communities of identity, such as the AIDS community, will allow policy makers to work with that community for health promotion activities that are tied to social action. Similarly, knowledge about communities of place (e.g., neighborhood) forms a basis for social planning of health promotion activities.

For example, Katz and Krueter (1997) make the argument that utilizing the health promotion principle of community participation in mental health policy and program development is justified on the following grounds:

- Nonmedical factors, including volitional behaviors, social conditions, and community values, have a major influence on health and mental health status.
- Policy makers must actively engage the community in the development of solutions to local social problems (e.g., homelessness) and health problems (e.g., drug addiction and HIV/AIDS among mental health populations).
- Mental health policy development requires active involvement of the clients and families who are affected by the programs and policies (p. 148).

In other words, the principle of community participation holds in esteem the belief that people have a right to fully participate in their community in the least restrictive setting and to the best of their abilities.

This important principle is further illustrated in the report *Healthy People 2010: Healthy People in Healthy Communities* (U.S. Department of Health and Human

Services, 2000). This document serves as a framework for a national health initiative and reminds health and mental health professionals of the interdependence of the community with the health and mental health care delivery systems. See Chapter 11 for an expanded review of this report.

Principle of Empowerment of Local People

The principle of empowerment of local people is based on two assumptions: *community power* and *local control*. First, members of a community have the power to assume control for defining their own problems, setting their own priorities and developing their own (self-help) programs and, as necessary, challenging the political structure to remove obstacles or to make resources available (Green & Kreuter, 2005). Empowerment, in this context, extends beyond activities that involve taking action to help oneself (e.g., personal empowerment) to activities that involve working with others and accessing mechanisms of public decision making (political empowerment) (Fellin, 2001a). This is especially true in communities of color who typically do not engage in traditional mainstream mental health programs. For example, the tradition of self-help or mutual aid are important features in African-American and Latino communities and are seen as a way to gain power and control to overcome local health, mental health, and social problems (Fellin, 2001a; Okazawa-Rey, 1998).

A second assumption is that local people, rather than outside experts, know best their needs and should be involved in the creation of health and mental health policies and services that are specific to their community. In this context, "local people" generally means any group of individuals who share a common geographic location along with a common interest and or ideology. Self-help groups, also known as mutual-aid groups and neighborhood associations, are one way that local needs are addressed.

According to O'Neill (2003), empowerment is more than the undertaking of simple knowledge and skill acquisition; it is a social and political endeavor in which the community sets its own agenda. Navarro (2003) suggests that this principle can be seen as a health option whose focus is to enable the empowerment of populations in facilitating their active participation in shaping their communities and larger society in general.

Principle of Integrative Primary and Mental Health Care

The principle of integrative primary and mental health care is based on the assumption that mental health clients and families want and benefit from a holistic approach to health care that combines mental health and physical care using a team approach to wellness. This principle asserts the crucial role that primary care plays in promoting the mental and physical well-being of people with mental illness. In other words, integrating primary care medicine with mental health treatment increases the potential that clients with mental illness and their families will receive comprehensive treatment services, experience less stigma, and recover more rapidly, with fewer disruptions due to a fragmented systems of care (New Freedom Commission on Mental Health, 2003; Felkner *et al.*, 2004).

The merits of this principle have been supported through research, which finds that people who have a diagnosis of a major mental disorder are two times more likely to suffer from a chronic, sometimes severe health condition (e.g., diabetes, respiratory distress, hypertension, substance abuse, obesity, HIV/AIDS) than the general population (U.S. Department of Health and Human Services, 2000; Dixon *et al.*, 1999). Left undiagnosed or untreated, these coexisting disorders thwart even the best psychotherapeutic efforts of mental health clinicians.

This principle has particular relevance for women with mental illness who are of childbearing age and may face many difficulties related to reproductive health. Research has found that women with serious mental illnesses, primarily depression, are at increased risk for higher rates of reproductive loss than their well counterparts (Coverdale *et al.*, 1997). Nicholson and Henry (2003) note that mothers with mental illness have numbers of children consistent with the general population or slightly higher yet health providers often lack the requisite knowledge and skills to serve women with mental illnesses who are contemplating pregnancy or are motherinvg already. Given the public health information campaigns about the negative effects of drug and alcohol use on fetal development, many women of childbearing age who take prescription psychiatric medications are concerned about medication's effects and pregnancy. Some women have even decided to avoid pregnancy due to fear of "passing on their mental illness" or fear of "going crazy" if not on medications while pregnant. Needless to say, there are myths and fears about pregnancy and mental illness that need to be allayed. This principle highlights these concerns by endorsing the need for integrative systems of primary care with mental health care. An example of an integrative primary and mental health care intervention is Women's Wellness, which is taught by nurse practitioners and delivered on site at either the woman's home or local health or mental health clinic. A detailed discussion of women, pregnancy and mental illness can be found in Chapter 9.

Principle of Intersectoral and Interagency Collaboration

The principle of intersectoral and interagency collaboration is based on the notion that a healthy community is the result of "the adoption of a unifying language with which to work across sectors, a partnership approach to allocation and sharing of resources and a strengthening of capacity across the individual, organizational and community dimensions " (WHO, 2004a, p. 55). This principle affirms that community members who are mentally and physically healthy are assets to a community and as such should be embraced by public and private sector organizations. When public mental health and private health sectors combine their efforts, they help promote community health by creating conditions that enable persons in need of mental health services to receive them, through elimination of barriers to access as well as through assertive delivery outreach. Navarro (2003) sees this principle actualized in a global health system that is "linked with redistributive policies within each country and between countries, complemented by full employment policies that ensure adults have the right to satisfactory work in an environment friendly system of production and distribution guided by public interventions and regulations" (p. 116).

This principle is important in addressing the sweeping changes that most private and public sector health and mental health systems are experiencing. Despite a legacy of separate service systems and faced with sweeping structural changes and fiscal constraints, public and private entities are now presenting new opportunities for partnerships to improve the health of the communities they serve (Kingsbury, 1999).

One example of how different systems can engage in intersectoral and interagency collaboration is illustrated in the lessons learned from a project initiated in Minnesota. Kingsbury (1999, pp. 225–227) summarizes 10 lessons learned from a collaborative regional network of managed care organizations and public health agencies. Using this principle and community organizing strategies, they identified the following 10 "lessons"—carefully noting that these are not steps because not enough is known about this process to articulate actual steps. These are summed up as follows:

- Develop a clear purpose
- Encourage a shared belief in and place high value on working for the common good
- Place a high priority on developing relationships between members and stakeholders
- Use consensus decision making whenever possible
- Conduct productive meetings
- Recruit talented and committed members with the reliable capacity to follow through with tasks
- Be able to stay on focus
- Share leadership
- Celebrate and recognize group successes
- Be willing to work hard in the hope and expectation of eventual success

Recognized as effective guidelines, these lessons highlight that no one organization or sector acting alone has the necessary resources to effect the changes needed to improve the mental health and health of a community (Kingsbury, 1999). Mental health and health are the responsibility of the entire community—both public and private—and require the intersection of various sectors and interagency collaboration.

■ From Principle to Policy to Programs

Overview of Mental Health and Health Promotion Policy and Programs

In the preceding section, our discussion focused on how core health promotion principles or beliefs provide the framework necessary to approach individual and community change. Our next step is to explore how these health promotion principles drive mental health policy development.

Policy Defined. When we refer to *policy*, we are referring to both a *process* and an *outcome*. Policy is a *process* that provides authority for the allocation of resources (Green & Kreuter, 2005). As an *outcome*, policy is also the expression of a group of general principles by which a governmental body guides the management of public affairs, the legislature, and programs (*Black's Law Dictionary*, 1979). Understanding how policy shapes and determines the implementation of health promotion programs is essential background knowledge for administrators, clinicians, clients, family members, and the community.

Policy as Process. Keisler and Sibulkin (1987) help distinguish two kinds of mental health policy processes: *de jure* policy and *de facto* policy. *De jure* mental health policy is both intentional and legislatively grounded in law, whereas *de facto* refers to the net outcome of all mental health practices whether intended or not. An example of de jure (or intentional) mental health policy can be seen in efforts at deinstitutionalization and community-based care—the Mental Retardation Facilities and Community Mental Health Centers Construction Act of 1963 (known as the CMHC Act). The intent was to depopulate state hospitals and to do so required legislative support. An example of de facto mental health policy is the current deluge of homeless mentally ill individuals whose benefits have been eliminated by revised state policies calling for reduced funding for housing, medications and service eligibility for low-income individuals and families. When federal and state government attempts to reduce costs for health and mental health care through reduced funding policy, the net result is an unintended increase in hardships for large populations of vulnerable mental health clients. While the intention was not to increase hardships for mentally ill clients, the outcome of a shortsighted policy effort has proved tragically otherwise.

Policy as Outcome. As an *outcome*, policy can provide a set of goals, objectives and rules guiding the activities of a mental health organization or administration. In other words, policy can be a collection of governmental, state, or agency goals designed to reflect the values of the stakeholders and to meet social objectives (e.g., the improvement of the health status of the populations of individuals who experience mental illness). For example, as discussed in Chapter 3, Oregon's state legislature enacted a policy, commonly referred to as "Senate Bill 267," which mandated that all state-funded agencies, starting with the Department of Corrections and the Department of Health and Human Services, institute evidence-based interventions into at least 75% their treatment programs by the year 2007. The goal of this policy was to ensure that agencies were offering interventions that were considered "best practices" and supported by science, as opposed to continuing to provide services that showed no improvement or were of dubious therapeutic benefit (e.g., long-term insight-oriented counseling for individuals diagnosed with schizophrenia or most other mental health conditions).

What Is Public Mental Health Policy?

Mental health policies come under the general headings of social policy, public policy, and health policy. Mental health policy is generally the result of governmental activities concerned with the prevention and treatment of mental disorders, the living situations of individuals with mental illness, and, more recently, activities that promote healthy lifestyles (Fellin, 1996). Mental health policies are largely a product of *legislative* (e.g, laws), *regulative* (e.g., regulations) and *judicial* (e.g., court decisions) processes (DiNitto, 2007). Table 5.1 illustrates these categories.

At the *legislative level*, the major government unit granted responsibility for mental health policy development is the National Institute of Mental Health (NIMH). The NIMH was established with the passage of the National Mental Health Act of 1946—P.L. 79–487. This broad based federal policy emerged out of a health promotion principle that called for intersectoral and interagency collaboration.

At the *regulatory* level, states implement and regulate federal policies based on interpretation and funding mechanisms. For example, most states are required to create a state plan for comprehensive community mental health services in order to receive funding from the community mental health services block grant. This mandate meets the requirement of Title V of the Public Health Service Act [42 U.S.C. 300x-1 et seq.]. Two health promotion principles are identified as the foundation of the Public Health Service Act—Comprehensive Community Mental Health Services. These are the principle of feedback (e.g., based on role that consumers and families play in community mental health organizations) and the principle of participation (e.g., given the emphasis on consumer driven services).

At the *judicial level*, there have been numerous court cases over the last 40 years that have affirmed health promotion principles. Examples of some of these court cases are *Lake v. Cameron[1966], Covington v. Harris [1969], Wyatt v. Stickney [1971], Dixon v. Weinbverger[1975]* and *Olmstead v. L.C. [1999]*(Sands, 2001; DiNitto, 2007). It is this last case, *Olmstead v. L.C.* 527 U.S. 581, 119 S. Ct. 2176 (1999), which has garnered the most recent attention in mental health settings and is a direct reflection of a key health promotion

TABLE 5.1. ***Intersection of Health Promotion Principles, Processes and Public Mental Health Policies.***

Processes	Policy Examples	Health Promotion Principles
▪ Legislative	National Mental Health Act of 1946 (P.L. 79–48)	*Principle of Intersectoral Collaboration*
▪ Regulatory	State Plan for Comprehensive Community Mental Health Services – Title V of the Public Health Services Act [42 U.S.C. 300x – 1 et seq]	*Principle of Feedback & Principle of Participation*
▪ Judicial	Olmstead v. L.C. 527 U.S. 581, 119 S. Ct. 2176 (1999)	*Principle of Community Participation*

principle: community participation. This principle, which affirms the right to live and participate fully in community settings, is based on the notion that people with mental illness have a right to humane treatment—including a safe environment and appropriate treatment interventions—that offer the least restrictions necessary to achieve treatment goals. In the Olmstead case, described further on in this chapter, the U.S. Supreme Court ruled that keeping individuals with mental disabilities in institutional facilities who are capable of living in community settings constitutes a form of discrimination under the Americans with Disabilities Act. In its ruling, the Court gave states the power to influence the process of determining who is eligible for community placement and a directive to place individuals in community settings following an assessment and consideration of a range of programs including assisted living and community integration. The emphasis of this judicially influenced policy is on community reintegration and participation.

Mental Health Programs

Referring to the conceptual model described at the beginning of this chapter, policy is implemented through programs. Let's review what we mean by a "program" and review examples of mental health programs that have been influenced by various health promotion principles and the policies that have emerged from them.

Programs. Mental health programs and their services are the consequence of public mental health policies (Fellin, 1996). Programs consist of a set of services (i.e., health, psychiatric, social and medical supports) that are delivered through administrative procedures (i.e., policies and procedures manuals) and meet predetermined goals and objectives (e.g., enhance quality of life, promote wellness behaviors among populations, reduce inpatient admissions by 20%) (Fellin,1996). Health promotion and mental health programs can be viewed as configurations of interventions and activities directed toward the implementation of mental health policy goals; they include a range of social, medical, and clinical mental health interventions (Fellin, 1996). Generally, mental health programs are implemented in either community (e.g., outpatient) or hospital (e.g., inpatient) settings. Community based mental health programs are generally a part of a local community mental health center, whereas hospital programs generally refer to state mental hospitals, units of local general hospitals or private psychiatric hospitals.

Most mental health programs, either community or hospital based, generally share the common goal: symptom reduction and management. Similarly, health promotion programs can be seen in some mental health clinics but are mostly situated in schools, workplace settings, and health care institutions (Poland, Green, & Rootman, 2000). They typically address lifestyle issues, maintenance of health, chronic pain, diet, exercise, and substance /tobacco use. Overall, mental health and health promotion programs can trace their origins directly back to key policies, which were, in turn, influenced by the principles held by the policy makers (Dandoy, 1997). The next section reviews the history of mental health policy through legislative actions.

History of Public Mental Health and Health Promotion Policies and Programs

Historically, shifts in health and mental health policy can be traced to changing societal mores and to a lesser degree, scientific knowledge (McCubbin, LaBonte & Dallaire, 2001). This is particularly the case in the evolution of care targeted toward the treatment of individuals with mental illness. This section will review the timeline of key mental health and health promotion policies and programs influenced by the health promotion principles we have discussed.

Mental Health Policies: The Early Years

Early Colonial America. In early colonial America, social mores or beliefs asserted that people with mental illness were more of a social or economic problem and should be cared for by the family or the local community (Fellin, 1996). The idea that mental illness was a medical condition was nonexistent. When families could not care for their mentally ill family members, care was transferred to almshouses or poorhouses and hospital asylums. These settings housed mixed groups of people who were indigent, physically and mentally ill, immigrants, developmentally disabled, troubled youth, and the aged.

Policy of Moral Treatment. A major shift in the public's attitude about care for mentally ill individuals came slowly through the efforts of the French physician Philippe Pinel, who worked in a Paris hospital for the "insane" (Fellin, 1996). Beginning in 1793, he introduced the concept of *moral treatment.* Originally conceived as a response to the inhumane treatment of patients in public mental hospitals, the approach was based on the principle that individuals with a psychiatric illness could benefit from humane care and should be treated with sympathetic and personal care using psychologically oriented therapeutic approaches. Moral treatment, in this context, referred to a moral approach, not moralistic content. However, in the United States, the approach was interpreted with a moralistic overtone and translated into the idea that bad habits lead to tendencies toward mental disorders (Fellin, 1996); this, ironically, is what large portions of mental health policy and health promotion efforts continue to emphasize today.

Mental Health Legislation in the Nineteenth Century (1800–1900)

Although existing health policy for people with mental illness at the beginning of the nineteenth century was more informal and driven by the medical community, public policy sentiment began to shift to more punitive measures.

Illegal-Entry Legislation. Spurred on at the request of local charities, the U.S. Congress, under President Pierce, enacted legislation in 1882 making it illegal for individuals with mental illness to enter the country. Pierce is also noted in mental health history as the one who vetoed Dorothea Dix's land grant bill to fund state mental hospitals.

New York State Care Act of 1890. States began to assume responsibility and care for the treatment of individuals with mental illness, mainly by building and maintaining mental institutions (Trattner, 1999). This trend, initiated by Dorthea Dix in the 1840s, culminated in the passage of the New York State Care Act of 1890. Under its provisions, New York State assumed complete care for all of the state's "insane" people. Programs were generally asylums or institutions; they were called asylums because that was what they were to provide, asylum from the burdens of society.

Mental Health Legislation of the Twentieth Century (1945–1999)

In the last 50 years, mental health legislation and programs in the United States have been primarily focused on deinstitutionalization, acute treatment, and diversion from inpatient settings. From this legislation, only a handful of policies and programs have emerged that incorporated health or health promotion as part of their mental health mandate. These include the *National Mental Health Act of* 1946, *Mental Retardation Facilities and Community Mental Health Centers Construction Act of* 1963, *State Comprehensive Mental Health Services Plan Act* (1986), *Steward B. McKinney Homeless Assistance Act* (1987), *Americans with Disabilities Act* (1990), *Ticket to Work and Work Incentives Improvement Act of* 1999, and the *Olmstead Act—Community Based Alternatives for Individuals with Disabilities*(1999). These policies are displayed on the the timeline of Figure 5.3.

The following section provides an overview of these policies and examples of programs that were the offspring of the policies.

National Mental Health Act of 1946 *(P.L. 79–487).* Mental illness was recognized as a major social problem for the United States when prior to World War II, approximately 25% of men (or 1,100,000 out of 4,800,000) were rejected from military service because of a mental or neurologic disease–or at least as mental and neurologic diseases were defined at the time. Of those inducted into the military and later discharged for medical reasons, approximately 40% were dismissed for psychiatric disorders (Trattner, 1999). Recognizing the prevalence of mental illness among the population of pre- and postwar veterans, the National Mental Health Act was created in response to the American people's concern about these conditions.

Programs. At the end of World War II, The National Mental Health Act of 1946 established a research center within the Mental Hygiene Division in the Public Health Service. This act provided for a critical program that is still in operation today: the National Institute of Mental Health (NIMH), founded in 1949. Although the initial purpose of NIMH was to pursue research on child development, juvenile delinquency, alcoholism, suicide prevention, and war-related problems (e.g., battle fatigue), its

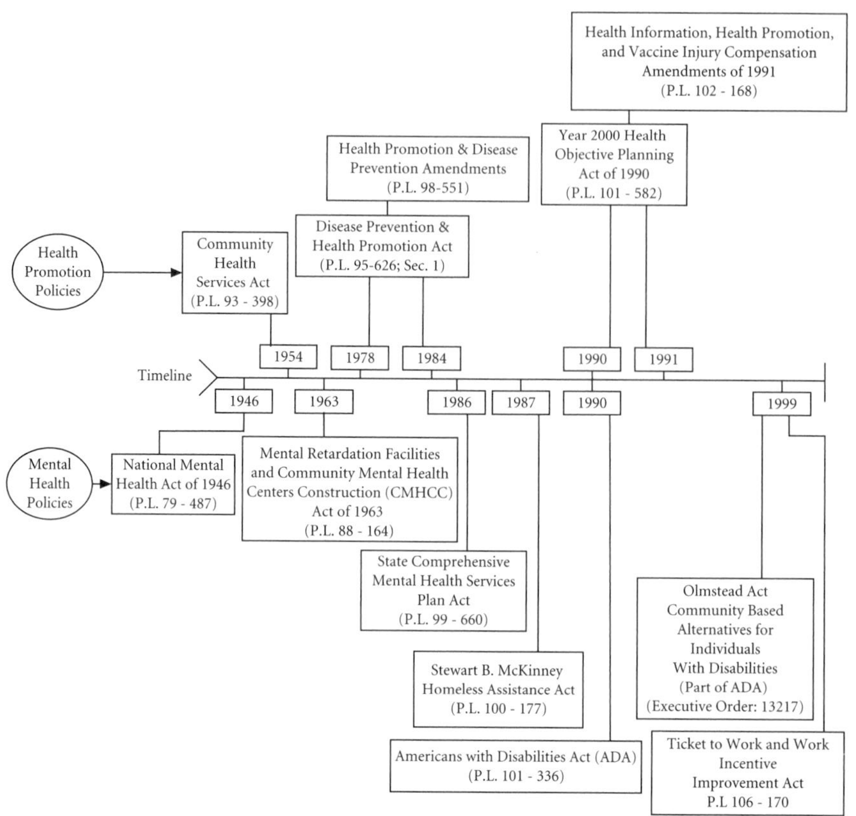

FIGURE 5.3. Timeline of key U.S. mental health and health promotion policies; 1945-1999.

ultimate goal was to promote mental health through research, education, and training (Moniz & Gorin, 2007).However, in recent years, congress reorganized NIMH such that it primarily focuses on research. Other agencies, like the Substance Abuse and Mental Health Services Administration (SAMSHA), have now assumed the role of training and services—at least that was the mandate when this manuscript went into publication.

In its early years, NIMH was also essential in establishing a well-known program still in use today: the *Community Support Program* (CSP), from which emerged the *Program for Assertive Community Treatment (PACT)*. The CSP, established in 1977, was meant to facilitate a federal–state partnership that would encourage state initiatives to focus on the needs of people with severe and persistent mental illness (Moniz & Gorin, 2007). Solomon and Stanhope (2006) point out that after deinstitutionalization, the Community Support Program movement laid out a network of essential services to support persons with severe mental illness in the community. Although many of the services were focused on symptom reduction (e.g., medication monitoring) and treatment compliance (e.g., case management), others program components were compatible with the goals of community-based health promotion approaches: enhancement of daily living skills, teaching life skills, supporting vocational goals, housing stability, securing income and benefits—all of which were components of the PACT Program.

The Mental Retardation Facilities and Community Mental Health Centers Construction (CMHHC)Act of 1963 *(P.L.* 88–164*).* This act was the landmark, albeit controversial, legislation that called for the building and staffing of community mental health centers across the country in response to national efforts at deinstitutionalization of state hospitals (DiNitto, 2007). The idea was to provide funds to states to close the state hospitals and replace them with community-based services in the least restrictive environment. What emerged was the development of community-based mental health programs. In 1968, the CMHCC Act was amended to include funding for the development of alcohol treatment programs (Moniz & Gorin, 2007). This amendment was later followed by a state wide mental health services plan.

State Comprehensive Mental Health Services Plan Act of 1986 *(P.L.* 99–660*).* The state plan allowed states to use federal block grant funds to expand their community-based mental health services. This legislation emphasized needs assessments (e.g., determining numbers of mentally ill individuals in the region) and helped to focus on homeless individuals who were mentally ill. This legislation was quite explicit in its recognition of health promotion as a basis for its programs.

Programs. Fellin (1996) notes that under this act, funding for special programs for homeless mentally ill individuals came from two sources: Housing and Urban Development and Health and Human Services. One of the unique programs to emerge from this act was "Shelter Plus"—which provided housing and long term supportive services to individuals with serious mental illness who also had comorbid conditions of substance abuse, AIDS, and related medical diseases (Fellin, 1996). Both pieces of legislation allowed for the development and expansion of community mental health centers.

The Stewart B. McKinney Homeless Assistance Act of 1987 *(P.L.* 100–77*).* Stewart McKinney provided block grant funding to states for the purpose of providing assistance and services to homeless individuals. This was one of the few policies that recognized the importance of an integrated system of health, mental health, and substance use services. Health promotion efforts were key in assisting homeless individuals to maintain basic levels of physical health despite significant environmental hardships from street life.

Programs. From this act, community programs were developed which provided the following services: emergency shelter, food, housing, health and mental health services, alcohol and drug abuse prevention services, education, and job training (Moniz & Gorin, 2007; DiNitto, 2007). One controversial program, at least in the United States, that dealt with homelessness and drug use is the Needle Exchange Program, located in a number of cities such as the one sponsored by the Multnomah County Heath Department in Portland, Oregon. This program is targeted to intravenous drug users, many of whom are homeless, with the goal of preventing the spread of HIV. The program is funded through county funds and uses a variety of outreach efforts. Based on the health promotion principle of using multiple methods, street outreach workers carry clean syringes to exchange for dirty needles used by homeless people and those working in the sex industry. The Needle Exchange program meets the principle of multiple methods test in that the program triages users needs in terms of housing, health, and education specific to safe needle use.

One of the main exchange sites is located at a shelter for homeless youth. Services offered at this exchange site include on-site HIV counseling and testing, referral to social services, detoxification, substance abuse treatment services, and distribution of hygiene products. Data for the second year of operation report that the exchange program distributed over 40,000 clean syringes and collected almost the same number of used syringes.

Americans with Disabilities Act of 1990 *(P.L.* 101–336*).* The American Disabilities Act (ADA) recognized the special needs of individuals with physical or mental disabilities and the need to offer protections against discrimination. The ADA defines disability as "one who has a physical or mental impairment that substantially limits one or more major life activities, a record of such impairment or being regarded as having such an impairment" (DiNitto, 2007, p. 182). The act was created in response to the fact that people with health and mental health disabilities, as a group, often face discrimination and are often severely disadvantaged socially, vocationally, economically, and educationally (Fellin, 1996). Primary responsibility for enforcing the ADA lies with the Department of Justice (DiNitto, 2007). The act has had significant implications for addressing employment discrimination as well as promoting community-based employment opportunities—which has been an ancillary focus of health promotion efforts.

Mental Health Legislation of the Twenty-First Century

Most recently, the *Ticket to Work and Work Incentives Improvement Act of* 1999 were designed to address many of the work disincentives (e.g., loss of cash benefits and medical coverage), faced by people receiving disability income [e.g., supplemental security income (SSI) and social security disability insurance]. This policy is unique in that it recognize the value of work, but only if health benefits can be retained.

Programs. Given the newness of employment-benefits maintenance disability-related legislation, one promising program that is currently being proposed by the Centers for Medicare and Medicaid Services (CMS) is the Medicaid Infrastructure Grant Program (which provides financial assistance to states to coordinate approaches between

Medicaid and non-Medicaid programs) (Substance Abuse and Mental Health Services Administration, 2005). This program would be one of the first to support the transition of individuals with mental illness into the workforce without the crippling threat of removing their health benefits. To do so will require coordination of multiple partners from the business sector, vocational services, and health and mental health organizations.

Olmstead Act: Executive Order 13217: Community-Based Alternatives for Individuals with Disabilities (2001). Another landmark effort in support of rights for individuals with mental illness is seen in the Supreme Court case *Olmstead v. L.C.* 527 U.S. 581, 119 S. Ct. 2176 (1999). In the Olmstead case, fundamental constitutional rights were at stake. The case originated in Georgia, where a suit was brought against the state on behalf of two women with mental disabilities who were institutionalized. They were denied placement in the community even though their treating professionals said they were ready for such placement. By denying them community placement, the courts deemed that they were discriminated against and thus segregated from daily life activities, which included contact with individuals, family relations, social contacts, work options, economic independence, educational advancement, and cultural enrichment (Wilkinson, 2002). Specifically, the Supreme Court construed Title II of the Americans with Disabilities Act to require states to place qualified individuals with mental disabilities in community settings, rather than institutions, whenever treatment professionals determine that such placement is appropriate, the affected persons do not oppose such placement, and the state can reasonably accommodate the placement. The Supreme Court determined that confinement in an institution severely diminishes everyday life activities of individuals, including family relations, social contacts, work options, economic independence, educational advancement, and cultural enrichment. It is now referred to as the *Olmstead Act*, and President Bush has issued Executive Order 13217: Community Based Alternatives for Individuals with Disabilities (2001) requesting selected federal agencies, including the U.S. Department of Labor, to support states in their implementation of the *Olmstead* decision. For a detailed description of this act and its implications, see www.worksupport.com.

Programs. In addition to supporting the efforts of people to participate as citizens in their own communities, the act also supported efforts of individuals with mental illness to obtain skills, training, and experiences in community-based employment opportunities. Community mental health centers have been active in developing a variety of Supported Employment Programs that emphasize job coach support for real-world employment training. Recognizing that many individuals with mental illness have a strong desire to work in spite of significant health issues (e.g., diabetes and chronic fatigue due to medications), clients and employers, with the assistance of job coaches, can be educated about the benefits of augmented work arrangements (e.g., frequent rest and snack breaks, modified hours).

The Olmstead Act had several consequences related to health promotion principles. In addition to supporting the efforts of people to participate as citizens in their own communities, the act also supported efforts of individuals with mental illness to obtain skills, training and experiences in community based employment opportunities. Furlong and colleagues (2002) describe one unique work program, Thresholds Bridge North Pilot, which uses the individual placement and support model of employment promoted by Robert Drake and his colleagues (see Drake *et al.*, 1999). Table 5.2 illustrates the interrelationship of principle-policy-program.

TABLE 5.2. ***Interrelationship Between Selected Health Promotion Principles, Federal Mental Health, and Health Promotion Policies and Programs.***

Health Promotion Principles	Policy Examples	Program Examples
Individual Level		
▪ Principle of Multiple Methods	-Stewart B. McKinney Homeless Assistance Act	→ Needle-Exchange Program
	-State Comprehensive Mental Health Services Plan Act	→ Shelter Plus
Community Level		
▪ Principle of Community Participation	-Americans with Disabilities Act: Olmstead Act (Employment)	→ Supported Employment Programs
▪ Principle of Empowerment of Local People	-Year 2000 Health Objectives Planning Act 2000	→ Promoting Healthy (Native) Traditions
	-Community Health Services Act of 1946	
▪ Principle of Integrative Primary & Mental Health Care	-Year 2000 Health Objectives Planning Act – Healthy People (2010)	→ Promoting Healthy Traditions → Preconceptual Health Promotion
▪ Principle of Intersectoral & Interagency Collaboration	-National Mental Health Act of 1946	→ National Institute of Mental Health: Community Support Programs (CSP) & Program for Assertive Community Treatment
	-Ticket to Work & Work Incentives Improvement Act of 1999	→ Medicaid Infrastructure Grant Program

Key U.S. Health Promotion Policies and Programs of the Twentieth Century

We now shift from a review of mental health policies to health promotion policies. In this section, we also show the link between health promotion policies and related principles discussed earlier in this chapter. Example of programs are described when possible.

In the United States, health promotion policies in the twentieth century were typically distinct from mental health policy despite the mutually shared goal of protecting and promoting the nation's health—in which mental health was certainly a factor. Key health promotion policies of the twentieth century that had relevance to mental health include the *Community Health Services Act of* 1954, *U.S. Disease Prevention and Health Promotion Act of* 1978 (with subsequent amendments in 1984), *Year* 2000 *Health Objective Planning Act of* 1990, and the *Health Information, Health Promotion and Vaccine Injury Compensation Amendments of* 1991. Of these four, the Community Health Services Act and the Year 2000 Health Objective Planning Act had the most influence in mental health and are discussed below.

Community Health Services Act of 1954 *(P.L. 96–398).* The Community Health Services Act of 1954 permitted local communities to establish their own mental health boards, which could use state funds to partially support the delivery of community based inpatient or outpatient care (Moniz & Gorin, 2007). This policy reflects the principle of empowerment of local people.

The 2000 *Health Objective Planning Act (P.L.* 101–582*).* This act paved the way for the initiative *Healthy People* 2000 (1990), which later expanded to *Healthy People* 2010 (2003). This initiative helped establish a 10-year policy framework and guidelines for building a healthy society. Two unique programs emerged from this effort: Promoting Healthy Traditions and Preconceptual Health Promotion.

Programs. In the United States, one example of a community's effort to create its own program for addressing health and mental health is the American Indian Health Care Association (AIHCA) (Ashton, 1992). McGinnis and Maiese (1997) describe how the AIHCA transformed the large government-sponsored health document, *Healthy People* 2000, into a user-friendly handbook entitled *Promoting Healthy Traditions.* Based on the principle of empowerment of local people, the purpose of the handbook was to "support the community's efforts to develop their own health/mental health objectives by using methods congruent to Native tradition style of communication. The handbook raised tribal awareness of health issues using questions like "Who are the healers in your community? How would you describe the concept of wellness? What are the healthy traditions of your community?" (p. 143).

Another program to emerge from this initiative is the Preconceptional Health Promotion program. Bennett and Cross (1997) describe an emerging health promotion approach that is applicable to women who have a mental illness and are of childbearing age. Referred to as *Preconceptional Health Promotion*, this is a supportive and educational approach to women's mental and physical health that focuses on optimizing health status through good nutrition, exercise, and vitamins while minimizing hazards to the uterine environment (e.g., drug and/or alcohol use) prior to pregnancy. This type of program can be offered as a portion of a women's wellness class or group at the local community mental health center or in partnership with personnel from the client's local primary care clinic, health clinic, or ob/gyn clinic.

The benefit of the partnership between primary care staff and mental health staff is that it provides a holistic approach to women's health care and mental health care that helps dispel the implicit message that women with mental illness should not have children. The partnership model between mental health personnel and primary care personnel helps women clients make informed decisions about family planning that is steeped in education and support rather than stigma and paternalism. This program can be directly linked to the principle of integrative primary and mental health care.

■ Global Policy Initiatives

Globally, the concept of health promotion is increasingly finding its way into the psyche of national governments and nongovernment organizations that consider health a basic human right. Most notably, Canada, the United Kingdom, and New Zealand have advanced the concept of health promotion by integrating it directly into public health policy. The following section provides a review of health promotion policies for these three countries.

Canada. Two such policy efforts can be seen in the Canada Health Act of 1984, which included health promotion in its preamble and later, the Ottawa Charter for Health Promotion of 1986. Other policy initiatives include *A New Perspective on the Health of Canadians* and *Achieving Health for All: A Framework for Health Promotion.* By taking the concepts of health promotion and wellness and embedding them in the constitution, health was placed squarely on the agenda of policy makers in all sectors and all levels. This effort was designed to encourage policy makers to (1) identify obstacles to the adoption of healthy public policies in non-health sectors, (2) identify ways of removing obstacles, (3) be aware of the health consequences of their decisions, and (4) accept their responsibilities for the health of Canada's citizens (Lupton, 1995; WHO, 2001, 2004a).

In the Canadian approach, health promotion policy aims to foster greater equity by coordinating the actions of legislation, fiscal measures, taxation, and organizational change. By using diverse but complementary approaches, health promotion policy is intended to result in healthier goods and services, healthier public services, and cleaner, more enjoyable environments (WHO, 2004a)—all of which are known determinants of mental health.

United Kingdom. The United Kingdom, particularly North Cumbria, has taken the concept of health promotion and broadened it to include *mental* health promotion. Several policy initiatives have been developed and are available in governmental publications. These include *Health of the Nation* (1992), *Our Healthier Nation* (1997), *Saving Our Lives: Our Healthier Nation* (1999), and *National Service Framework for Mental Health: Modernizing Mental Health Services* (1999). Specifically, Saving Our Lives, a national contract for mental health, outlines the integrated action that government and communities can undertake to reduce mental disorder and improve health (North Cumbria Health Department, 2002). A second and equally visionary document is the National Service Framework (NSF), which describes the key framework that the government is using to guide mental health services. This framework details the standards and service models for delivering safe, sound, and supportive mental health services. For example, standard one of the NSF offers the following directive for Health and Social Services: ". . . to promote mental health for all, working with individuals and communities, and to combat discrimination against all individuals and groups with mental health problems and promote their social inclusion" (North Cumbria Health Department, 2002, p.6).

The NSF has designated the Health Authority as the lead organization with key partners including local authorities, local education authority, consumer/user and caregiver/family forums, the voluntary sector, and employers. While the focus of this national strategy is primarily concerned with the mental health of working-age adults, young people, and schools, the approach is based on building alliances, developing multiagency approaches, encouraging community ownership, and supporting monitoring and evaluation efforts—all of which exemplify the health promotion principle of intersectoral and interagency collaboration. In addition to the NSF, there are a variety of other national policies in North Cumbria that refer explicitly to mental health, these are the National Healthy Schools Standard and Health Action Zones. For a full review of these initiatives, see mike.graham@nlhc-tr.northy.nhs.uk.

New Zealand. New Zealand has developed an extensive array of national health policies that can be categorized into seven distinct strategies, all of which reflect a commitment to health promotion principles and practices. These include the *New Zealand Health Strategy, Public Health Strategy, Mental Health Strategy, New Zealand Disability Strategy, Mental Health Promotion, Inequalities Strategy and the Youth Health Strategy.* Of these seven national policies, three have direct significance for mental health populations and issues: *Disability Strategy, Mental Health Promotion,* and *Youth Health Strategy.*

The New Zealand Disability Strategy, which is supported by the National Health Plan, is based on the social model of disability and human rights, which describes disability as "a process which happens when one group of people create barriers by designing a world only for their way of living" (O'Hagan, 2003, p. 4). One of its key programs is a project called *Like Minds, Like Mine.* This program was developed as a 5-year project to counter stigma and discrimination associated with mental illness.

The slogan "Like Minds, Like Mine" is a play on the phrase "We are all of like mind." In essence, it means we are all the same in that mental illness can happen to anyone. The project identifies its vision as "a nation that values and includes all people who experience mental illness." The project has three key aims: to enable all people with experience of mental illness (1) to gain equality and respect and to enjoy the same rights as others, (2) change public and private sector policy to value and include all people with experience of mental illness, and (3) create greater understanding, acceptance, and support for all people with experiences of mental illness.

Mary O'Hagan, Mental Health Commissioner of New Zealand, offers a uniquely worded goal for the project: "put value back into madness" (O'Hagan, 2003). While at first this phrase may seem awkward, O'Hagan gently argues that "all discrimination stems from devaluing madness." She asserts:

> the wider community often responds by excluding mad people and madness from its cultural, social, economic and political activities. Friends and families sometimes respond by excluding mad people from intimacy, companionship, social networks and family responsibilities. Mental health services too often use the rituals of diagnosis to devalue the people they are supposed to serve. Thus, to move forward, policies and programs need to challenge the root of discrimination by putting value back into madness. (p.iii).

She recommends that while we should not deny the pain of mental illness, society needs to amplify the voices of people who experience mental illness in different ways. This includes seeing "madness" or mental illness as a crisis of being, a reasonable response to trauma, and a transformation of identity or a protest against oppression. Programs like "Like Minds, Like Mine" are part of New Zealand's efforts to advance toward being a fully inclusive society. In essence, it illustrates how some people accomplished what they did in spite of their mental illness and some others because of their mental illness.

The *Mental Health Promotion Strategy* is a national initiative which seeks to promote health and reduce inequalities by enhancing the mental health and well-being of people affected by their socioeconomic status and who are vulnerable as a result of their social isolation and mental status. The framework for this strategy is a document called *Building on Strengths*. This document establishes a platform for continued improvements in mental health for all New Zealanders using two approaches: building community cohesiveness through activities that make people safer and developing partnerships to improve access to conditions that promote positive mental health, such as education, meaningful employment, and suitable housing (Ministry of Health, 2002).

The *Youth Health Strategy* is a national policy effort sponsored by the Ministry of Health and the Ministry of Youth Affairs (Ministry of Health, 2003) and is designed to address the rates of suicide and attempted suicides by young people. The strategy will focus on developing mental health programs that focus on wellness, developing intersectoral work to reduce youth suicides and attempted suicides, improving the range of accessible and appropriate services for youth, including Māori and Pacific Peoples. Examples of programs that this initiative is supporting are one-stop shops and Youth Health Centers (p. 31). These documents can be accessed on the Ministry of Health's Website: http://www.moh.govt.nz.

In addition to these country-specific initiatives, the most recent multination collaboration for health promotion can be found in the Bangkok Charter for Health Promotion (World Health Organization, 2005) and first introduced in Chapter 1. This charter, a product of many organizations, networks, and individuals in multiple countries is designed to call for health promotion policy coherence across governments, international organizations, civil society, and the private sector. One key goal will to be address determinants of health by engaging a variety of prominent health care stakeholders.

■ Strategies for Integrating Health Promotion Principles into Mental Health Policies and Programs

To meet the mental health challenges described in Chapter 1, mental health advocates and all stakeholders—including consumers, family members, clinicians, administrators—must work with policy makers in strategic ways. The challenge: convincing policy makers to embrace health promotion principles as the foundation for mental health policy development. Recommended strategies include educating policy makers directly and advocating at national, state, program, and individual levels. These strategies are discussed below.

Strategy 1: Educate Policy Makers

Gostin (2000) recommends that mental health policy makers need to better understand the principles of health promotion, how it works, what results are produced, and at what costs, particularly since society spends so much of its resources on regulations. In a study by Shumway and colleagues (2003), 100 state public policy makers (i.e., 40 administrative decision makers, 40 state legislators, and 20 legislative aids) from the U.S. were asked to rate the importance of key schizophrenia treatment outcomes. Participants rated schizophrenia-related health states using six domains: psychotic symptoms, deficit symptoms, medication side effects, productive activity, daily activity, and social activity. There ratings were then compared with ratings provided by 53 primary stakeholders (i.e., 20 consumers diagnosed with schizophrenia, 13 of their family members, and 20 of their health care providers). The authors found that while both groups placed similar values on functional outcomes, policy makers did not place as much importance on medication side effects. The authors caution that the differences in importance placed on medication side effects may lead to conflicts in the allocation of resources for the provision of newer and more expensive medications, which were, until recently, thought to be associated with fewer side effects (Shumway *et al.*, 2003). However, emerging research has challenged this notion with findings that for adults diagnosed with schizophrenia, newer antipsychotic medications show no difference than older-generation medications on quality of life, symptoms, and cost over a 1-year period (Jones*et al.*, 2006).

Although it is very encouraging that this group of policy makers and stakeholders value treatment outcomes in similar ways, mental health providers still have much to do in terms of informing policy makers of the detrimental social and health costs of medication side effects. For example, if policy makers appreciated the health promotion principle of multiple methods (which supports the use of multiple assessment and treatment interventions), they could see the link this principle has to mental health agency policies of paying nurses and doctors to help monitor health side effects. These medication monitoring services are implemented through community mental health programs that provide services such as health and medication education courses. These courses, in turn, result in a better-informed consumer who is more likely to report adverse medication side effects that, in turn, could save money due to hospital aversion, less chronic physical illnesses, and community stability.

There are several factors that mental health advocates should be aware of in attempting to influence policy makers to distribute resources for health promotion efforts. Borrowing from social psychology research, Corrigan and Watson (2003) note that policy makers' decision to allocate mental health resources are most heavily influenced by three factors: *perception*, *political ideology*, and *political accountability*.

In terms of *perception*, policy makers are most likely to weigh the following factors in forming mental health policy decisions and determining resource allocation: scarcity of resources, effectiveness of specific programs, needs of people who have problems who are served by these programs, and extent of personal responsibility for these problems.

In terms of *political ideology*, policy makers are typically members of one party and, depending on that party's "leaning" or orientation (e.g., often defined in terms of liberal, conservative, leftist, right wing, green, centrist, moderate), will be influenced by the belief systems held by that party. For example, in the United States, the republican party's ideology is typically characterized as one of fiscal constraint and low government intrusion, whereas the democratic party is known for its belief in human capital investment (e.g., such as social or entitlement programs). However, these are not hard and fast differences—particularly when it comes to political ideology, which can also be another way of speaking about personal ideology.

And finally, we cannot forget that policy makers are *politically accountable* to their constituents and thus sensitive to their desires. Despite mounds of empiric evidence for a particular health promotion approach (e.g., motivational interviewing for substance use), they may end up supporting one value (e.g., zero tolerance for drug use) over another value (e.g., harm-reduction approach to drug use) if it fits the constituents value base (Gostin, 2000; Corrigan & Watson, 2003). Given the power of perception, mental health advocates are still well advised to understand the psychological processes that affect policy makers' decisions about resource allocation.

So how do mental health advocates convince policy makers of the value of supporting and funding health promotion efforts for individuals, families, and communities who experience mental illness? There are four strategies: national, state, program, and individual.

Strategy 2: Advocate at the National Level

If health promotion principles are to drive mental health policies and programs, a first step is in legitimizing them as part of a national agenda. The Canadian experience with the Ottawa Charter for Health Promotion offers a rare glimpse into successful policy reform using the principles discussed in this chapter. These reform efforts can be summarized into four key strategies:

- *Develop a conceptual basis for action that is founded upon principles.* For example, Canadian policy makers developed three key documents that were instrumental in guiding health promotion agendas for health and mental health programs. These documents, mentioned earlier, were *A New Perspective on the Health of Canadians, The Ottawa Charter,* and *Achieving Health for All: A Framework for Health Promotion.* These documents helped distill the key principles of health promotion and the rationale behind policy reform efforts.
- *Cultivate a strong and enlightened leadership.* For example, governmental appointments included directors and ministers who had had experience with community development approaches to programming.
- *Demonstrate the ability to translate concepts into action.* For example, great effort was given to public dialogue, marketing, and program announcements that led to research initiatives.
- *Ability to understand the need to influence health system reform.* For example, given the rising costs of health care and the federal move from cost sharing to block funding, health promotion was identified by federal and provincial/territorial ministers as a priority for joint policy action. This large-scale understanding by government leaders of health economics and the impact of a new method of financing would eventually result in the most progressive of policy initiatives: health promotion was included in the preamble of the Canadian Health Act of 1984 (IUHPE, 2000, p. 123).

Even in the United States, The Institute of Medicine (IOM, 1988, 2003) has long recommended that public health and mental health leaders combine efforts to strengthen the linkages between the two fields, starting with the integration of services and programs at the local level.

Strategy 3: Advocate at the State or Provincial Level

Healthy People 2010 has called for state mental health systems to be based on health promotion principles. According to HP 2010 (U.S.DHHS, 2000), a mental health system that has made the commitment to operate under health promotion principles will (1) build on the World Health Organization's principles of access; (2) take into account broader population health and mental health issues; (3) create the conditions for effective provision of services to individuals, families, and communities who experience mental illness; and (4) organize integrated systems of care that include primary health care and educational opportunities. In other words, by focusing on principles—such as participation, community empowerment, and access to primary health care—state mental health systems and their provider agencies can help ensure success in reaching out and responding to the health and mental health needs of clients, families, and communities (U.S. Department of Health and Human Services, 2001).

Strategy 4: Advocate at the Program Level

Assuming that the state or province is on board with the broad-based principles of health promotion, it seems reasonable that local mental health agencies and their programs would soon follow the lead. It is generally recognized that mental health programs have to be planned on the basis of a thorough assessment of the evidence from epidemiologic, behavioral, and social science research. This evidence indicates reasonable linkages between the short-term impact of interventions (e.g., health promotion outcomes) and subsequent changes in the determinants of health (e.g., stable housing and access to health services) and health outcomes (e.g., reduced comorbidity rates—decrease in untreated diabetes and depression).

There are two key recommendations to ensuring the successful implementation of mental health programs with a health promotion focus: (1) ensuring that there is sufficient public and political awareness of the issues and the need for action and (2) developing capacity for program delivery through the training of personnel and securing the resources (i.e., budget) to implement and sustain the program (UIPHE, 2000, pp. 29–41). See Box 5.2 for an example of how a mental health agency budgets for health promotion services.

Box 5.2. *At the Forefront: A Principle Driven Agency*

How do we know if health promotion principles have been effectively integrated into public mental health policy and programs? Just look at the budget.

The budget is the single most important policy statement of any government or program and lies at the heart of all public policies (DiNitto, 2007). "Budgets determine what policies and programs are preserved, renewed, continued, cancelled, amended, and initiated. The expenditure side of a governmental or agency budget tells us who gets what in public money and the revenue side of the budget tells us who pays the cost (p.16)." In order for health promotion principles to realistically guide mental health policies and programs, they need to be rooted in the economic and philosophical realities of the institutions they are targeting.

The following example illustrates how one community mental health center has been able to integrate the principles of health promotion into the mission statement, philosophy, policy strategies, programs and finally, the budget. If we work backwards from the budget, one notices that the revenues for this organization are from a diverse stream: housing authority, vocational rehabilitation, state hospital transition, grants and school districts. The expenditures, while mostly consisting of salaries, show that the primary expense that a community mental health agency has is its personnel with miscellaneous expenses going into interpreter services, staff development, and lobbying efforts—all of which serve to keep the agency in a position of reinvesting in its staff and clients while maintaining necessary political visibility. These revenues, in turn, support the programs that evolved from the policies that were shaped by the agency philosophy (aka principles) which emerged from the mission statement. One can easily connect a number of health promotion principles discussed in this chapter to this organization.

Example of a Community Mental Health Center whose policies and programs reflect the Principles of Health Promotion as illustrated through their mission statement, philosophy, policy strategies, programs and budget.

Case Example: Arcadia Behavioral Healthcare, Inc.

Mission Statement

Arcadia, a community-based behavioral healthcare organization, provides high-quality innovative services to strengthen the health of individuals, families, and communities.

Core Philosophy

Arcadia's approach to community treatment is based on the recovery philosophy, which encourages independence and draws on the unique personal and environmental strengths that every individual possesses. While intensive outreach and support may be needed periodically, recovery is best achieved when consumers/clients can draw on natural systems of support such as family, friends, and spiritual and support groups. A primary goal is to provide the least restrictive treatment and avoid unnecessary hospitalization.

Policy Strategies

- We use teamwork and outreach to reduce barriers and help those who are most in need of our services.
- We design our services to enhance independence by focusing on strengths and natural supports.
- We use a variety of evidence-based best practices to assure the fastest and most positive outcomes for our clients.

Continued

- Given essentially equally effective treatment methods, we recommend the least costly services so that we are able to provide services to more of those most in need.
- We communicate how and why our service recommendations will be helpful.
- Recovery must address both substance abuse and mental health symptoms.
- The cultural, gender, sexual orientation, and spiritual context of the client's life are honored.
- Recovery support in the consumer's own community is an important part of our array of services.

Programs

These policy strategies are implemented through the following programs:

- Crisis (Discharge and Transition Team—DATT, Urgent Walk-in Services, Project Respond/Mobile Outreach for Mental Health Emergencies for homeless and uninsured individuals)
- Community Support Services (Case management, employment programs, consumer run services and Assertive Community Treatment Team)
- Integrated Treatment for concurrent mental health and addiction (Gambling, DUII, programs for bilingual youth and families in rural counties)
- Housing (development and management of 600 units at 50 different sites)
- Outpatient Programs (Individual, Child and Family, School based services, Sexual Minority Youth Resource Center, Older Adults)
- Medical Services (Medication Support for mental and physical health issues, child and adolescent psychiatry, forensics, geriatrics, and addictions)

Selected Budget Items Report for Community Mental Health Center

Revenues

HUD Contract	388,097
Indigent Funds	370,941
Vocational Rehabilitation Division	99,632
Acute Care Contract	4,288,369
Passages (state hospital transition monies)	69,499
Transitional Housing	18,075
City of Middle Earth	256,254
Middle Earth Public Schools	14,500

Volunteers of America	510,018
Medicare	572,244
Medicaid	8,416,037
Sponsorships	7,000
United Way Pledges	39,346
Donations	35,312
Expenses	
Salaries and wages	18,003,782
Interpreter	44,570
Clinical supervision	3,430
Lobbying expense	30,000
Staff development	49,847
Other (building, equipment, repairs, computers, rent)	

Strategy 5: Advocate at the Individual Level

McKee (2000) reminds us that people working in mental health programs can play an important role in promoting health. They may do this by providing examples of what can be done to achieve healthy environments and by using their authority to act as advocates for healthy public policies and as a source of advice on healthy behaviors to individuals with mental illness and their families (IUHPE, 2000, p. 123).

■ Limitations of Health Promotion Policy Advocacy

As the previous discussion illustrates, advocacy is the most political of health promotion strategies and, at the same time, has the smallest evidence base (McCubbin, Labonte, & Dallaire, 2001). Overviews of the efficacy of policy advocacy as a replicable health promotion technology or strategy has mostly been based on views expressed by policy authors or advocates and by circumstances reflecting a policy change. Little has been done to systematically assess the body of available evidence (McCubbin, Labonte, & Dallaire, 2001). McCubbin and colleagues (2001) provide one of the first exhaustive reviews of policy advocacy and conclude that: "Given the extremely limited portions of the required evidence base, it would be presumptuous to conclude that policy advocacy is, or is not, an effective health promotion technology for advancing population health. However, we do have quite a convincing body of evidence that a sense of control or 'power' is a major determinant of population health, which suggests that 'empowering' interventions are called for" (p. 16).

Two reasons for the limited science are methodology and newness of strategy. McCubbin and colleagues (2001) note that, like many health promotion strategies, evaluation of advocacy efforts tends toward case studies that are anecdotal or opinions rather than analytical or scientific methods—similar to the level 5 EBP referred to in Chapter 3. Case study descriptions, while helpful for future planners, typically describe how actions were planned or taken and the resulting immediate effects. Additionally, advocacy is a relatively new health promotion strategy and thus does not have a large evaluation literature from which to draw data. The authors recommend that future policy advocate practitioners take rigorous account of their efforts in order to build a scientific evidence-base.

■ Rational Mental Health Policy Development

Mental health policy development can be both a political process and a rational process. DiNitto (2007) notes that rational policy making would be straightforward, identify key social or organizational problems that impact mental illness (e.g., social, environmental, economic), explore all solutions to the problems, forecast all the benefits and costs of each solution, compare benefits to costs for each solution, and select the best ratio of benefits to costs. In essence, "a policy is rational if the ratio between the values it achieves and the values it sacrifices is positive and higher than any other policy alternative" (p. 5).

Until "mental health" is valued as a necessary condition for quality of life for all citizens, it will continue to be marginalized in the political process and its funding process. There will continue to be disagreements about the nature of causes of mental disorders, about what should be considered acceptable benefits and costs to funding mental health programs, who is entitled, who is to blame, and whose responsibility it is to fund services for vulnerable populations.

Although policies are generally defined as a "standing decision" characterized by behavioral consistency and repetitiveness on the part of those who make it and those who abide by it, most governmental policies are neither consistent nor repetitive (DiNitto, 2007). Mental health policies are no exception. Callicutt (1997) asserts that mental health policies and their outcomes often lack a unified, comprehensive direction to the field of mental health, which is due in part to the multitude of competing philosophies, values, and assumptions that create these policies. The very process of debating the merits of certain health and mental health policies is value-laden. Policies are influenced by moral, social, and cultural values such that government often uses its power in the form of economic supports or sanctions. This is seen in the form of supporting funding for substance abuse prevention programs with an abstinence-only approach and denying funding for needle exchange programs—despite evidences that the latter works over the former. This scenario is illustrated in Box 5.3.

Final Points

Gostin (2000) notes that government has a number of "levers" to promote the population's health—namely policies that emerge from laws and regulations. One lever is in

Box 5.3. Case Study: When Good Policies Go Bad: The Legacy of Substance Use Policy in the United States

The Issues. Drug use and abuse constitutes a huge public health problem not only in terms of its cost to users but also its cost to families, communities, and society. Relapse rates for individuals with drug and alcohol problems continue to be high, and the rate of HIV infection is high as well.

Public Health Strategies. However, we do know what works. For example, research has established that needle exchange programs are effective treatment approaches for injection drug users in that they save lives by reducing or stopping the transmission of HIV, discourage new users and do not encourage illegal drug use (CDC, 1993; National Academy of Science's Institute of Medicine, 1995; NIH,1997). Additionally, HIV drug infection rates are decreased when these programs are made available. Methadone maintenance programs are known to reduce crime and assist heroin addicts maintain more stable lives (DiNitto, 2000).

Policies of the 1970s: Treatment (The Good). Efforts to stem drug use through public policy have been controversial. Early policy efforts viewed alcohol and drug dependence as treatable illnesses. This ideology set the stage for the creation of *Comprehensive Alcohol Abuse Prevention, Treatment and Rehabilitation Act of* 1970. This act established the National Institute on Alcohol Abuse and Alcoholism (NIAAA) and later the establishment of the National Institute on Drug Abuse (NIDA) (DiNitto, 2007). Most public health practitioners considered these policy efforts a good thing.

Policies of the 1980s: Punishment (Beginning of the Bad). In the 1980s the ideology changed from substance use treatment to a law enforcement approach with an emphasis on interdiction (stopping the flow of drugs) and severe legal penalties for drug related crimes. The 1988 Anti-Drug Abuse Act, along with Nancy Reagan, First Lady and wife of then President Ronald Reagan, offered the public the phrase "Just Say No" which reflected a simplistic response to the now declared "war on drugs" mentality.

Contemporary Policies: The Slow Descent To Very Bad. Since 1988, there have been four key statutes in the United States that contained provisions prohibiting or restricting access to sterile injection equipment and funding for syringe exchange programs (SEPs). These statutes are Controlled Substances Act, the Anti-Drug Abuse Act, Model Drug Paraphernalia Act, and Federal Mail Order Drug Paraphernalia Control Act (prohibits the sale and transportation of drug paraphernalia via interstate commerce) (DiNitto, 2000; Gostin, 2000).

(continued)

While a minority of states have laws that permit syringes to be dispensed or possessed with a valid medical prescription (i.e., to treat diabetes with insulin), virtually all states have drug paraphernalia statutes that ban the manufacture, sale, distribution, and possession of syringes or advertisement of services that describe the procedures for introducing illicit substances in the body (Gostin, 2000). In other words, current laws on drug paraphernalia or syringe prescription make it a crime to give a drug misuser a clean needle. The exception to prosecution using drug paraphernalia laws is in the case of pharmacists who sell syringes over the counter believing that the syringes will be used for "lawful" purposes—like insulin use for the treatment of diabetes. Consequently, harm-reduction programs, such as needle exchange programs, have met with controversy despite scientific evidence that they work.

Public Health Impact (The Sad). Providers and outreach workers often testify to the harmful health conditions and safety implications that have arisen for individuals with mental illness, HIV, and substance abuse issues since the provision of the 1988 act. For example, the act supports the eviction of public housing residents who engage in or permit drug use on or near the premises and has instituted a federal funding ban on SEPs—despite studies showing that SEPs and pharmacy access to syringes reduce the incidence of HIV (Gostin, 2000).

Gasin (2000) points out that, taken together, these laws and funding restrictions, make it difficult, but not impossible, for public health agencies and community mental health clinics to reduce the incidence of HIV in their populations, coordinate services with SEPs, and help injection drug users with mental health diagnoses to access sterile equipment in pharmacies. These restrictions also impose limitations on the ability to conduct research to substantiate the relationship between access to syringes and greater drug use among mental health populations. Additionally, restricted federal funding and potential criminal penalties forces health and mental health providers to rely on state, local, or philanthropic funds for harm-reduction programs—which is problematic, given the precarious legal and social status of such community programs (Gostin, 2000).

the form of health policies that focus on individual behaviors (e.g., the ban on smoking in public facilities). The emphasis on funding has been on prevention programs—like alcohol and drug prevention, mental illness prevention and tobacco prevention. The irony is that prevention does not really address those segments of society who already have the illness or disability. Here is where health promotion fits in. As identified earlier, Canada recognized that promoting a population's health was worthy of political and ideologic investment. Until government recognizes that health promotion is a viable approach to achieving health for all, mental health polices and programs will continue to be crisis-driven, focused on pathology and deficiencies, and fragmented.

Too often, people outside a community insert themselves in decision-making roles for groups that they do not even understand. As Katz and Kreuter (1997) point out, policy and program planners may propose scientifically sounds solutions to mental health problems, such as the use of evidenced-based practice manuals for all treatment programs. However, they are unlikely to be implemented if they do not reflect the values, beliefs, and perceived needs of the community they are intended to affect.

■ Conclusion

Navarro (2003) says it best in implying that policy makers must possess a shared philosophy when it comes to linking health promotion principles and mental health policy with the citizens they serve. He states that "We have to recover holistic, comprehensive views of health in which the merit of an intervention is not evaluated by its contribution to economic growth but rather the reverse—the merit of an (economic) policy is measured primarily and exclusively by its impact on the health and welfare of the population" (p. 116).

Health promotion has three goals: lifting the health status of people, improving the quality of life of all people, and providing cost-effective solutions to mental health problems (Green & Kreuter, 2005). Policy planners and program administrators would do well to ask if their current policies and programs are achieving these goals. The driving challenge will be demonstrating that mental health policy change that is undertaken in the name of health promotion actually improves or protects the health and mental health of the individuals and communities it targets. Despite these gloomy warnings, we can see that health promotion certainly has the will (i.e., policies) and the way (principles); now it just needs the want.

In Our Own Words… Family and Consumer Perspectives on Mental Health Treatment Services: Focus Group Feedback

Topic: Designing Mental Health Services

Summary

As Chapter 5 argues, principles (e.g., beliefs) drive the policies that create the programs. In other words, the programs in place are a result of policies (e.g., either through legislative mandate or judicial directive) that have emerged from the values and beliefs of constitutients, politicians, and other stakeholders. Staying with this theme, consumers and family members were asked what they believed would be the most important features of a newly designed mental health system. Their suggestions can be captured in a single phrase: The five C's: choice, cordial (e.g., user-friendly), convenient, communication, and contact. Consumers added "holistic" (with an emphasis on spiritual) as another important component of any mental health system. It is notable that these suggestions are similar to survey results from business communities—which suggests that consumers and family members want the same kind of quality experience that nonconsumer groups do.

What Can We Learn?

Based on these suggestions, policy makers and program developers can invite consumers and family members into the planning process for mental health service system (re)design—as suggested Chapter 1. This inclusive effort would lay the groundwork for revising or developing a new mental health system shaped by the principles identified and valued by potential users and providers (i.e., choice and communication).

The following section details results of the focus group meetings as reported by family members and consumers.

Focus Group Question: " *If you could design a community based mental health system with all the right services, what would it look like?*"

Family Perspectives

Core Themes	Summary of Experiences	Comments
(Ranked in order of priority)		
First— Choice	A fully integrated mental health system would have a	"A mental health clinic should have a variety of services that

Focus Group Question: " *If you could design a community based mental health system with all the right services, what would it look like?" (continued)*

	broad array of choices for consumers and family members; it would have a menu or map of services that family members and consumers could use to select services that they considered appropriate for themselves.	consumers and family can choose. In particular, they should have more than religious based treatment—like A.A.—which can scare away some consumers." (S., *spouse*)
Second—Accessible	Services would be available at times convenient for working families	"Outpatient services should be accessible, culturally competent, located in clean facilities and provided based on need rather than availability of funding, space, or limited hours." (M., *sibling*)
Third—Communication	Communication and coordination among and between staff (case managers nurses, and doctors) should be the cornerstone of each clinic—like having a one stop shopping approach where one phonecall could activate services rather than having a consumer or family member making dozens of calls	"By having one head case manager or family advocate to communicate with, consumers can get the help they need. Most consumers have problems understanding too much information and will often give up before they can reach the help they need." (J., *parent*)

Consumer Perspectives

Core Themes	Summary of Experiences	Comments
(*Ranked in order of priority*)		
First—Flexible services that incorporate complementary	Consumers felt that they had more options when services were more diverse and holistic—like using naturopathy and	"Treatment approaches should be flexible—less demanding—for such a flexible condition as

(continued)

Focus Group Question: " *If you could design a community based mental health system with all the right services, what would it look like?" (continued)*

or alternative treatments	horticulture and less dependent on traditional treatments—medications.	mental health. For example, there were times that I longed to dig in the dirt and plant a flower. One day I went on a pass bought flowers and brought them back to the unit." (J.V.S., *consumer*)
Second—Integrate spirituality into practice	Spirituality should be a part of any program—starting at intake.	"Our spirits are broken and we need healing. Consumers need retreats too." (J., *consumer*)
Third—Increase community contact with case managers and nurse practitioners	More home visits from case managers and nurses	"The case manager and nurse practitioner could do home visits and try to find out if there is food in the house, if the walls need painting, does client have a good support system, health, health care, recreation." (J.V.S., *consumer*)

PART III

INTEGRATION AND APPLICATION

6. Using Health Promotion Principles to Guide Clinical and Community-Based Mental Health Assessments

It's not what you ask, but how you ask it. When you ask me about my spiritual, family and community support system, you convey you care. Also, just by offering me a cup of tea makes me feel like a person rather than my illness.

—J., consumer

■ Chapter Overview

This chapter continues to focus on the notion that health promotion principles are a guiding influence in mental health practice. Just as in policy development (Chapter 5), health promotion principles may be used as a means of influencing and directing mental health assessments. This chapter is intended to provide an in-depth review of various mental health assessment models/strategies derived from health promotion principles, with the understanding that these principles are the foundation of mental health assessment. Our chapter begins with a review of various definitions of *assessment* and discusses its various features—from evidence-based to culturally sensitive. Next, six health promotion principles (first introduced in Chapter 5) and their characteristics are matched to corresponding mental health assessment models and strategies. These include goal assessment using stages of change/motivational interviewing, health beliefs, substance abuse, biopsychosocial-cultural, asset-based, and community health assessment. Each of these models/strategies is accompanied by case examples. The chapter concludes with a summary of a focus group discussion held by consumers and family members who responded to the question: What kinds of information should mental health practitioners ask for during the assessment or intake portion of your first visit to the clinic?

Learning Objectives

When you have finished reading this chapter, you should be able to:

1. Explain the features of four kinds of mental health assessments: evidence-based, individual, community and culturally sensitive
2. Describe six health promotion principles and their relationship to individual and community-based assessment models

3. Describe six mental health assessment models derived from health promotion principles: goal assessment using stages of change/motivational interviewing, health beliefs, substance abuse, biopsychosocial-cultural, asset-based community development, and community health assessment
4. Identify core themes and recommendations expressed through consumer and family focus groups when they were asked what kinds of assessment information is important to be asked during the intake interview

■ Introduction

Chapter 5 suggested that health promotion principles can provide the backdrop for guiding mental health policy development. In this chapter, the same reasoning is applied but with a different goal in mind—the assessment process. It is argued that health promotion principles can guide the clinician in choosing the most appropriate assessment approaches based on the presenting issues of the client or community.

The ability to conduct a comprehensive, well-reasoned, empirically supported, multilevel biopsychosocial assessment is arguably the single most important activity that a clinician will perform. A comprehensive assessment sets the stage for connecting the client and or family members to the appropriate services, resources and treatment. In this regard, the clinician will benefit from having a broad-based conceptual framework in which to conduct an assessment. And just like policy makers who promote policies based on beliefs, values, and hopefully scientific data, clinicians also operate from a set of personal beliefs and knowledge—most often derived from their own professional training. An understanding of various assessment approaches coupled with health promotion principles is one way to ensure that clinicians will conduct assessments that are broad-based and compatible to the needs and experiences of the client or the community and not merely reflective of a narrow training model or an agency intake format. Let's now explore what is meant by *assessment* and the different ways to construct an assessment.

■ Assessment: An Overview

Accurate and appropriate assessment is the springboard for all clinical and community based mental health interventions (Vandiver, 2002; Bowen *et al.*, 2004). But what is assessment?

In general, it has been defined as the:

- "Process of systematically collecting, organizing, and interpreting data related to a clients functioning in order to determine the need for treatment, as well as treatment goals and intervention plan." (Roberts & Yeager, 2004, p. 972).
- "Thoughtful application of generalizable knowledge in the service of understanding a clients unique experiences" (O'Hare, 2005, p. 27)

- "Cornerstone of effective treatment and is an ongoing process that is interwoven with treatment" (Mueser *et al.*, 2003, p. 49)

Why Do Assessment?

Clearly, a variety of assessment strategies are needed to understand the health and mental health needs of individuals. These include chart reviews; laboratory tests; direct client interviews using structured and unstructured formats; information from collaterals like family, friends, and/or significant others; and clinician-based reports (Mueser *et al.*, 2003).

In situations of crisis, mental health practitioners often provide the first line of assessment. How they conduct the initial screening and assessment can influence both the immediate and long-term outcomes for clients and their families. For example, people who have been exposed to traumatic events will need to be assessed further for posttraumatic stress disorder (Bordick, Graap, & Vonk, 2004). Research has found that untreated trauma can progress from initial symptoms (e.g., lack of appetite, anxiety) to full-blown symptoms (e.g., posttraumatic stress disorder, depression, family distress, substance abuse, and physical health problems). From a health promotion perspective, accurate assessment and early identification of traumatic event(s) (e.g., physical abuse, automobile accidents, workplace accidents) and related problems (e.g., anxiety, mood swings, anger, increased fear, headaches, and upset stomach or GI distress) can lead to better coping and physical wellness. Bordick and colleagues (2004) point out that traumatic events can be ubiquitous and that therefore clinicians will need to develop a basic understanding of trauma and its associated symptoms in order to conduct a valid clinical assessment.

Broad-based mental health assessments that incorporate health status are increasingly important in the care and treatment of individuals with mental health conditions. Meyer and Nasrallah (2003) argue the need for more comprehensive medical assessments in patients with schizophrenia. In their review of the literature, they note that quality of life and indices of psychopathology are both adversely affected by the burden of medical illness and that patients with schizophrenia suffer from increased rates of multiple medical problems due to lifestyle circumstances (e.g., heavy smoking, high-fat diet), effects of medications (e.g., obesity and diabetes mellitus related to the use of certain atypical antipsychotics), and inherent neglect of personal care and barriers to treatment of physical illness (p. xi).

What Makes for an Evidence-Based Assessment?

Evidence-based assessment is a procedural framework that uses current scientific knowledge to guide evaluative questions. O'Hare (2005) describes evidence based assessment as having the following three attributes: (1) informed by current human behavior research, (2) emphasizes multidimensional and functional analysis, and

(3) enhanced by qualitative and quantitative tools. In conducting evidence-based assessments, O'Hare (2005) recommends these guidelines for the practitioner:

- Use problem-specific knowledge, such as research findings on schizophrenia, to identify important biopsychosocial risk and protective factors that cause and maintain the client's concerns.
- Assess clients' well-being on multidimensional levels (e.g., psychological, social, health, and behavioral).
- Employ functional analysis to describe how more proximate cognitive, behavioral, physiologic, interpersonal, and social factors interact over time and across situations.
- Incorporate the client's unique understanding and appraisal of the problem as part of the assessment.
- Use multiple methods of data collection from multiple sources.
- Focus on practical areas of change.
- Employ instruments and indexes to enhance the reliability and validity of the assessment and provide a baseline for monitoring and evaluation (p. 7).

Of these practitioner guidelines, two important organizing concepts are considered the heart of evidence-based assessment: *multidimensionality* and *functionality.*

Multidimensionality refers to an understanding of the nature and severity of the client's difficulties; multiple factors—both present and past—interact systematically over time and across situations and measurement across multiple psychosocial domains of living. Some of these domains include mental status (e.g., psychiatric symptoms); substance abuse; social functioning with regard to relationships with partners, family, and extended community relationships; access and use of environmental resources (e.g., housing, employment or volunteer activities); general health status; leisure; legal involvement; and sense of personal and spiritual well-being. A multidimensional assessment also considers personal issues and life circumstances that are influenced by gender, age, cultural identity, and other factors referred to as "person factors" (O'Hare, 2005).

A *functional* assessment refers to an understanding of the client's unique experiences based on a variety of sources: self, family, professionals, and other collateral sources. A functional assessment will focus on thoughts, feelings, behaviors, and social-environmental events over time, also referred to as *temporal sequencing;* the frequency, intensity and duration of issues, contingencies (e.g., rewards and punishments) in the environment that influence behavior and well-being; the establishment of client priorities and progressive stages of intervention on those priorities; the client's perception of problems and expectations for change; defining and measuring change and evaluating progress that is meaningful to client (O'Hare, 2005).

Overall, multidimensional and functional mental health assessments that use a health promotion perspective help increase the awareness of needed interventions and advocacy for greater access to necessary community services.

Focus of Assessment

Regardless of the breadth of issues or severity of symptoms, the establishment of health promotion goals and interventions are predicated on a variety of evidence-based individual and community assessments. These two kinds of assessments are distinguished accordingly.

Individual-oriented assessments allow both clinician and client to formulate a coherent, specific, and realistic treatment plan based on a comprehensive evaluation. Mueser and colleagues (2003) note that although assessment begins at the first contact, typically called the engagement stage, it should continue throughout the treatment, evaluation and follow-up phases. They note that information regarding the client's history, lifestyle, and functional, mental, and physical status are all gathered during the assessment phase, along with evidence regarding the effects and perceptions of proposed interventions. Treatment plans are then modified accordingly.

Although the types of questions in an individual-oriented assessment will vary based on the type of service the person is seeking, there are generally five core domains that are included in traditional, individually oriented mental health assessments: psychological, social, environmental, biological and cultural. The psychological domain typically follows the components of the mental status exam and includes presentation of self, behavioral, cognition, affect, clinical problems, and diagnostic impression checklist (Corcoran & Vandiver, 1996). The social domain may include information about occupation, education, social networks, and family. The environmental domain looks at housing, income, and other community variables. Biological domains consider health status, which includes current and past medical history of the individual and family and substance abuse history. The cultural domain looks at ethnicity or ethnic identity, cultural influences, language, home country if immigrant, views toward health and illness, to name a few.

Community-oriented assessments are valued for their focus on multiple stakeholder information and empowerment (Hancock & Minkler, 2005). Information in this respect refers to collecting hard data and stories that describe inequities in housing, food, transportation, employment, or access to health services and medicine for people with mental illness. Practitioners will want to gather information that has the benefit of both stimulating the need for change and then assessing the impact of that change. For example, affordable, mixed housing is considered to be one measure of a healthy community. Yet research continues to highlight the plight of individuals with mental illness who cannot afford to live anywhere. A community health assessment can be used to point out the lack of affordable housing for adult women who are homeless and have mental illness. Assessing the change (or not) in affordable housing in a region provides information that serves as a baseline of the individual and community dimensions of a community's health. In this example, community surveys and other instruments can be conducted to assess change.

■ Culturally Sensitive Assessment Processes

When assessing the needs or concerns of diverse (e.g., cultural, ethnic, racial, sexual orientation, or gender) individuals, families, or communities, there are several considerations to keep in mind. For example, Westbrooks and Starks (2001) recommend that providers who work with African-American individuals and families focus on assessment strategies that help clients reconnect with their identity, worth, and value. One method is the "Strength Perspectives Inherent in Cultural Empowerment"—also known as the SPICE model. This model suggests that by simply acknowledging strengths, this leads to cultural empowerment, which in turn leads to achievement and then to the validation of those strengths, with leads back to cultural empowerment. The authors graciously invite readers to "add a little SPICE to your training and practice as you acknowledge the gifts and strengths that you and your clients bring to the assessment process." (p. 117). Other recommendations to support culturally sensitive assessments are to remind providers to value diversity, understand the dynamics of difference, institutionalization of cultural knowledge, and adaptation to diversity, encouraging them to acknowledge and respect the predominance of cultural values like cooperation, sharing, and spirituality. Further, any "community assessment should include the stages of community engagement, group cooperation, information dissemination and professional involvement" (Manning, 2001, p. 129). For an excellent review of the assessment process for communities of color, readers are referred to the work of Fong and Furuto (2001).

Cross-cultural research suggests that mental health assessments with ethnic or culturally diverse populations begin with soliciting information about the cultural identity of the individual and family (e.g., clan, tribe, country of origin, preferred language) and then move on to individual and family health information. Although the conventional approach to assessment begins with identifying the problem and working toward a diagnosis, culturally sensitive assessment approaches work backwards by looking first at culture, then at health, and finally moving to problems. The diagnosis is the last step and is applied in a manner that accounts for language, cultural, and ethnic differences. An example of this assessment approach is illustrated in Table 6.1.

The guide is one example of how to incorporate cultural information right at the beginning of the assessment interview. For example, given that many ethnic people will describe psychological distress as physical ills, the interviewer can comfortably begin the interview asking about current health. This will appear less threatening to the client and the family. In order to improve diagnostic specificity in cross-cultural assessments, the *Diagnostic and Statistical Manual IV-TR* (APA, 2000) offers an appendix on culture-bound syndromes and glossary. This appendix provides an outline of five categories to consider when assessing the individuals cultural and social reference group. These categories are:

- Cultural identity of the individual (e.g., ethnicity and preferred language)
- Cultural explanation of the individual's illness (e.g., what are individual's explanation of symptoms in relation to the norms of the cultural group)

TABLE 6.1. *Multicultural Biopsychosocial Interview Guide for DSM-IV Use*

Interviewer Instructions: The following interview guide is designed to help the interviewer make a culturally competent assessment and diagnosis that is respectful of the patient's or client's background. The categories correspond with Axes I through V of the DSM-IV-TR (APA, 2000) but are listed in a sequence meant to facilitate conversation as the first part of the interview process – such as first learning about the client's ethnic/cultural background and then moving to health issues (Axis III) and concluding with cultural and diagnostic considerations and recommendations. You may make notes in the open sections or simply use the categories as a mental guide for your interview questions and final assessment.

Categories of Questions	Comments/ Narrative	DSM-IV Notes
A. Establish Cultural Identity ___ Ethnicity ___ Preferred language ___ Clan/tribe/faith ___ Country of origin ___ Family/ community identity ___ How long in host country?		
B. Cultural Explanation of (Physical) Illness/ Symptoms ___ Use of folk words to describe/explain illness (refer to DSM glossary) ___ Meaning and explanation of client symptoms ___ Context of "illness" (location, frequency, situation) ___ Types of help sought (traditional healers, potions)		**Axis III – Medical**
C. Cultural Factors Related to Psychosocial Environment and Level of Functioning Psychosocial environment: What are the perceived stressors? ___Support ___ Legal/criminal ___Educational ___ Violence/trauma ___ Occupational ___ Access to health care ___ Housing ___ Racism/discrimination ___ Spiritual ___ Other		**Axis IV – Psychosocial & Environmental Problems**
Level of Functioning (Wellness or Unwellness) ___ Degree of acculturation/biculturalism/ assimilation ___ Level of family/community stability		**Axis V – Global Assessment of Functioning**
Level of Interpersonal Functioning ___ Degree on interpersonal stress or tension with employers/family/neighbors		**Axis II – Personality Disorders**

(continued)

D. Cultural Factors Related to Psychological Health/Status ___ Symptoms linked to traumatic event (torture; escape; immigration) ___ Role of substances and rituals ___ History of unique behaviors/ cognitions as interpreted/reported via self, family, and community		**Axis I – Clinical Disorders**
E. Cultural Elements of Provider and Client Relationship ___ Gender issues ___ Age issues ___ Social status ___ Race/ethnicity ___ Language ___ Credibility within ethnic community ___ Any other issues to influence how symptoms would be expressed or how diagnosis/treatment would be affected		
F. Overall Cultural Assessment (Diagnosis and Care) ___ How can cultural considerations influence diagnosis and care? ___ What is the potential for compliance to the health care plan? ___ Has the family and/or significant community members (elders) been consulted?		
G. Summary **Recommendations:**	**Cultural Considerations** ________ ________ ________ ________ ________ ________	**Diagnostic Considerations** Axis I: ________ Axis II: ________ Axis III: ________ Axis IV: ________ Axis V: ________ ________

Adapted from Corcoran, K., & Vandiver, V. (1996). *Maneuvering the Maze of Managed Care: Skills for Mental Health Practitioners*. New York: Free Press.

- Cultural factors related to psychosocial environments and level of functioning (e.g., interpretation of stressors and available social supports)
- Cultural elements of the relationship between individual and the clinician (e.g., noting differences in cultural and social status between individual and clinician and how this may affect symptom expression, diagnosis and treatment)
- Overall cultural assessment for diagnosis and care (e.g., how cultural considerations specifically influence diagnosis and care) (pp. 897–898).

The interview guide is developed directly from the five categories listed in the DSM's Appendix I—"Outline for Cultural Formulation and Glossary of Culture-Bound Syndromes," and is particularly useful for individuals who are recent immigrants or refugees to the host country and may be at risk for being incorrectly identified as having a mental disorder when, in fact, the assessment may reveal other factors of concern.

With regard to sexual orientation and or gender, O'Hare (2005) cautions against the tendency for assessment to overgeneralize about women, sexual orientation, or class differences. He observes that findings on white males have historically been overextended to assessment and intervention guidelines for women and people of color, and that new evidence points to the differences associated with gender, race, and other individual factors. For example, research on urban African-American youths has demonstrated the impact of poverty and violence on racial minorities and their families (Gorman-Smith & Tolan, 1998). Similarly, women of color may share the common experience of oppression but will vary radically in the manner in which this experience is expressed within their racial or ethnic group. An under assessment of any of these psychosocial, economic, and environmental factors can lead to an inappropriate assessment of the needs of a client and his or her family.

■ Health Promotion Principles

Why Should We Use Health Promotion Principles to Guide Our Mental Health Assessments?

Chapter 5 reviewed nine health promotion principles and their influence on policy and programs. The present chapter argues that the principles of health promotion can be used to guide practitioners in the process of assessment. This argument is based on the emerging trend in mental health practice that favors person-and community-centered assessment and treatment—both of which reflect health promotion principles. Let's begin by suggesting that health promotion principles can provide a sort of checklist of key elements to guide the formulation of an evidence-based mental health assessment. Two examples of these principles and their relationship to assessment are discussed below.

Principle of Multiple Methods. You will recall from Chapter 5 that the principle of multiple methods implies that a variety of methods and interventions are necessary for holistic care and treatment given the multidimensional needs of individuals with mental disorders. This principle is supported through research, which finds that multiple methods of assessment are critical to understand the interactions of health conditions with symptoms of mental illness and distress. For example, research has shown that certain psychiatric conditions, like posttraumatic stress disorder (PTSD) and schizophrenia, are associated with high rates of medical service use and self-reported poor health (O'Hare, 2005; Holmberg & Kane, 1999). Numerous studies of combat veterans diagnosed with PTSD have found high rates of physical symptoms associated with osteoarthritis, diabetes, heart disease, comorbid depression, obesity, and elevated lipid levels. Tobacco-related diseases have been found to be the leading cause of death in patients who have been treated for substance abuse (Center for Substance Abuse Treatment, 2005). Yet few clinical reports feature detailed assessments of comorbid medical conditions and health risk factors.

Additional research has shown that psychiatric populations have high morbidity and mortality rates and are at increased risk for multiple and chronic social, cognitive, and behavioral issues that may lead to inadequate health and self-care practices. Untreated health conditions (e.g., HIV), which includes substance abuse, can worsen the outcome of severe mental illness, such as clients continuing to engage in unhealthy lifestyle behaviors that aggravate their mental illness (e.g., intravenous drug use and unprotected sex). Holmberg and Kane (1999) point out that several factors contribute to increased risk of physical illness in these populations: limited knowledge about health needs, low socioeconomic status, and inadequate detection of physical illness by providers. Understanding and assessing how health conditions affect mental health conditions can lead to treatment plans that specifically address these areas. Mueser and colleagues (2003) suggest, for example, that if a client's substance abuse is related to coping with symptoms of anxiety, he or she may benefit from learning more effective coping strategies or developing new social activities. These reasons alone highlight the need for providers to utilize multiple methods of information gathering in conducting assessments in mental health populations.

Principle of Feedback. The health promotion principle of feedback is a driving influence for assessing individuals with substance abuse issues. This principle implies that in order for individuals to learn from treatment, they need opportunities for direct and immediate feedback that is based on quantitative and qualitative measures. Providing clients with personalized feedback on the risks and benefits associated with aspects of their lifestyles and behaviors can be a powerful way to develop motivation. For example, The Consensus Panel on Enhancing Motivation for Change in Substance Abuse Treatment (1999) recommends "giving clients personal results from a broad based and objective assessment, especially when the results are compared to the norm, can not only be informative but also motivating" (p. 65). This has particular relevance for substance abuse; here numerous studies show that consumption is risky in terms of specific health problems (e.g., cirrhosis) and physical reactions. Other data can be used to support healthy lifestyle choices that enhance quality of life. Overall, findings from an assessment can become part of the therapeutic process if the client understands the practical value of objective information and believes that the results will be helpful (Center for Substance Abuse Treatment, 1999, 2005).

■ Assessments Used in Mental Health

This section discusses six mental health–oriented assessment models/strategies (e.g., goal assessment, health beliefs, substance abuse assessment, biopsychosocial assessment, asset-based community development and community health assessment) that are influenced by key health promotion principles. As Chapter 5 (Connecting Health Promotion Principles to Mental Health Policies and Programs) indicated, health promotion principles are divided into two levels: individual and community. Individual-oriented health promotion principles, discussed further here, include hierarchy, participation, feedback, and multiple methods. Community-oriented health promotion principles include community participation and empowerment of local people. In addition to reviewing these categories (principles and characteristics), this discussion also includes corresponding assessment models. See Figure 6.1 for an illustration of these assessment models and strategies.

■ Individual-Oriented Health Promotion Principles and Mental Health Assessments

Principle of Hierarchy

The principle of hierarchy can be characterized as focusing on motivation. This principle asserts that the beliefs and motivations of clients and family must be understood first before any treatment can begin.

Model: Goal Assessment. One assessment model that supports this principle is the *goal assessment approach*, which uses a motivational assessment approach based on stages of change.

FIGURE 6.1. Individual-and community-oriented health promotion principles, characteristics, and assessment models.

Description. Goal assessment is a nondirective, qualitative approach of assessing those factors that motivate or discourage decisions that clients make in regard to behavioral change. However, this assessment approach probes further than the traditional information-gathering format, which looks at risky behaviors (e.g., drug use), poor health habits (e.g., smoking), or symptom-management issues (e.g., medication compliance). Corrigan and colleagues (2001) emphasize that the focus of the goal assessment is to support client's efforts to identify behaviors that would enhance his or her quality of life. For example, information would be gathered on goals related to employment, dating, exercise, returning to school, living in one's own apartment, or developing hobbies. This assessment approach is derived from the stages of change model, which suggests that people typically progress through a sequence or hierarchy of stages as they think about, initiate, and maintain new behaviors. Their ability to change or seek a specific change strategy is linked to their motivation. In this sense, motivation is defined as the probability that a person will enter into, continue, and adhere to a specific change strategy (Center for Substance Abuse Treatment, 1999, pp. xix–xxiii).

Purpose. The purpose of goal assessment is to help people identify specific barriers as well as benefits related to achieving their goals.

Assumption. The goal assessment approach is based on four key assumptions, as described by Corrigan and colleagues (2001). These are (1) psychosocial therapies are more effective when they reflect the goals identified by the persons with psychiatric disability, (2) treatment should be driven by the consumer's goals as reflected through his or her perceptions and interests, (3) it is more effective to increase the frequency of behaviors that serve personal goals rather than to decrease the frequency of inappropriate or otherwise risky behaviors, and (4) the motivation to pursue goals is considered key to change and is influenced by individual and social factors. In this approach, internal factors are recognized as the basis of change; external factors are the conditions of change. An individual's motivation to change can be strongly influenced by family, friends, emotions, and community support. Behavioral change is a longitudinal process that is achieved only through a person's identification and assessment of the costs and benefits of making the change.

Design/Major Constructs. Conducting a goal assessment based on a motivational emphasis can be visualized using the stages-of-change framework. This framework consists of six stages: precontemplation, contemplation, preparation, action, maintenance, and recurrence. As described in Chapter 4, *precontemplation* suggests that the client is not yet considering change or is unwilling or unable to change. *Contemplation* refers to the idea that the client acknowledges concerns and is considering the possibility of change but is ambivalent and uncertain. *Preparation* acknowledges that the client is committed to and planning to make a change in the future but is still considering what to do. *Action* is when the client is actively taking steps to change but has not yet reached a stable state. *Maintenance* refers to the phase of accomplishment in which the client has achieved initial goals (e.g., employment) and is now working to maintain gains. *Recurrence* recognizes that a client has experienced a recurrence of symptoms or loss of desired goal and must now reorganize in an effort to decide what to do next (Center for Substance Abuse Treatment, 1999; Prochaska & DiClemente, 1983). Specifically, the clinician would help the client identify several goals and then use a cost-benefit analysis, which is rewritten as an "advantages and disadvantages" inventory list, to discuss each goal. This list would prompt the client and the clinician to engage in a dialogue that would determine the person's readiness or motivation to engage in the behaviors necessary to achieve that goal. Corrigan and colleagues (2001) reminds us that the "to be changed" behavior must be well defined for the stages of change to be accurately described (p. 115).

Administration/Technique. The goal assessment can be administered as early as the first session and later as part of the ongoing clinical work. Whether early in the relationship or later, the idea is for the client to take charge of identifying the desired goals and then determining the costs and benefits (advantages and disadvantages) of pursuing those goals. This helps lay the groundwork and determine the clients readiness for change and potential responsiveness to strategic feedback.

Source. For further information on this model, see www.ucpsychrehab.org.

Case Example. Box 6.1 provides an example of the goal assessment model.
In this example, client would decide if the cost of moving would outweigh the benefits of staying. Clinician and client would work from each concern to an eventual change in

Box 6.1. Case Example: Ms. Robinson—a Goal-Assessment Worksheet Using Stages-of Change-Motivational Interview Strategies

Background. Ms. Robinson is a 68-year-old woman who lives with her adult daughter. She reports a history of depression, suicidal thoughts complicated by a health history of severe diabetes and heart problems. She has requested counseling to address increasing conflicts between herself and daughter regarding her wish to move out of their shared home.

■ Goal Assessment Worksheet

Name: *B. Robinson* **Date:** *May 11, 2006*
Instructions: Write down a list of disadvantages and advantages of *"moving out of daughter's house"*:

(continued)

Box 6.1. Case Example: Ms. Robinson—a Goal-Assessment Worksheet Using Stages-of Change-Motivational Interview Strategies (Continued)

Disdvantages	**Advantages**
1. "*may get lonely*"	1. "*finally, freedom from a bossy daughter!*"
2. "*no one to take me to doctor's appointments*	2. "*privacy*"
	3. "*no more chores*"

Client assessment of disadvantages and advantages

1. "*stay put but work on privacy issues*"

Source: Format adapted from Corrigan, P., McCraken, S., & Holmes, E. (2001). Motivational interviews as goal assessment for persons with psychiatric disability. *Community Mental Health Journal, 37*, 2, 113–122.

one or more areas. Similarly, each advantage and disadvantage could be worked on as separate but related issues. As the case illustrates, Ms. Robinson completed the inventory and assessed that her best strategy at this point would be not to move from her daughter's home and instead work on negotiating issues of privacy—which upon later discussion was considered a central reason for wanting to move out in the first place.

Principle of Participation

The principle of participation can be characterized as consumer-driven in that it holds that people will be more committed to initiating and upholding behavioral changes if they have participated in the design of their treatment such that it suits *their* purposes and circumstances, not just the provider's (Green & Kreuter, 1999, p. 457)

Model: Health Beliefs Assessment. The health beliefs model supports the health promotion principle of participation by focusing on the daily activities people participate in which address their wellness, well-being, education, and recovery. Although this model is typically used in health settings, it is remarkably appropriate for use in mental health settings. This assessment has practical clinical utility in that it helps clients focus on the well parts of their lives and how they actively *participate* in their own self-care (or not). It also helps identify to the client where certain daily activities are ample and where others need to be promoted or enhanced.

Description. The health beliefs assessment model is a qualitative, multilevel, holistic assessment approach developed to understand health-related behavioral change using a conscious decision-making process (IOM, 2003). In this model, *health* is described as a state of balance of the person's mind, body, and spirit in conjunction with his or her family and community and forces of the natural world. The model allows both the client and the clinician to explore six interlocking behavioral facets of health strategies that individuals use to address their health and mental health needs. Clients are asked to describe the activities they use for maintaining, protecting and restoring their health in relation to their physical (body), mental (mind), and spiritual (spirit) selves. Neither etiology nor cause is explored using this type of assessment (Spector, 2000).

Purpose. The purpose of the health beliefs assessment is for both client and clinician to gain an understanding of the client's health beliefs, perceptions, and traditions. Clinicians who employ the health beliefs model in the assessment phase of clinical work can start with the assumption that individuals with mental illness and their families are already actively participating in activities that they believe are helpful in achieving health and stability. It is up to the clinician to learn of the details of these activities so that a thorough assessment can incorporate these day-to-day features into the intervention plan.

Assumption. This model is based on two major assumptions that are likely to influence whether a person will adopt a recommended health promotion/health protective behavior. These are that (1) in order for behavioral change to occur, a person must feel susceptible or threatened by the illness or condition and a high level of severity much characterize the condition and (2) people must believe that the benefits of taking a recommended action outweigh the perceived barriers and costs to performing the desired behavioral change (IOM, 2003, p. 342).

Design/Major Constructs. The design of the Health Beliefs Assessment is divided into nine interrelated sectors or perspectives derived from the following categories: *maintain health, protect health*, and *restore health—physical, mental*, and *spiritual.* In terms of the categories of maintaining health, clients can explore the active and everyday way they go about living and attempting to stay well. In terms of protecting health, clients are asked to describe the activities they choose to do that protect or preserve their physical, mental, and spiritual health. In terms of restoring health, it is known that once psychiatric symptoms have occurred, clients and families often adopt a variety of ways to promote or restore their return to health.

From a physical health perspective, the individual describes what they do to maintain, protect, or restore their daily health (e.g., nutritional needs, exercise, and sleep). From a mental health perspective, the individual describes what he or she does to maintain, protect, and restore his or her mental health (e.g., hobbies, therapy, friendships). From a spiritual health perspective, individuals are asked to describe the activities they do to maintain, protect, and restore their spiritual health (e.g., explore beliefs, rituals, and traditions associated with home, family, church, or self).

Administration/Technique. The health beliefs assessment is very easy to administer. It can be used as the basis of discussion during the clinical interview or given as a blank form and to be completed at a later date. This model is a useful example of the value of understanding how clients participate in their daily health practices and how their participation can be expanded to activities that maintain, protect, and promote their overall health.

Source. For an exemplary book on how to use the Health Beliefs Assessment, see Spector, 2000.

Case Example. Box 6.2 provides an example of how such an assessment would be written.

In this example, the client would fill in the blank boxes with examples of activities that she performs or participates in that address these multiple domains. The idea is to

Box 6.2. Case Example: Ms. Tenor—Use of Health Beliefs Model Worksheet

Background. Ms. Tenor is a 40-year-old unemployed woman who lives with her disabled elderly mother. She reports history of depression mixed with angry outbursts at family members as well as feelings of isolation and exclusion. She reports the beginning stages of adult-onset diabetes. She has requested counseling to address recurring fatigue and general feelings of depression.

Health Beliefs Model Worksheet

Name: *Ms. Tenor* **Date:** *June 6*

Instructions: In the boxes, write down as many activities you can think of that you do daily (or weekly) that you believe maintain, protect, and restore your physical, mental, and spiritual health.

(Daily/weekly)	Physical	Mental	Spiritual
Maintain health	"not much; eat"	"play solitaire"	"attend temple"
Protect health	"eat vitamins"	"read books"	"pray"
Restore health	"sleep and rest"	"nothing really"	"attend temple"

Client Beliefs. **What does this information tell you about yourself?**
"When I looked at the boxes, I realized that I don't do too much for my physical or mental health, which is maybe why I feel so bad all the time. My prayers help; maybe I need to do something else."

Adapted from Spector (2000).

use the self-assessment information as a visual tool to show strengths and gaps in self-care and wellness activities. Clinician and client would work from the identified areas–physical, mental, and/or spiritual—that the client acknowledged as areas needing attention. As the case illustrates, Ms. Tenor was surprised to see how little attention she paid to her physical and mental well-being and concluded that one of these areas could be the first thing to work on. For the first time she considered that perhaps her recurring fatigue, depressive cycles mixed with angry outbursts at relatives, and onset of diabetes could be all be contributing to her general feeling of malaise and poor physical health. She was equally pleased to see that her beliefs in her spiritual health were strong and influenced her mental health positively. The clinician would first work with Ms. Tenor on her physical health concerns (as identified on the health beliefs model) and then move to family counseling as a possibility at a later date. This case is an example of a consumer-driven approach to health and wellness assessment based on the principle of participation.

Principle of Feedback

The principle of feedback is characterized by its focus on quantitative and qualitative data exchange. This principle asserts that individuals have opportunities for direct and immediate feedback on their treatment progress and the effects of the intended change on desired outcomes (Green & Kreuter, 1999, p. 459).

Model: Substance Use Assessment Model for Clients with Severe Mental Illness. The *substance use assessment model* supports the health promotion principle of feedback by focusing on quantitative and qualitative measures. These measures explicitly recognize the principles and techniques associated with health promotion, particularly as it relates to feedback, behavior change and shared decision making.

Description. Mueser and colleagues (2003) offer a useful assessment model for working with adults who experience substance use and mental illness. The substance use assessment model is conceptualized as a five-step process with each step having a unique goal, specific assessment instruments, and various strategies for achieving client goals. These steps are detection, classification, functional assessment, functional analysis, and treatment planning. In each of these steps, feedback is provided in the form of quantitative and qualitative measures.

Purpose. The purpose of this assessment model is to provide a comprehensive, data-driven, multistep framework for exploring substance use disorders in clients with mental illness. Using extensive feedback measures in the form of self-reports, the assessment format is designed to detect substance abuse in the psychiatric population, classify substance use disorders according to DSM criteria, assess clients' functioning in different domains of life, understand the role that substance use plays in clients' lives, explore motivation to change substance abuse behavior, and offer guidance for developing a treatment plan that addresses substance use, mental illness, and their interactions.

Assumption. Using the substance use assessment model with individuals who have been diagnosed with a coexisting mental health and substance abuse condition rests on three assumptions: (1) co-occurring diagnoses of substance use and mental illness is the rule, not the exception (2) feedback in the form of empirically driven assessments can help move a precontemplator (someone who believes there is no problem or is not ready to change) through a fairly rapid change process without further need for counseling and (3) assessments that use feedback provided in a motivational style enhances commitment to change and improves treatment outcomes (Mueser, Noorsdy, Drake, & Fox, 2003; Center for Substance Abuse and Treatment, 1999).

Design/Major Constructs. The steps of the substance use assessment model are described briefly below.

- *Detection* refers to the ability to correctly detect or identify people who are experiencing the dual problems of mental illness and substance abuse. Research suggests that between 60% and 90% of clients with a mental health diagnosis also have co-occurring substance use issues. Yet, most clients are identified and treated as having one or the other but not both. The assessment strategies used at this stage include gathering a history of substance use before current use, conducting lab tests (e.g., drug screens), evaluating for the presence of negative consequences using DSM criteria for substance dependence (e.g., missing work) and abuse (e.g.,driving while intoxicated).
- *Classification* refers to the process of using the DSM to determine if individual meets the criteria for substance abuse using DSM criteria. When assessing for substance use, the DSM identifies four criteria sets which are applicable across classes of substances. These are substance *dependence, abuse, intoxication*, and *withdrawal.* According to DSM (APA, 2000):

  Substance *dependence* involves a maladaptive pattern of substance use that leads to clinically significant distress or impairment. The criteria for dependence can be made if the individual meets three of seven criteria over a 12-month period: tolerance (e.g., need for increased amounts of substance to achieve desired effect), withdrawal (e.g., the same substance is taken to relieve or avoid withdrawal symptoms), substance is taken in increasingly larger amounts over time, persistent desire or efforts to cut down or control the substance, extended efforts to obtain the substance (e.g., doctor shopping) or recovering from the effects (e.g., missed work days), important social, occupational, or recreational activities are eliminated or reduced due to substance use and continued use despite knowledge of negative consequences (e.g., diagnosis of liver disease as a direct result of alcohol consumption). The criteria for substance *abuse* also involves a maladaptive pattern of substance use leading to clinically significant impairment or distress over a 12 month period. The criteria for abuse includes meeting one of four criteria: recurrent substance use resulting in failure to fulfill major work obligations at work, school or home (e.g., poor work performance, suspensions or neglect of child), recurrent substance use in situations that are physically hazardous (e.g., driving a vehicle while impaired), recurrent legal problems (e.g., arrests), and/or continued substance use despite recurrent social or interpersonal problems (e.g., physical fights or disagreements with partner or spouse over use of substances). Substance *intoxication* refers to the development of a reversible substance specific syndrome due to recent ingestion of or exposure to a substance. Substance *withdrawal* refers to the development of a substance-specific syndrome due to the cessation of or reduction in substance use that has been heavy or prolonged, causes clinically significant distress or impairment in social, occupational functioning (APA, 2000, p. 201).

With all criteria, consideration must be given to whether the symptoms are due to a general medical condition or disorder. The assessment strategies used in this stage include using repeated assessment measures every 6 months, tap multiple sources (e.g., family, friends, employers,) for information (as appropriate), and focus on evidence rather than hearsay.

- *Functional assessment* refers to the process of gathering information about the individual's adjustment and functioning across varying domains (e.g., work, school, hobbies). There are five categories of information to be obtained: background information, psychiatric illness, physical health and safety, psychosocial adjustment, and substance use (e.g., description, motive, insight). Strategies for achieving this assessment include identifying client strengths, needs, utilize multiple information sources, and obtain information about client background, illness and treatment, physical health, and psychosocial adjustment.
- *Functional analysis* explores the role played by substance use in the client's life and the factors that may contribute to maintaining ongoing substance use. There are five characteristics of a functional analysis: *behavioral, constructive, contextual, maintaining factors*, and *empiric validation*. Functional analysis focuses on specific, observable behaviors and not on personality characteristics. It looks at constructive ways to address substance use behaviors through skill development rather than focusing on eliminating behaviors. Substance use is examined in the context of specific situations rather than assuming that substance use is an unchanging force in a person's life. The functional analysis evaluates factors in a person's life that seem to maintain substance use rather than focusing on the etiologic factors that first led to substance use. Finally, treatment is based on testable hypotheses that are supported by empirical validation (e.g., changes in scores on standardized measures).
- *Treatment planning* refers to the process of combining and integrating information obtained during the previous four assessment steps. Muesser and colleagues (2003) break down treatment planning into six steps: (1) evaluating current needs,

(2) determining client motivation, (3) selecting target behaviors as goals for change, (4) selecting most appropriate interventions for achieving desired goals, (5) choosing measureable outcomes to evaluate intervention outcomes, and (6) scheduling follow-up and booster sessions to review progress toward desired goals.

Administration/Technique. The substance use assessment model, including the treatment plan, can be completed in a 4- to 6-week period. Mueser and colleagues (2003) recommend the clinician allow for 1 to 2 weeks for the detection and classification steps, 2 to 3 weeks for the functional assessment and 1 to 2 weeks for the functional analysis and treatment planning steps. While some providers may consider this too long a period given the demand for quick turnaround assessment data, it can be argued that extra time spent in the assessment phase in the front end of the treatment process can actually be cost-saving down the road (Vandiver, Johnson, & Christofero-Snider, 2003). For example, if clinicians underestimate the clients motivation for change at the engagement phase, the best laid interventions will prove disappointing as the client drops out of treatment. As Mueser and colleages (2003) point out, many clients who have co-occurring disorders (i.e., substance use and a mental health condition) are often not motivated to address their substance use issues and thus will not engage in interventions designed for their needs. The authors eloquently recommend that if assessment is approached as a "desire to understand clients as they are, without prejudice or preconceived agendas, most clients will be able to participate with growing cooperation" (p. 54). The goal for the clinician then is to work on understanding how clients perceive their own problems and goals.

Mueser and colleagues (2003) recommend that the assessment be coordinated by a lead clinician but be conducted using an interdisciplinary team of individuals who will ultimately be providing services to the client. This team would consist of a case manager, psychiatrist, primary care physician (when available) nurse, and therapist. The lead clinician consolidates the information obtained from multiple sources (e.g., self-report data, lab tests, collateral information from family or others), discusses results with the treatment team and client, and continues the treatment plan follow-along up through completion or termination. The benefit of using a team-based approach increases the likelihood that treatment providers and client will work in tandem given the shared endorsement of the goals and strategies utilizing the most effective approaches (Mueser *et al.*, 2003).

The strengths of this assessment model lies in the variety of quantitative and qualitative self-report measures, rating scales, screening instruments, and standardized assessments used to provide feedback to the client and clinician. However, the assessment model is not without its limitations. Mueser and colleagues (2003) identify common obstacles to substance use assessment that can be directly applied to difficulties with integrated assessment models. These are failure to take a proper history; cognitive, psychotic, and or mood distortions; and premotivational state. Solutions to these obstacles require that providers ask clients directly about health and substance use issues, be aware of distortions without ruling out self-reports, ask collaterals for information, and recognize that low motivation is common in the early stages of treatment.

Although there are numerous measures that are user-friendly and easy to administer, clinicians will need to be sure that their measurement tool has been applied to populations with co-occurring disorders. Mueser and colleagues (2003) note that a common problem with many of the alcohol and drug use instruments is that they were developed for the general population and lack strong predictive utility for identifying substance use in clients who present with severe mental illness.

Source. Readers interested in a detailed review of this model are referred to Mueser *et al.*, 2003. See Box 6.3 for a description of two feedback tools (life style and functional assessment) used for these steps.

Box 6.3. Case Example: Mr. Goodyear—Quantitative and Qualitative Substance Abuse Assessment Instruments

Background. Mr. Goodyear is a 50-year-old man who lives with his wife and stepdaughter. Although he is currently employed as a mechanic at a tire dealership, his employer has threatened him with termination if he does not get help for "my little alcohol problem." Mr. G. does not believe that he has a "problem," but he is willing to go in for an assessment in order to please his employer . . . and wife, or, in his own words, ". . . to get them the hell off my back." Mr. G. completed two assessments, the DALI at intake and later the functional assessment. Examples of two of his responses are listed below.

Examples of Items from Substance Abuse Assessment Instruments

	Quantitative	**Qualitative**
Instrument.	Dartmouth Assessment of Lifestyle Instrument (DALI)	Functional Assessment Interview
Purpose.	detection of substance abuse	to gather information about functioning across multiple domains.
Example of Items.	Q.7 "Have close friends or relatives worried or complained about your drinking in the past 6 months?"	Categories: • Background Information • Psychiatric Illness • Physical Health & Safety

"Yes" = O
No = -1.
Refused = -0.78.
NA = -1
Don't Know = -0.78
Missing = -0.78.

- Psychosocial Adjustment
- Substance Use
- Goals
- Strengths: Example - "What do you see as your personal strength or abilities?"

"I'm a good provider and husband."

Adapted from Mueser *et al.* (2003).

In this case example, the client would complete at intake the Dartmouth Assessment of Lifestyle Instrument (DALI). The DALI is a quantitative, brief, 18-item self-report instrument used to detect if there is an issue of substance use, which includes alcohol, cannabis, and cocaine. The scored information is provided back to the client during the interview session. The client is encouraged to comment on these data and to take action accordingly. In the case of Mr. Goodyear (Box 6.3), he indeed scored high on a number of items indicating a problem with alcohol. Although he stated that he "was not really surprised," he just didn't expect to see the results in "black and white." He continued for additional sessions and later completed the Functional Assessment, a multi-item questionnaire with seven categories consisting of open- and closed-ended questions. Using the qualitative information from the functional assessment, Mr. Goodyear was able to put into his own words his self-observations (e.g., "I am a good provider and husband"). These personal reflections ended up being the motivating impetus to deal with his alcohol use secondary to his family and employer relationships. This case example illustrates the potency of the principle of feedback.

Principle of Multiple Methods

The principle of multiple methods is characterized by its holistic approach to data gathering. This principle asserts that a variety of data gathering methods are necessary to support the formulation of holistic assessment and treatment plans. It is worth noting here that many of the characteristics of the multiple methods principle are also found in the principle of feedback, which also relies heavily on the blending of quantitative and qualitative assessment information.

Model: Biopsychosocial–Cultural Model of Assessment. This assessment model supports the principle of multiple methods by stressing the importance of obtaining multiple perspectives in the data gathering phase. Given the high morbidity rates of physical illness with mental health conditions, it is helpful for the practitioner to utilize a broad-based framework that is atheoretical and embraces multidisciplinary input.

Description. The biopsychosocial-cultural model of assessment offers a holistic interview framework that utilizes a variety of qualitative and quantitative assessment procedures. The qualitative assessment portion incorporates the use of the Axis I through Axis V of the Diagnostic and Statistical Manual IV- TR (APA, 2000); the quantitative utilizes a variety of screening tools, self-report, and standardized measures.

Purpose. The purpose of a biopsychosocial-cultural assessment is to provide a holistic,comprehensive, multifaceted assessment of a client's life. One of the most useful aspects of the biopsychosocial-cultural assessment is that the model pushes the clinician to consider multiple perspectives that aid in formulating a flexible yet tailored treatment plan. The biopsychosocial assessment model is based on two assumptions: (1) client issues are multicausal and reflect their attempt to cope with stressors given existing vulnerabilities, environment, and resources, and (2) physical and mental health issues are intimately tied to overall health status and require holistic, comprehensive assessment approaches (Vandiver & Corcoran, 2002).

Design/Major Constructs. The assessment interview is framed around four systems: biological, psychological, social, and cultural. The biological system deals with the physiologic aspects of the person's health (e.g., such as blood pressure, oral health, weight, and sleep patterns). The psychological system explores the effects of psychodynamic factors (e.g., such as trauma, developmental impasses, motivation, and personality) on the experience and reaction to illness or distress. The social system explores issues relating to relationships, environment, family, employment, and community. The cultural system examines cultural identity as well as stressors, vulnerabilities, resources, and familial experiences on the expression and experience of coping with mental health issues (Vandiver & Corcoran, 2002).

While a detailed review of DSM categories is beyond the scope of this section, the reader is referred to the DSM for a thorough review of these categories. Axis I refers to clinical, psychological, and physiological conditions along with other codes that may be the focus of clinical attention (e.g., V codes). Axis II is used to record personality disorders, mental retardation, and defense mechanisms. Axis III is used to record general medical conditions. Axis IV refers to psychosocial and environmental problems that exacerbate distress. Axis V refers to global assessment of functioning (GAF), which is determined for the client's current state and highest level of functioning over the preceding year. For an example of each of these diagnostic categories, see Chapter 5, Figure 5.2. Overall, the biopsychosocial assessment format recommended in this section promotes the use of multiple methods: a framework that is organized around biological, psychological and social/environmental categories using Axes I through V of the DSM.

Administration/Technique. As mentioned at the start of this chapter, the clinician begins the biopsychosocial assessment process with the *bio*. The clinician gathers qualitative information on current health status (e.g., hypertension) and past health history (e.g., diabetes) or injuries (e.g., brain injury). Additional information is obtained on current medication use (e.g.,including over-the- counter, prescription, nonprescription, complementary), health, and lifestyle behaviors (e.g., exercise, nutrition, sleep pattern, and substance use) and family health history. Quantitative measures include a variety of health screening tools (e.g., SF-36 Health and Mental Health) (Ware, Kosinski, & Keller, 1994) and sleep charts. Genograms (e.g., similar to genealogy or a family tree) are also useful tools to track family health history (both positive and negative) and certain genetic disorders (e.g., schizophrenia) and to assess family patterns that may influence the achievement of client goals. Axis III of the DSM corresponds with information gathered in this section. It is important to note here that most mental health assessments are problem focused with an emphasis on Axes I and II, with little regard given to Axes III, IV, and V. However, by reversing the order of the axes and beginning with Axis III—General Medical Conditions—the provider can report medical or health conditions that may be relevant to understanding the individual's mental health. By starting off with Axis III, the clinician will discover that some medical conditions, also referred to as comorbid conditions, may be directly related to the mental disorder and must be further assessed for their prognostic or treatment implications. A detailed discussion of comorbid conditions is offered in Chapter 9.

The next step is to explore the psychological status of the client. This includes a broad range of topics including appearance, behavior, thought processes and content, mood, affect, and cognitive functioning. Common screening tools are self-reports (e.g., the Clinical Anxiety Scale) and the brief mental status exam. Axes I and II corresponds with information gathered from this section.

The "social" part of *biopsychosocial* refers to environmental connections (e.g., community ties, living conditions, neighborhood, economic status, and housing) and social relations (e.g., family, friends, employers). Useful assessment tools are ecomaps which, like genograms, facilitate an understanding of how the social environment maintains the problems and may aid or impede goal attainment (Vandiver & Corcoran, 2002, p. 298). The Global Assessment of Functioning (GAF) scale, as listed in the DSM, provides a numerical score for Axis V; other instruments such as Perceived Social Support—Friend Scale and Family Scale (Procidano & Heller, 1983) can be used for Axis IV of the biopsychosocial assessment.

The final section of the biopsychosocial includes information on the cultural experiences of the client. Broadly speaking, the clinician gathers information on cultural background (e.g., ethnicity, language), cultural explanation of physical illness/symptoms (e.g., folk words to explain illness), cultural factors related to psychosocial environment (e.g., racism, discrimination, access to health care system, spiritual), and level of functioning or wellness or unwellness (e.g., degree of acculturation). The reader is referred back to Table 6.1 for an example of how an assessment format would look when cultural considerations are primary.

Source. For a detailed review of a multiple method biopsychosocial assessment see Vandiver and Corcoran 2002. See Box 6.4 for an example of a biopsychosocial assessment model, using Axes I through V diagnostic categories and corresponding assessment tools.

*Box 6.4. Case Example of Ms. Belvedeer–Biopsychosocial -Cultural Assessment Model and Screening/Assessment Tools for DSM-IV-TR Axes I through V**

Background: Ms. Belvedeer is a 25-year-old married woman who lives with her husband next door to her parents. She was referred to the outpatient clinic through the encouragement of her mother and employer. She reports insomnia ("only sleeps 3 to 4 hours per night") for the last 6 months and feels anxious about losing her job as an assistant manager at a local restaurant. In one reported work incident, she was written up for "throwing a pancake at a coworker who criticized the way she handled customers"; she later denied that this happened or that a problem existed. The employer, however, provided background information that this event did indeed happen. She reports that she "frets all the time," dislikes her coworkers because they do not appreciate her fundamentalist religious background; lately she has questioned the value of her role in her church.

■ Biopsychosocial Cultural Assessment Model: Ms. Belvedeer

	Assessment Model ⟶	*Diagnosis* ⟶	*Quantitative & Qualitative Assessment Tools*
BIO	. Axis III: General medical Condition	Axis III: None, but evaluate for sleep apnea	. Sleep chart . General health work-up
PSYCHO	. Axis I: Clinical Considerations . Axis II: Personality disorders, defense mechanisms, & mental retardation	Axis I: V62 Religious or spiritual problem Axis I: 300.02 Generalized anxiety disorder (primary) Axis II: 799.9 Diagnosis deferred on Axis II but possible use of denial as defense mechanism	. Spiritual support scale* . Clinical anxiety scale * . Threat appraisal scale*
SOCIAL	Axis IV: Psychosocial & environmental problems Axis V: Global assessment of functioning	Axis IV: Occupational problem: discord with workers Axis V: GAF: 60 (moderate range; difficulty at work)	. Ecomap . Ecomap
CULTURAL	. Any or all of the above	. Considerations: sense of disaffection with church	. Spiritual Support Scale*

*All instruments may be found in Fischer & Corcoran (2007a)b.

In the case of Ms. Belvedeer, multiple assessment approaches can be offered to address each of the areas identified on Axes I through V. In this case example, the first step of the biopsychosocial would be to assess the physical health status of the client, particularly given the information that she had been suffering from sleep loss for 6 months. Sleep deprivation can cause significant dysfunction in social, cognitive and physical functioning. A simple sleep questionnaire assessment can be administered at intake with results to be reported over a 7-day period. The additional areas to be assessed using multiple methods are the psychosocial and cultural aspects of the client's life. Using the biopsychosocial framework, one can see how Axes I through V readily fit this model. What makes this a more holistic model is that all aspects of the client's life are considered—health, psychological, social, and cultural.

Although the intake information does not suggest that Ms. Belvedeer has a medical condition, as would warrant a notation on Axis III—general medical condition—her self-report of sleeplessness warrants further assessment. However, Ms. B.does meet the Axis I criteria for generalized anxiety disorder. This diagnosis can be corroborated by a second level of assessment which would include the use of the clinical anxiety scale; a 25-item scale designed to measure the amount, degree, or severity of clinical anxiety (found in Fischer & Corcoran, 2007b). Ms. B. is expressing concern about her religious convictions. This could be assessed using the Spiritual Support Scale (Nelson-Becker, 2006), a newly developed 18-item instrument used to measure spiritual supports in managing life challenges. While Ms. B. does not appear to meet any criteria for a personality disorder at this time (e.g., Axis II), she does tend to utilize the defense mechanisms of denial which is in relation to perceived threats to her self yet later denies the problem. One assessment tool to explore this coping style is the Threat Appraisal Scale, a 12-item situation-specific measure of the extent to which an individual perceives or appraises a situation as holding potential for harm to self (Fischer & Corcoran, 2007b).

Qualitative assessment methods for Axis IV (psychosocial and environmental) and Axis V (Global Assessment of Functioning) would include the use of ecomaps which are visual diagrams of the relationships between key elements of a person's life. The cultural piece for Mrs. B. includes the significant role that her faith has played in her life and the crossroads that she is at in terms of her professional life and her religious background. All of which speak to the importance of using a holistic assessment approach that includes the multiple methods of assessment embraced by the principle of multiple methods.

■ Community-Oriented Health Promotion Principles and Mental Health Assessments

Given the sociopolitical nature of problems like homelessness and mental illness, Yeich (1994) argues that solutions are found only through the participation of those most affected in terms of defining the problem and in subsequent organizing and social action. Unfortunately, many well-meaning health and mental health service professionals assume that people who are mentally ill are voiceless and or do not have the ability to articulate individual and community problems or concerns (Pilisuk, Mcallister, & Rothman, 1999). This section overviews two health promotion principles that can be used to guide community participation and empowerment based assessments.

Principle of Community Participation

The principle of community participation is characterized as focusing on the idea that individuals have the right to participate in their community in the least restrictive setting. This principle asserts that members of a community best understand their own needs and that community participation strengthens the capacity of community members to act collectively to exert control over the determinants of their health.

Model: Assets-Based Community Development. One model that supports the principle of community participation is the assets-based community development (A-B-C-D) model.

Description. The assets-based community development model (McKnight & Kretzmann, 1990) is a qualitative yet systematic approach to community building that utilizes individual and neighborhood participation. It refers to a range of approaches that work from the principle of community participation in that a community can be built only by focusing on the strengths and capacities of the citizens and associations that call that community "home" (Dewar, 1997, p. 1)

Purpose. The purpose of the A-B-C-D model is to assist low-income people, including those individuals living in facilities identified with having a mental illness, and their neighborhoods to develop policies and activities based on their self-identified capacities, skills, and assets. This is in contrast to typical community assessment approaches that focus on community risk factors which tend to be focused on deficits of residents (e.g., "drug users") and neighborhoods (e.g., economically depressed).

Assumption. This model works on three major assumptions: (1) community building must start with full participation by citizens from within the community; (2) if citizens control the community building agendas, existing and potential resources within the community will be put to good use; (3) communities can't be developed from the top down or from the outside in. Dewar (1997) reminds us that, historically, research has found that community building and development only takes place when local community people participate and are committed to investing themselves into local change.

Design/Major Constructs. The A-B-C-D model utilizes three categories of assets related to community building. Dewar (1997) describes these as (1) the gifts of individuals, (2) the power and direction of citizens' associations, and (3) the resources of local institutions. These are referred to as building blocks and are examined from the perspective of primary, secondary, and potential.

For example, *primary building blocks* refers to mapping the assets and capacities of individuals and organizations. *Individual* assets includes the skills, talents, and experiences of residents, individual businesses, home-based enterprises, personal incomes, and gifts of labeled people. *Organizational* assets includes a wide range of residentcontrolled associations including businesses, citizen's associations and cultural, communications, and religious organizations.

Secondary building blocks looks at assets located within the community but controlled by outsiders and include private and nonprofit organizations, public institutions and services and physical resources. *Private and nonprofit* organizations include institutions of higher education, hospitals, and social service agencies. *Public institutions and services* are public schools, police, fire departments, libraries, and parks. *Physical resources* refers to housing and vacant land.

Potential building blocks refers to resources which originate outside the neighborhood but can be embraced for community building purposes. These include welfare expenditures (e.g., enterprise development), public capital improvement expenditures (e.g., private investment), and public information (e.g., neighborhood information systems) McKnight & Kretzman, 2005, p. 166). These building blocks are illustrated in Figure 6.2.

Administration/Technique. McKnight recommends that community workers work with local residents to develop neighborhood assets maps. This can be done by using a map as a grid or inventory listings. These "data" can be organized around a series of questions and presented in a focus group forum. The case example in Box 6.5 illustrates how to combine the A-B-C-D model with a focus group format.

Focus groups are an excellent way to gather information derived from a qualitative approach yet also can yield quantitative results. Using a moderator, a small group of community members are assembled for purposes of having a discussion centered around a few questions (Kruger & Casey, 2000). Ultimately, the information gained from these techniques is not necessarily meant to be listed in a clinical chart but is intended to be used for social change and political advocacy. For example, if community

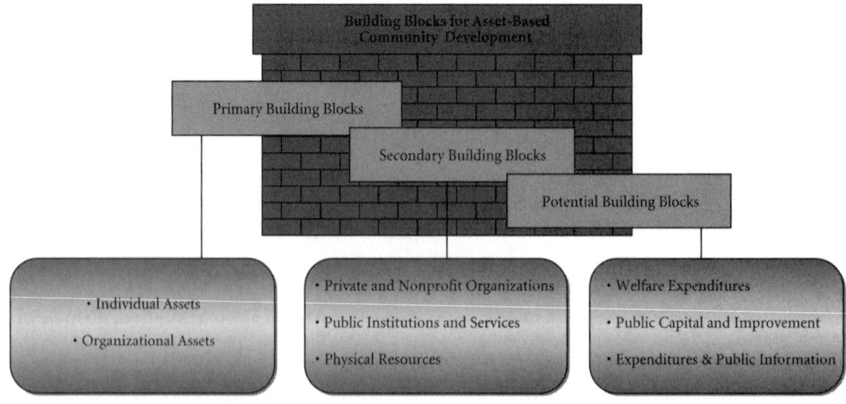

FIGURE 6.2. Asset-based community development model. Adapted from McKnight, J., & Kretzman, J. (1999). Mapping community capacity. In M. Minkler (Ed.), *Community organizing and community building for health*, pp. 157–174. New Brunswick, NJ: Rutgers University Press.

Box 6.5. Example of Focus Group Exercise Using Asset-Based Community Development—Primary Building Blocks—with Women in Residential Substance Abuse Treatment

Background. Harbor House is a community-based residential substance abuse treatment program for women and their children. The home is located in a suburban neighborhood and houses up to 10 women and 8 children. Recently the women residents expressed interest in getting involved in neighborhood safety campaigns that emphasize safe play zones for neighborhood children. In support of this effort, the neighborhood association has invited the women residents to attend an upcoming community/neighborhood focus group meeting. The following example illustrates how to integrate asset-based community development strategies into a focus group format. The content below can be used as a diagram for how to organize this process.

Focus Group Exercise

Steps	*Purpose*	*Facilitator Questions*	*Responses* (list on board)
1) Opening Questions	. used to identify commonalities	"Say your name and what skills, talents and or experiences you bring."	"I'm a gardner."
2) Introductory Questions	. introduces topic; encourages conversation and interaction	"We are concerned about the safety of our neighborhood. What assets do we already have that can be tapped?"	"day care already in place"
3) Transition Questions	. links introductory questions to key Questions; helps members see how others view topics	"What are the assets of our businesses & community organizations?"	"Active neighborhood association & local businesses."
4) Key Questions	. these questions drive discussion and allow reflection	"Of all the assets, which ones can we tap first to help us toward our goals?"	"Work with business to light walkway on playground."
5) Ending Questions	. bring closure to discussion and allow reflection		

	A. All things considered...	"Of all the items discussed, which one is most important to you?"	"Lighted walkways on playground."
	B. Summary Question...	"Is this an adequate summary?"	(refer to inventory list on board)
	C. Final Question...	"Have we missed anything?"	"No."
6) Closure	. helps establish agreement with outcome	"Let's summarize our discussion."	Can write or orally summarize

Steps 1 to 6 adapted with permission from Kruger & Casey (2000).

workers learn through this assessment process that the bulk of residential settings for women who have been homeless and are mentally ill is located in a dangerous neighborhood, action can be taken to relocate clients or to have the clients work with the neighborhood association to affect the crime.

Source. Kretzman & McKnight (1997). In the case example, a community of women in treatment for substance abuse and living in a residential setting wanted to participate in ongoing neighborhood organizing efforts targeting safety zones for children. Despite their marginalized status as "women drug addicts," members of the neighborhood association saw the women residents as concerned about their own children and wanted to support efforts for the entire community to have safe zones for all the children. True to the philosophy of the A-B-C-D model, the emphasis of the first community meeting was to look at the assets of the community and, in particular, what "gift, skill, talent, or experience" each resident brought to the table. Staying with the first portion of the A-B-C-D model—primary building blocks: individual and organizational assets—a focus group format was used to bring the various perspectives together. By the end of the meeting, an inventory list of assets was listed on the board and a group decision was made to contact the local businesses that could help. In this case, the community of residents decided on lighted walkways for sidewalks on the playground. This example illustrates how the principle of participation can be used to guide community reintegration efforts that include individuals with substance abuse problems.

Principle of Empowerment of Local People

The principle of empowerment of local people is characterized by the notion that the community sets its own strategy. This principle affirms the notion that individuals and groups in communities need to feel in control and need to be empowered to collectively control factors that influence their health and well-being (Bracht, Kingsbury, & Rissel, 1999, p. 84).

Model: Community Health Assessment. The Community Health Assessment supports the health promotion principle of local empowerment by focusing on three processes: (1) empowering the participants, (2) ensuring that knowledge is transferred back to the members of the community, and (3) actively involving community members into the research process (Hancock & Minkler, 2005). Community health assessments that embrace the principle of empowerment can be effective if they "respect both stories and studies and focus on eliciting high-level community participation throughout the assessment process" (p. 155).

Description. A community health assessment can be a combination of qualitative (ethnographic) and quantitative (data) approaches to gathering local information on the health and well-being of individuals in their identified community. The assessment can consist of health indicators (e.g., "number of neighborhood coffee shops" as one client described his perception of a healthy community; other indicators could be number of health and mental health clinics accessible via public transportation) or single factors reflecting the health status of individuals (e.g., number of days per week able to exercise in public spaces) or defined groups (e.g., sidewalks that are accessible to wheelchairs) (Rissel & Bracht, 1999). "Community" for this discussion, refers to the mental health community of residents who live throughout a geographical region.

Purpose. The purpose of a community health assessment is to assess health and well-being at the local level by empowering individuals to identify the strengths and resources in their communities.

Assumption. Community health assessments are based on two assumptions: (1) people know what is important to them and they have the ability to identify innovative and meaningful resources and measures of their health concerns and needs and (2) belief that community members have the power to assume control for defining their own needs, setting their own priorities and developing their own (self-help) programs as necessary.

Design/Major Constructs. The quantitative and qualitative methods used in the community health assessment approach is typically described as participatory research, which has significant relevance to health promotion (Hancock & Minkler, 2005). Participatory research has the benefit of using stories to form the basis of the study as well as providing hard documentation of health issues within and between communities. Both data sets can then be made readily accessible to policymakers who need to have "numbers."

Hancock and Minkler (1999) describes four key categories of information needed for conducting a local Community Health Assessment. These are (1) people's perceptions of community health, (2) local stories (3) data, and (4) epidemiological elements of place, time, and person. In terms of *perception*, community members are asked how they view their own individual health and well being in relation to their community as well as identify the strengths and resources of their communities.

Stories are another way of assessing the formal and informal processes of how communities transfer knowledge, history, and wisdom. Community stories can emerge from sitting around kitchen tables and on porch steps, attending community meetings, or writing local newsletters (Hancock & Minkler, 1999). Stories can provide insights into how community members define themselves, their interrelationships, what is important and strategies for maintaining health and well-being. As Hancock and Minkler (1999) point out "If one accepts that knowledge is power and that stories are a means of transferring knowledge between and within communities, the empowering potential of stories as a source of information becomes apparent" (p. 148).

A third category of information gathering for community health assessment is through combining qualitative (stories) and quantitative (data) procedures. Specifically, *data* and stories can reveal information about the community's physical and social environment, inequities in health, like access to mental health clinics, and the prerequisites necessary to address these inequities (Hancock, 1989). John McKnight is famously known for his eloquent understanding of the value of gathering local stories in combination with research studies as a part of a community health assessment. Said another way: "Institutions learn from studies and communities learn from stories." (Hancock & Minkler, 2005, p. 146).

Additionally, health status data that incorporates mortality, morbidity as well as quality-of-life measures (e.g., affordable, low income housing units) can be used to assess physical, mental and social well-being of an identified community.

Last, there is much to be learned about the health of a community using the *epidemiological* version of a mental status exam: person, place and time where *person* refers to the demographic profile of the community; *place* refers to the geography or environment of the community and *time* refers to the history and development of the community (Hancock & Minkler,1999). It is valuable for community mental health workers to have an understanding of the *demographics* of their clients community, especially in terms of age range of residents, gender distribution, racial/ethnic characteristics and socioeconomic status.

Understanding the composition of the neighborhood and its residents may provide a glimpse into health and mental health related issues facing the neighborhood. Also important is for community workers to understand the physical environment of the community where mental health clients live. For example, how accessible that neighborhood is to public transportation, parks, libraries, schools, cultural centers, health and mental health clinics. It is equally valuable for community mental health workers to have a sense of the economic, political and social forces that have shaped the history of the neighborhood—all of which can influence client's perception of safety and quality of life.

Administration/Technique. Marti-Costra and Serrano-Garcia (1983) describe a key process for conducting a community health assessment that reflects the empowerment principle. This process is referred to as *interactive contact methods* and includes techniques such as key informant interviews, door-to-door surveys and small group methods such as nominal group techniques. Specifically, the nominal group technique is a classic example of a structured group process that is designed to provide an opportunity for all community members to have a say about a particular set of questions or topics. It is designed to stimulate creative group decision making where agreement is lacking or members have incomplete knowledge of the nature of the issue or problem. It is also a means of enhancing creativity and decision making that integrates both individual work and group interaction with certain basic guidelines. As a method, it is typically used in situations where group members must pool their judgments to solve the problem and determine the course of action. The nominal group technique is most effective in generating large numbers of creative alternatives while maintaining group satisfaction (Delbecq, Van de Ven, & Gustafason, 1975; Lewis, Goodman, & Fandt, 2004).

Other examples of interactive methods involve the use of key informant interviews (McKnight & Kretzman, 2005; Dewar, 1997; Marti-Costra & Serrano-Garcia, 1983). This approach involves working with community leaders or spokespersons that are intimately involved in the community of interest—like the Buddhist monk at the local temple that works with the Laotian community. Key informant interviews can be con-

Box 6.6. *Example of Nominal Group Technique for Community Health Assessment of Transportation Issues for Mental Health Consumers*

Background: Members of a community-based peer helper program expressed concerns to clinic staff and later to city transportation leaders about the lack of bus lines available in their northeastern neighborhood, which could be described as a high-density low-income-housing area with a surplus of social service agencies and taverns. Many housing units were designated for Medicare- and Medicaid-eligible clients—most of whom were also clients of the local health and mental health clinics. The lack of accessible transportation created hardships for mental health clients with physical limitations when they had to walk over a mile to catch a bus for their clinic appointments. Many ended up just not going to their appointments. The issue became a top priority for mental health and community advocates when, during one summer month, three older adult mental health clients had to be hospitalized for heat exhaustion after walking long distances to get to the closest bus stop. Needless to say, they did not make it for their afternoon med-check appointments and the case managers ended up visiting

(continued)

them in the hospital. Consumer groups met with city transportation leaders to discuss conditions they felt were important for a viable, healthy community for all residents—which meant more bus routes to the northeastern sector of their city. The journey to this meeting began with a nominal group technique that embraced the principle of empowerment and was guided by the community health assessment framework.

Nominal Group Technique
Worksheet

Steps	*Methods*	*Example*
1) Identification Phase	On a piece of paper, individual members independently list their ideas on the specific issue, concern or need.	"no buses" "lack of transportation"
2) Idea Generation Phase	. Using a round-robin technique of introducing each other, each member is asked to present his/her 1 idea one at a time without discussion or comment	"meet with city officials to get more buses" "do a city map and show bus lines"
3) Recording	. Members ideas are recorded so everyone can see them	(Write all ideas on board/ flip chart)
4) Discussion & Clarification	Group discusses and clarifies ideas	(Have each member explain their idea)
5) Priority Setting	. Using a rank-ordering or rating procedure, each member votes (independently)	(From list on board, everyone votes for 1st and second idea)
6) Outcome	. Final outcome is determined by pooled individual votes and is thus mathematically derived	The top two ideas with most votes becomes the focus of community
	. Outcome will be the identification of two main (community health) issues for the community group to work on.	Main Community Health Issue: (1) "Convincing city planners of need to increase bus lines for 12 block area."

ducted using door-to-door surveys. These surveys consist of residents and community workers surveying the needs and or interests of local residents—like conducting a door-to-door safety survey among elderly, mentally ill residents in a housing complex.

Source. Readers interested in tools for community assessments and planning are referred to two resources: Community Tool Box (http://ctb.ku.edu) and Mobilizing for Action through Planning and Partnerships (MAPP) (http://www.naccho.org/tools.chm).

Case Example. See Text Box 6.6 for an example of nominal group technique.

In this community example, members of a mental health peer helper program became activists for an issue that was directly affecting the health and quality of life of not only their own members but those of an entire neighborhood community. The issue was lack of accessible public transportation in a socioeconomically impoverished area of town where many mental health consumers lived in low-income housing units. Called to action by the near deaths of three of its members due to heat exhaustion of having to walk long city blocks just to catch a bus, peer helpers worked with a facilitator to help them organize core issues and strategies. The group decided to conduct a community health assessment; one of the techniques for data gathering and strategizing was the use of the nominal group technique process. In this example, peer helpers met as a group, listed their issues, ideas and then through a priority ranking system, concluded with a single key strategy to present to city transportation planners: "Convince city planners of need to increase bus lines for a 12-block area." The power of this process was not limited to the outcome but to the empowering process that this technique and approach fostered for each of the participants.

■ Conclusion

As O'Hare (2005) points out, assessment is both art and science, inductive and deductive, idiographic and nomothetic. Effective intervention is contingent on accurate assessment and thus practitioners need to be assertive about obtaining accurate, thorough, and balanced views of clients, families, and community perspective of issues. In our review of six health promotion principles and their corresponding assessment models, we have illustrated a wide variety of techniques for gathering information relevant to mental health practice. These techniques are supported by an overarching health promotion philosophy that recognizes the importance of assessment that involves individual motivation, consumer-driven care, using quantitative and qualitative data gathering approaches, and conducting assessments in a holistic manner. Additionally, a health promotion philosophy also recognizes the power of community in providing a platform for clients to assess their own need for change in a manner that is meaningful and empowering. A quote that bears repeating is offered from John McKnight (1999): "Institutions learn from studies and communities learn from stories." In essence, the best mental health assessment will be guided by health promotion principles and reflect the best of the studies and stories. When our assessments have both of these attributes, we are all truly empowered.

In Our Own Words . . . Family and Consumer Perspectives on Mental Health Treatment Services: Focus Group Feedback

Topic: Content of Mental Health Assessments

Summary

As Chapter 6 illustrates, the assessment is the single most important activity in which client and clinician engage together. It sets the stage for all future services and potential relationships. Health promotion principles provide clinicians with a framework for posing questions and gathering information that is respectful, holistic, and collaborative. Staying with this theme, consumers and family members were asked to give suggestions about content that they would like to see go into the intake or first visit. Family members were clear that resource information (e.g., referral to support groups) would be helpful. Other important questions would involve the client's work and what kinds of support he or she needed. Consumers added to this by suggesting that questions about physical health were just as important. Both groups were clear that the approach or the process of the interview was just as critical as the information gained. Again, we see the request for respect, choice, and preference emerging as key issues for consumers and family members.

What Can We Learn?

Based on these perspectives, it is helpful for clinicians to remain mindful of the importance of the first meeting and that a gentle, respectful, yet helpful approach is valued and desired. While intakes are indeed occasions for fact finding and information gathering, they can still be conducted with tact and diplomacy and paced in such a way that consumers and family members feel "heard" during the process. The following section details the results of the focus group meeting as reported by family members and consumers.

Focus Group Question: *"What kinds of information should mental health practitioners ask for during the assessment or intake portion of your first visit to the clinic?"*		
Family Perspectives		
Core Themes	Summary of Experiences	Comments
(Ranked in order of priority)		
First—Support	Family members believed that intake staff should ask what kinds of support are available in times of crisis and what does that support structure look like. Support means different things to different people and workers should not assume that what's supportive for the family is supportive for the client.	"The family should be offered a referral to National Alliance of Mentally Ill (NAMI) for support as early as possible; also please ask us how active we want to be in our family member's recovery; we may need help ourselves first." (L., *parent*)
Second—Family History and Role	Family members believed it is important to ask what is the family history in terms of mental illness and what resources have been used for all family members.	"It is important to assess 'agreements' that are made in the family network system toward patients illness and care; our role may be different than you think." (S., *spouse*)
Third—Client Perspectives and Wishes	Family members were adamant that clients ideas and wishes about treatment should be respected, no matter how ill they might be.	"Good questions to ask include: when you are in crisis, what are your needs—like someone to watch out for your pet? Overall, it is important workers *believe* clients and family members and that we (family) are treated as a whole person, not as an interference." (M., *sibling*)

(continued)

Focus Group Question: "*What kinds of information should mental health practitioners ask for during the assessment or intake portion of your first visit to the clinic?*" *(continued)*		
Consumer Perspectives		
Core Themes	Summary of Experiences	Comments
(Ranked in order of priority)		
First—Approach	Interpersonal qualities (approach and attitude) were the most critical predictor of how well the intake was going to proceed; the most vital aspects of an intake were a compassionate and sensitive approach.	"Its not WHAT you ask, but HOW you ask it. When you ask me about my spiritual, family and community support system, you convey you care. Also just by offering me a cup of tea makes me feel like a person rather than my illness." (J., *consumer*)
Second—Consumer Perspective	Its more important to know the consumer's perspective than always going straight to the fact gathering.	"Its hard to be questioned by strangers when you are fragile. When I'm cognitively impaired, my senses are keen. I can look in your eyes and know if you care." (J., *consumer*)
Third—Physical Status	Consumers believed that more information should be gathered about their physical status; specifically, psychiatric symptoms should be screened through an examination of the clients' physical health, including history, family history, drug/alcohol, any brain scans or other physical exams that would show if anything else is contributing to the development of psychiatric symptoms.	"Intake workers should assess if there is a physical problem first—maybe the reason I'm so ill is that I'm not getting enough sleep." (J.V.S., *consumer*)

7. Integrating Health Promotion Strategies with Mental Health Interventions: The Role of Empowerment

As family, we need training too.

—*L., parent*

■ Chapter Overview

A central goal of health promotion is to empower people, families, and communities. In this chapter we focus on the importance of the role of empowerment as a guide in the application of evidence-based (EB) mental health interventions and health promotion strategies. Interventions are designed to enhance a sense of personal, familial, and community or societal empowerment. In order to do so, these interventions must have their impact at three levels: intrapersonal (individual), interpersonal (others), and intergroup (community and society). Within each of these levels, assessment issues influence the selection of EB practice interventions, which in turn are enhanced by health promotion strategies. These strategies reflect a combination of programs, initiatives, and efforts that illustrate the notion of empowerment-based health promotion and are used in conjunction with established EB interventions.

This chapter begins by first defining the term *intervention*, identifying examples of EB mental health interventions, and reviewing the distinctions between individual-and community-based health promotion strategies. Next, discussion centers on three levels of health promotion empowerment with corresponding examples of areas of interest (i.e., focus), assessment issues, evidence-based mental health interventions, and empowerment-based health promotion strategies. Within this discussion, readers are given an overview of key principles associated with a select group of EB mental health interventions. Limitations of EB mental health interventions are also reviewed. The chapter concludes with a summary of a focus group discussion held by consumers and family members who were presented the following question: What kinds of interventions have been helpful and not helpful?

Learning Objectives

When you have finished reading this chapter, you should be able to:

1. Apply three levels of health promotion empowerment (for individual, others, and community) to a variety of mental health areas (physical health, substance use, familial networks, social networks, employment, and stigma)
2. Understand how assessment issues (e.g., medication, co-occurring disorders, caregiver stress, relationships, employment, and marginalization) influence the selection of specific EB mental health interventions (e.g., illness management and recovery, psychopharmacology practice guidelines, integrated treatment using motivational interviewing, family psychoeducation, peer support, supported employment) and promising practices (e.g., media advocacy)
3. Identify empowerment-based health promotion strategies (e.g., wellness recovery action plan, coaching, family-to–family, health and wellness for family members, consumer as provider, workplace health promotion, and photovoice, and New Zealand national policy plan for stigma reduction) that can be used in conjunction with EB mental health interventions
4. Identify principles associated with selected EB mental health interventions (e.g., psychopharmacology, motivational interviewing, family psychoeducation, peer support, and supported employment)
5. Identify core themes and concerns expressed by consumer and family focus group participants when asked to describe what kinds of interventions have been helpful and not helpful

■ Introduction

In Chapter 6, we described how health promotion principles influence our choice of assessment models. Once the assessment has occurred, the next step is to select the most appropriate mental health interventions. Or more precisely phrased and worth repeating yet again: assessment drives intervention. The overarching goal of this chapter is to describe the process of integrating EB mental health interventions with empowerment-based health promotion strategies. But first, what is meant by the terms *intervention* and *EB mental health intervention?*

■ Defining the Terms

Over the years, the term "intervention" has been loosely defined in the mental health field as any activity that the clinician recommends for the client or consumer. The activity may be as straightforward as "After you take this medication, together we will monitor your blood level" or as broad as "When you feel stressed, try taking a walk in the park and writing down your feelings afterwards"—both of which, by the way, would be considered health promoting strategies. Generic definitions of the term "intervention" include the following:

- "Methods, strategies, tasks, or assignments that a clinician will use to assist the client in achieving the identified goals and objectives. Interventions define the *who;* the *what* will enable the specific responsibilities and actions to be taken by worker and client during the course of treatment " (Roberts & Greene, 2002, p. 839).
- "Activities engaged in by the practitioner, the client, and other collaborators for the purpose of solving specific problems, enhancing clients' psychological and behavioral coping abilities and modifying social-environmental contingencies to improve a client's psychosocial well-being" (O'Hare, 2005, p. 28).
- "Psychological, interpersonal and social approaches to improve the cognitive, emotional and daily functioning of individuals" (Leff, 2005, p. 142).

Ultimately, the main goal of any intervention is to help the client, the family, and in some cases the community achieve a state of physical, psychological, social, political, and environmental health, wellness, and/or well-being (Raeburn & Rootman, 1996). To achieve this goal, clinicians must now look beyond generic activities or recommendations and include interventions that have scientific evidence to support their use. These interventions are referred to as *EB interventions* and are defined as "a combination of skills and techniques that have been shown to be efficacious in controlled outcome studies with more serious and complex psychosocial problems" (O'Hare, 2005, p. 28).

■ What Makes for Evidence-Based Interventions?

As discussed in Chapter 3, interventions that are "EB" are those that meet the criteria for level 1 (two or more randomized controlled trials) and/or level 2 (one randomized controlled trial). In mental health, there are a few core set of interventions that meet the criteria for level 1 or 2. These interventions are: integrated treatment for co-occurring disorders, supported employment, illness management and recovery, peer support, medications prescribed within specific parameters, and family psychoeducation (Drake et al., 2003). Research has identified these interventions as helping persons with severe mental illness attain better outcomes in terms of symptoms, functional status, and quality of life (Torrey et al., 2003). Additionally, media advocacy has been identified as having empiric support as a means of dealing with stigma (IOM, 2000). These interventions are discussed at length later in this chapter. It is worth noting that there are many other solidly recognized EB mental health interventions (e.g., assertive community treatment and dialectical behavior therapy). However, our discussion here is restricted to the seven listed above.

■ Health Promotion Strategies and the Role of Empowerment

Health promotion strategies, as you will recall from Chapter 2, play a part in emphasizing positive outcomes that are oriented toward well-being and empowerment and not just symptom amelioration. Raeburn and Rootman (1996) make the argument that health promotion strategies "involve action, primarily on those factors that exert an influence on people's health" (p. 16). The World Health Organization (2004a) recommends that health promotion strategies become action through the following means: building healthy public policy, creating supportive environments, strengthening community action, developing personal skills, and reorienting health services. These action strategies can occur through individual and community approaches. Individually oriented health promotion strategies include recommending regular exercise, dietary modification, weight loss, smoking cessation, substance use moderation, stress reduction, anger management, sleep hygiene, and adherence to medications or dietary supplements (e.g., vitamins). Community-oriented health promotion strategies include small group development, community building, coalition building, advocacy, and political action (Green & Kreuter, 2005). In the next section we focus on the importance of empowerment as a guide in the application of EB mental health interventions and health promotion strategies.

■ Overview of Three Levels of Health Promotion Empowerment

As mentioned at the beginning of this chapter, one of the central goals of health promotion is to empower people, families, and communities. For a reminder of the promise of health promotion, let's return to the time-honored definition offered by the Ottawa Charter for Health Promotion: "Health promotion is the process of enabling and empowering people and communities to increase control over and to improve their health." (WHO, 1986, p. 1). Empowerment, from this perspective, may be described as emerging from three levels: *intrapersonal*, *interpersonal*, and *intergroup*. Raeburn and Rootman (1996) describe these three levels accordingly.

The *intrapersonal* level refers to the sense of self or the power within one's self to experience choice and take charge of and improve one's own health. For example, a client may be experiencing problems with physical health and substance abuse. Specifically, he or she may be concerned about medication side effects and problems of co-occurring depression (e.g., comorbid disorder). After a thorough assessment (see Chapter 6), the most appropriate EB interventions would be offered. These would be the *Illness Management Recovery Program* (Gingerich & Mueser, 2005) and *Integrated Treatment Using Motivational Interviewing* (Mueser et al., 2003). The provider would also be utilizing *Psychopharmacology Practice Guidelines* (Mellman et al., 2003). Empowerment based health promotion strategies would then be offered along side the EB mental health interventions. Two examples of empowerment-based health promotion strategies are the *Wellness Recovery and Action Plan* (Copeland, 2002) and *Coaching*

(McClay, 2004). Both of these strategies are designed to promote concepts of wellness through personal empowerment. See Figure 7.1A for an illustration of this process.

The *interpersonal* level refers to the power with or the experience of interdependency or connectedness with others. For example, individuals with mental health conditions and their family members often identify concerns about strained family and or social (e.g., peer) networks. After further assessment, these concerns may translate more deeply into issues of caregiver stress and complex social/peer relationships. Following a broad-based assessment, the most appropriate EB mental health interventions would be offered. From these examples, the following interventions would be *family psychoeducation* (Dixon et al., 2003) and *peer support* (Solomon & Stanhope, 2004; Minet al., 2007). Empowerment-based health promotion strategies would then be offered alongside each EB mental health intervention. Examples of empowerment based health promotion strategies would include a component on health and wellness from the National Alliance for Mental Illness (NAMI) Family-to- Family Curriculum and the *Consumer as Provider Program* (CAP) (McDiarmid et al., 2005). Both of these health promotion strategies are designed to enhance interpersonal empowerment through opportunities for educational attainment and advancement. See Figure 7.1B for an illustration of this process.

The *intergroup* level refers to the "cultivation of resources and strategies for personal and sociopolitical gains, enhancing advocacy and participatory democracy, and creating greater social equity." (Raeburn & Rootman, 1996, p. 16). In other words, intergroup development creates opportunities for individuals to develop resources, strategies and skills for participating in the political processes that moves one's self and community to a greater level of social equity. For example, individuals with mental health conditions frequently identify competitive employment and stigma as major obstacles to full community participation. Following additional assessment, it may be

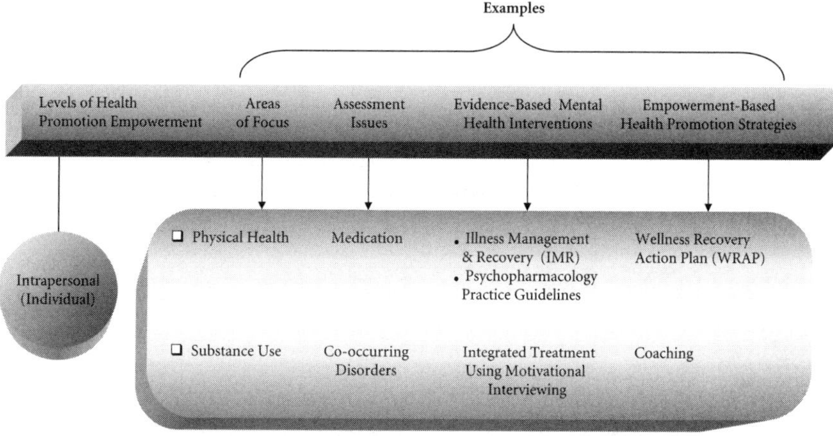

FIGURE 7.1A. Examples of the intrapersonal level of empowerment, areas of focus, evidence-based mental health interventions, and empowerment-based health promotion strategies.

determined that these obstacles are related to limited employment training opportunities and experiences with social marginalization. According to research on these two issues, the most appropriate interventions to offer would be enrollment in a *supported employment program* (Bond et al., 2003) and involvement in broad based *mass media advocacy campaigns* (IOMs) (Wallack, 2000b). Empowerment-based health promotion strategies would include workplace health promotion programs such as the *Wellness Toolkit*. Examples of empowerment-oriented health promotion strategies to address stigma *are PhotoVoice* (as described by Larry Wallack in the IOM report *Promoting Health: Intervention Strategies from Social and Behavioral Research* (2000b) and the National Stigma Awareness Plan (Ministry of Health, 2003) established by the New Zealand Ministry of Health. See Figure 7.1C for an illustration of this process.

The Institute of Medicine's report *Promoting Health* (Emmons, 2000c) advocates for an integration of all three levels. Specifically, the report acknowledges that individual-level interventions are "limited in their potential for health behavior change if they are conducted in isolation without the benefit of interventions and policies that also address interpersonal and societal factors that influence health behaviors" (p. 264). An expanded version of these levels and accompanying assessment, interventions, and strategies are outlined below.

■ Matching Evidence-Based Mental Health Interventions with Empowerment-Based Health Promotion Strategies

This section provides a detailed review of the three levels of health promotion empowerment (e.g., intrapersonal, interpersonal, and intergroup) and how these influence the choice of EB mental health interventions. Each level includes key areas that a client and provider would focus on, an overview of the literature on specific assessment issues

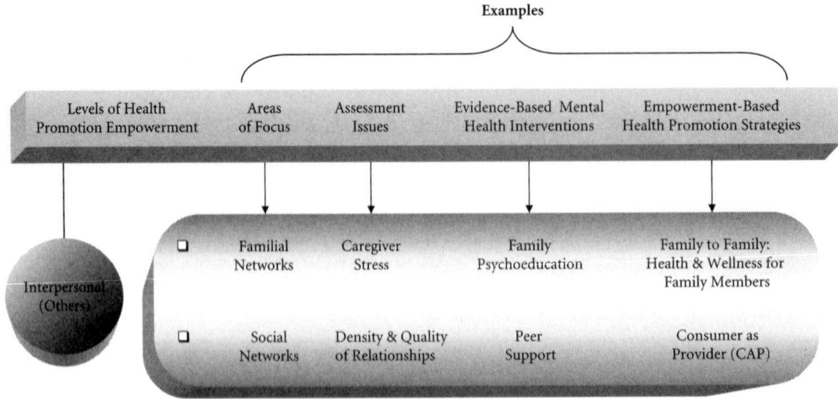

FIGURE 7.1B. Examples of the interpersonal level of empowerment, areas of focus, evidence–based mental health interventions, and empowerment-based health promotion strategies.

related to areas of focus, a description of the most appropriate EB intervention as identified by the assessment, and finally recommendations for complementary empowerment-based health promotion strategies for each EB intervention. Principles for five EB mental health interventions are provided (e.g., psychopharmacology, motivational interviewing, family psychoeducation, peer support, and supported employment).

Intrapersonal (Individual) Levels of Health Promotion Empowerment

Providers who work with clients at the intrapersonal (or individual) level will likely focus on two common areas of concern: physical health and substance use. Physical health is often assessed with an emphasis on medication; substance use is often assessed with an emphasis on the relationship with other co-occurring disorders. Let's look at both of these areas in detail.

Physical Health and Medication. In terms of physical health, let's look at the role that medication plays in the health status of clients, explore two recommended EB interventions (e.g., illness management and recovery and the use of psychopharmacology practice guidelines) and conclude with a review of an empowerment based health promotion strategy, wellness recovery action plan, that would be used in conjunction with the EB practices.

Key differences in health status continue to exist for men and women. Mowbray and colleagues (2003) summarize recent research on the differential experiences women and men have regarding the use of psychiatric medications. Women, for example, are prescribed psychiatric medications more frequently and in greater quantities regardless of diagnosis. Other research suggests that many mental health and rehabilitation programs do not address the possible gender-specific, long-term side effects of medications, which for women, include weight gain, amenorrhea, dysmenorrhea, skin and

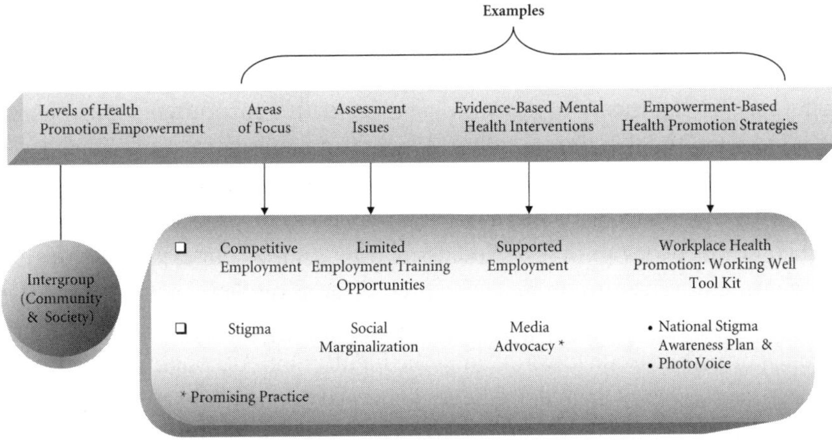

FIGURE 7.1C. Examples of the intergroup level of empowerment, areas of focus, evidence-based mental health interventions, and empowerment-based health promotion strategies.

hair problems, difficulties with lactation, and breast cancer. Men experience impotence and gynecomastia (e.g., the development of female breast tissue). There is increasing evidence to suggest that women experience more severe health problems that may be related to their increased use of psychiatric medications (Perese & Perese, 2003).

Psychiatric medications have been associated with poor diabetes-related health outcomes. Prevalence estimates for diabetes among people with schizophrenia have been estimated to be between 16% to 25%, compared to 4% among the general U.S. population (CDC, 2004). A recent review of the literature by Dixon and colleagues (2004) summarizes that newer antipsychotic medications (also referred to as second-generation agents), especially clozapine and onlazapine, have been linked to weight gain and dyslipidemia, thus possibly increasing the risk for developing or exacerbating diabetes.

Another issue regarding medication revolves around the issue of medication use. Medication nonadherence is one of the most preventable risk factors for relapse among people with severe and persistent mental illness. A key finding by Weiden and colleagues (2004) was that partial compliance with medication was associated with increasing risk of relapse in the long-term treatment of people diagnosed with schizophrenia. Using a retrospective review of California Medicaid pharmacy refill and medical claims of 4325 outpatients for whom antipsychotics were prescribed for the treatment of schizophrenia, the study showed a direct correlation between estimated partial compliance and hospitalization risk. Odds ratios found that gaps in medication days increased the risk accordingly: at 1 to 10 days, the odds ratio was 1.98; at 11 to 30 days, the odds ratio was 2.81; and at more than 30 days, the odds ratio was 3.96. Of most concern was the fact that even small gaps in medication use (e.g., 1 to 10 continuous days) in a 1-year period were associated with a twofold increase in hospitalization. Noncompliance, often perceived by health providers as "willfull cessation of antipsychotic medications," accounts for more than 40% of relapses among people with schizophrenia (Weiden & Zygmunt, 1997, p. 8). Compliance can be measured by patient self-reports, quantitative measures like the Medication Event Monitoring System (MEMS), or blood samples.

In terms of medication taking behavior among people with mental illness, recent research suggests that most outpatients diagnosed with schizophrenia are at least partially compliant with taking medications. Weiden and colleagues (2004) define partial compliance as a situation in which a person takes some but not all of his or her medications, takes an amount that is consistently less than the recommended amount, engages in irregular dosing behavior in which meds are taken "on-off," or experiences economic difficulty or cognitive confusion in having prescriptions refilled. They note that "partial compliance" refers to behaviors and does not reflect either the efficacy of the medication or the person's attitude toward taking the medication. Although the term "compliance" is used in this example to describe challenges to taking medications, the preferred term is "adherence," which is considered to be less paternalistic (pp. 886–887).

Medication treatment of individuals with severe mental illness has become the norm in many community mental health and primary care settings. Mellman and colleagues (2003) note that in the last 15 years, a number of new antipsychotics, antidepressants, and mood stabilizers have been approved for use in the United States. Along with favorable safety, side-effect profiles, and therapeutic advantages, there have been the unanticipated effects of weight gain, which has increased the risk for comorbid conditions such as hypertension and diabetes.

Research also indicates that despite gains in more efficacious psychopharmacology for mental health populations, individuals of color tend to be given less efficacious medications despite clinical guidelines that support the use of first-line treatments. Research on racial and ethnic variations in the practice of pharmacotherapy continue to find that African Americans do not receive first-line psychiatric medications as recommended by practice guidelines for the treatment of schizophrenia and other disorders. A review of the literature notes several disturbing practices. African Americans are less likely than white patients to receive second-generation antipsychotic medication even when their insurance plans provide access to such meds; when they do receive the older ones, the doses are typically higher than practice guideline recommendations and are given depot. These higher doses are known to increase the risk of tardive dyskinesia, emergency room visits, and hospitalizations while lowering the rate of adherence due to discomforting side effects (Herbeck et al., 2004).

Given the complexity of the issues described, it seems obvious that a multipronged approach is needed to address these issues. In looking to the research, two approaches emerge as meeting the requirements for EB interventions: illness management and recovery and psychopharmacology practice guidelines. These are described below.

Evidence-Based Mental Health Intervention: Illness Management and Recovery

Description. Illness management is defined as a professional-based intervention designed to help consumers and professionals collaborate in the treatment of mental illness, reduce susceptibility to relapses and develop coping strategies for the management of symptoms" (Gingerisch & Mueser, 2005, pp. 397–398). The Illness Management and Recovery Program (IMR) is a program out of Dartmouth College, funded by a grant from Substance Abuse and Mental Health Services Administration (SAMSHA). The program was designed to provide a cohesive package of services that have established empiric validity. The goal of the program is for consumers to learn information, strategies, and skills for managing their mental illness and to make progress in their recovery process. The format of the program is designed to offer weekly sessions either individually or as part of a small group (n = 8), with each session lasting between 45 and 60 minutes. The curriculum (or intervention) runs from 4 to 8 months. Consumers set and continue to refine their own goals throughout the program and actively practice the skills learned from each class while in the session and as part of homework assignments. Partners and significant others can attend sessions and be involved in various ways (e.g., helping the consumer complete homework assignments). The curriculum consists of 9 modules (e.g., recovery strategies, facts about mental illness, the stress-vulnerability model, building social support, using medication effectively, reducing relapses, coping with stress, coping with problems and symptoms, and getting one's needs met in the mental health system). These topics are taught through a variety of teaching methods: motivational and educational strategies and cognitive-behavioral techniques.

What Is the Evidence?

Although an extensive body of controlled research demonstrates the effectiveness of *teaching* skills related to illness management (Spaniol et al., 1994), little controlled research has been done to evaluate the *effects* of these programs (Gingerich & Meuser, 2005, p. 398). Mueser and colleagues (2002) provide an extensive review of the research literature on the effectiveness of illness management strategies. They reviewed over 40 randomized controlled trials of illness management programs for individuals with schizophrenia, schizoaffective disorder, or bipolar disorder. Their review, summarized here, concludes that illness-management programs that offered the following components were associated with positive benefits: psychoeducation, strategies for addressing medication nonadherence, relapse prevention training, and coping skills training for persistent symptoms.

Specifically, psychoeducation combined with other interventions has been successful at increasing consumers' knowledge of mental illness. It has not been associated with reduced relapses and rehospitalization. Strategies such as behavioral tailoring (e.g., placing medication next to a remote control) and motivational interviewing (e.g., articulating how medication can help an individual move toward goals) have led to improvements in medication regimes. Relapse prevention training that teaches stress management and environmental awareness (e.g., recognizing environmental triggers such as stressful events) has shown significant decreases in relapses or rehospitalizations.

Finally, coping skills training that employs cognitive-behavioral approaches (e.g., cognitive restructuring, role playing) has been effective in reducing the severity of troubling symptoms (e.g., psychosis, including auditory hallucinations). The IMR is, as of this writing, still undergoing systematic evaluation through the Implementing Evidence Based Practices Project funded through SAMSHA.

Evidence-Based Mental Health Intervention: Psychopharmacology Practice Guidelines and Algorithms

Description. The following section reviews four psychopharmacology practice guidelines applicable to medication issues. Mellman and colleagues (2003) describe four levels of pharmacology practice guidelines for use with psychiatric medication management. These are recommendations, comprehensive treatment options or guidelines, algorithms, and expert consensus guidelines. See Figure 7.2 for a review of these levels.

- Level one: Treatment recommendations report—usually published in the form of reports or guidelines are supported by extensive evidence of efficacy which is

	Level 1	Level 2	Level 3	Level 4
	Treatment Recommendations Report	Comprehensive Treatment Options	Medication Algorithms	Expert Consensus Guidelines
Example	Patient Outcomes Research Report (PORT)	Practice Guidelines	Texas Medication Algorithm Report (TMAP) & Texas Implementation of Medication Algorithms (TIMA)	Expert Consensus Guide for Treatment of Post-traumatic Stress Disorder (1999)
Source	U.S. Agency for Health Care Policy & Research	American Psychiatric Association	Texas Department of Mental Health & Mental Retardation	Volume 60:16, *Journal of Clinical Psychiatry*
Target Population	Individuals with schizophrenia	Individuals diagnosed with schizophrenia, bipolar, major depression, post-traumatic stress disorder	Individuals with schizophrenia, bipolar disorder, major depression	Wide range of disorders
Recommendations	Antipsychotic medications (Clozapine) are first line treatments followed by adjunctive medications for treatment resistive clients.	Recommend psychotherapy mostly as first line therapy followed by medications.	Recommend a range of stages such as Stage 1: new generation medications and Stage 2: Alternative medication treatment options.	Severe post-traumatic stress disorder: First line treatment is a combination of psychotherapy and medication.
Format	Describes dosing, maintenance, anti-psychotic medications, electroconvulsive therapy, and psychosocial recommendations.	Guidelines are comprehensive for all treatment modalities with solid sections on pharmacology.	Exclusive focus on medications	Medication guidelines for providers, patients, and families.
Classification	Very stringent evidence base	Less stringent than PORT	Broad based literature review and panels	Broad based review by experts
Contact		www.psych.org	www.mhmr.state.tx.us/centraloffice/medicaldirector/tmap	www.psychiatrist.org

FIGURE 7.2. Overview of Psychopharmacology Guidelines for Medication Management.

made available in the reports. An example is the *Patient Outcomes Research Team (PORT) Treatment Recommendations for Schizophrenia*. A recommendation would read: "Antipsychotic medications other than clozapine should be used as first-line treatment" (Lehman et al., 2004)

- Level two: Comprehensive treatment options—also known as "practice guidelines," are documents that are typically developed by professional organizations (e.g., the American Psychiatric Association) and generally have less stringent criteria for evidence than recommendations. An example is the practice guidelines for bipolar illness. A treatment option recommendation is: "For bipolar illness, lithium or the anticonvulsant valproate is endorsed for first-line therapy" (APA, 1994).
- Level three: Medication algorithms—this is a subset of practice guidelines and, like the DSM decision trees for diagnosing disorders, the guidelines are designed as a flowchart in which the provider is guided through a step-by-step approach to medication decision making. Relying less exclusively on randomized studies as a

central criteria for evidence, medication algorithms have been developed through a combination of expert panels, literature reviews, consumer input, academic and nonacademic clinicians, and consensus conferences. Examples of pharmacological algorithms come from the *Texas Medication Algorithm Project and the Texas Implementation of Medication Algorithms*. Recommendations are offered in terms of ranges or stages whereby, for a person who presents with mania, a stage 1 option of lithium and one of two anticonvulsants would be recommended, with continuation of stage 1 therapy contingent on adequate response (Crimson et al., 1999).

- Level four: Expert consensus guidelines. These are clinical guidelines based on the consensus of a panel of experts on a given topic or condition. The guidelines are not drawn from empiric literature reviews and were developed in response to criticisms that the empirically based reviews omitted many of the critical qualities to clinical management. An example is the expert consensus guideline for posttraumatic stress disorder. A guideline medication recommendation for the treatment of posttraumatic stress disorder suggests that the first line of treatment is combination psychotherapy and medication (Expert Consensus Guideline Series, 1999).

Steps for Psychopharmacologic Treatment. Mellman and colleagues (2003) recommends six steps that a clinician or health care team should take in considering prescribing medication for clients with severe mental illnesses. These steps are to (1) make an accurate diagnosis and specify target symptoms and severity; (2) choose a medication and dosage range that is supported by the research evidence; (3) monitor changes in symptoms and occurrence and tolerability of side effects using standardized rating instruments; (4) if side effects develop or symptoms do not remit, follow illness-specific guidelines that suggest dosage or medication change; (5) evaluate for co-occurring syndromes (e.g., hypertension) and make similar changes; and (6) evaluate treatment response and, if necessary, discontinue medications that have not improved therapeutic response and return to step one—reassessing the diagnosis.

Benefits and Limitations. Besides the assumption of improved quality of care, there are several economic *benefits* to using psychopharmacology guidelines in the treatment of individuals with severe mental illnesses (e.g., referring primarily to those individuals with diagnoses of psychotic disorders, mood disorders, and certain anxiety disorders—panic disorder and posttraumatic stress disorders). Mellman and colleagues (2003) suggest that guidelines may reduce costs by eliminating ineffective practices and providing greater value per health care dollar. Limitations noted are that there is not enough information on comorbid conditions.

Principles of Psychopharmacology. Kopelowicz and Liberman (2003) offer six principles that treatment programs and staff should adopt in the efforts to integrate pharmacologic and psychosocial interventions. Slightly modified here for purposes of this section, these principles reflect the distillation of numerous study results and practice guidelines. These principles are listed in Box 7.1.

Health Promotion Strategy: Wellness Recovery Action Plan

Now that the provider has identified two EB mental health interventions for addressing the health and medication needs of an individual with mental illness, the next step is to incorporate a health promotion strategy with the EB interventions. The strategy identified for our discussion is WRAP, which stands for *W*ellness *R*ecovery *A*ction *P*lan. Copeland (2003) describes the WRAP as "a system for monitoring, reducing, and eliminating uncomfortable or dangerous physical symptoms and emotional feelings" (p. 3). WRAP is a manualized self-management program in which participants identify internal and

Box 7.1. Principles of Psychopharmacology

- *Principle of Relapse Reduction:* Pharmacologic treatment consistently improves symptoms and reduces risk of relapse and should be a standard consideration for individuals who are at risk for relapse.
- *Principle of Basic Psychosocial Skills:* Medications alone will not give people the basic psychosocial skills they need to navigate their lives; medications can, however, remove the obstacles (i.e., symptoms) that impede the person's learning of new skills through psychotherapeutic or educational procedures.
- *Principle of Psychosocial Treatment:* Individuals who experience mental illness and their families benefit from psychosocial skills training in the areas of social, vocational, educational, family, recreational, coping, resilience, and self-care through symptom reduction, stress amelioration, and promoting adherence to psychopharmacologic and medication treatments.
- *Principle of Dose-Effect:* Both pharmacologic and psychosocial treatments have dosage-related therapeutics effects and side effects and both should be administered and measured over time to ensure their continued therapeutic impact.
- *Principle of Stability:* Stable levels of medication contribute to positive psychosocial responses.
- *Principle of Practicality:* Effective psychosocial treatments are those that contain elements of practicality: concrete problem solving for everyday challenges, strategies for incorporating medication into lifestyle and daily routine, incremental shaping of social and independent living skills and flexible goals.

Source: Adapted from Kopelowicz and Liberman, (2003, pp. 1491–1498).

external resources for facilitating recovery and then use these tools to create their own individualized plan for successful living (Copeland, 1997). Voluntarily taking psychotropic medications is one example of self-managed care. Individuals are guided to develop a personal "wellness toolbox" consisting of safe, free, or low-cost self-management strategies such as healthy diet, exercise, medication and vitamin schedule, and pursuit of adult life roles (Cook, 2005).

WRAP, which begins with "Getting Started" (gathering of writing materials and binder), has the following components:

Section 1: Daily maintenance list (describe when you are feeling all right, things you do to keep yourself feeling alright and things you might need to do to keep on track)
Section 2: Triggers (describe external events or circumstances that, if they happen, may produce serious symptoms—like not taking the correct dosage of medication)
Section 3: Early warning signs (list early warning signs that you recognize as potentially indicating future trouble)
Section 4: When things break down (list symptoms, what they mean to you and what you want done)
Section 5: Crisis planning (write down plan for yourself and others if you are in situation where others need to intervene; like medications you are currently taking, those that might help in crisis, and those that should be avoided)

One program that has fully incorporated WRAP is that of Boston University's Center for Psychiatric Rehabilitation—Rehabilitation and Recovery Services. Offered as one-to-one or classroom based formats for persons who have had psychiatric experiences, participants enroll in courses that they identify as supporting and facilitating their recovery process. For example, one entire curriculum module is entitled "Wellness." Course topics include the following: Coping with Stress, Personal Fitness, Healthy Lifestyles for Men, Healthy Lifestyles for Women, In Harmony Hatha Yoga, Building Your Wellness Recovery Action Plan (as described above), Meditation, Wu Style Tai Chi I and II, and Fruits and Vegetables. The programs or courses vary in length, cost, and commitment and all have a research component (Hutchinson & Hamilton, 2002).

As mentioned earlier, the essence of health promotion is the focus on empowerment of the individual. The WRAP program is a model of empowerment and patient-centered medical care as identified by the Institute of Medicine in its *Crossing the Quality Chasm* report (IOM, 2001). The goal of WRAP is to acquire new skills and information to better manage troubling symptoms and achieve higher levels of health, wellness, and functioning (Cook, 2005).

Substance Use and Co-occurring Disorders. In terms of substance use, let's look at the role that co-occurring disorders play in the lives of clients, explore one EB intervention (e.g., integrated treatment using motivational interviewing) and conclude with a review of an empowerment-based health promotion strategy, coaching, which would be used in conjunction with the EBP.

Substance abuse, which includes the criteria for abuse and dependence, is considered the most common and clinically significant comorbid disorder among adults with severe and persistent mental illness (Drake et al., 2003). The clinical literature refers to this combined clinical phenomenon as "co-occurring disorder," which generally means the co-occurrence of substance abuse and severe mental illness. Some of the key findings associated with co-occurring disorders are as follows:

- Nearly 50% of individuals with severe mental disorders also experience substance abuse.
- Negative outcomes associated with co-occurring disorders include high rates of relapse, treatment noncompliance, hospitalization, violence, incarceration, homelessness, and blood borne diseases, such as HIV and hepatitis.
- Treatment systems and funding continue to be fragmented.
- Most clients with co-occurring disorders have little readiness for abstinence-oriented treatment.
- Men are more likely to develop alcohol and drug disorders, but substance use among women may be underreported.
- Clients with co-occurring disorders have lower levels of educational attainment than clients with severe mental illness.
- Clients with antisocial personality disorders and co-occurring disorders tend to have an earlier age at onset of both psychiatric illness and substance use disorders, are more symptomatic, are more likely to have been arrested, and have greater impairment in independent living skills than clients with co-occurring disorders who do not have antisocial personality disorders.
- Clients with co-occurring disorders are more likely to drop out of treatment programs and experience medication side effects.
- Clients with co-occurring disorders who have a family history of substance use tend to have more severe substance abuse problems (New Freedom Commission on Mental Health, 2003; Meuser et al., 2003; Dixon et al., 2003; Drake et al., 2003).

Of all the negative outcomes, relapse and treatment nonadherence have been the most studied and are the most responsive to health promotion interventions. Individuals with substance use disorders and mental illness are reported to have high relapse rates and treatment noncompliance. In turn, these individuals will often be labeled with pejorative terms such as "noncompliant," "difficult to treat," "resistant," and "in denial" for not fully participating in their programs. The consequences for relapse and treatment nonadherence may be program termination or even worse, jail, particularly for those on probation. Ironically, research has found that relapse rates and treatment noncompliance for heroin dependence, alcohol, and nicotine are nearly identical to those of patients who present with diabetes, asthma, and hypertension—all conditions that can be seen as chronic, relapsing medical conditions (McLellan et al., 2000; Marlowe & DeMatteo, 2003). Figure 7.3 shows these comparisons.

Diagnosis	Relapse Rates (2) %	Treatment Non-Compliance (3)
Substance Use (Dependence) (alcohol, heroin, nicotine)	40%–60%	40%–60%
Asthma	50%–70%	40%–60%
Hypertension	50%–70%	40%–60%
Diabetes	30%–50%	40%–60%

(1) Data reported from McLellan, A., Lewis, D., & O'Brien, C. (2000). *Journal of American Medical Association,* 284, 1689–1695.
(2) Relapse rates refers to recurrenece of symptoms that requires professional intervention.
(3) Treatment non-compliance refers to not adhering to medication regimes, dietary schedule and behavioral programs and or dropping out of (drug abuse) treatment before receiving a minimally adequate dosage of service.

FIGURE 7.3. Comparisons of relapse and treatment non-compliance for four patient groups: substance use, diabetes, asthma and hypertension. (1)

McLellan and colleagues (2000) scanned the research literature and found that in general, rates of relapse and treatment noncompliance for these disorders hovered around 50%. In particular, all patient groups, meaning those diagnosed with substance use (e.g., heroin, alcohol, nicotine), type I diabetes mellitus, hypertension, and adult-onset asthma had high rates of lack of adherence to their medication regimes, dietary changes, and behavioral changes and had high rates of recurrence of symptoms within 1 year. This suggests that adhering to health related treatment regimes is challenging to all patient populations. One theory for these similar rates could be that patients were not ready or not motivated to participate in the treatment programs they were referred to, thus leading them to drop out or, at best, achieve only modest behavioral changes. Individuals with co-occurring disorders may often deny or minimize their mental health issues or problems related to substance abuse and may believe that alcohol or other drugs are actually helping their mental health. Mueser and colleagues (2003) suggest that individuals with co-occurring disorders may be legitimately confused about causality because they perceive the substance as making them feel better as opposed to the negative feelings (e.g., fatigue, lethargy) that some neuroleptic drugs induce. Drake and colleagues (2003) point out that the net result is a lack of motivation to pursue treatment and thus undertreatment by mental health clinicians.

Women and men also experience substance use differentially. For example, ongoing research has found that, in comparison to men, women are more likely to abuse licit drugs such as benzodiazepines (mild tranquilizers), stimulants, and sedatives. They begin and continue using substances (e.g., marijuana and heroin) due to social influences, which includes family or male partners; tend to become dependent more quickly, develop problems with alcoholism after or during episodes of depression, drink alone at home and often end up in substance use treatment facilities as a result of co-occurring psychiatric and or physical problems. Additionally, research indicates that women tend to enter inpatient psychiatric treatment at a younger age, having had a history of drug abuse, unemployment, medical problems, and currently being parents with children living with them and active users of self-help services (Mowbray et al., 2003, p. 105.)

Evidence-Based Mental Health Intervention: Integrated Treatment Using Motivational Interviewing

Description. Motivational interviewing is based on the larger assumption that change involves not a discrete event but rather a cycle of stages or phases through which people pass through. (Miller & Rollnick, 2002). As discussed throughout this book, most behavioral health professionals will recognize these stages as emerging from the transtheoretical notion of change as first described by Prochaska and DiClemente in their landmark book *The Transtheoretical Approach: Crossing the Traditional Boundaries of Therapy* (1984). As an intervention, motivational interviewing is a client-centered, gently directive way of being with people in a way that seeks to move them toward change by eliciting and strengthening their reasons for change (Miller & Rollnick, 2002). At a practical level, it is recognized as any clinical strategy designed to support an individual's readiness to change. Ironically, most behavioral change programs that clinicians offer to clients are appropriate for people in the action stage of change

Components. A review of the literature by Drake and colleagues (2003a) found that integrated treatment programs, meaning mental health programs that incorporate substance abuse interventions, are more effective than nonintegrated programs. Based on a review of eight studies of comprehensive co-occurring disorders or dual diagnosis programs that used experimental or quasi-experimental designs, Drake et al. (2003a) identified seven EB practice components that were associated with effective treatment for co-occurring disorders. The components of integrated treatment include:

- Staged interventions or stages of treatment (e.g., engagement, persuasion, active treatment, relapse prevention)
- Assertive outreach (e.g., intensive case management and home visits)
- Motivational interventions (e.g., helping client identify own goals and examine ambivalence)
- Counseling (e.g., motivational sessions and cognitive-behavioral interventions are used in individual, family, group formats)
- Social support intervention (e.g., focus on strengthening and supporting social environment using social networks—friends, employers—and family interventions)
- Long-term perspective (e.g., recognizing that improvement occurs over months and years, is community-based, and requires a rehabilitation perspective that supports gains, promotes health, and prevents relapse)

- Comprehensiveness (e.g., making available a seamless array of services: inpatient hospitalization, assessment, crisis intervention, medication management, money management, laboratory screening, housing, vocational services, health-based care)
- Cultural sensitivity and competence (e.g., making integrated services that serve populations with co-occurring disorders accessible to individuals and communities of color while still maintaining fidelity to known treatment effectiveness [pp. 41–42]

Essential Skills of Motivational Interviewing. There are four essential skills inherent in motivational interviewing:

- Ask open-ended questions that help elicit change talk.
- Listen with empathic reflection.
- Affirm what the client has expressed.
- Summarize the discussion in a way that gathers together the client's own change motivations using his or her words (Center for Substance Abuse Treatment, 1999).

Motivational Interviewing and Health Promotion. Miller (2004) describes three ways in which motivational interviewing (MI) can be used as a health promotion intervention in the treatment of substance use: (1) brief, opportunistic intervention; (2) motivational catalyst prior to other interventions; and (3) cost-effective, minimally intrusive, first (and possibly sufficient) level of intervention within a stepped sequence of care.

As a brief intervention, MI can be effective if it is delivered in the first session or reoccurring sessions. Research has found that positive change usually occurs between one and four sessions (Miller, 2004; Center for Substance Abuse Treatment, 1999). Introducing MI at the first and sometimes only session can serve as a catalyst for change. Additional research shows that MI can improve adherence and participation in more conventional treatment programs simply by correctly gauging and supporting the stage of change the client is in. Basically, motivational interviewing involves helping the client to identify his or her own goals and to explore the ambivalence that accompanies their achievement. An implied strategy may be to help them recognize that their current way of managing their health and illness could be interfering with the attaiment of those goals.

What Is the Evidence?

How does it work? Research has found strong evidence that behavior change (e.g., giving up drug use) is predicted by the extent to which the client's statements during counseling show increasing commitment to change (Miller, 2004). In other words, clients go from a precontemplation level of "I don't see any problem with using cocaine on the weekends—as long as I can go to work on Mondays" to a contemplation level of

"You know, maybe doing meth on the weekends is not such a good idea; I miss my family time."

To date, more than 60 clinical trials of motivational interviewing have been published. Miller (2004) summarizes these findings as follows:

- **Alcohol**: Of 18 clinical trials addressing alcohol use, 15 have reported that MI has beneficial effects on treatment retention, motivation, and adherence; combining MI with cognitive behavioral interventions for alcohol treatment has shown positive outcomes, but MI has been shown to be contraindicated for heavy-drinking college students when delivered in a group format.
- **Drug use**: Of 15 clinical trials addressing illicit drug use and related problems, 11 have reported beneficial effects of motivational interviewing; 4 have reported no differential effect on treatment entry by drug users.
- **Smoking**: In six clinical trials reviewed on tobacco smoking, MI had no discernible impact on smoking cessation with adolescent smokers, women in prenatal care, general practice patients, and children's exposure to a parent's secondhand smoke; it is notable that the criteria for total abstinence rather than reduction may have adversely impacted the outcomes.
- **HIV risk behavior**: Two clinical trials reported positive benefits of MI (when compared with health education or placebo) in reducing risk taking (e.g., unprotected intercourse, substance abuse before sex) behavior for women and lower rates of unprotected sex and higher rates of condom use for African-American men.
- **Health**: Although clinical trials are quite limited for health, MI has shown encouraging findings in the areas of cardiovascular rehabilitation, diabetes management, physical activity among middle-aged adults seen in primary care settings, and nutritional intake among African-American adults.
- **Mental health**: Although the evidence is limited, clinical trials with mental health populations exposed to MI indicates beneficial effects in the areas of treatment retention and adherence for adults with mental disorders and a reduction in problem gambling. However, no outcome differences have been found for the use of motivational enhancement therapy and cognitive behavioral therapy with bulimia patients.

There is evidence that change in one behavioral risk factor may serve as a stimulus or gateway for change in other health behaviors (Emmons, 2000). Unger (1996) found that smokers who recently quit reported intentions to become more physically active and tended to limit alcohol consumption more than continuing smokers did. Additional resedarch by Abrams and colleagues (1994) found that smoking cessation may benefit alcohol relapse among alcoholic smokers. Miller (2004) concludes that "MI is generally more effective than no treatment; adding MI to an active treatment often improves outcomes. and when MI is compared with other established outcome methods, outcomes are often similar despite the lower intensity of MI" (p. 6).

Principles of Motivational Interviewing. Miller (2004) provides an overview of the principles of motivational interviewing. These are listed in box 7.2.

Health Promotion Strategy: Coaching

Drake and colleagues (2003) note that some clients who are demoralized, symptomatic, or confused may mistakenly believe that alcohol and heroin are actually helping them cope better than their provider prescribed medications. When this is the case, providers can look to a variety of health promotion strategies that offer information, education, and support as a means for clients to determine their readiness for change or treatment.

Miller (2004) suggests that a major emerging strategy for health promotion involves coaching individuals over time into new patterns of behavior. He notes that within routine health care, for example, repeated visits provide opportunity to do brief counseling or coaching to promote motivation to change. If introduced at the beginning of care, this may yield more rapid change and can reduce inappropriate referrals—particularly if the person is not concerned or ready.

Health coaching can be defined as a service or strategy in which providers facilitate participants in establishing and attaining health promoting goals (van Ryn & Hearney, 1997). Other terms that may refer to the same phenomenon include *executive coaching, personal health management program, personalized coaching, health education coaching,*

Box 7.2. *Principles of Motivational Interviewing*

- *Principle of Ambivalence:* Understand that ambivalence and/or resistance is normal and that the clinician should adjust to this rather than opposing it directly or confrontationally with the client.
- *Principle of Client Values:* Ambivalence can be resolved by understanding the client's values and working with his/her intrinsic motivations.
- *Principle of Partnership:* Both client and clinician are considered collaborative partners in the change process and each brings important expertise to the relationship.
- *Principle of Empathy:* An empathic, supportive, yet respectfully directive counseling style supports the conditions in which change can occur.
- *Principle of Discrepancy:* Motivation for change is enhanced when clients recognize discrepancies between their current situation or behaviors and their desired future or desired behaviors.
- *Principle of Support:* Foster a setting and relationship that supports self-efficacy, optimism. and recovery.

Source: Adapted from Center of Substance Abuse Treatment (1999, pp. 40–49).

therapeutic coaching, systemic coaching, and *lifestyle counseling* (McClay, 2004). Coaching also involves the use of tailored intervention strategies that include a two-pronged approach: provider prompting and tailored interventions. *Provider prompting* refers to contacts between client and provider in which the provider (either in person or over the phone) assesses the individual's issues and his or her readiness to change and then tailors or personalizes an intervention to make it relevant to the individual's unique issues. The tailored intervention can include the provision of printed materials (e.g., newsletters, birthday cards, messages about life changes, information about bus routes).

The evidence for this health promotion approach is increasing. An Institute of Medicine report—*Promoting Health* (2000c), concludes that printed materials, when tailored to the needs of the individual, can influence behavior change (p. 281). It suggests that materials in print tend to attract notice and readership. In one randomized study, a combination of provider prompting, tailored print materials, and tailored telephone counseling was used to promote smoking cessation among a sample of low-income African-American outpatients who attended a local health clinic. Surprisingly, the interventions that were most effective in promoting smoking cessation at the 16-month follow-up were the dual combination of provider prompting plus tailored print materials. Telephone counseling combined with the other two interventions was not that helpful. In this example, more does not mean better. Although this example is taken from a community health clinic, the process of tailoring mental health interventions to include health promotion approaches like this one are promising. The principle of motivational interviewing still sets the stage for determining the level of readiness to receive information. Once the information is received, the person can privately explore this information as they consider whether to move in the direction of behavioral change.

Typically seen as a form of motivational interviewing, coaching involves the use of in-person, computer, telephone or email interventions and is designed to lead to the initiation and maintenance of behavior change. The Institute of Medicine (IOM, 2000c) identifies several individual level interventions that reflect a coaching model; these are combining in-person counseling sessions with community-based modalities—mailed materials and telephone counseling; home visitation, and computer-based interventions. The typical method in health coaching involves a trained "health coach" who begins by facilitating a discussion with the client about his or her interests and goals (e.g., quitting smoking, nutrition, balancing medication with exercise). Each session can last 30 minutes and contact can range from a single visit to regularly weekly visits. Computer technology offers several new options for the delivery of health promotion interventions that use coaching as a strategy. The American Internet User Survey (1999) report estimates that 33% of all adults have online access and 38% have used the internet for health and medical information in the past 12 months. Individuals with substance abuse disorders and mental illness can visit chat rooms or simply gather more information about health and wellness as it relates to substance abuse.

Health coaching is presumed to provide assistance to individuals who wish to improve the quality of their lives. Research has found that motivational interviewing is an effective method of facilitating this health-oriented behavior change approach. Overall, health coaching has potential for the mental health field as a method of addressing behavior change or lifestyle modifications for improved health and quality of life. It is a method in which individuals can get professional assistance in improving their health without seeking expensive and often limited medical and psychiatric attention (Woodlard et al., 1995).

Interpersonal Levels of Health Promotion Empowerment

For providers who work with clients at the interpersonal (or others) level, they will likely encounter two common areas of concern: family (or familial) networks and social networks. Family networks are often assessed in terms of caregiver stress. Social networks are often assessed in terms of number of friends and social relationships that client is involved with. Let's look at both of these areas in detail.

Familial Networks and Caregiver Stress. In terms of family networks, let's look at the role of caregiver stress experienced by family members, explore a recommended evidenced based mental health intervention (e.g., family psychoeducation), and conclude with a review of an empowerment based health promotion strategy, the Family to Family—Health and Wellness for Family Members program, which would be used in conjunction with the EBPs.

In the recent IOM report, Emmons (2000c) notes that there has been relatively little work utilizing family interventions to affect health behaviors among adults. A study by Magana and colleagues (2004) found that African-American mothers who were providing care for their adult children with mental illness had higher rates of chronic health conditions, such as high blood pressure, arthritis, and eye problems than African-American mothers who were not caring for a mentally ill relative. Their findings suggest that black mothers who care for an adult child with schizophrenia may be emotionally resilient but physically vulnerable.

The family experiences of caring for a relative with mental illness are differential and can be discussed from four perspectives: *parents* (fathers and/or mothers), *siblings' relationships*, *children caring for adult parents with mental illness*, and *spouses*. These distinctions are important, particularly in trying to set up targeted programs based on the needs and role of the caregiver. Understanding these distinctions can also assist in the development of health promotion strategies that are unique to the life stage and role of the caregiver.

In terms of parental caregivers (i.e., typically a mother and father), research into the experiences of family members or caregivers who have a relative with mental illness report that families often provide care with little to no information or training about mental illness, problem-solving strategies, coping with the ongoing physical and emotional stressors of caring for an ill relative and resources for social service, health benefits, or psychiatric services. To make this more complicated, most of the caregiving responsibilities tends to done by mothers who report that they often feel unsupported and unprepared to care for their ill relative (Pickett-Schenk, 2003). Lefley (1996) has written extensively on the burden of providing care to an adult child with mental illness. These burdens include the stressors of providing continuous instrumental support (e.g., financial assistance, transportation, and housing) as well as subjective feelings of guilt, depression, anger, and grief.

When education and support programs are offered for families, the majority of participants are women (51% to 96%) who report caring for an adult male relative (57% to 90%) (Pickett, 2003). Sibling relationship also plays a role in caregiving. Studies have found that adult sisters were more likely to report greater feelings of stigma, to have frequent contact, and to offer emotional, caregiving, and direct support to their mentally ill sibling than non-ill adult brothers. Sister siblings were also more likely to assume future care for an ill sister but not a brother (Greenburg et al., 1997, 1999).

Although there is minimal research on the role of adult children caring for a mentally ill parent, Marsh and colleagues (1993) found that adult children of parents with mental illness report a variety of psychological experiences ranging from low self-esteem, resentment, sense of robbed childhood, fear of intimacy, and unresolved grief to increased levels of compassion and empathy. In both groups, adult children expressed a need for concrete information and explanations as well as coping strategies to help improve their emotional well-being.

Spouses experience distress in much the same way as parents except that issues of loss and grieving are more for the loss of the adult relationship. Often these losses are economic such as when the primary wage earner becomes ill or in reverse, the primary wage earner has to take assume full care for an ill spouse or partner. The marital relationship is even more distressed when one spouse may have to initiate court-ordered hospitalization proceedings in order for the ill spouse to receive needed help.

Evidence-Based Mental Health Intervention: Family Psychoeducation

Description. Psychoeducation is an EB treatment modality that has reported positive outcomes in clinical trials, primarily for schizophrenia and cancer (Lukens & MacFarlane, 2004). It is a flexible model that incorporates both illness-specific information and tools for managing related circumstances. *Family psychoeducation* is also an EB treatment approach that has been shown to reduce relapse rates and facilitate recovery of persons who are mentally ill and whose families have received psychoeducation (Dixon et al., 2003). Numerous studies have found that families who participate in family education and support programs report improvement in their psychological well-being, reduction in feelings of isolation, improved ability to resolve problems related to their relatives' illness, more positive relationships with relatives, increased knowledge of the etiology and treatment of mental illness, and decreased levels of medical illness among family members (Pickett-Schenk, 2003).

The term *family psychoeducation* refers to a professionally delivered treatment modality that integrates psychotherapeutic and educational interventions and is based on the values of health, collaboration, coping, and empowerment (Lukens &

MacFarlane, 2003). It may be delivered as part of a multifamily group meeting, single-family group meeting, or mixed session. It may be located in a clinic, home, family practice, or community setting. And it may be delivered in a variety of formats: educational, supportive, didactic, or with a cognitive-behavioral emphasis. The goals of a family psychoeducation program are to work with the caregiver and client in a collaborative process for the purpose of supporting the caregiver—family member in their efforts to care for their relative with the mental health condition. Thus, no one method can be used for every family member or client/consumer but there are some consistent structures that need to be adhered to.

Structure of a Single-Family Psychoeducation Program. Mueser and colleagues (2003) describe a single-family psychoeducation program used in conjunction with behavioral family therapy where co-occurring disorders are the concern. Although their description is used for a single family, the topics may also be applied to multifamily sessions with some variation on the content. There are three goals of a family psychoeducation program: (1) provide basic information to family members about mental illness, substance abuse, drug interactions and treatment approaches, (2) offer family members strategies to work together, and (3) develop strategies for family members to improve family and client communication. The focus is educational and the content is developed around seven basics topics ranging from understanding psychiatric diagnosis to communication skills. Each session can be offered in a 90-minute time frame and is generally offered over seven sessions that can be weekly or monthly.

What Is the Evidence?

In this section, let's explore the evidence for general psychoeducation and family psychoeducation. Lukens and McFarlane (2004) reviewed the research literature on 16 psychoeducation studies and concluded that they met the research criteria for a "probable or possibly efficacious intervention and that the design was a treatment compared with a wait list." These criteria do not conventionally qualify as meeting the criteria for evidence-based practice—which is generally considered as "established, efficacious, specific intervention, including two rigorous randomized trials conducted by independent investigators" (p. 208). They are worth mentioning to illustrate how broadly psychoeducation is used across populations, disciplines, and conditions and the variety of techniques offered through this model.

Briefly, Lukens and MacFarlane (2004) reviewed the literature on four sample populations and or diagnostic categories and the treatment protocols: *mental health conditions*, *caregivers of persons with mental health conditions*, *medical illness*, and *other clinical settings*.

- *For mental health conditions*, a psychoeducation program was provided to individuals diagnosed with bipolar I and II, adults with depression in the community, children with mood disorders, women diagnosed with postnatal depression, women diagnosed with binge eating disorders and persons with bipolar disorder. The *treatment protocols or curriculums* consisted of a combination of describing symptoms, communication enhancement, coping skills and strategies, relaxation, positive thinking, social skills, stress management, expanded social supports, cognitive-behavioral techniques, problem-solving training, homework, and as-needed crisis intervention.

- *For caregivers of persons with mental health conditions*, a psychoeducation curriculum was offered to informal caregivers of persons with dementia and parents with children with intellectual disability. The curriculums involved topics on stress, appraisal, coping, and interactive group participation.
- *In terms of medical illness*, a psychoeducational curriculum was offered to women aged 30 to 35 preparing for elective hysterectomy, women with obesity, people with chronic physical pain, and adolescent girls with type I diabetes and disturbed eating attitudes and behavior along with their parents. *Psychoeducation strategies* for these groups included information plus cognitive intervention, education about obesity, problem solving, body image work, assertiveness training, definitions of pain, myth busting, cognitive behavioral techniques, pain management, group problem solving, communication skills, and mutual support.
- *With regard to other clinical settings*, psychoeducation was provided to antisocial youth in a medium security youth correctional facility, to women with a history of a partner abuse plus posttraumatic stress disorder, and in an eating disorder prevention program for adolescent girls in an affluent high school. The curriculums for these groups involved strengths-based peer group mediation, skills training, anger management, moral education, exploration of trauma history, stress management, assertiveness, managing contact with batterer, strategies for self-advocacy and avoiding victimization, focusing on normal developmental transitions, risk factors for eating disorders, social challenge, body shape and weight (adapted from Lukens & McFarlane, 2004).

With regard to family psychoeducation, the empirical support seems more favorable. Research has summarized the salient elements of effective family psychoeducation programs. These are as follows:

- Individual consultation may be more beneficial than group psychoeducation for families who are already in a support group (e.g., women's group) or for those who already have a strong support network.
- Combining assertive community treatment, family psychoeducation, and supported employment has been associated with better competitive employment outcomes than conventional vocational rehabilitation.
- Education, support, crisis intervention, and training in problem solving should be offered to available family members over a period of at least 9 months.
- Single- or multiple-family psychoeducation groups are beneficial to a variety of clinical disorders: bipolar disorders, major depression, obsessive-compulsive

disorder, anorexia nervosa, borderline personality disorder, and chronic physical illness.
- Relapse rates are reduced when information is presented to families and clients that includes skills training, ongoing guidance about illness, and self-management and emotional support for family members (Greenburg, 1995; Lukens & McFarlane, 2004; Dixon, et al., 2003).

Principles of Family Psychoeducation. Dixon and colleagues (2003) note that all treatment models that are supported by evidence of effectiveness are guided by a set of principles that incorporate families of persons who have a mental illness. Although modified slightly from those principles thoroughly identified by Dixon et al. (2003), the core elements remain as guidelines for health promotion strategies. See Box 7.3 for description of family psychoeducation principles.

Health Promotion Strategy: Family-to-Family: Health and Wellness for Family Members

As suggested by the research, caregiver burden is quite extensive for family members who care for an ill relative. While the existing education and support group programs provide extensive psychological and social support, one thing that is missing is an emphasis on the physical health status of caregivers themselves. Family members report

Box 7.3. Principles of Family Psychoeducation

- *Principle of Listening:* Providers need to listen to families' concerns in order to truly involve them as equal partners in the care and treatment of the family member with mental illness.
- *Principle of Discovery:* Explore family member's expectations of the treatment program and team members as well as expectations for the consumer.
- *Principle of Strengths:* Assess the strengths and limitations of the family's ability to support the consumer and themselves.
- *Principle of Education:* Provide the family and consumer relevant information and resources at appropriate times while providing training for the family on topics such as structured problem-solving techniques, health, and wellness.
- *Principles of Participation:* Encourage family members to expand their social networks beyond the health and mental health care systems.
- *Principle of Flexibility:* Remain flexible and present for the family and clients as they move through their new understanding.

Source: Adapted from Dixon et al. (2003, pp. 199–201).

changes in weight and sleep which can additionally take a toll on their ability to provide support. One health promotion strategy is to include health and wellness information in the existing NAMI-sponsored program entitled Family-to-Family (see www.NAMI.org). This program is a 12-week course for families and friends of individuals with serious mental illness. The traditional curriculum focuses on six disorders: schizophrenia, panic disorder, obsessive compulsive disorder, clinical depression, and schizoaffective disorder. The course includes sessions on the latest medications and treatment, effective communication skills, problem-solving techniques, and how to advocate with the system. In order to expand this with a health promotion perspective, a supplement could be added that is entitled: *Promoting Health and Wellness for Family Members.* Topics could include coverage of what families need to take care of themselves as defined by members: issues of family substance use as well as recommendations for exercise, stress reduction, diet, respite and meditation, and counseling. Health promotion may focus on supporting the wellness of the members of the support system, be it parent, spouse, or sibling. An example of what this would look like is given in Table 7.1, which illustrates a typical outline for a psychoeducational program.

Social Networks and Density and Quality of Relationships In terms of social networks, let's assess the role of friends and social support in the lives of individuals with mental health conditions, explore a recommended evidenced based mental health intervention (e.g., peer support) and conclude with a review of an empowerment-based health promotion strategy, consumer as provider (CAP), which would be used in conjunction with the EBPs.

Individuals with mental health conditions often voice concern about their lack of friends and love interests. Goldberg and colleagues (2003) reports that people with mental illness frequently experience feelings of loneliness, rejection, discrimination, and frustration. In turn, most clinicians operate from the perspective that supportive relationships help contribute to positive adjustment and buffers against stressors and adversities, including medical and psychiatric problems (Walsh, 2000). However, research has found that not all social relationships are beneficial. Lin and Peek (1999) reviewed research findings on women and social networks and found that having a large network actually increased women's exposure to stress, which in turn elevated their distress levels. Density, or the extent to which members in a network are connected, has varied results in the literature. Research on the effects of density in mental health varies from positive effects (e.g., decreased distress or increased life satisfaction) to negative effects (e.g., poor adjustment to a life event) to no effects (Lin & Peek, 1999). The cautionary note here is to avoid assuming that more is better; more friends do not necessarily mean better quality of life or friendships. Lin and Peek (1999) provide an extensive literature review of the research on social networks and conclude that the quality and array of social networks varies depending on the individual's social position, stage of life, and the composition of role relationships in his or her network. They note that it is accepted that stronger or more intimate ties tend to provide better support along most aspects of the life course.

TABLE 7.1. *Topical Outline for Single Family Psychoeducation Program for Co-occurring Disorder with a Health Promotion Component**

Family Psychoeducation Curriculum Outline

Week	Topic	Content
Session 1	Psychiatric diagnosis	Overview consumer's diagnosis, symptoms and characteristics
Session 2	Medication	Summarize main medications and overview benefits, side effects, issues of adherence and consumer ambivalence
Session 3	Understanding mental illness: the stress-vulnerability model of psychiatric disorders	Overview of biological (medication, substance use, neurochemical) and environmental (stress and coping)
Session 4	Alcohol and drugs 101: basics facts	Fact-filled session reviewing common substances and effects—both positive and negative
Session 5	Alcohol and drugs 201: motives and consequences	Focus on reasons for use and accompanying consequences
Session 6	Treatment of co-occurring disorders and related health issues	Introduce stages of change; explore motivation, discuss health related issues (e.g., HIV) and behaviors (e.g., I.V. drug use)
Session 7	Communication skills	Overview strategies for enhancing communication between all family members
Session 8	* Promoting health and wellness for family members	Discuss issues of family or caregiver substance use; strategies for diet, exercise, respite, counseling, and stress reduction

* Session 8 focuses on the health and wellness of family or caregiver, which is an overlooked aspect of most traditional psychoeducation programs.
Source: Content for Sessions 1–7 adapted from Mueser K., Noorsday, D., Drake, R. & Lindy, F. (2003). *Integrated treatment for dual disorders: A guide to effective practice* (pp.191–201). NY, NY: Guilford Press.

Evidence-Based Mental Health Intervention: Peer Support

Description. For over 30 years, peer support has been recognized as an essential component of the support network for individuals with mental illness (Solomon, 2004). Peer is defined as "an individual with severe mental illness who is or was receiving mental health services and who identifies as such" (Solomon, 2004, p.393). In a review of the literature, Solomon (2004) describes the two most common definitions of peer support as:

- A social emotional support, frequently coupled with instrumental support that is mutually offered or provided by persons having a mental health condition to others sharing a similar mental health condition to bring about a desired social or personal change (Gartner & Reissman, 1982).
- A system of giving and receiving help founded on key principles of respect, shared responsibility, and mutual agreement of what is helpful (Mead et al., 2001, p. 393).

Peer support as reviewed by Solomon (2004) is conceptualized into six categories: self-help groups, Internet support groups, peer provided/delivered services, peer run or operated services, peer partnerships and peer employees.

- *Self-help groups:* voluntary, small, mutual aid groups that are formed by peers who have come together for a mutual or shared purpose.
- *Internet support groups:* anonymous support systems offered through email or bulletin boards whose membership can be open (anyone can join) or private (application to owner of group) (Perron, 2002).
- *Peer provided/delivered services:* services offered by persons who identify as a consumer of services themselves and are delivered in the form of peer-operated peer partnership or peer employee service system (Solomon, 2004).
- *Peer-run services:* Services based on the values of choice and peer control; embedded within a formal organization but freestanding in terms of structure; staffed by volunteers and some paid staff; and planned, operated, administered, and evaluated by people with psychiatric disorders.
- *Peer partnerships:* A partnership between the dominant provider organization and a peer-run program in which the administration and governance of the peer program are shared mutually between peers and nonpeers but primary control is held by the peers (Solomon & Draine, 2001).
- *Peer employees:* Individuals with a history of receiving mental health services who are hired by mental health agencies in positions like case manager aids, peer advocates, peer companions, consumer case managers, or peer counselors. While the term *consumer* is used to designate someone who participates in mental health services and thus can be considered a peer, Solomon (2004) describes another term for the individual with a psychiatric disorder who also is trained professionally as a social worker, nurse, or psychologist: prosumer. Prosumers generally identify themselves to their clients as also having a psychiatric disorder (Frese & Davis, 1997).

What Is the Evidence?

Of the six categories of peer support listed above, *peer provided/delivered services* has the strongest evidence for effectiveness; in other words, the criteria have been met for more rigorous studies that use experimental or quasi-experimental designs. Research on peer provided services suggests the following benefits: reduced use of hospitalization and or crisis services; recipients had improved social functioning, improved self-esteem, fewer significant life problems, reduced substance use, and improved quality of life. Having a consumer peer on intensive case management resulted in fewer and shorter hospitalizations, higher rates of employment, higher earnings, and positive participation in vocational rehabilitation outcomes (Solomon, 2004; Clark et al., 2000; Klein et al., 1998.).

Similarly, research on self-help groups reports positive outcomes in areas of reduction of and fewer hospitalizations, increase in individuals' social networks and quality of life and improved outcomes related to skills deficits and diagnostic related issues—like depression (Davidson et al., 1999). It is notable from a health promotion perspective that self-help groups showed effectiveness when they focused on skill building rather than addressing lifestyle habits likes smoking and drinking (Gould & Clum, 1993). Although these study results must be interpreted cautiously given the limited number and scientific rigor, they still point to useful information regarding the effectiveness of peer support.

Overall, it is reasonable to conclude that peer support (1) enhances the number of people that a person with a psychiatric disorder can turn to for support and assistance, (2) provides a sense of belonging, and (3) provides opportunities for positive feedback of a person's own self-worth (Solomon, 2004).

Principles of Peer Support. Peer support operates with a set of principles that can be categorized into three areas: service elements, characteristics of peer providers, and characteristics of mental health service system. Although modified somewhat from the original excellent overview by Solomon (2004), these principles can serve as guideposts for the inclusion of health promotion strategies. After each summary is an indication of the amount of empirical evidence (i.e., randomized designs) to support the principle. This information is listed in Box 7.4.

Health Promotion Strategy: Consumer As Provider (CAP)

Now that research substantiates the importance of peer provided/peer delivered services, how can organizations support peer providers in these valuable roles? An empowerment based health promotion approach would explore opportunities for education and training outside the mental health system. One strategy that exemplifies a health promotion orientation is the Consumer as Provider (CAP) Training Program. This supported education program, as described by McDiarmid, Rapp, and Ratzlaff (2005) was designed to prepare consumers for direct service employment in community mental health programs. CAP fosters a partnership between colleges and community mental health centers where students experience classroom and internship activities. Preliminary outcome studies from a 2-year longitudinal study of CAP graduates indicates increased employability, especially in the social services field and higher

Box 7.4. *Principles of Peer Support and Corresponding Level of Empiric Support*

Service Elements

- *Principle of Experiential Learning:* Peers who have experience with serious mental illness use themselves as the instrument of change and are the best role models for recovery (*high level of empiric evidence*)
- *Principle of Mutual Benefit:* Peers who help others gain much for themselves and serve as effective role members in self-help groups (*moderate to high level of empiric support*)
- *Principle of Natural Social Support:* Peer volunteers are typically further along in the recovery process and offer important opportunities for social and recreational activities to participants (*high level of empiric evidence*)
- *Principle of Voluntary Nature of Service:* Services should be offered in a manner that promotes choice and supports self-determination (*limited empiric evidence*)
- *Principle of Peer Control:* Peer-provided services need to be peer-driven in order to support a consumer-run approach (limited empiric evidence)

Characteristics of Peer Providers

- *Principle of Experience with Mental Health System Service Delivery System:* Peer team members' knowledge of the workings of mental health service systems is essential to engaging individuals with psychiatric disorders (*no empiric evidence*)
- *Principle of Peer in Recovery and Stable:* Peer providers need to be in a stable phase of their recovery in order to provide services (*weak evidence*)
- *Principle of No Substance Use or Dependence:* Peers must be free of any substance dependence in order to perform their duties and serve as good role models (limited evidence)

Characteristics of Mental Health Service Delivery System

- *Principle of Diversity and Accessibility of Various Types and Categories of Peer-Provided Services:* There is value in offering a variety of peer-run services across the mental health system and not locating them in one setting (*no direct evidence*)
- *Principle of Cultural Diversity from a Community Perspective:* Peer services need to provide a variety of services that meet community needs such as those of the homeless, minority groups, or gender-specific groups (*limited evidence based on observations and researcher interpretations*)
- *Principle of Availability of Adjunctive and Alternative Peer-Provided Services:* Peer-provided services offer an alternative to traditional services for individuals who are cautious about engaging (e.g., homeless) (no direct empiric evidence; limited evidence mostly inferred from research findings)

Source: Adapted from Solomon (2004).

post–secondary educational involvement (p. 3). The four main components of the program include class room instruction (e.g., University of Kansas School of Social Welfare), group supervision, internship (e.g., 128 hours), and assistance to community support programs to hire consumer-providers. The curriculum boasts a strong health promotion orientation by virtue of its contents: Basic Helping Skills, Strengths Model Practice, Recovery and Wellness, Rights-Responsibilities, and Ethics and Mental Health Services. This program has strong implications for women recovering from mental illness. Nikkel (1994) suggests that women who are balancing the demands of parenting and living with a mental illness can serve as peer role models for those who are new to the experience. He notes that recovery can occur through empowerment when people can offer their own experiences as a way to contribute to the recovery of others.

Intergroup (Community and Society) Levels of Health Promotion Empowerment

Providers who work with clients at the intergroup (or community and societal) levels will likely encounter two common areas of client concern: employment and stigma. Employment concerns are typically assessed within the context of limited training opportunities. Stigma is often assessed in terms of social marginalization. Let's look at both in detail.

Competitive Employment and Limited Employment Training Opportunities In terms of competitive employment concerns, let's look at the issues of limited employment training opportunities for real-world job experiences, explore a recommended evidenced based mental health intervention (e.g., supported employment), and conclude with a review of an empowerment-based health promotion strategy, Workplace Health Promotion: Working Well Tool Kit, which is a program model that could be used in conjunction with the EBP.

Employment is viewed by society as a high priority and valued outcome (Bond, 2004). Research into consumer preferences suggests that most consumers of mental health services want to work, consider employment as key to recovery, prefer competitive employment over sheltered work and desire community jobs that "any person can apply for, in regular places of business, paying at least minimum wage and with mostly nondisabled coworkers." (p. 346). Despite these desires, many approaches to offering employment to individuals with psychiatric disabilities have been based on unfounded ideas. Although now disputed by research, typical formats for providing employment experiences to mental health populations have in the past consisted of (1) providing extensive vocational preparation and training to consumers before placement; (2) separating rehabilitation, vocational and mental health treatment services from each other; (3) using transitional employment or protected work, like serving as program secretary for the day in a treatment program; and (4) using vocational specialists who also worked as clinical specialist (Anthony & Blanch, 1987; Biegel et al., 2007). Many of these formats were offered through day treatment programs, which at the times were reasonable settings to begin this process. However, new thinking about employment and emerging research has recommended converting day treatment services to supported employment services.

Evidence-Based Mental Health Intervention: Supported Employment

Description. Supported employment (also known as individual placement and support, or IPS) is an evidenced-based practice approach to employment for people who have experienced severe and persistent mental illness (Bond et al., 2001). By definition, "supported employment" refers to either a status of employment or a type of program (Bond, 2004). The Rehabilitation Act Amendment (1998) as quoted by Bond (2004) distinguishes the difference: "*employment status* refers to competitive work in integrated work settings consistent with the strengths, resources, priorities, concerns, abilities, interests and informed choice of the individuals, for individuals with the most significant disabilities for whom competitive employment has not traditionally occurred or has been interrupted or intermittent as a result of significant disability" (p. 346).

As a *program*, supported employment refers to a structured, free standing program designed to help people with disabilities find and keep jobs. It is also recommended that the supported employment program hire employment specialists who maintain a caseload of 25 or lower and who spend at least 70% of their time in the community. For an expanded review of the research on supported employment, the reader is referred to the work of Gary Bond (see references). For readers interested in obtaining a tool kit on supported employment, see Becker and Bond, (2002).

What Is the Evidence?

In support of this transition, recent findings from studies that examined the conversion of day treatment to supported employment and randomized controlled trials comparing supportive employment to a variety of alternative approaches found that between 40% and 60% of consumers enrolled in supported employment obtain competitive employment while less than 20% of similar consumers do so when not enrolled in supported employment (Bond, 2004). Research that has the strongest evidence, which refers to RCTs, direct experimental and quasi-experimental, and correlational evidence, includes the following:

- There is no evidence that attendance in day treatment is a useful strategy for preparing consumers for competitive employment (Becker & Drake, 2003).
- There are higher rates of employment for consumers who received "personal therapy" than for controls receiving supportive therapy. Personal therapy refers to a theoretically grounded psychotherapy emphasizing gradual phases of change (Hogarty, 2002).
- Case management, in the absence of specific vocational efforts, has little impact on employment (Bond et al., 2001).

- Sheltered workshops that help individuals progress to competitive employment are ineffective (Drake et al., 1999).
- There is strong empiric support for rapid job placement (Bond et al., 2001).
- Cognitive interventions as a means to improve work performance on the job that are concurrent with job placement are showing success (Bell et al., 2003).
- Studies have failed to find any specific client factors (e.g., diagnosis, age, symptomatology, gender, disability status, prior hospitalization, education, or dual diagnosis status) that warrant exclusion of a client from enrolling in a supported employment program, although there is evidence for the need to titrate the type and level of support needs based on job suitability, symptoms, or cognitive impairments (Bond, et al., 2001; McGurk & Mueser, 2003).
- Overall, the benefits of competitive jobs include improved self-esteem and better symptom control. However, enrollment in supported employment programs has no systematic impact on nonvocational outcomes such as rehospitalization or improved quality of life (Bond, 2004).

One area of concern that is not identified in the above research is how supportive employment programs work differentially with women and people of color. Mowbray and colleagues (2003) note that most employment programs for people with psychiatric disabilities provide training for outside the home, usually in janitorial or other service positions that often do not have on-site child care—which may prove difficult for women with children. In an earlier study, Menz and colleagues (1989) found women tended to be disadvantaged in terms of vocational rehabilitation services, representing only one third of those on active caseloads with vocational rehabilitation programs.

Principles of Supported Employment. Becker and colleagues (2005) offer six principles that treatment programs and staff can apply to developing supported employment programs. These are listed in Box 7.5.

Health Promotion Strategy: Workplace Health Promotion-Working Well Tool Kit

Now that people are employed, how do they stay healthy? A new movement is occurring in the field of health promotion that is referred to as Workplace Health Promotion (WHP). WHP is a process aimed at both the individual behavior and the level of organizational conditions (IUHPE, 2000). Based on the notion that traditional occupational health and safety practices are limited regarding their impact on well-being at work and ill health, WHP has gained attention in Europe for its successes. Research by Breucker and Schröer (2000) argue that WHP: supports health-related practices, is crucial for health-promoting job and organizational design, contributes to building social capital by strengthening individual and organizational resources conducive to health, and reduces illness-related absenteeism. Although research on WHP has been limited due to variability in evaluation conditions and organizational designs, there are some core elements of WHP that can be considered relevant for the employment needs of individuals with mental health conditions. For purposes of this discussion, WHP will

Box 7.5. Principles of Supported Employment

- *Principle of Eligibility:* Employment is based on client choice and not on work readiness or abstinence or other screening out measures
- *Principle of Seamless Services:* Supported employment is integrated with mental health treatment and coordinated through team work
- *Principle of Competitive Employment:* Competitive employment is the goal in settings that are integrated work environments
- *Principle of Rapid Placement:* Job search begins immediately with assistance of job coach and pace of individual seeking employment
- *Principle of Individual Placement:* Job finding is individualized and based on persons preferences, strengths, and experiences and to provide a living wage through competitive employment
- *Principle of Continuous Follow-Along:* Individuals are offered follow-along for the time that fits the individual, rather than a set point

Source: Adapted from Becker et al. (2005).

focus on intervention areas for the individual along with types of health-promoting interventions. For example, the following intervention areas are available to address individual concerns or matters: smoking cessation, weight control, nutrition/cholesterol, stress, fitness/exercise, alcohol, injuries, depression, cancer detection, and HIV/AIDS. The following health-promoting interventions are made available to workers to address these concerns: material information (e.g., medical self-care books, newsletters, videotapes, monthly mailings, self-help manuals), classes and social support (e.g., training, counseling, employee assistance programs, buddy system, health education classes, group clinics), and supportive environments (ergonomic improvements, fitness facilities, smoking policy, access to nutritious meals, and incentives).

An example of a WHP is a program called *Working Well: The Tool Kit.* This tool kit was developed by Working Well, the workplace mental health promotion division of the New Zealand Mental Health Foundation (www.workingwell.co.nz) is an innovative tool kit of resources for enhancing organizational and personal wellbeing and success. Designed with input from New Zealanders, the tool kit is grounded in the idea that employees and employers want practical, helpful tools to help improve workplace productivity and to create work environments of respect, dignity, and success. Offered in a curriculum-based approach, the tool kit covers the following categories:

- Mentally Healthy Workplaces (defined, rationale, case and models of health outlined)
- Working Well Together (step by step tips on communicating well and resolving conflict; strategies for building a robust workplace that promotes all around wellbeing for all—employers, employees and community)

- A Policy For Working Well (policy frameworks to apply to organizational values)
- Check How Well You Are Working (surveying your workplace and monitoring progress)
- Working Well From The Start (good workplace practices and tips)
- Working Well Through Difficulties (individual and organizational stress and distress; handling concerns about workmates, boss or other employees)
- Getting Help to Work Well (using employee assistance programs, therapists, mentors and agencies for further help)

Stigma and Social Marginalization In terms of stigma, let's look at the issues of social marginalization, explore a promising practice (e.g., media advocacy) and conclude with a review of two empowerment-based health promotion strategies, Photo Voice and the National Stigma Awareness Plan, both of which could be used in conjunction with media advocacy.

The stigma of mental illness carries not only negative moral connotations (e.g., "lazy") but results in social marginalization, isolation, withdrawal, a devalued sense of self, and lower self-esteem for those diagnosed with a mental disorder (Link & Phelan, 1999). What do we mean by *stigma?* This term is described as a discrediting attribute involving stereotypes that can result in active discrimination. Unlike most medical diagnoses, which typically do not stigmatize the person who is ill, labels or diagnoses of mental illness are widely viewed as stigmatizing the person who receives them. From a sociological view, stigma is conceptualized as a sort of chain-reaction process that begins with the person perceived as being "marked" by a label, which for some means being given a diagnosis. This perceived labeling can lead to the person feeling set apart from others, which in turn, creates an image of the person having undesirable characteristics that then leads people to reject or avoid the stigmatized person (Thoits, 1999; Phelan & Link, 1999).

A review of the literature by Link and Phelan (1999) found that studies that compare mental illness with other stigmatizing situations (e.g., prostitution and ex-convict status) and conditions (e.g., epilepsy, alcoholism, drug addiction) report that mental illness landed near the most stigmatized end of the continuum. Diagnoses such as schizophrenia are often used incorrectly, which contributes to misunderstandings and misconceptions about mental illness (Horwitz & Scheid, 1999) and worse, are often considered the most stigmatizing of all medical conditions. Research by Mann and Himelein (2004) found that stigmatization of schizophrenia was significantly higher than stigmatization of depression. In their survey of 116 undergraduates, the authors examined the impact of diagnosis, attitudes about treatment, and psychiatric terminology on stigma associated with mental illness. They found that more positive attitudes toward treatment were associated with significantly less stigma; psychiatric terminology had no impact on attitudes toward mental illness and females tended to report less stigmatization of mental illness than males (p. 185).

Stigma and Sense of Identity. Empiric studies have found that the greater the concern about stigma by people with mental illness was associated with lower self-esteem, discontinuation of medications, social impairment, and discrimination associated with housing, jobs, and social interactions (Mann & Himelein, 2004). Research on the genetic or biological correlates of stigma actually has been associated with more negative views on the possibility of recovery. If one perceives that mental illness is genetic—or a permanent part of one's makeup—then recovery seems less likely. So the more one believes that a mental illness is genetic or biologically induced, the less controllability of the illness and the greater the sense of stigma. Mann and Himelein (2004) suggest that one way to decrease stigma is to educate people about treatment possibilities.

People with mental illness are commonly portrayed in the media as dangerous and distinctly different from mainstream society. Using content analysis of prime-time television dramas over a 17-year period, Signorelli (1989) found that 72% of mentally ill characters were portrayed as violent and 21.% were portrayed as murderers. Ten years later, Link and colleagues (1999) found that not much had changed. Results of a nationwide probability survey found that 75% of the public view persons with mental illness as dangerous. Corrigan and colleagues (2004) found an even more disturbing outcome of public education programs that addressed violence and stigma: participants who completed an Education-About-Violence program aimed at juxtaposing facts about mental illness were significantly more likely to report attitudes of fear and dangerousness, to endorse services that coerced persons into treatment and treated them in segregated areas, to avoid persons with mental illness in social situations, and to be reluctant to help persons with mental illness.

In the study, they examined how two types of public education programs (e.g., Education-About-Violence and Education-About-Stigma) influenced how the public perceived persons with mental illness, their potential for violence and the stigma of mental illness. A total of 161 participants were selected from a college campus and randomly assigned to one of three conditions: an Education-About-Violence program, an Education-About-Stigma program, and a control program in which issues related to mental illness or physical disability were not discussed. Programs were scripted and read verbatim, with each session accompanied by up to 12 slides. The Education-About-Violence program juxtaposed facts about mental illness and violence (e.g., "FACT: Annually, approximately 1000 homicides are committed by individuals with untreated mental illness") with accompanying vignettes of persons with mental illnesses. The Education-About-Stigma program was designed to review common myths about mental illness and challenge these myths; personal stories of consumers with mental illnesses were used. Three key measures were used that are specific to public education campaigns: attitudes, behavioral decisions and resource allocation. Although the sample size was small and generalizability was limited, the authors concluded that community groups should not use public education programs that emphasize the link between ment al illness and violence if they want to improve resources for mental health programs. In contrast, the anti-stigma education program produced more positive responses: participants in the Education-About-Stigma program were significantly less likely to endorse social avoidance than those in the control group, were more willing to help persons with mental illness than participants in either of the two groups and although nonsignificant, were more likely to support funding for rehabilitation services. Wahl (1995) notes that these images may be particularly potent at shaping attitudes and beliefs and that any antistigma campaign should aim to counterbalance these images by reducing the frequency, intensity, and inaccuracy of such negative fictional influences rather than promoting approaches that utilize competing destigmatizing messages.

Promising Practices Intervention: Media Advocacy

Description. Media advocacy is now emerging as a recognized approach to dealing with structural stigma. Structural stigma can be defined as a sociopolitical force in which public or private media outlets perpetuate prejudice and discrimination through negative reporting. The intervention strategy is for mental health consumers to educate reporters about issues of recovery, genetic causes and environmental stressors rather than personal and parental blame stories. The strategy is based on the notion that stigma emerges from societal attitudes and not the person. Using a method referred to as group-reinforced coping, consumer-based self-help groups are formed which utilize empowerment approaches. The potential success of consumer self-help groups in combating stigma supports the notion that when people with mental illness are empowered to "come out" and challenge negative stereotypes, the broader public may come to view mental illness differently than they now do (Link & Phelan, 1999).

What Is the Evidence?

Research has shown that individually oriented treatment approaches to deal with cultural or social stereotypes are not helpful. Typically, practitioners try to help individuals with mental illness cope with the stigma of mental illness by focusing on "inoculation" approaches (Link & Phelan, 1999). Examples of three common, individually oriented approaches are (1) *secrecy*—not telling people or coworkers about one's mental illness; (2) *withdrawal*—simply not associating with people who would not understand mental illness; and (3) *education*—strategies based on individual education about mental illness. A review of the literature by Link and colleagues (1991) argue that these three standard approaches are actually either ineffective or potentially harmful. In contrast, group-reinforced coping efforts (as described above) that utilize social support to reject cultural stereotypes may be more effective because the collective approach helps individuals see the problem as originating in the over generalizing attitudes of the stigmatizers rather than the problem originating within the person.

Corrigan et al. (2005) found positive results on the effects of advocacy efforts on the outcomes of newspaper stories about mental illness. Although the evidence for mass media campaigns is in the early stages of evaluation efforts, ongoing research suggests that newspapers are reporting fewer stories about persons with mental illness as being dangerous and more stories have advocacy related themes. As mentioned above, the media have a major role in creating and perpetuating negative stereotypes or promoting positive images of people with mental illness. Many efforts to change public attitudes used the mass media and studies of other health promotion campaigns confirm the benefit of mass media in creating a climate of opinion that can be supportive of healthy public policy. Overall, the evidence suggests that modifying cultural stereotypes through large scale public education efforts is a good start toward reducing the stigma of mental illness. Link and Phelan (1999) suggest that one means to this end begins with implementing smaller-scale experimental studies focused on the different sources of cultural stereotypes, assessing the effects of various types of messages and focusing on different means for conveying those messages.

Health Promotion Strategies

Health promotion strategies for reducing the stigma of mental illness include public reeducation efforts. This approach is based on the premise that if the public can view and react to mental disorders in the same way they do to other diseases (like diabetes) then the effect can be one of destigmatizing. Two examples illustrate these approaches: the National Stigma Awareness Campaign (New Zealand Ministry of Health) and Photovoice.

National Stigma Awareness Campaign. One example of a national health promotion strategy to address the stigma associated with mental illness can be seen in a document produced by the New Zealand Ministry of Health. The ministry is promoting a national plan entitled "Project to Counter Stigma and Discrimination Associated with Mental Illness" (O'Hagan, 2003). Based on the social model of disability, which sees disability as a process which happens when one group of people create barriers by designing a world only for their way of living, and a human rights approach, one of the objectives of this national plan is: "use the mass media, community education and other means to improve the social inclusion of people with experience of mental illness." (p. 12). The plan calls for a two-pronged strategy to achieve this objective: (1) work with news and mass media to foster and promote informed and nondiscriminatory reporting of mental illness and (2) develop community action, advocacy, education, training, and community activities to reduce stigma and discrimination.

At the *national* level, activities include:

- Educate journalism students about discrimination against people with experience of mental illness.
- Develop education resources for journalism schools.
- Provide training and support for working with the media for project providers and supporters, especially people with experience of mental illness.
- Coordinate national and local media monitoring.

At the *regional* level, activities include:

- Identify key target audiences and rationales for working with them.
- Develop community education approaches that work for the different target audiences.
- Monitor national and local media, and coordinate responses within regions by acknowledging enlightened coverage and complaining about inaccurate and stigmatizing reporting.
- Develop working relationships with local journalists and support spokespeople to talk to the media (p. 12).

Photovoice. Another health promotion approach that utilizes the media is Photovoice, which is the use of photography as a means to promote social change. A recent IOM report (2000b) describes Photovoice as a relatively new concept that emerges from feminist theory, empowerment theory, participatory research, and documentary photography. The goals of Photovoice are to (1) increase the participation of marginalized groups in the political process, (2) increase understanding of local issues and concerns through the perspectives of affected groups of people, (3) promote knowledge and critical discussion about significant community issues, and (4) connect with policy makers and others who can promote real change. To meet these goals, Photovoice uses photographs taken by local people rather than experts to present issues pertinent to the community, lead discussion groups and present visible data so that social change can occur (p. 355).

Using a grassroots approach, Photovoice is designed to engage the community to act on its own behalf and to enable people to create and discuss photographs as a means of catalyzing personal and community change (IOM, p. 354). Wallack (IOM, 2000b) overviews the key steps involved in applying the Photovoice program in community settings. The process begins with identifying and defining a project, targeting and engaging an audience of political or community leaders, and training facilitators to lead groups on the technology of photography. The facilitators, in turn, recruit community participants (e.g., people with mental health conditions) whose experiences reflect the issues at hand. These participants attend a series of workshops to learn the philosophical, ethical, and technological aspects of Photovoice. After community pictures are taken, facilitators and participants select pictures to share with journalists and policy makers. The presentation of the pictures in a community forum is used to increase awareness of community issues and act as a stimulus to provoke social change. Although Photovoice has not been subject to empiric evaluation, it is a powerful medium in which the power of local groups can be used to make the case for social change (IOM, 2000b). Two programs in which Photovoice has been used with success are the Language of Light Project in Ann Arbor, Michigan, which provided pictures of the homeless to city planners, and the Picture This project in Contra Costa County, California, which displayed pictures (e.g., closed hospital) at the county health clinic, illustrating the lack of health services for low-income people (Wang et al., 1999; Spears, 1999)

Limitations of Media Advocacy. Organizations like NAMI have worked actively to project the message that mental illness is a brain disorder with a biological origin and as such should be viewed and thus treated as any other medical condition. Media advocacy, in this sense, does nothing to promote the narrow biomedical view about mental illness. Although classifying mental disorders as medical diseases has helped to reduce stigma in some circles, Mechanic (1999) questions whether much has been gained by conceiving mental disorders as diseases in contrast to problems in living or societal discrimination. Link and Phelan (1999) found that this approach may actually result in merely describing psychiatric problems in terms of biological conditions and could result in less favorable evaluations of and behavior toward the person with the mental illness.

■ Conclusion

Throughout this chapter, we have illustrated how the concept of empowerment is woven throughout the application of EB mental health interventions and health promotion strategies. These interventions and strategies are designed to enhance a sense of personal, familial, and community or societal empowerment. In order to do so, these interventions were considered at three levels: intrapersonal (individual), interpersonal (others), and intergroup (community and society). Within each of these levels, assessment issues influence the selection of EB practice interventions, which, in turn, are enhanced by health promotion strategies.

Limitations of EB Interventions. As discussed earlier in this book, there are barriers to the application of EB mental health interventions. These stem from the fact that individual service providers may lack the necessary knowledge and skills to assimilate these practices and that organizational dynamics may undermine a treatment teams' ability to implement and offer innovative approaches (Corrigan et al., 2004). The challenge of implementing these interventions lies at many levels. Thus it is important for providers to ensure that client preferences for treatment and autonomy are honored.

Another point to consider is the value of the intervention to the client. While the statistical value of an EB intervention can be established as justification for its use, what about the social value of these interventions? By *social* we mean the value these interventions have for the person who is receiving them. Here is where empowerment-based health promotion strategies enter the clinical picture. The various health promotion strategies that have been discussed in this chapter share a common element: recognition of the value of empowerment based choice. In other words, these strategies combine the best of the EB interventions with empowerment-based health promotion strategies that are client-, family-, and community-centered.

Sylvia Nasar, author of *A Beautiful Mind*, describes a conversation in which a psychiatrist at a conference asked John Nash, the winner of the Nobel Prize for his work on equilibrium points in game theory, if he felt that his triumph over schizophrenia was a miracle. While John agreed it was great not to be plagued by delusions, he said that he really wished he could work again (Nasar, 1998). This poignant comment is a gentle reminder that mental health interventions should be as much about promoting health and restoring wellness as they are eliminating symptoms. In Nash's case, the most meaningful intervention was one that promoted his health and wellness—a job.

As clinicians we have a professional obligation to provide the very best of empirically supported, evidence-based interventions; we also have a moral obligation to coordinate interventions that are meaningful to the person, or, in the words of Winston Churchill, "Give us the tools and we will finish the job" (1874–1965).

In Our Own Words . . . Family and Consumer Perspectives on Mental Health Treatment Services: Focus Group Feedback

Topic: Mental Health Interventions

Summary

As Chapter 7 illustrates, a central goal of health promotion is to empower people, families, and communities. As such, mental health interventions should be selected and applied in a manner that enhances a sense of personal, familial, and community or societal empowerment. Staying with this theme, consumers and family members were asked to identify the kinds of mental health interventions that have been helpful (i.e., empowering) and those that have not. As noted below, both groups acknowledged the benefit of specific kinds of interventions; for family members it was peer support and medication training, for consumers it was recreation. One noteworthy intervention, suggested by a consumer, suggests that an empowerment-oriented approach is the option for respite or voluntary hospitalization. With regard to interventions that were not helpful, both groups had experienced the negative (and frightening) impact of police encounters (e.g., legal intervention) when a health intervention was really needed. A second area, and relative to this chapter, is the role of medication monitoring. An evidence-based intervention of such magnitude is potentially harmful if not properly followed up by medical personnel.

What Can We Learn?

Based on theses experiences and perspectives, mental health providers are encouraged to continue offering empowerment-oriented interventions such as educational information and social outreach (e.g., peers and recreation). The most critical matter to try to influence is the (re)training of first responders (e.g., police or emergency medical personnel) who are called to the home of a person with a mental health condition who has a medical emergency.

The following section details the results of the focus group meeting as reported by family members and consumers

Focus Group Question: ***"What kinds of interventions have been helpful and not helpful?"***

Family Perspectives

Core Themes	Summary of Experiences	Comments
(Ranked in order of priority)		
First—Helpful: Peer Support	Peer support (group therapy) was valuable for consumer in eyes of family because it provided a support group of people who understood and could relate the best	"A circle of peers worked for my daughter; they understood her and she could relate to them the best of all." (J., *parent*)
Second—Helpful: Medication Training	Family members valued training on medication usage and side effects that was offered by caseworkers and nurse practitioners.	"As family, we need training too." (L., *parent*)
First—Not Helpful: Legal Interventions	Family members concerned about volatility of legal interventions in response to 911 crisis calls. Several family members described encounters with police during a crisis situation in which their son or daughter had almost been shot by authorities for "not doing what they were told to do"—like put down the knife—during a psychotic episode.	"Mental illness is the only disease you can have in which a call for help can result in you or your loved one being killed." (M., *parent*)
Second— Not Helpful: Lack of Medication Monitoring.	While medications were helpful, the big concern was the diminishing medication follow-along and monitoring for their relatives placed on high dose, high powered psychiatric medications.	"Heavy dosing with medications with no follow-up is just plain wrong." (K., *parent*)

Focus Group Statement: "*Describe your experiences with the mental health system when you have a health problem.*" *(continued)*

Consumer Perspectives

Core Themes	Summary of Experiences	Comments
(Ranked in order of priority)		
First—Helpful: Interpersonal Approach	Consumers all agreed that the most important part of an intervention is not necessarily the TYPE of intervention—like "homework" or "skills training" but the way it is delivered by the caseworker; examples of interpersonal approaches are when therapist conveys caring (offers tea), uses empathy, allows venting, is non-judgemental, meets client at their level and has listening skills.	"When I was symptomatic, I could call my case manager 5 days a week for 10 minutes each day just to check in. Just being able to call in frequently and know that someone was there and cared made all the difference in my life—this was the best intervention." (J.V.S., *consumer*)
Second—Helpful: Respite or Voluntary Hospitalization	Consumers felt that respite in the form of voluntary hospitalization was vitally helpful and had, at times, served as a respite by providing a warm, safe, and encouraging environment.	"Hospitalization was helpful but not the 'holds.'" (J.,*consumer*)
Third—Helpful: Recreation	Opportunities for recreation, like outings or drama class, have helped with depression and provided something to do on weekends.	"We need opportunities to do normal things—like attend plays. We need help with this because it may be a new experience. Best of all, when we get help, we do things like start our own theatre troupe." (J.V.S., *consumer*)
First—Not Helpful: Legal Interventions	Similar to family members, consumers expressed dread recalling negative experiences with police authorities,	"When one of my roommates was getting sick and delusional, we called 911 asking

(continued)

Focus Group Statement: "*Describe your experiences with the mental health system when you have a health problem.*" *(continued)*

	especially when a family member or friend called for help on behalf of the consumer.	for help. Following the crisis call, police barged into our house, started frisking my housemate, ripping out his billfold from his back pocket. They thought they had every right to intimidate him due to a previous legal record. They created so much negative energy that by the time he went to the hospital, he was sicker than when we had called. This behavior by police would never have happened if he had called in with a heart attack. The police situation is the only place where if a 911 call comes in for a physical illness, they send paramedics. If a 911 call comes in for mental illness, they send the police. Mental illness is just as much a physical illness such as a heart attack but look at the differences in treatment interventions." (J.V.S., *consumer*)
Second—Not Helpful: Medications & Forced Hospitalization	Forced medication and hospitalization were considered a violation of their civil rights and often more destructive than the symptoms themselves.	"I know when I need to go in the hospital; but taking my clothes, holding me down while injecting me with medication is hardly treatment, its physical abuse." (J.V.S., *consumer*)
Third—Not Helpful: Authoritative Approach	The least helpful approach for any intervention was when the worker delivered it in an authoritative or demeaning manner, no matter how obvious the recommendation was—like stop using drugs—it was the attitude of the worker that was offensive more than the actual recommendation.	"Telling me to stop doing certain things—like I don't know." (R., *consumer*)

8. Evaluating and Measuring Health Promotion Strategies for Mental Health Interventions

All interventions should have some practical outcome measures—the things that influence day-to-day successes or struggles.

—*S., spouse*

■ Chapter Overview

Assessment, intervention, and evaluation are interrelated approaches in health promotion practice. Assessment drives the intervention, which, in turn, determines the evaluation approach. The importance of evaluating the success or failure of mental health interventions and health promotion strategies cannot be overstated. Clinicians and clients need to know whether change has occurred and had the intended effects. This chapter begins by examining the various approaches used in evaluation efforts, beginning with an overview of qualitative and quantitative methodology and moving to a review of conventional research designs—single-subject, group, quasi-experimental, and experimental. Next, an overview is provided on the critical issues experienced in health promotion measurement—reliability, validity, snapshot measures, understandings, time course and perspectives. The remainder of the chapter reviews six measures appropriate for health promotion strategies and provides a discussion on the limitations and benefits of evaluating mental health interventions and health promotion strategies. The chapter concludes with a summary of a focus group discussion held by consumers and family members who responded to the following question: "What kinds of information do you think are important for the evaluation of mental health interventions, services, or programs?"

Learning Objectives

When you have finished reading this chapter, you should be able to:

1. Describe the various types of evaluation designs typically used to evaluate health promotion strategies and their limitations; these are qualitative and quantitative approaches, which includes single subject designs, group designs, and quasi-experimental and experimental research designs

2. Discuss six measures used to evaluate health promotion strategies: adherence determinants questionnaire, adult health concerns questionnaire, perceived stress scale, self-efficacy scale, organizational climate scale, and empowerment evaluation
3. Understand core challenges of measuring health promotion activities: multiple understandings, time course, multiple perspectives, and cultural relevance
4. Identify core themes and concerns expressed by consumer and family focus group members when asked to identify information that could be used to evaluate interventions, services, or programs

■ Introduction

No assessment or intervention is complete until its impact has been evaluated. Evaluation is beneficial because it encourages the clinician (and client) to establish criteria for judging the success of an intervention before, during and after treatment. Evaluation of past interventions as well as other information should drive future decision making as part of an ongoing decision-making feedback loop. The evaluation process helps clinicians and clients both observe the impact of the interventions as objectively as possible and take further corrective action if it becomes necessary. Let's first explore just what is meant by *evaluation.*

■ Evaluation Overview: Definitions

Evaluation can be described as a *process*, a *method*, and a *communication tool.* As a *process*, evaluation is used to determine the effectiveness of a particular intervention or program and to inform clinicians, funders, and agency and system policies. Effectiveness data may come from a variety of sources (e.g., rapid assessment tools, surveys, and case records). Effectiveness studies are investigations that attempt to replicate the positive findings obtained through prior efficacy studies conducted in practice contexts. These studies involve a clinical mix of individuals (e.g., multiple diagnoses) who can present with multiple problems (e.g., from poverty to trauma) and are naturally occurring treatment groups (e.g., seen at different settings and receiving different interventions) (Thyers & Myers, 2003).

As a *method*, evaluation uses qualitative and quantitative methods to update the assessment, adjust the intervention and measure client progress and aggregate data for the purposes of quality assurance and program evaluation (O'Hare, 2005, p. 7).

As a *communication tool*, evaluation sets in motion the opportunity for clients, families, and communities to have feedback about their growth and progress. And as we know from Chapter 6, feedback is a core health promotion principle. The principle of feedback "ensures that individuals have opportunities for direct and immediate feedback on their treatment progress and the effects of the intended change on desired outcomes" (Green & Kreuter, 1999, p. 459).

■ Types of Health Promotion Evaluation

Mental health interventions that incorporate health promotion approaches typically use two kinds of evaluation approaches: qualitative and quantitative.

Qualitative Approaches. Health promotion has long used the qualitative approach to data gathering because of its flexible and person-centered approach. Qualitative evaluation uses an array of observational data collection techniques and methods of analysis to obtain highly textured descriptions of individual, family, and community perspectives (O'Hare, 2005). Some of the techniques for qualitative data gathering include focus group techniques, nominal group methods, in-depth interviews, case studies, and semistructured questionnaires. Although qualitative approaches have been criticized for a variety of reasons—susceptibility to personal bias (Gambrill, 1995), extremely labor intensive and low yield of generalizable results—they do provide for excellent naturalistic analysis and often serve as a guide for developing a more systematic evaluation protocol (O'Hare, 2005). Qualitative approaches are often perceived as more culturally sensitive approaches to data gathering for some ethnic or communities of color who appreciate the relational aspect of information gathering and who may be more put off by the systematic, pen-and-paper evaluation process of quantitative data gathering approaches.

Quantitative Approaches. Two major forms of inquiry for evaluating health promotion outcomes are single-system designs and group designs. In a single-system design, the clinician and client can measure a single clients (or small number of clients) functioning before, during, and after intervention. Group designs use inferential statistics to look at outcomes on larger groups of clients.

Single-Subject Designs. Single subject designs empirically measure client functioning repeatedly over time. Measures are taken in three phases: baseline, treatment, and follow-up. Measures taken at the assessment stage and prior to the intervention are referred to as baseline. Data gathered during the course of the intervention are referred to as treatment-phase data and data collected at the end of treatment is referred to as follow-up.

Single-subject designs provide information about the treatment so that changes may be made and progress monitored. Measures are usually administered repeatedly, usually weekly. Data can be collected by the client, significant others, the practitioner, or a combination of interested individuals. Data are collected systematically through the course of treatment using the same measurement instrument in all phases of the case.

Analysis is often by eyeballing (i.e., visual analysis) or by observing the level, trend, and stability of the data in the different phases with various statistical procedures (Fischer & Corcoran, 2007b). Sattler (1992) recommends matching client style and preferences to the type of assessment tool used, which requires practitioners to have a broad repertoire of quantitative and qualitative assessment tools. In single-subject designs, the goals are to specify the problem, learn its extent and severity, and track the issues throughout the course of the treatment (Jordan & Franklin, 2003). Clinicians can use standardized self-report measures (e.g., Medication Adherence Determinants Questionnaire, or ADQ), self-anchored rating scales ("On a scale of 1 to 10, where one is calm and 10 extreme agitation, please rate daily how you feel about your job") or goal-assessment rating scales ["On a scale of 1 (not much) to 5 (a whole lot), describe how much you practiced mindfulness each day"]. There are three common designs that are easy to import into most health promotion evaluations. The A-B design is the simplest form of single-subject design. This measure simply involves the clinician and client taking a baseline measure of client functioning (A) before and (B) during the intervention. The A-B-A/follow-up design is the continued collection of data after the intervention is discontinued. The A-B-A-B design involves the collection of reliable and valid data using first baseline, initial treatment, second baseline during which treatment is halted, and then the second treatment phase when intervention is reinstated (Thyer & Myers, 2003). Examples of these designs are illustrated in Figure 8.1.

Group Designs. Group designs typically constitute the "gold standard" for conducting efficacy studies. Efficacy studies represent a research design that is tightly controlled, using carefully screened clients who meet certain inclusion criteria and are treated by specially trained clinicians (Thyers & Myers, 2003). Group designs explore relationships among intervention and outcome variables that exist in a number of configurations. For example, the researcher may compare an experimental treatment to standard intervention (i.e., control) or an alternative intervention (i.e., comparison group) to treatment as usual.

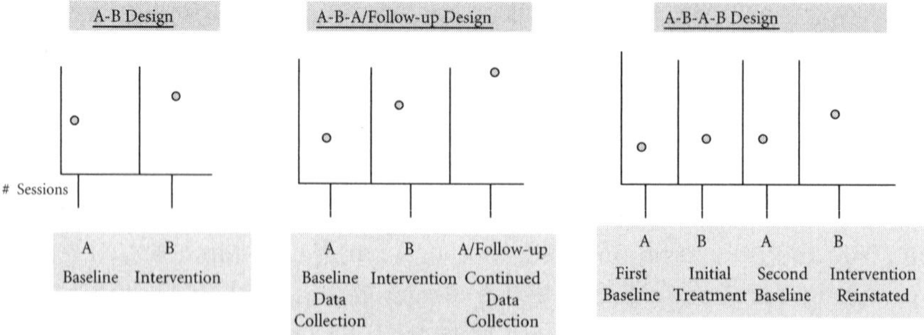

FIGURE 8.1. Examples of single-subject designs for measuring health promotion interventions.

For statistical purposes, the minimum number of clients is 10 or more for each condition (O'Hare, 2005), which is necessary for statistical purposes but may not be generalizable to a population. Unlike single-subject designs, which rely on consecutive measurements taken from one or a few clients, group designs typically rely on a few repetitions of measurement on a larger number of clients. Group designs typically use inferential statistics such as *t*-tests, analysis of variance, or chi square to determine if change has really occurred. Group designs are used in health promotion research—for example, with large numbers of clients (e.g., in a Supported Employment Program that used Workplace Wellness Tool Kits).

Thyer and Myers (2003) provide a thorough review of three types of group designs recommended for health promotion evaluation. These are: *preexperimental (e.g. post-test only and pre-post test)*, *quasi-experimental*, and *experimental.*

Preexperimental Group Research Design. An example of a preexperimental group research design is the posttest-only group design. In this design, a group of clients are formally assessed after they have participated in a health promotion intervention. The design could be labeled X-O, with X representing the exposure to the intervention and O representing a reliable and valid assessment of client functioning.

Case Example: Post test only. A sample of 50 clients could be contacted 6 months after participating in a Wellness Recovery Action Plan (WRAP) workshop. They would fill out questionnaires on well-being, quality of life, medication management skills, and other measures. An example of a questionnaire would be the (medication) Adherence Determinants Questionnaire (ADQ; Dimatteo, et al., 1993).

A slightly more robust example of a preexperimental group design is the O-X-O, where O is the assessment before the intervention, X is the intervention, and O is the assessment again after the health promotion intervention.

Case Example: Pre and Post Test Design. A sample of 25 "students" were identified to be enrolled in the Consumer as Provider Program (described in Chapter 7). Before enrollment in the training program, they completed a rapid assessment instrument on self-efficacy (e.g., Self-Efficacy Scale), (O), then enrolled in the program (X), and then were assessed again just before they "graduated" (O). A simple t -test would be used to determine any change in scores (e.g., higher scores mean greater sense of self-efficacy or competence). Higher scores, indicating a greater sense of self-efficacy, would reflect a health promotion outcome. Although limited in its predictability, the design does provide some preliminary individual and programmatic evaluation data.

Quasi-experimental Group Research Design. Quasi-experimental group research designs typically have some sort of control group (e.g., no treatment or alternative or other treatment). The design is based on the premise that if improvements are seen in the treated group but no improvement is noted in the no-treatment group, there is tentative evidence that the health promotion intervention caused the improvement. The diagram for such a design looks like this: O-X1-O and O-X2-O, where X1 refers to standard program and X2 refers to the standard program plus intensive program; O refers to measure.

Case Example. Fifty family members had contacted NAMI to register for Family-to-Family Psychoeducation classes. An astute mental health worker wanted to see if the new curriculum addition of a health promotion unit (e.g., Unit 8: Health and Wellness for Family Members) was helpful for family members and decided to test this assumption with the new cohort. After much publicizing the event and getting permission from participants, 25 family members were enrolled in the standard family psychoeducation curriculum (X1) and the remaining 25 later enrolled in Family Psychoeducation with an Intensive Session of Family Health and Well-being (X2). The two groups were matched on the basis of equally assigning males and females to each treatment condition (X1 and X2); no random assignment occurred. Measures of family wellness and health (e.g., Perceived Stress Scale) were administered prior to the sessions and then at the end of the 7-week curriculum. Differences in reported stress, well-being, and health were indeed noted for the participants who received the additional specialized health promotion module on family self-care.

Experimental Group Research Design. Considered the gold standard, experimental designs can be quite complex with a number of treatment variations. True experimental designs involve the random assignment of clients to differing conditions. To maintain quality, cases are randomly assigned to three groups: treatment group, treatment as usual, and no treatment. This design could be diagramed thus: R → O X1 O, R → O X2 O, R → O X3 O, where R represents random assignment; O represents measurement or assessment, also known as observation; X1 represents experimental conditions, also known as standard treatment; X2 represents standard treatment with intensive health promotion treatment feature added; and X3 represents control group, also known as a wait list or delayed-treatment group. When client or practitioner factors are controlled for, these are called factorial designs (O'Hare, 2005). Controlled comparisons—where clients are well chosen, researchers well trained, and instruments reliable and valid—provide the most robust of evidence to support the effectiveness of an intervention. Despite the strong rigor of their design, experimental designs have notable limitations for health promotion research. One is generalizing the results to the real world, where people and feelings are anything but controlled. On the positive side, they do provide much higher levels of internal validity, which permit stronger statements about whether the health promotion intervention caused any observable improvements.

Case Example. The community mental health center had just received funding to evaluate a new health promotion intervention called coaching. The method is used as a supplement to existing motivational interviewing (MI) techniques for the integrated treatment program for individuals with dual diagnosis. Wanting to offer the very best in evidence supported interventions, a talented mental health worker in consultation with potential consumer enrollees developed an experimental design. Over a 2-month period, approximately 60 clients were assigned (R), 20 were enrolled in the standard MI (X1) course, another 20 were enrolled in the MI course with coaching (X2), and the third group of 20 were placed on a delayed-treatment list (X3). All three groups were given a rapid assessment instrument: Adult Health Concerns Questionnaire (HCQ). Services were made available to the waitlist in the form of case management contacts so that clients would not be without some support. Scores at the end of the combined intervention (e.g., X2; motivational interviewing with a coaching component) indicated a positive response to recognizing a need to address several health and mental health issues (as identified from the HCQ). There was no change in scores for the delayed-treatment group. Each of these designs is illustrated in Table 8.1.

■ Measurement and Design Issues

There are three key issues to consider when applying any of the above evaluation approaches. These are: snapshot measurements, reliability and validity.

Snapshot Measurement. Snapshot measurements are measures that use quantitative methods (e.g., single-subject designs) to evaluate outcomes. These snapshots, while looking at single points in time, do not take into account the nuances of health promotion interventions that focus on increasing knowledge, improving life and coping skills, creating infrastructure, and garnering human resources (Ebbesen et al., 2004).

Reliability and Validity. Roper and Mays (2000) provide a review of two methodologic issues to be addressed in order to use public health performance measurement processes for scientific inquiry: reliability (which is simply instrumental consistency) and validity (which refers to accuracy of the instrument to ascertain what it is intended to measure). Although the authors focus their discussion primarily on general approaches in public health evaluation efforts, their examples can easily be generalized to issues in health promotion evaluation in mental health practice. The use of reliable and valid instruments to measure health promotion interventions is limited by the lack of a gold standard. For example, validity can be compromised because of the lack of sufficient coverage of the attributes of a variable, such as too few symptoms of depression. Let's put the matter in simple terms.

Reliability. Reliable health promotion measures are those that reflect performance consistently across observations, over time, and between two forms of the same instrument. The instrument must be consistent between items (i.e., internal consistency), over time (i.e., test-retest reliability), between forms (i.e., parallel forms reliability), and between the individuals who may be making the observations (i.e., interrater reliability). Roper and Mays (2000) offer the following recommendations to increase the reliability of health promotion performance measures:

TABLE 8.1. *Examples of Group Designs Used in Health Promotion Research*

Design	Format	Key	Example
Posttest only	X-O	X = exposure to intervention O = measurement of client functioning	X (*Intervention*) *WRAP Workshop* - O (Measure) Medication Adherence Determinants Questionnaire
Pre- & Posttest design	O – X – O	X = intervention O = measure before/after intervention	O (Pretest Measure) Self-Efficacy Scale - X (*Intervention*) *CAP Program* - O (Posttest Measure) Self-Efficacy Scale
Quasi-experimental design	(M) O-X1-O (M) O-X2-O	M = matching X1 = standard program X2 = standard program + intensive component O = measure	(M) (n = 25) O (Pretest Measure) Stress Scale - X1 (*Intervention*) *Family Psychoeducation Group* - O (Posttest Measure) Stress Scale (M) (n = 25) O (Pretest Measure) Perceived Stress Scale - X2 *Intervention Family Psychoeducation Group + Intensive Health Promotion Module* - O (Posttest Measure) Perceived Stress Scale

Experimental	(R) O-X1 – O	R = random assignment to 1 of	(R)	O	X1	O
design	(R)O– X2 – O	3 treatment conditions;	(n = 20)	(Pretest)	*(Intervention)*	(Posttest)
	(R) O-X3-O	X1 = traditional treatment (MI);				
		X2 = traditional treatment (MI)		HCQ	*MI*	HCQ
		+ Intensive Intervention	(R)	O	X2	O
		Coaching – C;	(n = 20)	HCQ	*MI+C*	HCQ
		X3 = Control Group also	(R)	O -	X3	- O
		known as delayed treatment	(n = 20)	HCQ	Control	HCQ
		group – Case Management;			(*Case*	
		O = measurement or assessment			*Management*)	
		Adult Health Concerns				
		Questionnaire (HCQ)				

Key: Interventions are noted by *italics;* measurements are underlined.

1. Provide clear and specific definitions for each measure in order to reduce differences in interpretation.
2. Use detailed reporting requirements that are periodically verified by audit.
3. Survey directly the clients or organizations that are involved in health promotion activities rather than relying on government agency reports or key informants.
4. Implement interrater reliability tests, in which multiple independent raters (including survey participants) review the reports or data.
5. Collect repeated observations of the same measure over time and test for longitudinal consistency.
6. Conduct external audits and direct-observation site visits to confirm the reliability of self-reported measures (pp. 67–76).

The authors caution that, in some cases, health promotion data can be used beyond the purposes of scientific inquiry. For example, if data from health promotion activities are used to allocate resources or enforce contracts, respondents or researchers may face incentives to up-code their reports or findings. To correct for this potential conflict, one strategy is to require respondent compliance with rigorous data collection and reporting standards. The disadvantage of requiring rigorous reporting standards is that they can be perceived by respondents or clinicians as being the antithesis of the wellness and empowerment approaches so prized by health promotion practitioners. A negative perception can, in turn, lead to failure to complete interviews or self-report measures, thereby diminishing the degree of participation and representation of the intended populations.

Validity. Valid measures must be accurate (Fischer & Corcoran, 2007a). In other words, they measure accurately what they intend to measure. Performance measures for health promotion activities can include indicators of structure (e.g., personnel, scope of expertise), process (e.g., types of services and interventions used), and outcomes (e.g., morbidity, community satisfaction, quality of life, risk reduction, healthy lifestyle). Health promotion measures may focus on activities like health education (e.g., Wellness Class), health conditions (e.g., depression due to hypothyroidism), risk factors of interest to mental health systems (e.g., co-occurring disorders such as substance use and mental disorders), as well as specific populations (e.g., Native Americans, who tend to have high rates of diabetes and substance use).

The qualities of a valid health promotion performance measure, according to Roper and Mays (2000) should

1. Reflect a structure, process, or outcome with a large expected impact on health at the individual and/or population level
2. Reflect a process or condition that is substantially within the control or influence of the individuals or organization under study
3. Measure substantial variation—or have the ability to detect meaningful differences in performance—across individuals or organizations over time

4. Be sensitive to the elements of the intervention during the period of observation (p. 71)

Many core health promotion activities are influenced by factors outside the domain of mental health services. Outcomes may be influenced by a variety of nonintervention variables: housing, transportation, medical care, environment, legal, and family influences. Roper and Mays (2000) suggest that when health promotion measures are the dependent variables of interest (e.g., alcohol use), it is recommended to use multivariate methods such as least-squares regression and logistic regression analysis to control for confounding factors. Conversely, when health promotion measures are the independent variables of interest (e.g., does health status predict employment success?), structural equation methods such as instrumental-variables estimation are recommended. This method is used to control for factors that jointly influence health promotion performance and the dependent variable of interest.

■ Challenges of Health Promotion Measurement

Researchers in the field of health promotion evaluation have identified three conceptual challenges to keep in mind in attempting to conduct health promotion evaluation research. These are multiple understandings, time course, and multiple perspectives.

Multiple Understandings. A common challenge among research personnel is making sure that everyone has a consistent understanding of commonly used terms across the project. Often there is a lack of consistent understanding of health promotion terminology by individuals, across settings and organizations. For example, the terms enhanced well-being and quality of life are two goals of health promotion. But for some clients and practitioners, these terms may seem dated and be so overused as to have lost meaning, whereas others may find the terms too lifestyle-oriented and thus restricted for measurement. These multiple understandings of terms have implications in the design and format of measurement tools and data analysis (Ebbersen et al., 2004).

Time Course. Time course for change refers to the need to understand the longitudinal nature of change associated with many health promotion interventions. Many health promotion outcomes do not fit into set time frames and thus may impede the ability of researchers to provide a quick turnaround report on data collected.

Multiple Perspectives. Perspective is a critical challenge in the measurement and evaluation of health promotion performance. In measuring and evaluating health promotion activities, one should ask: From what or whose perspective will this activity be measured? The appropriate perspective for measuring and evaluating health promotion activities will depend on whether the measures are to be used for governmental accountability, quality improvement, scientific inquiry, policy reform, or individual change.

Perspective also determines the unit of observation (e.g., members of a medication education group compared with clients receiving no medical education) and the level of analysis (e.g., single-subject or quasi-experimental).

Roper and Mays (2000) identify three standard audiences or perspectives: *federal and state governmental perspectives, client perspectives,* and *societal perspectives.*

Federal and state governmental perspectives may want health promotion measures that provide outcome data that address accountability for public investment in mental health activities. For example, data derived from the SF 36 (Ware et al., 1994), a measure of the health and mental health status of multiple populations, may be used to justify funding for at-risk populations in need of mental health services. Client perspectives may be concerned with issues of access, affordability, and satisfaction. Health promotion measures for these issues could be in the form of satisfaction surveys. Societal perspectives may focus on the evaluation of health promotion activities in terms of their net effect on social well-being and or the need for policy reform. Measures for these perspectives or concerns could focus on national stigma campaigns.

■ Measures for Health Promotion

In Chapter 7, we reviewed six evidence-based mental health interventions and one promising practice. These were, respectively, illness management and recovery, psychopharmacology practice guidelines, integrated treatment using motivational interviewing, family psychoeducation, peer support, and supported employment; media advocacy is considered a promising practice. In turn, each of these mental health interventions had a corresponding health promotion strategy. These were the wellness recovery action plan, coaching, family-to-family, health and wellness for family members, consumer as provider, workplace health promotion, workplace wellness kit, photovoice, and national stigma campaign.

The following section describes measures for each of these health promotion strategies. Some of the health promotion strategies already have undergone solid empiric testing, and there exists a strong body of support (e.g., wellness recovery action plan), whereas others (e.g., consumer as provider) have preliminary data. The purpose of this review is to offer recommendations of potential measures for health promotion strategies.

Evaluating health promotion outcomes must involve two fundamental prerequisites: (1) the provider must have practical, reliable, inexpensive, and valid outcome measures that can be used to evaluate results and (2) it must be possible to administer the outcome measure at a minimum of two or more occasions (Thyer & Myers; 2003, p. 387). Five quantitative measures are described that meet these prerequisites: the Adherence Determinants Questionnaire, Adult Health Concerns Questionnaire, Perceived Stress Scale, Self-Efficacy Scale, and Organizational Climate Scale. Empowerment evaluation uses a qualitative evaluation approach that incorporates community organizing strategies. Each of these measures, along with recommendations for closely related measures, are described briefly in the next section. See Table 8.2.

TABLE 8.2. *Measures for Health Promotion Strategies*

Health Promotion Strategy	Recommended Measures
• Wellness Recovery Action Plan (WRAP)	(Medication) Adherence Determinants Questionnaire (ADQ; DiMatteo, et al, 1993)
• Coaching	Adult Health Questionnaire (HCQ; Spoth & Dush, 1988)
• Family Psychoeducation: Health and Wellness for Family Members Module	Perceived Stress Scale (PSS; Cohen & Williamson, 1988)
• Consumer As Provider (CAP)	Self-Efficacy Scale (SES: Sherer, Maddux, & Mercandante, 1982)
• Workplace Health Promotion: Working Well Tool Kit	Organizational Climate Scale (OCS; Thompson & McCubbin, 1996)
• PhotoVoice • National Stigma and Awareness Campaign	Empowerment Evaluation (EE; Israel, Checkoway, Schulz, & Zimmerman, 1994)

■ Overview of Strategies

Wellness Recovery and Action Plan (WRAP)

Medications are an important element of illness self-management programs, such as WRAP. A core goal of the WRAP program is for individuals with mental health conditions, using self-designed tool kits, to acquire new information and skills to better manage troublesome symptoms associated with medications (Copeland, 2002). Previous evaluation efforts of WRAP done by the Vermont Recovery Education Project (www.mentalhealthrecovery.com) have focused on the following outcome measures: ability to create crisis plan, knowledge of early warning signs of psychosis, recognition of prodromal symptoms, use of wellness tools in daily routines, and sense of hope for recovery and self-advocacy. An additional measure considered was voluntary adherence to medication programs or regimes. The concept of patient nonadherence to medication treatment has been identified as a widespread phenomenon in both the health and mental health fields, with prevalence rates that range up to 93% for some patient groups. Medication usage, unless monitored properly, can have life-threatening consequences. WRAP incorporates this concern into its program design and thus can easily be considered a health promotion outcome measure.

Health Promotion Measure: The Adherence Determinants Questionnaire

The Adherence Determinants Questionnaire (ADQ) (DiMatteo, et al., 1993) is a 38-item questionnaire designed to assess seven aspects of patient adherence to medication regimes.

These seven aspects are presented as subscales and consist of interpersonal aspects of care, perceived utility (benefits/costs and efficacy), perceived severity, perceived susceptibility, subjective norms, intentions and supports, and barriers. It has been normed with clinical samples (n = 316) consisting of patients who were members of different medical treatment programs (e.g., rehabilitation program, head and neck cancer study program, low-fat diet program). The ADQ has fair internal consistency, with alphas that range from 0.63 to 0.94; validity is reported as fair to good as determined by evaluations of the subscales in regression analysis. Responses are scored using a 1-to-5 Likert scale, with categories ranging from 1 (strongly disagree) to 5 (strongly agree). A typical question is: " Sometimes the doctors and other health professionals use medical terms without explaining what they mean." Although originally designed to assess cancer-control regimes, the ADQ is equally appropriate to administer to clients who are receiving medications for psychiatric and physical health problems. It can be used as a self-report measure in a single-subject design.

Additional Measures. Other measures that are more broadly related to health and mental health and could be used with WRAP are the following:

- Health Survey Short Forms (SF-12) (Ware, 1996)
- Multidimensional Desire for Control Scales (MCDS) (Andersonet al., 1989)
- Health Promoting Lifestyle Profile (HPLP) (Walker et al., 1987)

Coaching

Individuals who are experiencing substance use issues may initially respond better to approaches like coaching, whereby they can get professional help without seeking expensive and often limited medical and psychiatric care. A core goal of coaching, a derivative of motivational interviewing, is to help individuals establish and maintain health-promoting goals through the use of prompts and specific interventions. Previous evaluation efforts of coaching have focused on behavior change related to smoking cessation, with the most effective intervention consisting of provider prompting using individually tailored printed materials.

An additional measure to consider for coaching would be the use of a biopsychosocial symptom checklist that identifies a host of health and mental health related concerns. Research by Drake and colleagues (2003a) notes that some individuals who are demoralized or symptomatic may believe that their substance use is actually helping them more than medications. Coaching would incorporate this perspective into its approach without challenging it while at the same time offering information, education, and support as a means for the individual to determine his or her readiness to change. This approach can begin with the use of a measurement tool designed to assess a variety of symptoms.

Health Promotion Measure: Adult Health Concerns Questionnaire (HCQ)

The Adult Health Concerns Questionnaire (HCQ) (Spoth & Dush, 1988) is a 55-item symptom checklist designed to assess multiple domains related to health, mental health, and psychosocial issues. The HCQ has a two-level response format. First, the respondent underlines any concern that apply to him or her and then rates the underlined items on a 5-point Likert scale regarding severity or distress. The HCQ has been normed with a variety of populations: college students (n = 15), pain clinic patients (n = 32), psychology outpatients (n = 82), and inpatient and outpatients of a private hospital (n = 167). Although actual norms are not presented, means for the most frequently (0.95 to 1.90) and 10 least frequently (0.09 to 0.35) checked items were reported. The HCQ has fair concurrent validity, with several scales of the Minnesota Multiphasic Personality Inventory (MMPI) being correlated with both number of items complete on the HCQ and the total distress score. Distress responses range from 1 = mildly distressing to 5 = severely distressing. Examples of checklist items include marital distress, problems at work/school, upset stomach, too many drugs, and legal problems. Although originally designed to measure psychiatric symptoms, the HCQ is equally appropriate to administer to individuals to begin the conversation about their perspective of their issues and what information they would like the "coach" to offer them. This measure can be used as a self-report measure in a single-subject design.

Additional Measures. Other measures that could be used to support the evaluation of coaching efforts are the following:

- Client Motivation for Therapy Scale (CMOTS) (Pelletier et al., 1997)
- Multidimensional Health Locus of Control Scales (MHLC) (Wallston et al., 1978)

Family Psychoeducation: Health and Wellness for Family Members Module—Family-to-Family Education Program

Good mental health and physical health are important goals for any person, but they become particularly salient to the caregiver of a person with mental illness. A core goal of a health and wellness for family members module is to teach family members to recognize and attend to their own physical health and wellness. Previous evaluation efforts (Dixon et al., 2003) of the traditional family-to-family program have focused on the following outcome measures: subjective and objective illness burden, empowerment, and depression. Favorable results were found in all categories of psychological and social support immediately after the training and 6 months later. For future evaluation efforts, it is recommended to add in health and wellness content specific to the caregiver in order to address underlying health issues that are the consequence of exposure to stressful conditions or events—like caring for an ill relative. It is well documented in the research literature that a global perception of stressful events, when appraised as threatening or demanding, can increase risk of health problems. By adding in an educational component on health, wellness, and well-being, a family psychoeducation program can take on an added health promotion perspective to address this concern.

Health Promotion Measure: Perceived Stress Scale (PSS)

The Perceived Stress Scale (PSS) (Cohen & Williamson, 1988) is a 10-item instrument designed to measure the degree to which one's life is appraised as stressful. The PSS provides information about the processes through which stressful events influence the stress–illness relationship and health (Fischer & Corcoran, 2007a). The instrument has been normed with a national probability sample of 2388 respondents, which was compared to the census data for the entire United States. The overall mean for the PSS was 13.02 (SD = 6.35); the mean for males as 12.1 (SD = 5.9) and for females 13.7 (SD = 6.6), with higher scores indicating greater levels of perceived stress. The PSS has good internal consistency, with an alpha of 0.78 and good construct validity. Responses are scored using a 0-to-4 Likert scale, with categories ranging from 0 = never to 4 = very often. A typical question is: "In the last month, how often have you felt nervous and stressed?" Given that the frequency of physical illness and symptoms of physical illness are positively related to reports of stress, this measure has particular utility for caregivers of people with mental illness.

Additional Measures. Other health promotion measures closely related to caregiver health and wellness concerns are:

- Family Adaptability and Cohesion Evaluation Scale (FACES-III) (Olson, 1986)
- Family Assessment Device (FAD) (Epstein at al., 1983)
- Family Attachment and Changeability Index 8 (FACI-8) (McCubbin et al., 1996)
- Family Crisis Oriented Personal Evaluation Scales (F-COPES) (McCubbin et al., 1991)

Consumer as Provider (CAP)

Self-efficacy, defined as the individual's belief that he or she has the psychological, biological, cognitive, and social capacity to execute a desired behavior, has been shown to moderate the effects of depression and coping responses for persons with severe and persistent mental health conditions (Fischer & Corcoran, 2007). Given that the expectation of being efficacious is related to social skills and competence—both of which are needed to participate in an educational program such as CAP—enhanced self-efficacy is generally considered to be a valuable outcome. Although the ultimate goal of CAP is to increase the employability of consumer participants through a college-based training program, evaluation efforts to date have concentrated on vocational and educational status (McDiarmid et al., 2005). An additional measure to consider is self-efficacy as a subjective measurement.

Health Promotion Measure: Self-Efficacy Scale

The Self-Efficacy Scale (SES) (Sherer et al., 1982) is a 30-item instrument designed to measure general expectations of self-efficacy. The instrument is useful as an index of progress, since expectations of self-efficacy should change during the course of intervention. The SES consists of two subscales, general self-efficacy and social self-efficacy. It has been normed on two populations: undergraduate psychology students (n = 376) and inpatients from a Veterans Administration alcohol treatment unit (n = 150). The SES has fairly good internal consistency, with an alpha of 0.86 for the general subscale and 0.71 for the social subscale. The SES has good criterion-related validity by accurately predicting that people with higher self-efficacy will have greater success in vocational, educational, and monetary goals than those who score low in self-efficacy. Responses are scored using five categories: A = disagree strongly to E = agree strongly. A typical question is: "When I make plans, I am certain I can make them work." This instrument is adaptable for individual or group measures of health promoting interventions, such as CAP.

Additional measures that are closely related to consumer education and self-efficacy are:

- Social Support Behaviors Scale (SSB); Vaux, Riedel & Stewart, 1987)
- Self-Efficacy Scale for Schizophrenia (SESS) (McDermott, 1995)
- Self-Esteem Rating Scale (SERS) (Nugent & Thomas, 1993)

Workplace Health Promotion: Working Well Tool Kit

When it comes to the health and wellness of newly hired employees who have mental health conditions, worker wellness programs would seem to offer a perfect complement to a holistic health promotion approach. Not only are wellness programs like the Working Well Tool Kit a "normal" part of worker or employee life, they are focused on health management, which is a critical part of clinical treatment. A core goal of the Working Well Tool Kit is to serve as a resource for enhancing organizational and personal well-being and success. Traditional types of worker wellness programs offer the following components: exercise and physical fitness, smoking control, stress management, back care, nutrition, high blood pressure, weight control, off-the-job accidents, job hazards/injury prevention, substance abuse, AIDS education, cholesterol, mental health, cancer detection/prevention, medical self care, STDs and prenatal education (Linnan et al., 2006). What makes the Working Well Tool Kit distinguishable from traditional programs and gives it a health promoting perspective is that it is driven by employees' and employers' desires to obtain practical, helpful tools that will foster workplace productivity and work environments based on respect, communication, and participation. These are illustrated in the curriculum topics (e.g., mentally healthy workplaces, working well together). Although as the authors note, evaluation efforts of the tool kit have been minimal. One measure that can more directly evaluate the impact of Working Well Tool Kit is the measure of organizational climate.

Health Promotion Measure: Organizational Climate Scale

The Organizational Climate Scale (OCS) (Thompson & McCubbin, 1996) is a 30-item questionnaire designed to measure the problem-solving and communication patterns of individuals in the workplace who are sensitive to organizational change (Fischer & Corcoran, 2007a). The OCS has two problem-solving and two organizational communication subscales. These address four dimensions: challenges, control, conflict, and support. The challenge factor examines the organization's emphasis on working together to solve problems, plan and define difficulties as challenges. The control dimension characterizes problem solving with the organization's emphasis on an internal locus of control, having a shared belief that problem solving is within the employees' and the organization's control and abilities. The conflictual communications dimension assesses the degree to which the organization emphasizes confrontation, embarrassment, becoming strained and ultimately making issues more incendiary. The supportive communication dimension focuses on the degree to which the organization emphasizes respect, sensitivity, affirmation, listening and seeking of positive conclusions.

The OCS was normed with a sample of employees from a large insurance company (n = 1346). The OCS has very good internal consistency, with alphas of 0.82, 0.83, 0.87, and 0.89 for challenge, control, conflictual communication, and supportive communication. The OCS reports excellent stability, with 1-year test-retest correlations that range from 0.49 to 0.68 (Fischer & Corcoran, 2007). The OCS has good concurrent validity as established through significant correlations among all subscales. Responses are scored with categories that range from 0 = false, 1 = mostly false, 2 = mostly true and 3 = true. A typical item is: "We work hard to be sure colleagues/coworkers are not offended or hurt emotionally." This measure is one of the few organizational evaluation measures that focuses on dimensions considered important to health promotion efforts: worker input, bottom-up approach to problem solving, and a positive work force climate.

Another health promotion indicator closely related to work-related wellness or illness behaviors is the Illness Behavior Inventory (IBI) (Turkat & Pettegrew, 1983).

■ Empowerment Evaluation: A Community Organizing Approach

Photovoice and the National Stigma Awareness Campaign

As discussed in Chapter 7, two health promotion approaches have proved strategic in the public campaign to reduce stigma and discrimination towards individuals with mental illness: Photovoice and the National Stigma Awareness Campaign. Both have in common the following elements: empowerment and education oriented, use of media (e.g., news, film, photography; journalists), community organizing activities; unfortunately, neither has been subject to rigorous evaluation.

Photovoice is a media approach to social change and a core component of health promotion (see Wallack in IOM, 2001). Using photography as a means to promote social change (i.e., reduce stigma), two central goals of Photovoice are to increase the participation of marginalized groups (i.e., mental health consumers) in the political process and increase understanding of local issues and concerns through the perspectives of affected groups of people (e.g., homeless individuals who have a mental illness).

The National Stigma Awareness Campaign is a national campaign organized through the New Zealand Ministry of Health. The project is entitled "Project to Counter Stigma and Discrimination Associated with Mental Illness." A central goal of this national plan is to use the mass media, community education and other means to improve the social inclusion of people who experience mental illness (O'Hagan, 2003). The project aims to approach these goals at two levels: national and regional. At the national level, activities will include working with highly visible journalists, journalism schools, and various media outlets. At the regional level, activities will include local involvement with media while developing community education approaches and local responses to inaccurate or stigmatizing reporting.

Health Promotion Measure: Empowerment Evaluation

So how does one evaluate large-scale community and national initiatives that use an empowerment orientation such as these two health promotion strategies? Israel and colleagues (1994) point out that while there are several quantitative and qualitative measures applicable to evaluating community-based health promotion interventions that use an empowerment approach, only one is truly designed for assessing the multilevel concept of community empowerment: empowerment evaluation.

Unlike the other evaluation instruments described in this chapter, which are typically self-reported rapid assessment instruments, empowerment evaluation is a multistage, community-based evaluation approach. For example, specific empowerment-oriented approaches used to collect information for antistigma campaigns and the Photovoice approach are personal interviews, surveys, public presentations, advertising, videotaped documentation of the perceptions of local leaders after viewing Photovoice presentations, focus groups, community mapping of housing and neighborhoods, and community forums.

Community empowerment evaluation ideally would use methods for assessing the extent to which community empowerment exists in a specific community and then document its development and change over time (Israel et al., 1994). Minkler (1999) describes this approach as "an interactive process through which individuals (e.g., residents of a local homeless shelter) work with a support team (e.g., county commissioners, case managers and media personnel) in identifying their concerns (e.g., lack of affordable housing for people with mental health disabilities), determining how to address them (e.g., public awareness using photodocumentary), measuring their progress toward the goals they have set (e.g., present at city council meetings), and using information gained to increase the viability and success of their efforts" (p. 289).

Although initially developed for evaluating specific programs and community based initiatives (Coombe, 1999), this approach can be used by self-identified groups (e.g., consumers of mental health services) to determine, design and own their intervention and evaluation efforts. Coombe (1999) articulately describes three principles that under gird the use of an empowerment evaluation approach:

- Principle 1. Authority over and execution of research is a democratic process that is shared between community participants and professional groups who are assisting.
- Principle 2. The process of evaluation is incorporated into the continual planning, action, and feedback of the participants to the targeted community.
- Principle 3. The ultimate goal is to help community participants use self-evaluation and research to effectively impart their message.

In empowerment evaluation, participants determine what kinds of issues are investigated and how this information is delivered back to the community, whether it's through the use of photodocumentary techniques (i.e., Photovoice) or national initiatives in which consumers work with national media networks to change the media presentations of people who have mental illness. This approach is one of both process and outcome. The process includes participating in the steps; the outcome is determined by the achievement of the process steps and review of the original goal. Empowerment evaluation is a form of participatory research, which, in itself, is a health promotion research approach that emphasizes community and individual empowerment by involving community members in the research process.

Steps of Empowerment Evaluation

Coombe (1999) describes six steps of empowerment evaluation. See Figure 8.2 for an illustration of these steps.

- *Step 1: Assess the community's concerns and resources.* With the assistance of a support team (e.g., case managers and community consultants) participants determine where they are now, how their organizing efforts stand and thoughts about ideas for future progress (i.e., mission). Methods include focus groups, interviews, surveys, community/agency meetings, and community mapping.
- *Step 2: Set the mission and how the objectives will be achieved.* This step defines what people want to accomplish. Efforts are made to ensure that mission is consistent with current local needs (e.g., housing shortage), criteria for evaluation is established (e.g., expected results, establishing intermediate and long-term outcomes), strategies for assessing performance. Methods include brainstorming sessions and prioritizing of agreed upon goals.
- *Step 3: Develop strategies and action plans.* Participants, in consultation with their support team, develop the strategies for achieving their goals; in this case the strategy selected is Photovoice. This step requires concrete planning in terms of who will do what and when. Methods used are typically small group strategy meetings.

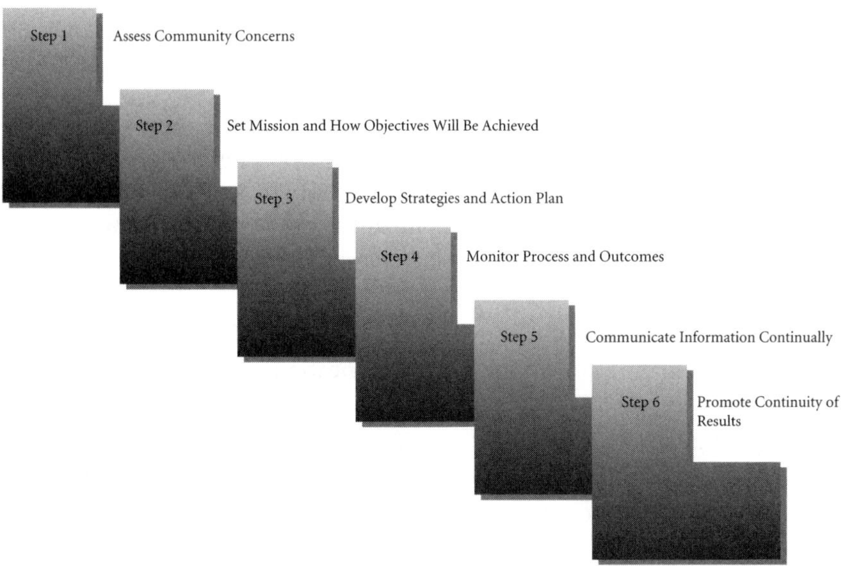

FIGURE 8.2. Steps for empowerment evaluation. Adapted from Coombe, C. (1999). Using empowerment in community organizing and community-based health initiatives. In M. Minkler (Ed.) *Community organizing and community building for health*, pp.291-307. New Brunswick, NJ: Rutgers University Press.

- *Step 4: Monitor process and outcomes.* This step requires the group to define the measures, collect the data and interpret the findings. Documentation methods include the use of portfolios, interviews, media spots.
- *Step 5: Communicate information and findings to relevant audiences as they emerge.* This step poses the question: who needs to be notified along the way? A unique component of this step is that participants are encouraged to provide ongoing feedback to community members about findings—unlike traditional approaches to community evaluation, which may involve a report submitted months or years later. Methods for this step include attending community meetings, writing newsletter articles, obtaining media coverage, and making presentations at local neighborhood or professional associations.
- *Step 6: Promote continuity of results.* This step is modified from the original outline by Coombe (1999s) which states: "Promote Adaptation, Renewal and Institutionalization." It seems reasonable to suggest that a final step for participants is to reflect on their accomplishments while at the same time determining a strategy for how the project results can continue to live in the minds of the targeted audience. In other words, how can the projects impact achieve sustainability? Methods for this step include combination planning meetings of targeted audience members, participants, and support team members to problem-solve identified issues.

Limitations and Benefits of Empowerment Evaluation

By following these guidelines, it is assumed that participants will have achieved their initial goal of increasing public awareness of a housing shortage for people with mental health disabilities who are now homeless. However, as Coombe (1999) points out, empowerment evaluation has many limitations: it is a vague concept, little is understood about the relationship between individual and community empowerment, and it is difficult to attribute empowerment outcomes to specific interventions—as in the example of Photovoice.

Despite these limitations, there are numerous benefits: the step-by-step process for empowerment evaluation is a useful guide in delineating a blue print for mental health clients who wish to participate in activities that promote community awareness and social change, it builds individual and community competence through opportunities for collaboration of citizens, community planners, and recipients of mental health services and homeless shelters. Finally, when empowerment evaluation is used to assess a national or community-oriented approach that is consumer-driven, health promotion strategy, it can reveal important findings that could be overlooked by conventional evaluation methods (Coombe, 1999).

■ Recommendations

In leaving this chapter, there are a number of recommendations for building a future for health promotion evaluation in mental health practice. This is not an exhaustive list but rather just a few suggestions. These are:

Ensure Culturally Competent Evaluation. In evaluating the success of a health promotion intervention for consumers and families from diverse cultural groups, Siegel and colleagues (2005) suggest that the results need to be judged in terms of culture-specific outcomes and usual outcomes (Siegel et al., 2005). Cruz and Spence (2005) describe four criteria that Oregon tribal communities use to evaluate the efficacy of treatment programs: cultural validated, cultural replicated, science validated, and science replicated. An example of one program that is used among several tribes and meets all four evaluation criteria is the "Parents Who Care." This is an evidence-based parenting curriculum for parents/caregivers of Indian children that teach protective factors, setting guidelines, refusal skills, anger management and governance. Evaluation measures are considered culturally relevant and endorsed by the tribal community.

Build Trust across Diverse Groups. Building trust refers to the importance of building a trusting relationship between researchers and organizational or community representatives in order to ensure high-quality data. Often health promotion strategies used in mental health practice settings will be new and may be be perceived as unconventional, providing information that is considered sensitive to personnel or organizational issues. As Ebbesen and colleagues (2004) note, if a trusting relationship is established between researchers, participants, and staff, then potential areas of participants or organizational resistance can be minimized.

Conduct Empirically Based Evaluation. As Thyer and Myers (2003) note, if providers anticipate that health promotion strategies are to affect individual and family functioning in meaningful ways, then it is critical to conduct efficacy and effectiveness studies. Efficacy studies are tightly designed experimental investigations, usually using carefully screened clients meeting certain inclusion criteria; specifically trained therapists offer interventions delivered in accordance with a treatment manual or other structured protocol and with repeated administration of reliable and valid outcome measures. Effectiveness studies are investigations that attempt to replicate the positive findings obtained through prior efficacy studies in practice contexts that are most similar to real-world settings (p. 386).

Thyer and Myers (2003) recommend the following evaluation principles, humorously referred to as Thyer's axioms:

- Axiom 1: If something exists (e.g., a client need, strength, or problem), it is potentially measurable.
- Axiom 2: If you measure client functioning, you are in a better position to treat client functioning.
- Axiom 3: If you treat and measure client functioning, you are in a better position to evaluate clinical outcomes (p. 388).

Measure the Community within Its Environment. Given the growing attention to the effects of a spectrum of environmental determinants on health (e.g., access to health care, outdoor green spaces, transportation) and mental health (e.g., access to mental health care, safe housing), local communities are likely to become more important in health promotion research and evaluation. This represents another opportunity for mental health professionals and researchers to collaborate in developing evaluation measures and efforts that will have a significant effect on the well-being and health of individuals who experience mental health conditions while living in communities.

Use of the Multimethod Approach for Evaluation. The health and mental health status of individuals and communities in the context of health promotion must be studied using a variety of methods. For example, combinations of quantitative (e.g., single-subject designs that use self-report measures) and qualitative methods (e.g., empowerment evaluation) are fruitful approaches for illuminating the complex experiences of people with mental health conditions and the communities in which they live. When decisions about people's lives are based on data points obtained through objective, quantitative measures (e.g., like whether an individual scores high on a suicide risk assessment and thus the decision is made to hospitalize), having subjective, qualitative data (e.g., empowerment assessment) becomes even more important.

As Labonte (1996) argues, there remains a practical need for seeking more generalizable measures of health promotion. But in the same sense, what makes generalizability practical for specific community groups? A take-away point is that without a qualitative dialogue, quantitative measures would lack any meaning or relevance to the group engaged in the empowerment project (Labonte, 1996, p. 140).

Evaluate the Economic Costs of Health Promoting Activities. Health-related costs are increasingly being used to evaluate the cost-effectiveness of health promotion interventions for mental health problems. Anderson (2004) states that key goals of health promotion research and evaluation is to understand the effects of change in health (e.g., lowered blood pressure) and mental health status (e.g., depression) and on changes in important health-related cost outcomes (e.g., health care utilization and lost work days). He argues that in order to evaluate health promotion activities, we need to understand the relationship between health risks and health-related costs. Yet determining the relationship between health risks and health care costs is a challenge that health-promotion researchers and evaluators have not quite mastered. Anderson recommends that in order for individual- or community-oriented health promotion activities to be properly evaluated with the rigor afforded evaluation efforts in the medical field, interventions must demonstrate that they reduce modifiable risk factors (e.g., stress, smoking, alcohol use). By reducing modifiable risk factors, it is presumed that a chain reaction occurs whereby health is improved, which leads to reduced health care costs and improves productivity-related outcomes and quality of life.

One way to demonstrate a change is through the use of evaluation techniques, such as self-report instruments that use single-subject design measures. It is worth restating here that not all risk factors are within the control of the individual and thus amenable to change and measurement. Poverty, racism, stigma, and unsafe housing are all risk factors that contribute to increased health care costs and should not be viewed as amenable to individual efforts of change.

■ Conclusion

Use of the scientific method for evaluating health promotion strategies has lagged behind comparable efforts in mental health and other fields of practice. Consequently, mental health providers who utilize health promotion strategies have few truly evidence-based tools and guidelines available to evaluate outcomes. Further, most behavioral health care organizations have limited ability to demonstrate accountability for public funds and to allocate scarce mental health resources for research and program evaluation using reliable and objective decision criteria. In a review of the literature, Perrin (1998) found that what is measured often bears little resemblance to what is relevant. Often the very goals measured have nothing to do with what is deemed valuable by the participants but rather reflect what the social scientists know how to measure. In order to generate accountability, researchers often build monitoring systems that can be time-consuming, requiring extra training and expense that may not be justified by the benefits of the expected results.

Ideally, health promotion strategies should be linked to changes in health and mental health outcomes. The difficulty in measuring these outcomes occurs when a number of system influences (e.g., institutions, providers, community partners) all contribute to the overall health status of the individuals, families, and communities.

If the field of health promotion is to advance its status through a science base, it must be able to demonstrate, "with legitimate data that are credible to others" (Thyer & Myer, 2003, p. 386), that its strategies are genuinely capable of helping the individuals, families, and communities served. Roper and Mays (2000) offer the argument that research can advance the accumulation of scientific knowledge and enhance the production of information to build the knowledge base of evidence-based practice for health promotion. The research and evaluation of health promotion strategies will become increasingly important as consumers and communities call for more involvement in the very evaluation efforts that are meant to be used with them. So rather than designing health promotion evaluation efforts *for* individuals with mental health needs, why not design *with* them. Or as Mme. du Deffand (1697–1780) reminds us, "The distance is nothing; it is only the first step that is difficult."

In Our Own Words . . . Family and Consumer Perspectives on Mental Health Treatment Services: Focus Group Feedback

Topic: Evaluating Mental Health Treatment Outcomes

Summary

As Chapter 8 illustrates, evaluation is a collaborative process between clinicians and clients that establishes whether change has occurred and had the intended effects. Staying with this theme, consumers and family members were asked to describe the kinds of information that interventions, services, or programs should use for the purpose of evaluation. Both family members and consumers agreed that the very act of participation in a real manner, not token, is an important aspect of agency evaluation efforts. Family members identified three strategies: use of computer technology to track data, changes in levels of client functioning, and family input. Consumers felt that evaluation should also incorporate how successful an organization was on achieving the goal of client "choice." Another critical evaluation component was how well the agency provided services for diverse populations.

What Can We Learn?

Based on family and consumer preferences, agencies can provide consumer and family centered evaluation efforts by first ensuring that agency philosophy and services reflect the values of choice, diversity and authentic participation; followed by practical aspects of integrating computer technology into the tracking of client health and functioning status.

The following section reveals these perspectives in more detail.

Focus Group Question: *" What kinds of information do you think are important for the evaluation of mental health interventions, services, or programs?"*

Family Perspectives

Core Themes	Summary of Experiences	Comments
(Ranked in order of priority)		
First—Family input into program performance	Family members stressed that programs should be evaluated using family member input	"I am afraid to speak up if I don't think things are going well; there is no impartial mechanism for evaluating progress—so if a family member

Focus Group Question: *"What kinds of information do you think are important for the evaluation of mental health interventions, services, or programs?" (continued)*

		thinks things are not going well, it becomes my word against the case workers." (J., *parent*)
Second—Clients level of stability and daily living skills	Interventions should be based on data derived from functional outcomes evaluation—like hospitalization, livability and community stability.	"All interventions should have some practical outcome measures—the things that influence day to day successes or struggles." (S., *spouse*)
Third—Use of computer technology	The only way to achieve the above two evaluation strategies is to have capable computer technology systems that permit programmatic & clinical evaluation data to be collected.	"My daughter worked with one case manager for two years. She was finally stable on meds and everything was great. Now, here comes along a new doctor, doesn't look at history of care, changes the meds, adds Prozac, and then she started to go out of control again. If only they had had a system for monitoring her progress and tracking her care, this would not have happened." (M., *parent*)

Consumer Perspectives

Core Themes	Summary of Experiences	Comments
(Ranked in order of priority)		
First—Participation	Consumers approached this question differently than family members by suggesting that participation should be incorporated into all aspects of program, service and intervention evaluation. Agencies should be evaluated on how clients participate in developing their own treatment plan and participate in the governance of the organization.	"If clients are truly participating in services, then their health would be better and this would be your outcome." (J.V.S, *consumer*)

(continued)

Focus Group Question: *"What kinds of information do you think are important for the evaluation of mental health interventions, services, or programs?" (continued)*

Second—Choice	Agencies need to examine the philosophy of their program—did choice really exist or were sanctions imposed against clients—like termination—if they didn't go along with the program or take their meds.	"If clients are involved in a political action or policy making group, like a board, they can support the philosophy—but they need to be heard and respected. This allows an honest evaluation of what is happening." (J.V.S., *consumer*)
Third—Diversity	All services should be evaluated on the basis of commitment to diversity, which includes racial, sexual minorities, spiritual beliefs, and acceptance of culturally specific beliefs and norms.	"I look around the agency to see if they have resources that will help me access my LGBT community." (R., *consumer*)

PART IV

SPECIAL POPULATIONS

9. Health Promotion Strategies for Women with Comorbid Health and Mental Health Conditions

It's important that care integrates physical well-being with psychological well-being—we are one being, you know?

—*R., consumer*

■ Chapter Overview

In the last decade, there has been increased recognition of the link between mental health conditions and physical disorders—a relationship known as comorbidity. This nexus has had particular implications for women diagnosed with a psychiatric illness and receiving public sector mental health services. This chapter begins by defining and illustrating the terms *morbidity* and *comorbidity*, followed by a review of four core health- related concerns that women with psychiatric conditions present to mental health providers. They include psychosocial/personal history, medication-induced weight gain, pregnancy, and substance use. Next, the chapter describes four health promotion strategies (e.g., intentional recovery community, fitness program, health education, and gender-specific treatment groups) and model programs. The remainder of the chapter reviews barriers to the implementation of strategies (e.g., fiscal, clinical, and training) and provides recommendations for organizational shift to a health promotion philosophy. The chapter concludes with a summary of a focus group discussion held by consumers and family members who were asked the following question: "How can the mental health system improve your and your family members' health needs?"

Learning Objectives

When you have finished reading this chapter, you should be able to:

1. Define and describe examples of morbid and comorbid health and mental health conditions
2. Identify core health related concerns that women with mental health conditions present to providers
3. Apply health promotion strategies to these conditions
4. Describe barriers and recommendations associated with integrating health promotion strategies into mental health services

5. Identify core themes and concerns expressed by consumers and family members when asked to describe activities that mental health providers could do to assist with their health concerns

■ Introduction

Although both men and women with mental illness face medical challenges greater than those individuals without mental illness (Goldman, 1999, 2000; Perese & Perese, 2003), it appears that women have unique experiences, risks, and needs that must be considered when a clinician and client develop treatment strategies. For example, women who experience severe and persistent mental illness suffer from increased rates of multiple or comorbid medical problems due to history of trauma (e.g., sexual abuse, domestic violence), barriers to treatment of physical illness (e.g., poverty, lack of insurance, misdiagnosis or underdiagnosis), lifestyle choices (e.g., high smoking prevalence and substance misuse), effects of medications (e.g., obesity and diabetes mellitus related to certain psychiatric medications), and consequences of the illness itself (e.g., neglect of personal care). Additionally, quality of life and indices of psychopathology are both adversely affected by the burden of medical illness (Dickerson *et al.*, 2002; Brady, 1989; Dixon *et al.*, 1999; Meyer & Nasrallah, 2003; Cook, 1998).

From the service delivery end, mental health clinicians are experiencing an unprecedented increase in complex psychiatric cases in which women with serious medical, substance use, and social issues challenge the effectiveness of traditional, office-based approaches to mental health care. As a consequence of these multiple issues, clinicians and women clients are beginning to explore intervention strategies that embrace notions of wellness, partnership, quality of life, and recovery. Health promotion is one such strategy for addressing the link between these social issues and medical and psychiatric comorbidity. But first, what is meant by the term *comorbidity?*

■ Defining the Terms

Generally speaking, awareness of the medical morbidities seen in mental health populations is a vital step toward both intervention in the disease process and advocacy for greater access to necessary services for this medically underserved population (Meyer & Nasarallah, 2003). As previously discussed in Chapters 1 and 7, many terms have been used in the fields of health promotion and mental health to describe individuals who present with multiple health conditions and mental health disorders, including substance use. Some of these terms represent attempts to identify which problem or disorder is seen as more primary or severe, determine funding priorities, and/or target specific treatment interventions (DHHS, 2005). For purposes of our discussion, let's distinguish two commonly used terms when discussing health and mental health symptoms: *morbidity* and *comorbidity*.

The term *morbidity* is considered one of the classic indicators of health problems and generally refers to any disease, illness, or injury that is any departure, subjective or objective, from a state of physiologic or psychological well-being (Green & Kreuter, 1999). It can be measured in three units: (1) persons who are newly ill (e.g., incidence), (2) the illnesses themselves that these persons experienced (e.g., hypothyroidism or depression), and (3) duration of days, weeks, months, or years of continuing or surviving cases or people with the illness at a particular point in time (e.g., prevalence).

The term *comorbid* is defined as the presence of any coexisting condition (e.g., mental, physical, or substance use–related) in a patient/client with an index or primary disorder or disease (Kanzler & Rosenthal, 2003). Depending on whether the clinical setting is primary care or a mental health program, the term *comorbid* may be used to describe either a *comorbid psychiatric condition* or a *comorbid medical illness*.

When a person is said to have a *comorbid psychiatric condition*, this generally refers to a medically ill person who is also experiencing a co-occurring psychiatric disorder. One example of a comorbid psychiatric condition is depression secondary to coronary heart disease. In this case, a comorbid psychiatric illness of depression in a cardiac patient is often associated with increased frequency and severity of medical symptoms, along with the additive impairment in social and vocational functioning, increased health care costs and increased risk for mortality (Dwight & Stoudemire, 1997). An important point to remember is that whenever the clinician determines that the mental health diagnosis is related to a general medical condition, the health condition is coded on Axis III—General Medical Conditions of the DSM-IV-TR's diagnostic categories (APA, 2000). For example, when a mental disorder significantly affects the course or treatment of a general medical condition, it would be written in the medical record as follows:

- Axis I—316 Major Depressive Disorder delaying recovery from myocardial infarction (APA, 2000, p. 734)
- Axis III—410.90 Infarction, myocardial, acute (primary)

On the other hand, when a person is said to have a *comorbid medical illness*, this generally refers to a mental health client who is experiencing a medical condition. For example, is it is estimated that 50% of individuals with a mental illness (e.g., schizophrenia) have a known medical comorbidity (e.g., diabetes) while another 35% have a medical condition that has not been diagnosed (e.g., hypertension). Evidence shows that this population dies 10 to 15 years earlier than the general population, due in part, to complications from untreated medical conditions (Miller & Martinez, 2003).

When symptoms of a mental disorder and a general medical condition co-occur, it is important to determine whether the etiologic relationship is directly physiologic or another mechanism is involved. In some cases, the development of a medical disorder (e.g., osteoarthritis) or associated disability (e.g., inability to work due to pain) may exacerbate a mental disorder (e.g., adjustment disorder). For example, when a medical disorder significantly affects the course or treatment of a mental health condition, it would be written in the medical record as follows:

- Axis I—309.0 Adjustment Disorder, with depressed mood
- Axis III—715.90 Osteoarthritis
- Axis IV—Problems with Employment: lost job due to reemergence of medical disability—osteoarthritis

Readers interested in a more thorough review of the variety of diagnostic scenarios used to assess for comorbid medical and psychiatric conditions may see the following sections of the DSM-IV-TR (APA, 2000): Psychological Factors Affecting Medical Conditions, Medication-Induced Movement Disorders, Relational Problems, Personality Traits or Coping Styles Affecting General Medical Condition, Maladaptive Health Behaviors Affecting General Medical Condition, Stress-Related Physiological Response Affecting General Medical Condition, and Other or Unspecified Psychological Factors Affecting General Medical Condition.

With these definitions in mind, let's now review the research on women's comorbid health and mental health and how health promotion strategies can be applied as brief treatment approaches.

Four Core Health-Related Concerns

There are four areas of health-related concerns that clinicians need to be aware of when providing mental health services to women. These are: psychosocial/personal history, medication-induced weight gain, pregnancy, and substance use with complications of HIV.

Psychosocial/Personal History

More than half of women with severe mental illness report a history of childhood sexual abuse, and those with history of abuse have five times the rate of suicide and twice the rate of rape when compared with women who have psychiatric disorders who had not been abused as children (Miller, 1997; Miller & Finnerty, 1996). They also have double the rate of depression, twice as many gynecologic problems, and generally seek care in primary settings for insomnia, gastrointestinal problems, chronic pain, and multiple other problems. There are several explanations for these high rates: childhood sexual abuse frequently results in feelings of shame, lack of control, and difficulty trusting and relating to others (Brown & Jemmott, 2000; George, 2002; Perese & Perese, 2003). Additionally, women who have been abused may have difficulty accepting gynecologic examinations, which may trigger memories of abuse.

Early symptoms of mental illness may also have interfered with typical activities associated with adolescence, such as dating and developing skills necessary for negotiating healthy relationships, including boundaries. Consequently, some women with a history of mental illness may frequently be in relationships that are abusive and exploitative. They are seen in mental health settings for depression and self-destructive behaviors, such as suicide attempts and domestic violence (Perese & Perese, 2003). Poverty is considered a risk factor that may lead some women with mental illness to trade sexual favors for food, a place to sleep, and drugs. George (2002) noted that although these issues can explain some of the reasons why women have difficulty participating or engaging in health or mental health care, overall, women respond well to caregivers who treat them with respect and help them with problem solving. They often consider health and mental health care providers as an important source of support.

Medication-Induced Weight Gain

One measure of health status for adults and children is body weight. When people gain weight, they are at increased risk of developing diabetes mellitus, coronary artery disease, and endocrine disorders, not to mention negative health and self-image consequences (Umbricht & Kane, 1996; Kawachi, 1999). The clinical picture becomes more complex when weight gain is a side effect of pharmaceutical treatment for a primary mental health condition. Perese and Perese (2003) noted that psychotropic medication is implicated in more than just weight gain for women and includes comordid conditions such as amenorrhea, sexual dysfunction, breast cancer, and osteoporosis.

While both men and women with schizophrenia have higher mortality rates and lower rates of health-promoting behaviors than rates observed in the general population (Brown, 1997; Holmberg & Kane, 1999), suicide and obesity stand out as higher among women than men (Allison, Mentore & He, 1999). Although studies are mixed regarding the prevalence of obesity in mental health populations (Elmslie *et al.*, 2001), weight gain associated with some pharmaceuticals has become an increasing concern among women with mental illness and their prescribers (Brady, 1989).

There is a well-established relationship between psychiatric medications, appetite control, metabolism, and weight (Vanina *et al.*, 2002). For example, individuals who are taking psychopharmaceuticals have observed drug-induced changes in body weight of as much as 5%, or roughly 22 pounds per year. Vanina and colleagues (2002) highlight key issues associated with weight changes and psychotropic medication use:

- Medications with sedative properties may alter metabolism, compounding the problem.
- Patients who are receiving treatment often eat more as their appetite and well-being improve.
- Many psychotropic medications produce weight gain which can be distressing and result in noncompliance with or discontinuation of treatment.
- Weight gain is one of the most prominent difficulties associated with the use of certain psychotropic medications.
- Drug-associated weight gain does not regress easily.
- Weight increases are gradual and are often linked to the patient's personal characteristics and medication response history.

- Sometimes weight gain during pharmacotherapy can be a reflection of improvement in the clients mental status.

Additionally, the direction and extent of weight change also depends on the specific drug, the dosage, and the duration of treatment, as discussed in the next section.

Drug-Specific Weight Gain. In addition to overall weight changes, certain psychiatric medications have been implicated in very large weight gains (Yelena *et al.,* 2002). Vanina and colleagues (2002) have developed a consensus report on drug-induced weight changes associated with six categories of commonly used psychiatric medications: antipsychotic drugs, mood stabilizers, antidepressant drugs, antiparkinsonian drugs, psychostimulants, and other medications (e.g., buspirone). Of 69 significant papers reviewed, the authors rank-ordered weight change from "loss" to "very large gain." The medications most associated with very large weight gain emerged from three main groups: two antipsychotic drugs, chlorpromazine and clozapine; one mood stabilizer; valproate products; and one antidepressant drug, amitriptyline. Conversely, medications associated with weight loss were one antipsychotic drug, molindone; one mood stabilizer, topiramate; and three antidepressant drugs, isocarboxazid, bupropion, and nefazodone.

It is theorized that the mechanisms responsible for neuroleptic-associated weight gain with the use of antipsychotics is related to the blockage of certain cortical receptor sites (e.g., anticholinergic, serotonergic, and histaminergic) connected to appetite stimulation. These mechanisms will be different for each medication. In one study, patients who were treated with chlorpromazine increased their food consumption and gained an average of 10 pounds during the course of 3 months of therapy (Allison *et al.,* 1999). Ironically, while new antipsychotic drugs are associated with fewer neurologic side effects, they are known to increase weight gain, which may adversely affect glucose metabolism and have a diabetogenic influence. Of the mood stabilizers, valproate and its derivatives are associated with significant weight gain.

Overall, weight gain can be explained by increased food intake, decreased energy expenditure, low physical activity, reduction of thermogenesis, and greater availability of long-chain fatty acids. Antidepressants can enhance appetite, cause dry mouth, and induce a craving for carbohydrates and sweets—all of which can lead to increase risk for periodontal disease, dental caries, and excessive consumption of high-calorie beverages and food (Keene *et al.,* 2003).

Pregnancy

For women with schizophrenia, pregnancy carries a unique set of risks as well as options. Miller (1997) provides a comprehensive review of the research on pregnancy in women with schizophrenia. Research suggests that women diagnosed with schizophrenia, when compared to controls, were at increased risk of pregnancy due to reported higher rates of coerced or forced sex, higher rates of HIV-risk behavior (e.g., needle sharing or not insisting that partners use condoms), and limited knowledge about contraception, basic physiology, and anatomy.

Although women with schizophrenia averaged the same number of pregnancies as others who were not mentally ill, more of the pregnancies were unplanned and or unwanted. Additionally, several studies found that women with schizophrenia were less likely to receive prenatal care than women who are not mentally ill, and when prenatal care is offered, psychiatric symptoms are often underreported, partly due to fear of potential custody loss. Psychosis or psychotic denial may also contribute to underreporting due to delayed recognition of pregnancy, misinterpretation of somatic or bodily changes, failure to recognize labor, attempts at premature self-delivery, and precipitous delivery.

Compounding all these health risks is the challenge of finding agencies that will support the care of women with schizophrenia who are pregnant. Shelter or residential facilities may refuse admission to pregnant mentally ill women for a number of reasons, including concern for liability associated with obstetric complications, premature labor, or the risk of other residents harming a pregnant woman. When shelter or brief inpatient services are acquired, treatment policies may focus on consent to an abortion, custody issues, and medication management rather than counseling, nutrition education, or family planning and support (Nicholson & Henry, 2003; Miller & Finnerty, 1996)

For women with schizophrenia who are successfully managing their illness with medications, a pregnancy affects their ability to continue their pharmacotherapy. While the concern is focused on the potential effects of the medication on the fetus, withdrawing medication for the mother will likely precipitate a relapse during the pregnancy itself. The consequences of relapse may, in turn, lead to an acute psychosis, which is likely to adversely affect nutrition, self-care, and ability to access or utilize prenatal care. It has been estimated that 65% of women with schizophrenia who do not maintain medication will relapse during pregnancy (Casiano & Hawkins, 1987). Overall, high rates of obstetric complications and untreated psychosis increase the health and mental health risks for women with schizophrenia who are pregnant.

Other findings by Miller (1997) indicate that rates of obstetric complications are higher among women with schizophrenia than in the general population. This seems due to risk factors associated with low socioeconomic status and substance use. While rates of substance abuse are high among mental health populations in general, one study found that 78.1% of a sample of women with schizophrenia acknowledged substance abuse during pregnancy (Miller & Finnerty, 1996).

Substance Use with Complications of HIV

The role of mental illness, medical illness, and substance use in the lives of women presents a complex clinical picture. For example, in a large, cross-sectional prevalence study of 26,332 Medicaid recipients among whom half (n = 11,185) were noted to have been treated for a severe mental illness, three key findings emerged: (1) comorbid substance use increased risk for multiple medical disorders, (2) those with a psychotic disorder had two or more medical disorders, and (3) there was a significantly higher age- and gender-adjusted risk of key medical disorders compared with Medicaid beneficiaries who were not treated for severe mental illness (Dickey *et al.*, 2002).

Although prevalence data for men and women indicate that 41% to 65% of individuals with a lifetime substance abuse disorder also have a lifetime history of at least one mental disorder (Kessler *et al.*, 1996), the research is even more bleak for women. Research from the Center of Substance Abuse and Treatment (Sacks & Ries, 2005) reports that, when compared with the general population, 30% of women with mental illness have coexisting substance abuse problems and are at increased risk of HIV/AIDS, with rates of 5% in comparison to 0.17% among the general population. Additional factors that increased the risk for infectious diseases (e.g., HIV) included lifestyle practices (e.g., multiple sexual partners, unprotected sexual activity, or shared needle use, a history of intravenous drug use) or a diagnosis of depression, which was shown to independently predict seropositivity (Perese & Perese, 2003).

Blank and colleagues (2002) report that the rates of HIV infection is significantly elevated among persons with serious mental illness. Using a cross-sectional study of Medicaid claims data and welfare recipient files for persons aged 18 years or older, the authors estimated the treated period prevalence of HIV infection among the Medicaid population and the rate of HIV among persons with serious mental illness. They found that the treated period prevalence of HIV infection was 0.6% among Medicaid recipients who did not have a diagnosis of a serious mental illness and 1.8% among those who did.

The good news is that contrary to popular belief, there is no evidence that adherence to treatment for HIV infection is poorer among persons with serious mental illness than it is in the general population (Blank *et al.*, 2002). However, if professional bias enters into the clinical picture and providers think that women with serious mental illness are less likely to adhere to treatment, they may be less likely to prescribe a state-of-the-art treatment regime (i.e., highly active antiretroviral therapy combined with gender-specific support groups) for these clients than for women who do not have serious mental illness.

■ Health Promotion Strategies

Green and Kreuter (1999) identify nine personal health promotion practices that are associated with physical and mental health and are cumulative in their effect. Each may be seen as a goal of brief treatment. They are sleeping 7 to 8 hours daily, eating breakfast most days, rarely or never eating between meals, being at or near the recommended height-adjusted weight, being a nonsmoker, using alcohol moderately, participating in physical activity, and having social support and association memberships (p. 126). Yet these are practices that are frequently compromised in the lives of women with mental health conditions.

Overall, the data on positive health promotion practices or lifestyle lend credibility to the notion that at least 50% of all comorbidity can be modified by brief treatment to promote healthy behaviors. However, research also suggests that although knowledge itself is necessary, simply dispensing information has not been shown to influence levels of risk behavior (Wainberg *et al.*, 2003). For health promotion strategies to be effective in the lives of women with mental illness and comorbid health conditions, they need to be relevant, meaningful, sustainable, and brief.

This section discusses four health promotion strategies that address the clinical concerns described earlier. These strategies are, respectively, intentional recovery community, fitness program, health education, and gender-specific treatment groups. Each may be delivered in a time-limited or brief treatment format. For an overview of these strategies, see Figure 9.1.

The Intentional Recovery Community (IRC) is a program concept based on the notion that psychosocial recovery should be a multidimensional process of positive transformation in the areas of social functioning, employment, inter-personal relationships and social integration (Whitley, Harris, Fallot & Berley, 2007). Grounded in the health promotion principle of empowerment, the IRC model focuses on mutual support, peer education, and the idea that the "community" should serve the role as surrogate family and a place for safety and socialization. This philosophy is particularly salient for women who have difficulty maintaining safe housing and stable and mutually satisfying interpersonal relationships that are not dependent upon substance use communities (Fallot & Harris, 2002). Intentional communities, also known as recovery communities, are not a new concept and despite recent meta analysis reaffirming that these programs are an effective form of treatment, very few agencies provide this service (Lees, Manning & Rawlings, 2004).

Model Program. One program that illustrates the intentional recovery community model is the Women's Empowerment Center (WEC), a program sponsored by Community Connections, a private, not-for-profit mental health agency in Washington,

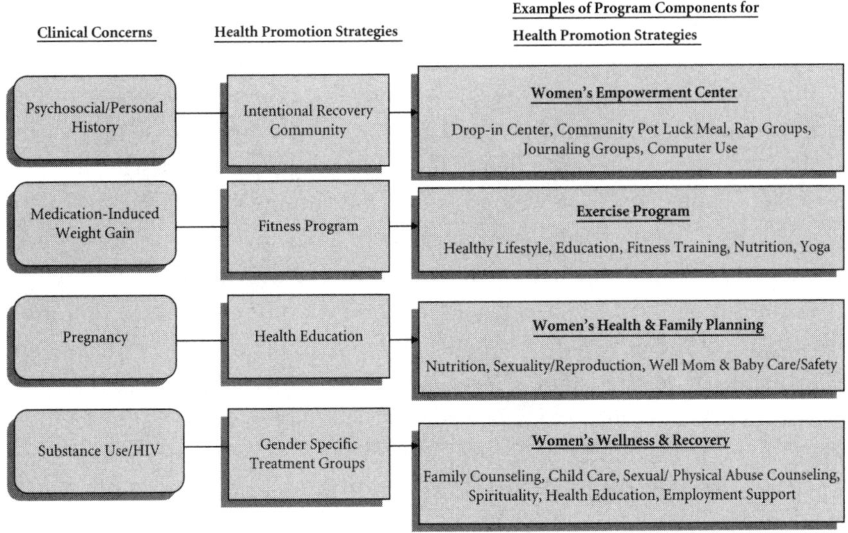

FIGURE 9.1. Clinical concerns, health promotion strategies, and program components for women with mental illness and comorbid health conditions.

D.C. The mission of WEC is to create a community of peers and professional helpers to foster the development of social support, self-esteem and belonging—all in a setting considered to be a safe, healing environment. The philosophy of the center is that it is run by women for women and any "professional" intervention is cautiously introduced so as not to violate the empowerment ethos of the center. However, members of a women's trauma team and case managers are available for support. The program is open to women who have experienced severe mental illness; a vast majority of these women also present with a history of physical and sexual abuse and a co-occurring substance-use disorder. The program operates as a drop in-center and is open daily with up to 15 women attending at any one time. It provides a mix of peer- or staff-led, structured activities (e.g., journaling, rap group or anger management classes) and unstructured activities (e.g., snacks, rest areas, pot luck meals, computer use). Future groups may include conflict resolution. For more information about this program, see www.communityconnections.org.

Fitness Program

Exercise is emerging as a recognized health promotion strategy for addressing medication-induced weight gain. By way of example, a national consensus panel on psychosis, obesity, and diabetes (Consensus Report, 2004) recommended physical activity and nutritional counseling for overweight clients taking antipsychotic medications. Richardson and colleagues (2005) found that the most effective fitness programs were those that tailored interventions to specific populations (e.g., women) and/or the individual's age, gender, socioeconomic status, cultural background, health status, barriers, or fitness level; they used motivational messages in printed form; provided physician-prescribed "exercise prescriptions" (e.g., walk around block two times a week); focused on moderate-intensity activities (e.g., walking); and used principles of behavior modification (e.g., goal setting, self-monitoring, social support, and shaping).

While Vanina and colleagues (2002) conclude there is no established treatment for medication-induced weight change, clinicians and clients can explore together the following health matters: (1) assess whether the client has gained or lost weight, the extent of the weight change (e.g., a few pounds or a lot), timing of the change (e.g., rapid, gradual, seasonal, holiday), any associations with illness or smoking history and lifetime patterns, (2) consider switching to a medication that is less likely to cause weight gain before clinically significant gains occur, and (3) explore treatment options based on the severity of the weight problem, the emotional impact of the problem, and the client's somatic or mental status. When an effective psychoactive agent has caused major fluctuations in weight and no appropriate alternative can be found, an informed client and clinician can discuss the risks and benefits of maintaining, discontinuing, or changing the dosage or the medications. As a time-limited, health promotion strategy, physical activity interventions have the benefit of being low in cost, valued, accessible, wellness-oriented, flexible, normalizing, and easily adopted into existing mental health programs or primary care settings (Richardson *et al.*, 2005).

Model Program. A Fitness class is one of many wellness-oriented classes offered through the Recovery Center at the Center for Psychiatric Rehabilitation in Boston and serves as a model for programs striving to incorporate physical fitness health activities into traditional mental health care. While the emphasis is on total health, clients learn about physiology and self-care issues specific to medication-induced weight gain. Based on the notion that weight changes have a powerful impact on medication adherence, body image, and health, the central aim of a fitness class is to provide a structured and supportive environment for exercise and fitness training. Clients work with their recovery advisor to develop individualized fitness goals and create wellness plans. The setting also provides an opportunity for socializing, mutual support, and education, particularly as students receive guidance for understanding and managing weight changes associated with the use of psychotropic medications.

Based on an adult education model, the fitness class or exercise program consists of three supervised 45-minute exercise sessions each week for 20 weeks. Sessions are held in a university fitness room and participants can utilize stationary bicycles, stair-climbing machines, and treadmills. They are offered instruction on measuring their heart rates, and for warm-up and cool-down periods. Preliminary findings from this program indicate that participants showed statistically significant improvements in their cardiovascular fitness and psychological fitness, such as self-esteem, quality of life, mood, and depression (Hutchinson, 2005).

Health Education

Incorporating women's health and family planning into traditional mental health care delivery systems has many benefits. These include enhancing the physical and mental well-being of women with mental illness who are in their childbearing years, pregnant, and or currently parenting. Women can be helped to explore sexual relationships and strategies to reduce unplanned pregnancies. Miller (1997) advocates for a multipronged health promotion approach to support women with mental illness who are pregnant or at risk of pregnancy due to lifestyle or educational needs. Examples of health promotion strategies that specialize in health content that is specific to personal health and family planning are classes in family planning and women's health, active consultation with ob-gyn physicians and nurse practitioners, access to day care, and enrolling clients in a women's health and wellness center.

For women who are pregnant and taking psychiatric medications, thebenefit of addressing pregnancy with a health promotion strategy is that a health-oriented approach helps reduce the stress, guilt, and or fear of the pregnancy—regardless of whether the pregnancy was planned or unplanned. It also provides an opportunity for the pregnant woman to explore support systems, medication options, and life planning with case managers who are already familiar with her life. Although critics would claim that agency mental health staff do not have the time or expertise to provide such education, they should be reminded that their women clients are already experiencing these issues and will need their assistance regardless of the agency's preparedness. Mental health agencies can tap into in-house nurses or nurse practitioners to provide these trainings or local public health nurses or student interns from nursing programs. As Miller (1997) states, "mental health practice that considers sexuality, reproduction, and parenting can be highly effective in lessening risks for women with schizophrenia who are pregnant and soon to be parenting" (p. 631). Health education programs are, by design, usually short-term and time-limited. Women who participate in health and family planning programs typically participate in sessions that are relevant to their specific concerns and interests.

Model Program. One program that has obtained success in working with mothers considered "at risk" is the Nurse-Family Partnership Program. This program began as a research project in rural New York in the late 1970s and now operates programs in 22 states. The program was developed for first-time low-income expectant mothers who were at risk for substance use and abuse. Additionally, other factors were targeted, such as behaviors that influence family poverty, dropping out of school, failure to find work, subsequent pregnancies, and poor maternal and infant outcomes (Kitzman *et al.*, 2000). Most nurse-family partnerships are funded through special projects or through state and federal appropriations (e.g., National Center for Children, Families and Communities). A key feature of the program is that it is administered by licensed nurses, while nonnursing or paraprofessional staff have been found to be ineffective (Olds *et al.*, 2002). Two central goals of the program are to improve pregnancy outcomes by helping mothers adopt healthy behaviors and improve families' economic self-sufficiency. A nurse visits the homes of high-risk women when pregnancy begins and continues for the first year of the child's life. Home visit protocols are in place and are designed to help women learn new health-oriented behaviors (e.g., nutrition) and to care for their children responsibly. Recent research by Kitzman and colleagues (2000) found that the program increased employment by 83%, reduced maternal substance abuse by 25%, and reduced abuse of children by mothers by 80%.

Gender-Specific Treatment: Women and Substance Use/HIV

In order to deal with the diversity of comorbid issues that women with mental health and substance abuse conditions experience, health promotion strategies should emphasize gender specific treatment. This recommendation is based on the knowledge that most therapeutic community programs for the treatment of substance abuse are typically tailored to men. The clinical approaches are often confrontational with little regard given to the needs of family and children. Bride and Real (2003) summarize the following benefits of gender-specific treatment services for women:

1. They provide women with an opportunity to concentrate on their own needs and desires away from their traditional concerns of social approval and the welfare of others.

2. They offer safe environments to discuss topics that they might not discuss in mixed gender settings.
3. Such programs are more likely to provide services specific to needs of women.
4. They tend to be more supportive, less confrontational, grounded in women's experiences, and to focus on empowerment and women's strengths.

Components of gender-specific health promotion strategies incorporate a broad range of activities that includes therapists and nurses collaborating closely with outside caregiving agencies and assisting clients in linking their medical services, which may include HIV/AIDS conditions, to ongoing mental health and substance abuse services. The needs of women who experience co-occurring mental illness and substance abuse complicated by health conditions will require a long-term, flexible, integrated care model. However, many aspects of gender specific treatment can be delivered in a brief treatment format, such as time-limited, women-only groups and/or counseling. These services are typically provided by female therapists in conjunction with nurse practitioners (Copeland *et al.*, 1993, p. 84).

Model Program. Project Assist is an example of a model health promotion program that works solely with women who are homeless, mentally ill, abusing substances, and having HIV/AIDS conditions. Project Assist is an eight-bed, modified therapeutic community for chemically dependent homeless women with HIV/AIDS. The program is organizationally linked with St. Jude's Recovery Center, a private nonprofit substance abuse treatment agency in Atlanta (Bride & Real, 2003). Project Assist was developed with a new set of principles to address the unmet health, mental health, and substance abuse needs of women. Based on the principles of mutual aid, recovery, and the therapeutic community, Project Assist provides a variety of health promotion interventions that are specific to the needs of women. Health promotion interventions include HIV support, education and health services, groups on spirituality, meditation, psychoeducation, the 12-step program, relationships, addiction, employment, and health education.

■ Barriers to Implementing Health Promotion Strategies

Practitioners of brief treatment who wish to offer these four health promotion strategies to their women clients will face a complex set of challenges. Three areas in particular are *fiscal*, *clinical*, and *training*.

From a *fiscal* standpoint, insurance plans are increasingly using carve-out behavioral health plans that separate psychiatric care from health care. While some research has shown that carve-outs may in some ways ensure focused mental health care, the medical needs of women with psychiatric disabilities may not be met. Further, these carve-out models continue to perpetuate mind-body dualism, which is the antithesis of health promotion strategies, as well as run counter to progressive medical and mental health practices.

Given the strong association between mental illness and medical comorbidity, health administrators have hypothesized that adequate treatment of mental illness will lead to a reduction in medical expenditures (Olfson *et al.,* 1999). In other words, if only more money could be allocated to treat mental disorders, there would be lower expenditures for medical care. Simon and colleagues (1995) found just the opposite: medical care costs were actually higher, not lower, when adults with mental illness were properly treated. However, Jeste and colleagues (1996) speculated that inadequate medical treatment, rather than a comorbid condition, may explain some research findings that people with schizophrenia have more severe physical illnesses but not necessarily more so than the general population.

From a *clinical* standpoint, some women with mental illness may be reluctant to seek medical care due to previous negative clinical experiences with mainstream health providers. Integrating medical and mental health treatment may encourage greater continuity of care but not improve communication between the primary care provider and the woman client who needs treatment for both the mental health and health condition. For example, research has found that people diagnosed with schizophrenia are reported to have a high tolerance for pain and are thus unlikely to report pain as a symptom. Women with mental illness are sometimes unwilling to seek medical help or, when they do, frequently have difficulty describing their problems to a physician. Other clinical barriers can include inability on the part of the woman with mental illness to recognize or describe physical symptoms perhaps because psychotic symptoms interfere with her ability to communicate with the physician. On the other hand, a physician may focus on the mental illness and miss symptoms related to the medical disorders (Dickey *et al.,* 2002).

From a *training* standpoint, most mental health professionals are not trained in the philosophy or practice of health promotion, nor are they trained to identify medical problems. Without some form of specialized public health training, front-line mental health workers and case managers may be overlooking potentially life-threatening health symptoms that their women clients are experiencing or are at risk for. So even though an integrated medical and mental health system would encourage greater continuity of care and coordination of different health promotion strategies (Dickey *et al.,* 2002), much still needs to be done to both enhance the health education of the mental health provider and to improve communication between the practitioner and women clients who present with mental health and medical needs.

■ Recommendations

Despite these barriers, much hope exists for the integration of health promotion strategies into mainstream mental health practice, particularly in those settings that recognize the unique needs of women clients. To do so, however, requires a shift in organizational philosophy and practice. For example, one way that an organization can address fiscal issues is to advocate for insurance parity in the treatment of health and mental health conditions. This position is in line with the health promotion philosophy that sees health and mental health on the same continuum of care. Dickey and colleagues (2002) take this argument further by recommending that (mental) health care organizations, rather than focusing on lowering medical expenditures, emphasize better medical treatment, not less. Better medical treatment could be achieved by integrating substance abuse, health services and mental health. While the result may not initially lower medical costs, integrated treatment may lead to early identification of medical illnesses among mental health clients, which in turn, may direct clients to health promotion strategies aimed at wellness and lifestyle changes. This philosophical shift has the potential to reduce comorbidity which, in itself, is likely to be a cost savings.

Another area of organizational change can occur in the way that providers initially communicate and engage with women clients who present with medical and mental health issues. One of the defining hallmarks of the field of health promotion is its emphasis on a holistic, person-centered, empowerment-oriented approach to assessment and treatment. When medical providers and mental health practitioners listen to women clients with this philosophy in mind, the potential for miscommunication or under communication is lessened. To offset negative clinical encounters, better communication on the part of providers can result in openness on the part of women clients to participate in some of the evidence-based health promotion strategies, like Health Education for Health and Family Planning as described in this chapter. These specialized tailored interventions might improve their understanding and self-management of certain types of comorbid health conditions—like depression and diabetes—that could affect pregnancy.

Cross training and pairing mental health workers with public health nurses is an excellent way to increase the skill set of traditionally trained mental health workers. Agencies that commit to interdisciplinary training and staffing (e.g., social workers, out reach workers, nurses, psychiatrists, psychologists, nutritionists, fitness trainers) provide an important service to women clients who have multiple psychosocial, mental, and physical health needs. Scully (2004) reminds practitioners that "mental illnesses are medical illnesses, and the use of biological treatments such as medications involve multiple body systems beyond the central nervous system and require knowledge of biology, biochemistry, anatomy, and physiology" (p. 24). The mental health practitioner today needs to have an appreciation of the psychosocial lives of women clients as well as pharmakinetics (how the body handles a drug) and pharmacodynamics (the effects of a drug on the body). We are reminded that psychotropic medications affect many organ systems beside the brain, including the gastrointestinal, hepatic, renal, and circulatory systems.

■ Conclusion

The philosophy of health promotion is not a new concept. Martial (A.D. c. 40–104), a first-century Roman poet, stated "Life is not just being alive but being well." More recently, an endorsement by the New Freedom Commission Report (2003) stated that "mental health is key to overall physical health" (p. 21). In short, the integration of health and mental health services has become, in a sense, recognized as "best practices." Health promotion is one framework that helps unite these two areas.

Health promotion strategies are also not a new or radical practice approach. Good mental health practice has always called for health promotion approaches—e.g., supporting client or consumer empowerment, organizing opportunities for fitness, providing health education, conducting outreach, providing gender sensitive services, arranging interagency coordination, and ensuring that mental health staff are cross-trained. Now the data are quite clear that clients want these types of interactions and consider them beneficial. As Sheridan and Radmacher (2003) write: "A treatment cannot be effective if a client fails to utilize it, or its effectiveness may be reduced by actions taken by patients or by the failure of professionals to administer the treatment appropriately" (p. 5).

What is new about health promotion is the idea of formally embedding health promotion strategies into mainstream mental health practice. The ultimate goal of this combined approach is best summed up by Green and Kreuter (1999): "Health promotion seeks to promote healthful conditions that improve the quality of life and health as seen through the eyes of those whose lives are affected. Though health promotion might have instrumental value in reducing risks for co-morbidity, its ultimate value lies in its contribution to quality of life." (p. 54). For women clients who believe there is more to treatment than just a plan and that wellness, empowerment, and quality of life can be the expectation rather than the exception, health promotion is one idea whose time has arrived.

In Our Own Words . . . Family and Consumer Perspectives on Mental Health Treatment Services

Topic: Promoting Health in Mental Health

Summary

As Chapter 9 illustrates, women with mental illness have unique experiences, health risks, and needs that must be considered when a clinician and client develop treatment strategies. Staying with this theme, consumers and family members were asked to identify ways that the mental health system could help with these health needs. Family members acknowledged the need for support in order to stay healthy and to learn more about medication monitoring as a means to helping their family member. Consumers, all of whom were women, were quite specific about the ways in which their health issues could be addressed by the mental health system. Their suggestions included providing education and resources, integrating services, and conducting health assessments.

What Can We Learn?

Based on these suggestions, mental health providers can provide an important service to their women clients and their family members by providing basic health education and interpersonal support. The following section details the results of the focus group meeting as reported by family members and consumers.

Focus Group Question: ***"How can the mental health system improve your and your family members' health needs?"***

Family Perspectives

Core Themes	Summary of Experiences	Comments
(Ranked in order of priority)		
First—Family Support	When mental health staff provide support to family members, stress is reduced. Without support, family members agreed that their own physical health suffers when their loved one is ill; symptoms include weight loss, stress reactions and sleep deprivation.	"Families need to be cared for; our health would be better if these issues were addressed." (S., *spouse*)

(continued)

Focus Group Question: "*How can the mental health system improve your and your family members' health needs?*" *(continued)*

Second—Medication Monitoring	It is too challenging keeping up with medication side effects and more information is needed from staff about the negative aspects of medication and need for recognizing the signs before worse symptoms develop.	"Clinicians need to address the medication issues and side effects.... and the side effects of the side effects; don't mask the side effects with drugs that create more problems." (M., *sibling*)

Consumer Perspectives

Core Themes	Summary of Experiences	Comments
(Ranked in order of priority)		
First—Education & Resources	Agencies and providers need to provide education and resources that explain health conditions—particularly if diabetic; this means doctors and staff taking more time to discuss health concerns or pointing out risks.	"Caseworkers should be just as active in asking how clients take care of their health and then offering education, support, resources and suggestions." (J., *consumer*)
Second—Integrative Care Model	It is important that all clinicians treat the physical and "psychic" modes of well-being as one entity.	"It's important that care integrates physical well-being with psychological well being— we are one being, you know?" (R., *consumer*)
Third—Health Assessment	Providers could be more active in performing health assessments by asking about physical health issues, what other medications are being taken, and making sure that they had the resources to support healthy lifestyles—like special diet or a better diet.	"Workers need to ask people what they do to take care of themselves and don't always explain or dismiss symptoms as mental or psychological." (JVS—*consumer*)

10. Health Promotion Strategies for the Mental Health Needs of Children and Families

Catheleen Jordan, Maria Scannapieco and Vikki Vandiver

Please make the assumption that parents are really doing good work, have the best intentions, and are not to blame for abuse.

—*K., parent*

■ Chapter Overview

Children and family mental health has become an increasingly important focus for providers and community leaders who represent community mental health, health, and social service agencies. Part of this interest is related to the maturing of health promotion perspectives in the field of adolescent mental health (Pederson *et al.*, 1994) as well as an awareness of the importance of developing health promoting attitudes during adolescence. Additionally, research is moving away from a focus on the study of single problems (e.g., truancy) and toward examining clusters of problem behaviors (e.g., poverty, parenting needs). Despite this movement, knowledge is still needed about what constitutes a mental health condition for children, how to assess change in this condition, and approaches for helping children, families, and communities move beyond the diagnosis. One such approach is through the application of empirically supported health promotion strategies.

In this chapter, we begin with a description of children's health- and mental health–related disorders and a supporting theory: ecologic systems. Next we present information on assessment instruments for client and family functioning as well as five health promotion strategies and their limitations. We conclude the chapter with a summary of a focus group discussion held by consumers and family members who were asked the following question: "How can mental health providers help you address the health and mental health needs of you and your children?" Our goal is to provide information that can be used by providers to support the empowerment of children and families toward models of care that integrate health promotion practices with outcomes of health, wellness, and enhanced quality of life.

Learning Objectives

When you have finished reading this chapter, you should be able to:

1. Identify common children's health- and mental health–related disorders
2. Access quantitative measures useful for assessing children and their families in their communities
3. Identify health promotion strategies for different clinical issues experienced by children and their families in their communities
4. Describe the limitations of a health promotion approach
5. Identify core themes and concerns expressed by consumer and family focus group members when asked about ways in which they could be helped with their children

■ Introduction

Children in community mental health settings are seen for a variety of problems ranging from general medical conditions to emotional and behavioral problems. Findings from a report issued by the Health and Human Services Substance Abuse and Mental Health Services Administration (DHHS, 2005) suggest that 1 in 10 children in the United States has a serious emotional disturbance and 1 in 5 has a diagnosable mental disorder. For example, research on teenagers with bipolar disorder found that these youth are more likely to face major health risks through suicide, drug and alcohol abuse, and high-risk sexual activity and have significantly higher medical admission rates compared with adolescents with other behavioral health diagnoses (Borchardt & Bernstein, 1995; Peele *et al.*, 2004). Similarly, research by Jaffee and colleagues (2005) found that children with special health care needs have behavioral and emotional problems at much higher rates than other children. Despite a greater need for mental health services, these children often face significant barriers to health and mental health services due in part to community-level contextual stressors (e.g., poverty, unemployment, crime, and lack of social support). These stressors have been associated with an increased incidence of behavioral and emotional problems and inadequate mental health care (Jaffee *et al.*, 2005). Given these concerns, it seems evident that a broad-based assessment and intervention approach is needed to address health and mental health issues at multiple levels: child, family, and community. Let's now turn to a review of health and mental health conditions that providers are likely to encounter in working with children, adolescents, and their families.

■ Overview of Major Childhood Mental Disorders

This section describes selected diagnostic-specific health and mental health conditions of children and adolescents. These include anxiety disorders due to general medical condition, pain disorder associated with both psychological factors and general medical condition, depression, bipolar I, separation anxiety disorder, posttraumatic stress disorder, dissociative disorder, attention-deficit hyperactivity disorder, conduct disorder, oppositional defiant disorder, anorexia nervosa, bulimia nervosa, and substance abuse. These were selected as representing mental health conditions that providers would routinely see in clinical practice and that lend themselves to health promotion strategies. For a more extensive review of childhood diagnostic categories, readers are referred to the *Diagnostic and Statistical Manual of Mental Disorders* (DSM-IV-TR) (APA, 2000). For our purposes, a summary list of diagnostic categories, health promotion strategies, and programs is illustrated in Figure 10.1a to d.

These conditions are discussed using the following categories: mental disorders due to a general medical condition, emotional and social disorders, behavioral and emotional disorders, and health-related disorders.

Mental Disorders Due to a General Medical Condition

Two disorders are described in this section. These are *anxiety* and *pain disorder*.

Anxiety and General Medical Conditions. Everyone experiences anxiety at some point, but children with anxiety disorders experience tremendous and persistent fear and apprehension, which impairs their functioning in significant ways. Symptoms of children with anxiety disorders are expressed in three ways: cognitively, somatically, and behaviorally. Cognitive symptoms include, fears, intrusive thoughts, obsessions, dissociation, lack of self-confidence, hypersensitivity to criticism or rejection, and numbing. Somatic complaints include headaches, stomachaches, or fatigue, with symptoms that include motor tension; autonomic hyperarousal; rapid, shallow breathing; and increased heart rate. The child's behavioral symptoms may include shyness, social withdrawal, hypervigilance and avoidance of reminiscent stimuli, self-absorption, compulsions,

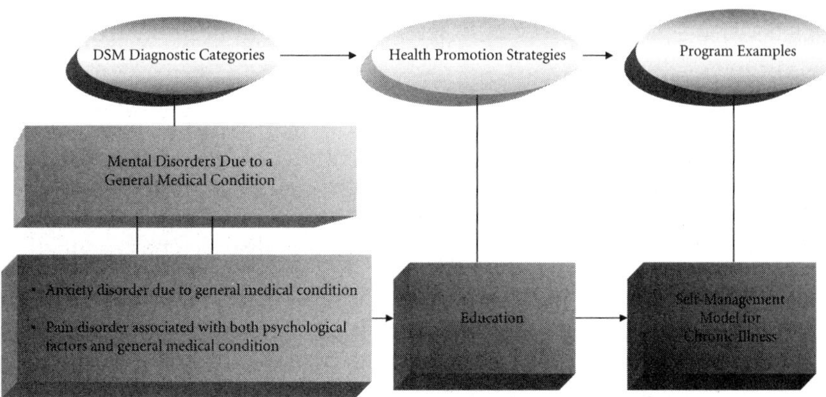

FIGURE 10.1A. Evidence-Based Mental Health Promotion Strategies and Program Examples for Diagnostic-Specific Mental Health and Health Conditions of Childhood and Adolescence: Mental Disorders Due to General Medical Condition.

and rituals. Because these children have fewer disruptive behaviors and often seek to please others, parents, social workers, teachers and physicians easily overlook their problems (Nelson-Gardell & Harris, 2003; Santos & Barrett, 2002). Anxiety disorders are among the most prevalent forms of psychopathology in children and adolescents, occurring about as frequently as asthma in the pediatric population (Santos & Barrett, 2002). Children and adolescents who experience anxiety disorders are frequently and intensely worried and apprehensive for considerable periods of time. Anxiety disorders are characterized by a heightened state of fear or nervousness in relation to an emotion or a stressful event.

The symptoms of anxiety disorder due to general medical conditions are the same as those of primary anxiety disorders such as panic disorder, generalized anxiety disorder, and obsessive-compulsive disorder (APA, 2000). The only differences is that the symptoms are caused by general medical conditions such as vitamin deficiency, diabetes, or anemia. Ironically, anxiety due to medical conditions is generally not discussed in the child and adolescent literature (Santos & Barrett, 2002; Sattler, 1998; Schroeder & Gordon, 2002).

Examples of DSM-IV-TR criteria for anxiety disorder due to a general medical condition include prominent anxiety, panic attacks, or obsessions or compulsions and evidence from examination that the disturbance is the direct physiologic consequence of a general medical condition (APA, 2000, p. 479).

Pain. Pain disorder is frequently encountered in children and adolescents. It is characterized by persistent or recurrent pain (e.g., recurrent abdominal pain, headaches) for which an adequate general medical explanation is not found and usual medical treatment is ineffective. Pain disorder symptoms cause substantial stress for the child or adolescent, which results in maladaptive functioning, such as inability to attend school, limited social interactions with peers, and frequent trips to the doctor (Kaye & Pataki, 2002).

Examples of DSM-IV-TR criteria for pain disorder associated with both psychological factors and general medical condition include pain in one or more anatomic sites, pain that is the predominant focus of the clinical presentation and is of sufficient severity to warrant clinical attention, and pain where psychological factors are judged to have an important role in its onset, severity, exacerbation, or maintenance (APA, 2000, p. 503). See Figure 10.1A

Emotional and Social Disorders

The two categories of disorders discussed in this section are *mood* (e.g., depression and bipolar I) and *anxiety* disorders (e.g., separation anxiety disorder, posttraumatic stress disorder, dissociative disorder).

Mood Disorders and Children

Depression. Depression is one of the most frequently occurring mood disorders. When we think about depression in children, we are often referring to symptoms rather than a full-blown disorder. Depression is among the most commonly occurring symptoms for children who have experienced any form of maltreatment, particularly sexual abuse (Kendall-Tackett, 2003). Depression can range from a symptom, such as fatigue, sadness, or insomnia to a group of symptoms that go together to form a disorder such as major depressive disorder (MDD). Children and adolescents may experience depressive symptoms without meeting the criteria for MDD. Although the DSM-IV-TR does not include MDD as a disorder of childhood, the criteria for diagnosing adult depression are valid for use with children (Kazdin & Marciano, 1998; Schroeder & Gordon, 2002).

Kazdin and Marciano (1998) indicate one criterion, irritability, within the DSM-IV-TR that varies for depression in children and adolescents. The majority of children will present with "irritable mood" and this symptom can be used in place of depressed mood.

Children may present different symptoms at different developmental levels. The following are some indicators of depression across childhood and adolescents (Sattler, 1998):

- Infants and preschool children (an estimated 1% are depressed): sleep disturbances, increased clinging, aggressive behavior, crying, sadness, apprehension, loss of appetite, and refusal to eat
- Middle childhood (an estimated 2% are depressed): all the above and loss of weight, temper tantrums, concentration difficulties, and sleeplessness
- Adolescents (an estimated 6% are depressed): all the above and loss of feelings or pleasure and interest, low self-esteem, excessive fatigue, and loss of energy, inability to tolerate routines, aggressive behavior, loneliness, irritability, running away, stealing, guilt feelings, and suicidal preoccupations.

Examples of DSM-IV-TR criteria for major depressive episode with emphasis on children and adolescents include five or more of the following symptoms: depressed or irritable mood nearly every day, diminished interest in activities, failure to respond to expected weight gains, insomnia or hypersomnia nearly every day, psychomotor agitation, fatigue daily, feelings of worthlessness (APA, 2000, p. 356).

Bipolar I Disorder. Bipolar disorder in adolescence is increasingly being identified as a significant public health problem (Peele *et al.*, 2004). Some of the key features of mood and behavior disturbances among children diagnosed with bipolar disorder are extreme mood variability, intermittent aggressive behavior, high levels of distractibility, and poor attention span (Sadock & Sadock, 2007). Although the average age of onset of bipolar I is 20 for both men and women, direct comparisons with other pediatric psychiatric disorders have highlighted the relative severity of new cases among prepubertal children and adolescents (Sadock & Sadock, 2007). Recent evidence indicates that pediatric bipolar disorder is a severe illness associated with high rates of impairment involving substance use, comorbidity, psychosis, and suicidality; a chronic or relapsing clinical course; two to three times the rate of psychosocial problems as in youths with a diagnosis of attention-deficit hyperactivity disorder; and more global impairment than in adolescents with unipolar major depression (Geller *et al.*, 2002; Lewinson *et al.*, 2000). At a prevalence rate of about 1%, approximately 10% to 15% of adolescents with a recurrent major depressive disorder will go on to develop bipolar I disorder.

Examples of DSM-IV-TR criteria for bipolar disorder, manic episode, bipolar disorder I, and single manic episode are listed below. According to DSM-IV-TR, the diagnostic criteria for a manic episode are the same for children and adolescents as for adults with the caveat that classic manic episodes are uncommon in this age group even when depressive symptoms have already appeared. The primary diagnostic criterion for manic episode is a distinct period of abnormality and persistently elevated, expansive, or irritable mood lasting 1 week. Some of the symptoms include inflated self-esteem or grandiosity, decreased need for sleep and more talkativeness than usual, distractibility, and an increase in goal-oriented activity (p. 362). The diagnostic criterion for bipolar disorder I, single manic episode are presence of only one manic episode and no past depressive episodes (APA, 2000, p. 388).

Children and adolescents who meet criteria for depression and bipolar disorders often meet criteria for one or more other disorders as well. This is referred to as "comorbidity," as discussed in Chapter 9. These other disorders may include anxiety disorders, addressed below.

Anxiety Disorder. Anxieties and fears of children manifest themselves across a number of disorders where the main feature is exaggerated anxiety. All children experience anxiety as a temporary reaction to a stressful experience. When anxiety is intense and persistent and interferes with the child's functioning, it may become a diagnosed anxiety disorder. The DSM-IV-TR's (APA, 2000) current system lists 12 categories of fears and anxieties related to children. The three major ones addressed here are *separation anxiety, posttraumatic stress disorder,* and *dissociative identity disorder.*

Separation Anxiety Disorder. Separation anxiety disorder is associated with a child's fear of being separated from home or a caregiver (attachment figure). Separation anxiety most often occurs at a transitional period, such as starting school or at the time of a loss of a caregiver either by temporary separation (foster care) or permanent separation (death). It is characterized by excessive anxiety beyond that which is developmentally appropriate for the child's age or developmental level.

Examples of DSM–IV-TR criteria for separation anxiety disorder include developmentally inappropriate and excessive anxiety concerning separation from home or from those to whom the child or adolescent is attached as evidenced by three or more of the following: excessive distress about harm to self or to attachment figures when separated and persistence in opposition to school attendance, physical complaints, opposition to being home alone, and shadowing of caregiver (APA, 2000, p. 125).

Posttraumatic Stress Disorder (PTSD). Children who experience an extreme trauma, such as sexual abuse, severe physical abuse, accident, or suicide, may develop PTSD. PTSD can develop following exposure to an extreme trauma or series of events in a child's life.

Symptoms cut across cognitive, emotional, and behavioral domains and must occur within 1 month of exposure to the stressful event.

Examples of DSM-IV-TR criteria for PTSD with children include information showing that the child has been exposed to a traumatic event in which the response was expressed by disorganized or agitated behavior, and the traumatic event is persistently reexperienced through repetitive play in which themes or aspects of the trauma are expressed (APA, 2000, pp. 467–468).

Dissociative Identity Disorder. The onset of dissociative identity disorder is believed to occur in early childhood, although it is rarely diagnosed in childhood. The lack of diagnosis in childhood is most likely attributed to the intricacy of the diagnosis for children, and the symptoms are often attributed to other reasons. APA (2000) defines the critical features of dissociative disorders as a failure in the normal integration of cognitive functions associated with consciousness, identity, memory, or perception of the environment (Wolfe, 1998). Dissociative identity disorder is a condition whereby the child develops amnesia, feelings of depersonalization, or two or more distinct identities or personality states that recurrently take control of her or his behavior (Sattler, 1998). Children with dissociative identity disorder may feel controlled by these identities, over which they have no control. Dissociative identity disorder has been conceptualized as a coping strategy used to reduce overwhelming stress and anxiety (Wolfe, 1998). Some dissociative experiences in childhood and adolescence are normal, such as imaginary playmates or other fantasy play, and need to be placed in a developmental context.

Examples of DSM-IV-TR criteria for dissociative identity disorder include the presence of two or more distinct identities or personality states (each with its own relatively enduring pattern of perceiving, relating to, and thinking about the environment and self) and at least two of these identities or personality states recurrently take control of the individual's behavior (APA, 2000, p. 529). Other features include recurrent amnesic periods or missing blocks of time, frequent trance-like states (being "spaced out"), or appearing to be in a daze, acting like a different person and being distracted, and showing major fluctuations in behavior, which may include dramatic changes in school performance or variations in apparent social, cognitive, or physical abilities (Sattler, 1998; Sadock & Sadock, 2007). (See Figure 10.1b.)

Behavioral or Emotional Disorders

Children with special health needs have behavioral and emotional problems at much higher rates than other children (Harman *et al.*, 2000). These children are at risk for chronic physical, developmental, behavioral, and emotional conditions and require mental health services beyond that required by children generally. Jaffee and colleagues (2005) summarize the research on these risk factors and suggest that they are due in part to economic stress and negative family interactions, both of which can have a negative impact on the mental health of children.

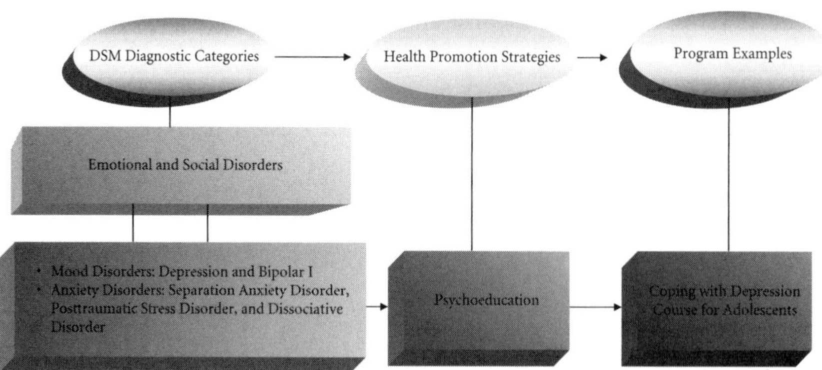

FIGURE 10.1B. Evidence-Based Mental Health Promotion Strategies and Program Examples for Diagnostic-Specific Mental Health and Health Conditions of Childhood and Adolescence: Emotional and Social Disorders.

Children and adolescent behaviors range from mild to serious and a child is said to have a "disorder" when her or his behaviors occur frequently and are severe. Research suggests that children with emotional or behavioral disorder refers to a condition in which behavioral or emotional responses of a child are so significantly different in degree from her or his generally accepted age-appropriate, ethnic, or cultural norms that they adversely affect educational performance in one or more areas: self-care, social relationships, personal adjustment, academic progress, or work adjustment.

There are three categories of emotional and behavioral disorders are attention-deficit/hyperactivity disorder (ADHD), conduct disorder, and oppositional defiant disorder.

Attention-Deficit/Hyperactivity Disorder. Children who show symptoms of inattention, hyperactivity-impulsivity that are not consistent with their developmental level may have ADHD. The inattention aspect of ADHD refers to difficulty sustaining attention to tasks or activities. *Hyperactivity-impulsivity* refers to difficulty in controlling inappropriate impulses and inhibiting activity level to meet the demands of the situation (Schroeder & Gordon, 2002).

Examples of DSM-IV-TR criteria for ADHD–inattention include the presence of six out of nine symptoms of inattention such that degree of impairment is maladaptive and inconsistent with the developmental level. Examples of these symptoms include: fails to give close attention to details, difficulty sustaining attention in tasks or play activities, does not listen when spoken to, has difficulty organizing task and activities (APA, 2000, p. 92). Hyperactivity–impulsivity is characterized as often fidgeting with hands or feet, squirming in chair, leaving classroom seat, running or climbing excessively in situations where it is inappropriate, often being "on the go," often blurting out answers before questions have been completed, difficulty awaiting turn, and interrupting or intruding on others (APA, 2000, pp. 92–93).

Conduct Disorder and Oppositional Defiant Behaviors. Research indicates that aggressive behavior among children is escalating, giving rise to disturbing increases in subsequent drug abuse, depression, juvenile delinquency, antisocial behavior, and violence in adolescence and adulthood (Webster-Stratton, 1997). Risk factors for these occurrences include increasing poverty, economic stratification, family isolation, fewer supports for families, and a declining sense of community (Sviridoff & Ryan, 1996). With regard to conduct problems, studies have shown that poverty, lack of social support, maternal depression, and family isolation are related to the onset of conduct disorders (Hawkins *et al.*, 1992).

Conduct Disorder. Children diagnosed with conduct disorder have a persistent and repetitive pattern of behavior that involves violating the basic rights of others or major age-appropriate social norms (APA, 2000). These behavioral features extend beyond the family to the school and community and involve serious aggression, violation of rules, and defiance of authority. Behavior patterns of staying out late, rule breaking, aggressive behavior, skipping school, and running away are characteristic of children and adolescents with conduct disorders. Conduct disorder is often associated with an early onset of sexual behavior, drinking and drug use, smoking, and risk-taking acts.

Examples of DSM-IV-TR criteria for conduct disorder include aggression to people and animals, destruction of property, deceitfulness or theft, and serious violation of rules (APA, 2000, p.99).

Oppositional Defiant Disorder. Behaviors categorized as oppositional defiant for a child or adolescent are less severe in nature than those for a children with conduct disorder and typically do not include aggression toward people or animals or destruction of property. Typical behaviors include arguing with adults, refusing to follow or defying adult directions, blaming others, being angry, annoying others, and being spiteful.

Examples of DSM–IV-TR diagnostic criteria for oppositional defiant disorder include a pattern of negativistic, hostile, and defiant behavior lasting 6 months during which four (or more) of the following are present: often loses temper, argues with adults, defies or refuses to comply with adults' requests or rules. and deliberately annoys people (APA, 2000, p.102). (See Figure 10.1c.)

Health-Related Disorders

The first two health-related disorders to be discussed are the eating disorders *anorexia nervosa* and *bulimia nervosa*, to be followed by substance use problems.

Eating disorders are characterized by severe disturbance in eating behavior and body image. Children and adolescents may excessively restrict food intake or engage in binge eating. Often this behavior is followed by compensatory behavior including excessive exercise, purging through vomiting, or the misuse of laxatives or diuretics. Eating disorders can be life-threatening and cause serious health risks. Eating disorders are

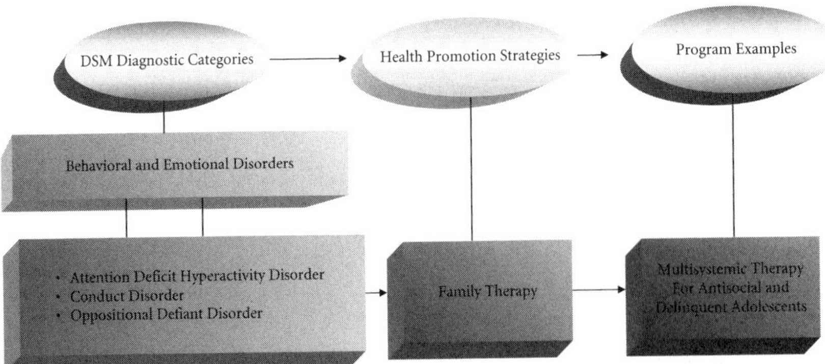

FIGURE 10.1C. Evidence-Based Mental Health Promotion Strategies and Program Examples for Diagnostic-Specific Mental Health and Health Conditions of Childhood and Adolescence: Behavioral and Emotional Disorders.

most common among adolescents and young women (Kendall-Tackett, 2003). Other eating disorders not covered in this chapter are pica, rumination disorder, obesity, and feeding disorder of infancy and early childhood. Anorexia nervosa and bulimia nervosa, the most common eating disorders, are currently recognized by specific sets of symptoms (APA, 2000).

Anorexia Nervosa. Anorexia nervosa rarely occurs before puberty and occurs mainly in teenage girls, but boys and young women and men may also experience this disorder, especially if they participate in sports with weight restrictions, such as wrestling or boxing. Adolescents with anorexia are obsessed with being thin beyond what may be considered socially desirable or attractive (Foreyt et al., 1998). Individuals with anorexia nervosa never see themselves as thin but always as being "too fat." Some key warning signs that a person has anorexia nervosa are deliberate self-starvation with weight loss; fear of gaining weight; refusal to eat; becoming disgusted with former favorite foods; limiting self to "safe foods" only, usually those with no fat; denial of hunger; obsession with clothing size; sometimes wearing baggy clothes or layers to hide fat or emaciation; spending a lot of time criticizing body parts; constant excessive exercising; developing greater amounts of hair on the body or face; having no or irregular menstrual periods; and, in boys and men, declining levels of sex hormones and loss of scalp hair.

Additionally, anorexia nervosa often coexists with other disorders or symptoms such as substance abuse, depression, self-mutilation, irritability, and withdrawal. Dieting may represent avoidance of or ineffective attempts to cope with the demands of a new life stage, such as adolescence. Individuals with either anorexia or bulimia are overly concerned with weight gain and becoming fat. Adolescents and young adults with anorexia starve themselves and avoid high-calorie foods while exercising constantly.

Examples of DSM–IV-TR criteria for anorexia nervosa include a refusal to maintain body weight at or above a minimally normal weight for age and height (e.g., weight loss leading to maintenance of body weight less that 85% of that expected) and intense fear of gaining weight even though already underweight (APA, 2000, p. 589).

Bulimia Nervosa. The prominent feature of bulimia nervosa is an excessive intake of food followed by "recurrent inappropriate compensatory behavior in order to prevent weight gain" (APA, 2000, p. 549). Some key warning signs that a person has bulimia nervosa are binge eating, usually done in secret, feeling out of control when eating, vomiting, misusing laxatives, exercising excessively, or fasting to get rid of calories. As a result of excessive self-inflicted vomiting, such individuals may experience sore throats, abdominal swelling and pain, and scarring or bite marks on the hand from inducing vomiting. Other difficulties include dental problems from the regurgitated stomach acid, which erodes enamel that protects teeth; weight may be normal or near normal unless anorexia is also present (Foreyt *et al.,* Sattler, 1998). Those with bulimia eat huge amounts of food, but they throw up soon after eating or take laxatives or diuretics to avoid gaining weight. Adolescents with bulimia usually do not lose weight as drastically as adolescents with anorexia.

Examples of DSM-IV-TR criteria for bulimia nervosa include recurrent episodes of binge eating in which eating (within any 2-hour period) any amount of food that is definitely larger than most people would eat during a similar period of time and a sense of lack of control over eating during the episode (e.g., feeling that one cannot stop eating or control what and how much one is eating) (APA, 2000, p. 594).

Substance Use Problems. Substance use, which includes dependency and abuse, include both alcohol and drugs. For many youth and adolescents, some alcohol and drug use is normal and should be expected. Developmentally, youth are experimenting with adult behaviors, and the substance use will not lead to addiction. This is not to say that adolescent alcohol and drug experimentation should not be taken seriously. Most drugs impair perception and thought process and a single dose of certain substances (e.g., inhalants)can lead to permanent damage or death.

Substance use disorders are associated with maladaptive use, abuse, or dependency that results in adverse social, behavioral, psychological, and physiologic consequences for the child or adolescent. For youth, consequences are most frequently expressed in deterioration in peer and family relationships, decline in school attendance and academic functioning, higher levels of negative affect (depression and anxiety), and involvement in antisocial behaviors (Myers *et al.,* 1998). There is much overlap in the symptoms and behaviors of adolescents with other mental disorders who are misusing drugs or alcohol. This makes it imperative to determine whether the presenting symptomatology is substance-induced.

Symptoms of substance-induced disorders for adolescents include but are not limited to physical signs (e.g., fatigue, repeated health complaints, red and glazed eyes, and persistent cough), emotional signs (e.g., personality change irritability, irresponsible behavior, sudden mood changes, low self-esteem, poor judgment, and depression), family (e.g., starting arguments, breaking rules and withdrawing from family activities), school (e.g., drop in grades, change in attitude about school, many absences, truancy, and discipline problems) and social problems (e.g., engaging in criminal activities, theft, vandalism, changes in dress style or appearance, and new friends who share similar signs).

Assessment of adolescent substance abuse problems relies on criteria that were originally developed for adults (Myers *et al.,* 1998). The DSM-IV-TR criteria are often used with adolescents and have been found to have some utility for diagnosing substance use disorders (Martin *et al.,* 1995).

Examples of DSM-IV-TR criteria for substance dependency and abuse are listed separately. Examples of diagnostic criteria for substance dependence include a maladaptive pattern of substance use leading to clinically significant impairment or distress over a 12-month period. This includes tolerance and withdrawal and an increase in the substance in larger amounts over a longer period than was intended (APA, 2000, pp. 197–198). Examples of diagnostic criteria for abuse are a maladaptive pattern of substance use over a 12-month period in which there is recurrence substance use resulting in a failure to fulfill major role obligations at work, school, or home (APA, 2000, p.199).(See Figure 10.1d.)

Ecological Systems Theory and Health Promotion

In order to understand children with the disorders described above, we must first appreciate the context of their environment. One way to do this is through a theoretical approach favored in the field of health promotion: the ecological systems theory. This theory, while not designed to guide intervention selection, has proved useful for organizing complex interventions for youth who are adjudicated and at risk for out-of-home placements (Jordan & Franklin, 2003).

Ecological systems theory is based on the notion that individuals use multiple ways to interact with, respond to and modify their environments (Dulmus & Wodarski, 2002). Examples include interactions with environment that may be physical, psychological,

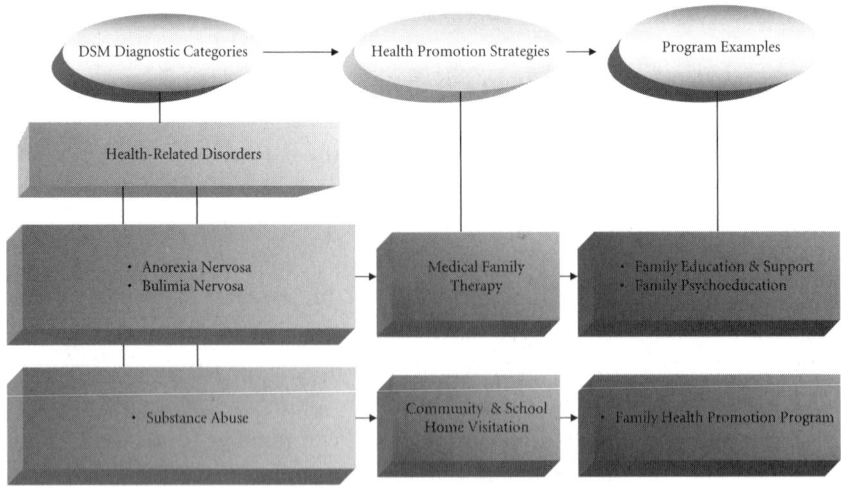

FIGURE 10.1D. Evidence-based Mental Health Promotion Strategies and Program Examples for Diagnostic-Specific Mental Health and Health Conditions of Childhood and Adolescence: Health-Related Disorders.

educational, and or social. An ecological systems view also considers client strengths and the context of multisystemic risk and protective factors (e.g., peers, family, school, neighborhood, community, organizations). These multiple contextual variables interact to complicate or support children's lives. For purposes of our discussion, we will focus on five important contextual variables: the *illness*, the *client*, the *environment/community*, the *family*, and the *health/mental health care setting*.

Illness

The type of disease as well as the long-term prognosis may have implications for a health promotion intervention. For example, a chronic versus an acute or terminal illness would be treated differentially. A chronic illness such as diabetes must necessarily involve long term planning for teaching the child self management skills to give his or her own insulin shots, monitor blood levels, adjust his or her lifestyle to the disease, and so forth. In contrast, adjustment to the terminal illness of a child may require child and family coping skills, such as grief counseling.

A different type of health promotion intervention is required if the illness is behavioral or emotional versus a physical illness as in the example above. For instance, a child with conduct or oppositional defiant disorder requires a more behaviorally oriented intervention aimed at helping the child and family to control the child's externalizing behaviors and to use the multisystemic therapies provided by agencies. These behaviors may include stealing, truancy and drug use. In sum, the type of condition and its unique characteristics leads to specific treatment options.

Client

Client functioning may be viewed in several domains including emotional, behavioral, psychological, and physiologic. Assessment should assess each area and treatment should be designed to intervene with the clinically significant areas in each domain. Emotional functioning may include under or over functioning in mood leading to depression, anger and so forth. Behavioral functioning includes surfeits or deficits in one's interaction with the environment. For example, children or family members may have skills deficits in communicating, problem solving, conflict resolution, and so on. Psychological functioning may include cognitive processing errors such as irrational thinking or other perceptual errors. Finally, physiological functioning includes organic limitations such as deficits in sensory skills (sight, hearing), and motor skills.

Environmental/Community

The environmental/community context is another important variable that may interact with and compounds response to children's problems. For example, families living in rural versus urban environments may have greater difficulty in obtaining appropriate services. Jaffee and colleagues (2005) found that community-level contextual stressors (e.g., poverty, unemployment, crime, and lack of social support), race, and child's health status were significantly associated with behavioral and emotional problems among children with special health and mental health care needs. Other community supports may or may not be available in specific environments. Churches, neighbors, support groups, and social service agencies are all examples of sources of support that may or may not exist in the child's environment.

Family

Families are a powerful influence on the health of their members, particularly in terms of the emotional support offered to its children. Family criticism and conflict has been shown to be strongly predictive of poor outcomes, while family closeness has a positive influence on the illness. Other sources of support for children with problems may or may not be forthcoming from parents, siblings, and extended family members. Parents' skill and coping level, as well as financial situation are factors in how well they respond to their children's illness. Parents must deal with their own feelings of guilt, anger, sadness, and so on when their child is diagnosed with a mental health condition. Siblings of children who are ill may have needs of their own that are not being met due to an over focusing on the ill child. Some siblings may be called upon to act as coparents to the ill child, losing out on their own childhood experiences (Galan, 1992). Extended family may or may not be available to support the family with an ill child.

Health and Mental Health Care Settings

Issues with health and mental health care settings include gaps in needed services, poor quality services, lack of insurance, and lack of client access to available services due to stringent inclusion criteria. Samaan (2000) examined race, ethnicity, and poverty and found that children who have mental health problems and are from low-income families were less likely to obtain mental health services. Primary care settings have increasingly become the de facto setting of mental health services for low-income families, particularly when the child has a combination of health and mental health conditions (Jaffee *et al.*, 2005). Client satisfaction is rarely measured in order to help social service agencies improve the level of services provided.

■ Assessment

The two areas for assessment include client and family functioning. These two areas encompass the important contextual issues discussed in the preceding section and are summarized in Figure 10.2.

Measurement is used to aid in assessing clinically and socially significant problems and, later, to monitor outcomes; thus measurement is a focus of the assessment areas presented here.

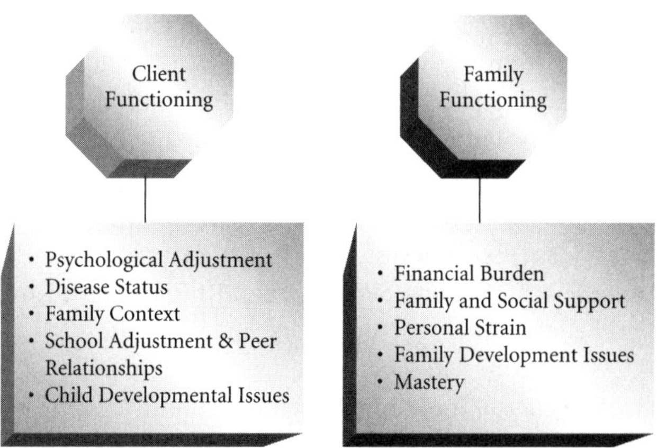

FIGURE 10.2. Assessment Areas for Client and Family Functioning.

Client Functioning

Six areas of client functioning are discussed here. These are psychological adjustment, disease status, family context, school adjustment, peer relationships, and child developmental issues.

Psychological adjustment. Fischer and Corcoran (2007a, 2007b) identify standardized measures with high reliability and validity that may be used to measure the psychological adjustment of children. These include the Hudson's scales, which measure the emotional health of the ill child and other family members. Examples include depression, self-esteem, impulsivity, eating behaviors, coping skills, and so forth. Commonly used scales that are reproduced in the Fischer and Corcoran (2007a,b) texts include the Depression Self-Rating Scale, the Hare Self-Esteem Scale, Impulsivity Scale, Compulsive Eating Scale, and Adolescent Coping Orientation for Problem Experiences.

Disease Status. Campbell (2002) suggests that interventions for assessing the impact of chronic diseases, diabetes, asthma, or hypertension, for example, may be measured by use of physiologic measures. Examples are glycosylated hemoglobin, pulmonary function testing, and blood pressure (p. 317). In the case where no physiologic measure exists, self-reports of symptoms or disability or adherence to medical treatment may be measured.

Family Context. Important to consider here is the issue of positive family support versus critical or conflict burdened family. Hudson's Index of Family Relationships may be used to assess overall family functioning (Fischer & Corcoran, 2007a). The Conflict Tactics Scale is an example of a measure of family conflict (Fischer & Corcoran, 2007a).

School Adjustment and Peer Relationships. Fischer and Corcoran (2007a) also reproduce scales appropriate for use in measuring school issues including adjustment. One example is the Hare Self-Esteem Scale which measures the child's self-esteem in three areas: home, school, and with peers. Other scales in the book measure behaviors thought to be indicators of success in school settings, such as problem solving and level of social support. Examples from the book are Problem-Solving Inventory and Social Support Appraisals Scale. Examples of other scales that may be used with a school population include Sexual Attitude Scale, Eating Attitudes Test, Compulsive Eating Scale, and Alcohol Beliefs Scale.

Child Developmental Issues. Traditionally, testing administered by psychologists has been used to assess children's development levels. Examples of scales often used include the Bayley Scales of Infant Development, Stanford-Binet Intelligence Scale, Kaufman Assessment Battery for Children, McCarthy Scales of Children's Abilities, Wechsler Preschool and Primary Scale of Intelligence, Leiter International Performance Scale, System of Multicultural Pluralistic Assessment, Bender-Gestalt, and Peabody Individual Achievement Test (Mash & Terdal, 1988).

Family Functioning

Assessment and measurement of family functioning should include interpersonal as well as contextual variables. Those discussed here include financial burden, family and social impact, personal strain, family developmental issues, and mastery.

Financial Burden. Fischer and Corcoran provide scales for helping to assess family issues including finances and other family maintenance behaviors. These include the Family Inventory of Resources for Management, Family Crises Oriented Personal Evaluation Scales, Family Responsibility Index, and the Family Inventory of Life Events and Changes.

Family and Social Support. Important areas to consider for family and social support include family relationship issues, especially critical and hostile behaviors. Examples of scales that help to measure family functioning are the Index of Family Relations, Conflict Tactics Scale, Family Adaptability and Cohesion Evaluation Scale, and Parental Nurturance Scale. To assess social impact, scale examples are Network Orientation Scale and Perceived Social Support Scales (family and friends versions) in Fischer and Corcoran (2007a).

Personal Strain. Stress responses with a corresponding need for coping skills are to be expected when the family is experiencing a child health problem. Examples of scales to measure both personal and family stress and coping are: Adolescent Coping Orientation for Problem Experiences, Adolescent-Family Inventory of Life Events and Changes, Family Hardiness Index, Impact of Event Scale, Index of Clinical Stress, Hopelessness Scale for Children, and Reasons for Living Inventory.

Family Developmental Issues. Families differ in their response to members' issues, in part due to family developmental issues such as relationship between parents and children, between child and siblings, and between family and extended family. Some appropriate scales for measuring the quality of these relationships are Parent-Child Relations, Child's Attitude About Parents, Index of Brother and Sister Relations, and Family-of-Origin Scale.

Mastery. Mastery has to do with how well the child and other family members are able to do for themselves and feel good about their level of achievement. Examples of scales include Separation-Individuation Process, Ascription of Responsibility Questionnaire, Belief in Personal Control Scale, Family Empowerment Scale, and Internal Control Index. These instruments are also reproduced in Fischer and Corcoran (2007 a)

In summary, the measures above are used to assess children and their families, to select the appropriate treatment, and to monitor client progress throughout the intervention process. Let's now focus on another aspect of this process: treatment, using health promotion strategies.

■ Health Promotion Strategies

Up to this point, we have reviewed a number of specific health and mental health conditions and discussed the use of ecologic systems theory as a framework for understanding the context for which mental health conditions develop. In addition, we have identified a number of client and family assessment measures useful for monitoring treatment progress and outcomes for health and mental health conditions of childhood and adolescence. Let's now turn to a review of evidence-based health promotion strategies and related programs that have been shown to be effective with children and adolescents who present with mental health conditions and their families. These strategies include education, psychoeducation, family therapy, medical family therapy, and community and school home visits. See Figure 10.1a to d for an overview of these strategies. As readers will note, each strategy and program example has a family-based component of treatment, which is considered a critical feature of any child- or adolescent-focused health promotion strategy.

Educational: Self-Management Model for Chronic Illness

The self-management model for chronic illness is a practice model that teaches clients, particularly those with chronic illness or a medical condition that is affected by a mental health condition, to perform the care necessary to maintain and control the symptoms of their illness. The techniques of this approach are from the behavioral (operant conditioning) and cognitive-behavioral approaches, which tend to be evidence-based and efficacious. These techniques, which are educational in design, may include but are not limited to self-monitoring, self-instruction, relaxation, and imagery. Self-efficacy, or mastery, as discussed above, is often used as the outcome measurement.

The process of self-management is a six-step process. These are goal selection, information collection, information processing and evaluation, decision making, action, and self-reaction. Empiric studies of self-management approaches report success in use of self-management skills, reduced medication use, improved exercise, and cognitive and physical symptom management (Creer *et al.*, 2004, pp. 726–727). This approach is particularly helpful for youth who are experiencing an anxiety disorder concurrent with a general medical condition such as diabetes. (See Figure 10.1a.)

Psychoeducation: Coping with Depression—A Course for Adolescents

The coping with depression course for adolescents is a psychoeducation model that assumes a cognitive and behavioral explanation of the depression (Kazdin, 2004). The treatment utilizes cognitive behavioral methods; clients are taught to recognize the cognitive features of their depression (i.e., negative thinking), to substitute positive thoughts, to elicit positive reinforcement from the environment, and to use specific social skills. The treatment is presented in a psychoeducational framework so that the stigma of being in treatment is reduced. The adolescents receive training in a group; parents receive group training, as well. They are taught to support the new skills acquired by their children.

The process of therapy includes brief assessment focused on skills and a 16-week group course followed by booster sessions offered at 4-month intervals for a 2-year period. Empiric research on this approach show decreased depression for adolescents, especially younger males. The parent group has not been shown to add to the basic intervention, but studies are continuing (pp. 555–556). Despite limited studies for the efficacy of the combined child and parent session, we would like to illustrate how a combined session would unfold. An example is illustrated in Text Box 10.1 A psychoeducational approach is particularly helpful for helping families and youth to understand the various symptoms, cues, and triggers associated with mood disorders such as depression and bipolar disorder. (See Figure 10.1B.)

Box 10.1. The Case of Carl and His Family: Using Psychoeducation as a Health Promotion Strategy for Treating Adolescent Depression

Background

The following is an example of a health promotion strategy, psychoeducation, used with a teenager, Carl, age 17, diagnosed with depression, and his family.

Assessment Summary

Carl Baker and his family recently moved to Dallas from a small town in West Texas. It had been a very difficult transition for Carl and he has not adjusted to life in an urban environment. Carl and his family were referred to the social worker by the Timberwolf Hospital staff hoping that the family could learn more about Carl's condition and how to support him. Carl's parents, Ted and Kay Baker, are at a loss as to how the family should be coping with Carl's diagnosis. Carl has six siblings, and they too are anxious to understand how to help and support their brother.

Carl and his family came to the office after he was released from Timberwolf Hospital. Carl had been admitted for threatening to hurt himself and others. He has been diagnosed with depression and has begun taking fluoxetin HCl (Prozac). His parents noticed that things were not going well when his grades began to fall and he was kicked off the football team. At school, he reportedly started several fights with other boys, leading to his suspension. While in the hospital, Carl frequently mentioned quitting school. He is also angry with his parents for moving him to a new town and school in his senior year.

Treatment Plan

Problems: (1) Depression. (2) Family conflict.

Goals: (1) Reduce depression. (2) Reduce family conflict.

Measurement: (1) Reduce depression on the Beck Depression Inventory to a level that is non-clinically significant. (2) Reduce family conflict on the Conflict Tactics Scale to a level that is non- clinically significant.

Intervention: (1) Psychoeducational treatment to educate family about depression (excerpt demonstrated below). (2) Cognitive behavioral family therapy to reduce conflict by improving communication and conflict resolution techniques.

Beginning Script

THERAPIST (T): Hi! It's good to see you again. Now that we have been apart for a couple of days, have you had a chance to think about what we talked about last time?

FAMILY (F): Yes.

(T): Do you have any comments or questions?

(F): We want to learn more about our son's depression.

(T): Great. That's just what our education topic is today. We are going to talk about depression and provide information about what depression is, its treatment

(continued)

and side effects, the effects that depression has on the family, and what each individual family member can do to help. Let's now begin by looking at exactly what depression is.
(Therapist places transparency on overhead projector)
"Session 1: LEARNING ABOUT DEPRESSION"*
Clinical depression is a serious illness affecting millions of Americans. Each year, more than 11 million people suffer from this illness, which is as common as it is misunderstood. Many people go through life suffering from clinical depression, never understanding that it is a medical illness or that effective treatments are available. Too often the illness has carried with it fear and shame that prevented people from asking basic questions about its causes and treatments. Please feel free to ask questions at any time during our session.

* Readers are referred to Chapter 7, Table 7.1, for an overview of a family psychoeducation session format; this example would be linked to Weekly Session 1: Psychiatric Diagnosis: Overview Consumer's Diagnosis, Symptoms and Characteristics.

Family Therapy: Multisystemic Therapy for Antisocial and Delinquent Adolescents

Multisystemic Therapy (MST) (Kazdin, 2004) is a family therapy approach which focuses on intervening with and altering behavior which is embedded. Kazdin (2004) reports on Henggeler's approach (p. 558) to treatment, which focuses on multiple systems (parents, peers, school, etc.) where the youth has problems. Assessing risk and protective factors such as parental discipline and child communication skills help to determine the appropriate intervention. Interventions are individualized and multifaceted and may include marital therapy, skills training, and contingency management.

The goals of treatment are "to help the parents develop the adolescent's behaviors, to overcome difficulties that impede the parents' ability to function as parents, to eliminate negative interactions between parent and adolescent, and to develop or build cohesion and emotional warmth among family members" (p. 558). Kazdin (2004) reports strong empiric support for MST. In addition to the child's relationships with parents and others and reducing child psychopathology, the approach has known cost effectiveness (pp. 558–559). This evidence-based strategy is particularly helpful in addressing the multiple systems that children and youth who are diagnosed with attention-deficit, conduct, and oppositional disorders come in contact with. What makes this a health promotion strategy is the emphasis on building supports among multiple systems and encouraging emotional and social wellness and warmth among family members. (See Figure 10.1c.)

Medical Family Therapy

Medical family therapy is a model of family therapy designed to help families with a member who is experiencing a health problem such as anorexia or bulimia. Two types of medical family therapy have been reported: *family education and support* and *family psychoeducation* (McDaniel *et al.*, 1992).

Family education and support provides information and emotional support to families whose child is experiencing a health problem. The program may be led by a professional or a peer counselor who has experienced the same illness as the family.

Family psychoeducation also provides education and support but adds a third component of therapy for family relationship issues that might arise as a consequence of the child's illness. This may be done by a family therapist but is often done by others with various backgrounds. These approaches are particularly supportive for families where the family member (i.e., youth) is experiencing an eating disorder.

Community and School-Based Home Visitation Program: Family Health Promotion Program (FHPP)

The Family Health Promotion Program (Rey, 1999) is a combination community- and school-based primary prevention and health promotion program targeted to children ages 3 to 8 and their families who are at risk for substance abuse. The program emerged from the coordinated efforts of the Greater Santa Rose Neighborhood and the Connie Chambers Early Childhood Education Center, who saw a number of unmet needs (e.g., quality child care, mental health services, basic health care, parenting help and transportation, risk for substance abuse) of the children and families living in the area. Most of the children and family members in this program are monolingual Spanish-speaking and living in Tucson, Arizona.

Treatment consists of two approaches; one for children, the other for parents. In an effort to develop resiliency skills, children were involved in a variety of developmentally appropriate activities in child care, school, and recreational activities. Parents were involved in activities that focused on empowerment and increasing protective factors. These interventions included: training in resiliency/protective factors by providing home visitation, parent advisory council meetings, support groups, family weekend activities, training for key school personnel and in-house staff, provision of daily transportation, and art therapy sessions. One example of a health promotion activity is a class that is offered to participants 20 hours per month and consists of activities involving body management, health awareness and self-care, communication and soci-alization. Evaluation measures included the use of a quasi-experimental, pretest–posttest comparison group design to assess the impact of these interventions. Outcome data were quite positive and included data showing a decline in parents' use of tobacco, alcohol, and amphetamines between pretest and posttest. Significant group improvement was seen in resiliency factors for children, which included school success, delayed onset or abstinence from alcohol, tobacco, and illegal drug use, and teacher ratings of conduct problems, hyperactivity, inattentive-passive and hyperactivity (Rey, 1999). What makes this program uniquely health promotion–oriented is the emphasis on a community approach to a variety of needs and resources. The holistic emphasis on community and family health addressed, by inclusion, substance abuse issues. (See Figure 10.1d.)

Limitations of Health Promotion

Campbell (2002) reviewed the research on health promotion strategies for children and families. His review indicates that family interventions, particularly family psychoeducational approaches, are superior to other types of interventions in promoting health. Campbell suggests that these family-oriented interventions improve the mental and physical health of all family members and are cost-effective as well; many have proven effectiveness for some types of problems while showing promise for others. He concludes: "Family interventions for childhood disorders, especially diabetes and asthma, are effective in improving medical … as well as psychosocial outcomes. Not surprisingly, family interventions are most effective at each end of the life cycle when much of the care is provided by family caregivers" (p. 331). Campbell goes on to assert that the limitations of the research include too few observational and intervention studies on families and health as well as too few family researchers and clinicians involved in the study of this area of practice.

Implications

Campbell (2002) suggested future directions for research on child and family health promotion interventions for health including:

1. More research of families and health; this area of study is in its infancy.
2. More research based on family theories and family science; much of the current research is atheoretical.
3. Research should systematically study interventions on one disease.disorder; then successful interventions may be tested on other diseases/disorders.
4. Multiple outcomes should be used in intervention studies.
5. Interventions should be flexible enough to adapt to individual families.
6. Cost–benefit studies should be done.
7. Intervention studies should describe interventions in more detail so that they may be replicated.
8. Gender effects should be studied.
9. Studies should include diverse populations (pp. 329–330).

Conclusion

Health promotion seems implicated in a wide range of child and family health-related behaviors. The goal of this chapter is to provide information that can be used by providers of health and mental health care to support the empowerment of children and families toward models of care that integrate health promotion practices with outcomes of health, wellness, and enhanced quality of life. By understanding the broad array of children's health- and mental health–related disorders, providers can conduct assessments that are more precise, develop outcomes that are measurable, and offer health promotion strategies and interventions that support health-enhancing environments for children and their families. In the words of Hillary Rodham Clinton, "There's no such thing as other people's children." We are thus reminded of our collective roles in the health and mental health of children and their families.

In Our Own Words . . . Family and Consumer Perspectives on Mental Health Treatment Services: Focus Group Feedback

Topic: Mental health and health needs of children and families

Summary

As Chapter 10 illustrates, child, adolescent, and family mental health is becoming an increasingly important focus for providers, who recognize the importance of developing health promoting attitudes and behaviors early on. Additionally, providers and researchers recognize that the lives of children with mental health conditions and their families are affected by an array of social issues (e.g., poverty, parenting needs, access to care). Staying with this theme, consumers and family members were asked to identify ways in which providers could help them to provide for the needs of a child with a mental health condition. As in previous reports, education (e.g., parenting skills) is the single most important activity that providers can offer both consumers and family members. Additionally, both groups mentioned the need for a respectful and collaborative relationship.

What Can We Learn?

Based on these recommendations, providers and agencies must continue to strive to build in educational sessions as part of the "regular" intervention—whatever that might be. As noted in this chapter, all six evidence-based health promotion strategies described had an educational component built into the intervention. Clearly this is an activity that meets the need. One cautionary note, though, is that "education" should not be perceived to be a top-down approach but one that is delivered with respect and invites a collaborative discussion with all members of the child/family/provider support team.

The following section details the results of the focus group meeting as reported by family members and consumers.

Focus Group Question: ***"How can mental health providers help you address the health and mental health needs of you and your children?"***

Family Perspectives

Core Themes	Summary of Experiences	Comments
(Ranked in order of priority)		
First—Education	Family members wanted more education from providers on the	"When asking about our child's history, we may not always

Focus Group Question: *"How can mental health providers help you address the health and mental health needs of you and your children?" (continued)*		
	topic of child development, medication, and mental illness; even teachers could benefit from an understanding of mental illness and help explain it to parents.	know the difference between normal adolescence and early signs of mental illness or what a 'precipitating event' even is." (J., *parent*)
Second— Partnership	It helps when mental health providers engage parents in a partnership that is respectful and collaborative.	"Please make the assumption that. parents are really doing good work, have the best intentions and are not to blame for abuse. The number one important thing is to treat us as real people, with respect and listen to family input; we really do know our children and we have valuable information." (K., *parent*)

Consumer Perspectives

Core Themes	Summary of Experiences	Comments
(Ranked in order of priority)		
First— Education	Consumers stated that education was the single most important core skill that providers can offer to parents with a child with mental illness. For example, a single mom might need parenting skills that would, in turn, help her child and reduce stress at home. Providers also can educate parents in the form of resource referral by letting families know the variety of providers available to assist them.	"WHO these providers are makes a huge difference. By cutting the bureaucracy that plagues health and mental health systems, parents could be more resourceful with the information they are provided by their workers." (R., *consumer*)

PART V

ORGANIZATIONAL LEADERSHIP, READINESS, AND CULTURAL COMPETENCE

11. Moving Health Promotion Forward: Culturally Competent Leadership, Strategic Planning, and Organizational Readiness

We are the best resource for an agency—if they would let us be.

—M., *parent*

■ Chapter Overview

If the field of health promotion and its accompanying philosophy, principles, and practice strategies is to move forward and be fully integrated into mainstream mental health organizations and practice, it's going to take a lot more that simply convincing students, academics, and providers of its merits—as I hope this book has done so far. It will require a fundamental shift in the way mental health organizations provide leadership, develop strategic plans, and plan for organizational change. Toward that end, this final chapter reviews some of the key ingredients necessary for moving health promotion forward into the field of mental health practice. As Chapter 1 emphasizes, there are a variety of stakeholders (e.g., consumers, family members, providers, agency administrators, and policy makers) who have an interest in mental health system reform. This chapter is written with that audience in mind. So whether you are currently in an administrative or leadership role, thinking about being in an administrative or leadership role, or simply want to be a part of an informed change process, this chapter is for you.

This chapter is basically about how leadership, planning, and organizational readiness to change are key ingredients in determining the integration of health promotion into mental health systems. Throughout the chapter are examples of various models of leadership, strategic plans, and practical stages and steps for doing an analysis of an organization's readiness to move health promotion forward in the field of mental health practice. The terms *leader* and *administrator* are used interchangeably, although admittedly they may not be so in reality.

The chapter is divided into six sections. The first section is a review of the transition that mental health and health promotion has undergone in the clinical, professional staff, fiscal, and outreach areas. Discussion is provided on the new trend in health promotion for tomorrow's leader: interactive health communication. The second section moves into the topic of leadership. Much emphasis is given to the role of the culturally competent leader, understanding their vision, and examining the roles that they assume within their organizations and communities. The third section discusses in practical detail the art of strategic planning—which is the cornerstone of how an organization fulfills its mission to integrate health promotion. The fourth section explores the reasons why a strategic plan may not work in some circumstances. This section explores organizational change, which includes resistance and challenges to change, change steps, and targets of change. The fifth section offers a challenge: Is your organization ready to change to a health promotion model? Based on the answers to this series of questions, you'll have your answer. Finally, the sixth section concludes with a summary of a focus group discussion held by consumers and family members who were asked the following question: "If you could make recommendations for improved mental health services for yourself or your family member, what would you want the agency director and providers to know?"

Learning Objectives

When you have finished reading this chapter, you should be able to:

1. Understand the historical changes in clinical, professional, fiscal and outreach efforts in the field of mental health and health promotion
2. Explore emerging trends in health promotion leadership and technology
3. Describe the characteristics and roles of a culturally competent leader
4. Develop a strategic plan that focuses on health promotion
5. Describe organizational change process that includes resistance, steps, targets, readiness to change.
6. Identify core recommendations for mental health agency improvement offered by consumer and family focus group participants

■ Introduction

For health promoters in mental health organizations, it is not enough to just "teach" people about lifestyle adjustments or behavior change to obtain better health and mental health benefits. The organization itself and its leadership have to be informed and supportive of health promotion activities. Much is needed in the way of organizational training and retrofitting to accomplish this task. What is clear is that administrators of mental health organizations are in a good position to influence a changing vision for the health and mental health of their client populations, their families, and the larger community. That vision is health promotion and there are three factors necessary to accomplish the integration of health promotion into the field of mental health practice: *effective leadership*, a *strategic plan*, and *organizational readiness/ flexible organization*—all subsumed under the umbrella of cultural competence. Let's look at how these factors have changed over time.

■ Mental Health and Health Promotion in Transition: Yesterday, Today, and Tomorrow

Let's briefly recap some of the changes in the field of mental health that are driving the move toward a new model of leadership, strategic planning, and organizational change that is oriented to health promotion practice. We'll begin by looking at features of mental health systems (e.g., clinical, professional staff, fiscal, and outreach) in the past and present and conclude with a review two key trends emerging in the health promotion field—communication technology, also referred to as interactive health communication (IHC), and an integrated care philosophy.

Clinical

In previous generations, many mental health administrators will have worked in systems that favored the more traditional approaches to mental health care. Examples of traditional approaches could be described as utilizing a psychodynamic and or case management model of practice, where the primary focus of care was directed to the individual, involved minor elements of teaching people new health related skills (e.g., relaxation techniques for stress reduction) and where the identified target of change was the behavior of the individual. The clinical approach was to work on isolated problems (e.g., substance use first and then mental illness) through a program designed to perform risk-based disease management or, in other words, to reduce the primary problem or risk factor that was identified as perpetuating the problem (e.g., alcohol use).

Today, administrators of mental health services are finding themselves facing a new array of client populations whose complex needs range from untreated mental health conditions (e.g., depression and substance abuse) and comorbid health conditions (e.g., medication-induced obesity, diabetes, hypertension) to extreme levels of poverty, history of trauma, and limited access to basic health and mental health care. Consequently, traditional models of mental health treatment (e.g., office based, long-term psychodynamic approach to care) are no longer acceptable, effective, or practical. Recent reports by the World Health Organization (WHO, 2001, 2004a,b) found that despite years of local, state and national public health education efforts to inform individuals on the risks of unprotected sex, tobacco use, and alcohol consumption, these risks remain in the top 10 categories of disease, disability, and death worldwide. This same report highlights that heart disease, the world's leading cause of preventable death, is caused by tobacco use, high blood pressure, and/or diet-related cholesterol. These reports suggest that these risks could be reduced with relatively modest lifestyle changes: stop smoking and stay away from second hand smoke, exercise, and eat right. However, simple lifestyle adjustments may not come in time if people cannot have access to basic medications to reduce hypertension, psychosis, depression, or even access to healthier food choices.

Although most administrators acknowledge that these areas/approaches will still occupy a clinical and organizational place in mental health systems, visionary leaders recognize a need to incorporate newer theoretical and practice models (e.g., health promotion, wellness, and recovery) that focus on families, groups and communities as well as individuals. These same leaders can encourage providers to retool their skills in order to move from single-problem focus and treatment to integrated service approaches (e.g., substance abuse, mental health, and primary care). They can also promote the idea that individuals and communities will be assessed for their assets rather than risks and that services offered reflect evidence-based practice and are appropriate for their clientele. This means, of course, that there will be an impact on staff, some who may continue to offer programming based on an outmoded model of treatment (e.g., long-term residential placement for children) or that reflect a clinicians unyielding loyalty to their previous decades old training (e.g., ego psychology or object relations) regardless of the client's, family's, or community's presenting problem. Other changes have included the demand for agencies to retool the way they do business—particularly in the areas of clinical services, such as filling a niche market in housing or child-, and family-, and community-based services.

Professional Staff

In years past, hiring practices for most mental health agencies has been dictated by a combination of reimbursement plans (e.g., in the United States, Medicaid reimbursement can occur only through services delivered by licensed or qualified mental health practitioners) and discipline and degree specific categories (e.g., licensed, master's level counselors/therapists who come from three discrete, and sometimes competing, disciplines: counseling, social work, and psychology). However, increasingly, today's leaders who embrace a health promotion philosophy and vision will ensure that providers will be less discipline-bound (e.g., social work) in their jobs and be more interdisciplinary in the connections to other providers (e.g., primary care physicians and mental health therapists and consumer peers).

Fiscal

For the last 15 years, the standard fiscal approach to mental health services has been cost containment through a variety of means: rationing care for clients such that they have limited clinic appointments, providing lower-level services (e.g., case contact rather than therapy) for some clinical situations, reduced services, and a move to more cost-efficient group treatment modalities. Today, reduced federal and state/provincial spending for mental health and addiction services has prompted organizations to prepare competitive budget packages and proposals to private-sector funding sources (e.g., business sector and foundations). There is considerably less reliance on federal matching of dollars spent on clients.

Outreach

In the past, outreach efforts were driven by market-based programming; in other words, what specific market niche did the organization command in the particular community? For example, the mental health organization may have done targeted outreach to schools and child welfare agencies in order to promote their children's residential services programs. In some organizations, children's residential might be seen as an agencies flagship service in which the organization was recognized for a particular approach (e.g., children's intensive therapeutic residential care); consequently, the outreach would be directed toward a market niche in the community to support that program.

Today, mental health administrators who advocate for an integration of health promotion with mental health practice are shifting their outreach efforts to community systems that are in partnership with client services. For example, childhood and adult obesity among mental health populations requires a collaborative partnership among school personnel and public health/mental health providers. Other partnerships include mental health systems collaborating with neighborhood pharmacies to arrange payment systems for clients who may be confused by copayments structures and thus decline to have prescriptions filled. These are two kinds of outreach that is much more likely to affect change than a single focus on individual clinical therapy and patient behavior change (Terry, 2003; Kersh & Morone, 2002).

Tommorrow: Future Trends

Two emerging trends in the field of mental health and health promotion are reflected in opposite ends of the spectrum. One is the trend toward new technology (e.g., communication technology such as web based interactive health tools) and the other is toward a new thinking (e.g., integrated care philosophy)—both of which involve significant changes in the way administrators, practitioners and clients interact. Let's first examine the trend toward a new form of communication technology.

Communication Technology. The mental health field has witnessed radical changes in the last decade related to technology. These changes include advances in information technology that have reshaped the way mental health organizations access information and communicate internally and externally. Examples include telemedicine, Internet technology, electronic decision support tools in health care, and consumer-oriented websites (SAMHSA, 2005). Administrators of mental health systems recognize the need to utilize a variety of information systems to communicate health promotion strategies to mental health "audiences." One trend that is gaining popularity in mental health circles is the use of computer-based information technology, referred to as communication technology.

Current practice has been to use media-based health communication strategies such as radio, television, printed text, and pictures, now referred to as "old media," to convey information that promotes healthful behaviors. New media, however, have potential advantages for communicating a variety of information based content that is user-friendly, easily tailored to individual concerns, and easily disseminated. This is part of a growing field of communication technology that is changing the nature of interactions between individuals, health and mental health professionals, and communities.

This form of communication technology is referred to as *interactive health communication* (IHC), defined as the "interaction of an individual—consumer, patient, caregiver or professional—with or through an electronic device or communication technology to access or transmit health information or to receive guidance and support on health related issues" (Robinson *et al.*, 1998, p. 1265). IHC refers to the use of operational communication and computer software programs or modules geared towards users or people who use IHC applications. IHC applications have three core functions: to relay information (e.g., websites, online services, telephone-based applications that use interactive voice responses, and fax-back technology); enable informed decision making (e.g., selecting a health care professional or health management plan), and promote healthful behaviors (e.g., modules on risk assessment and health promotion modules based on theories of behavioral change) (Robinson *et al.*, 1998).

IHC however, is not without its risks. Since IHC systems are now directly available to the public (via the Internet), minimal research has been reported about the risks associated with their widespread use. Potential risks include inaccurate or inappropriate health information, poorly designed applications, websites that do not keep updated information and present misleading claims that might lead to delayed treatment. Efforts are currently under way by the Office of Disease Prevention and Health Promotion of the U.S. Department of Health and Human Services to review these technologies and develop a standardized reporting template to evaluate the safety and quality of these resources.

Example. One example of an employee-focused, web-based IHC health promotion training program is *Prevention Connection: Substance Abuse Prevention Training for Health Promotion Practitioners.* Developed through a Small Business Innovation Research (SBIR) grant through the National Institute of Drug Abuse (NIDA), this program uses an interactive, multimedia approach to train wellness professionals to integrate substance abuse prevention materials and messages into health promotion programs. The program uses hands-on exercises that allow practitioners to build their own program outlines with topics ranging from stress management to healthy eating. (McPherson & Cook, 2004). For more information, the reader can visit the following website: www.drugabuse.gov/NIDA_notes/NNV0119N3/Tearoff.html

Integrated Care Philosophy. As discussed in Chapter 1, in the field of mental health care administration, health promotion is an emerging philosophy and concept that is driving many organizations to rethink the way their policies, services, and personnel interact with clients, families, neighbors, communities, businesses, funders, and even politicians. Moving beyond an illness focus, health promotion is becoming a powerful conceptual tool for administrators to build healthy environments for workers, clients, and even the community. Sometimes referred to as an "integrated care model" because of the blending of health and mental health practices, integrating health promotion into the field of mental health practice is a challenge and one that involves a new kind of leadership and management approach.

■ Leadership and Health Promotion

As already noted, mental health agencies have changed significantly over the last three decades. Fueling this change has been an increased expectation from consumers, family members, community partners, and policy makers that mental health leaders develop new skills and relationships to deal with a changing mental health care environment. The expected model for chief executive officers (CEOs) has become more of a collaborative manager who values diversity and participatory management and less of a professional manager who is hierarchal and uses a top-down decision-making style. The leaders in today's mental health environment must be ready to embrace change, encourage dialogue, use participatory decision making, instill a team-oriented culture and be able to build management teams that know how to execute the organizations strategies—all within a framework of cultural competence.

The research literature on leadership, like health promotion, is drawn from an eclectic set of management theories espoused by a multidisciplinary range of professions (Terry, 2003). This section overviews key aspects of leadership for the contemporary mental heath organization.

3 C's Leadership Model

Lewis and colleagues (2004) list the 3C's of a Leadership Model: competent, character and commitment. In order to be an effective leader, one must be competent, both culturally and intellectually, have character, and have a strong commitment to one's communities. Let's explore these further.

Competence

Competence refers to having requisite business acumen and professional skills to be effective. This means being able to understand financial statements, develop marketing skills, demonstrate policy-making skills, have good interpersonal and diplomacy skills, and be able to manage individual, team, and a variety of in-house and community relationships. Castro and colleagues (1999) identify seven factors linked with competent leadership. These include (1) garnering support for a program from the local community and funding agency, (2) strengthening staff morale and commitment to program goals, (3) maintaining fidelity in program implementation when necessary, (4) identifying serendipitous developments that can be added to the program evaluation data to aid in documenting program development and effectiveness, (5) meeting regularly with staff to assess program activities, (6) engaging in problem solving, and (7) planning for future activities and program growth (pp. 138–145).

Culturally Competent Leaders. Another aspect of a competent leader is one who models cultural competence, defined as "the integration and transformation of knowledge, information and data about individuals and groups of people into specific clinical standards, skills, service approaches, techniques and marketing programs that match the individual's culture and increase the quality and appropriateness of health care and outcomes" (Davis, 1997, p. 33). A culturally competent leader is one who supports the organization in its ability to provide services that are perceived by clients, their families, and the community as relevant to their lives. Culturally competent leadership is more than just directing the agency to work with racially and ethnically diverse groups. Such a leader is about embracing the strengths, assets, differences, and gifts of ethnic and minority communities. However, being competent means first being aware. In other words, administrators need to have an awareness (sensitivity) of issues and then skills to address those issues (competencies).

Dana (1993) suggests that *cultural sensitivity* is a precursor to cultural competence. He defines cultural sensitivity as awareness of another culture based on knowledge and first hand acquaintance. This awareness is cultivated through professional activities (e.g., internships) and exposure (e.g., participation in ethnic-specific events). In designing and implementing health promotion programs for ethnic or minority communities, culturally sensitive and competent administrators are vital to their success. Castro and colleagues (1999) describe qualities of effective administrators who work with Latino communities providing health promotion programs. These are listed in Table 11.1.

Call to Leadership:Workforce Training Issues. From the federal policy level down to mental health organizations, cultural competence has been endorsed as an integral part of best practices in mental health care (Stanhope *et al.*, 2005, p. 225). Despite this endorsement, research has found significant gaps in the competencies of mental health organizations ability to deliver best practices that are culturally competent. For example, the New Freedom Commission on Mental Health Report (2003) identifies the following workforce training issues:

1. Racial and ethnic minorities are underrepresented in the core mental health professions.
2. Many providers are inadequately prepared to serve culturally diverse populations.
3. Investigators are not trained in dealing with minority populations.
4. Gross errors in diagnosis and grossly inappropriate services and interventions have resulted from cultural and linguistic misunderstandings.
5. Clinicians who are unfamiliar with a client's culture and health beliefs may misinterpret symptoms, leading to diagnostic errors (Pi & Simpson, 2005; Manderscheid *et al.*, 2002; Peterson *et al.*, 1998).

What Leaders Can Do. Work-force training seems to be a key step for leaders to take to address the work-force crisis. Stanhope and colleagues (2005) reviewed the status of cultural competence training in agencies and found that many national, state, and local organizations have responded, albeit slowly, to the need to reach out to racially, ethnically, culturally, and sexually diverse people. Most settings are developing guidelines to implement culturally competent behavioral health services. They note that associations

TABLE 11.1. *Qualities of Effective Administrators of Health Promotion Programs Who Work with Latino Populations*

- Knowledgeable of local community
- Possess an organized vision of the program's purpose and direction
- Ability to communicate vision, purpose, and direction to staff on a regular basis
- Build commitment and morale among program staff
- Give all staff an appropriate voice regarding program policies and procedures
- Arrange and participate in meetings with community leaders and other stakeholders
- Build and maintain *personalismo* (personalized relations) and *confianza* (trust) with community partners
- Demonstrate a "commitment from the top" in giving an ear and a voice to the community in relation to program goals and objectives
- Maintain a balance between scientific agendas and cultural competence agendas in the ongoing evaluation of the program
- Proactive in anticipating problems and in searching for solutions that optimize program effectiveness given the available resources
- Inspire staff and community confidence that agendas are driven by the goal of enhancing the health and welfare of the local community
- Exhibit strength and integrity in responding forcefully on behalf of the program if and when the program is attacked by those harboring political and social opposition

Adapted from Castro, F., Cota, M., & Vega, S. (1999). Health promotion in Latino populations: A sociocultural model for program planning, development and evaluation. In R. Huff & M. Kline (Eds.), *Promoting health in multicultural populations. A handbook for practitioners,* p. 161. Thousand Oaks, CA: Sage.

like the American Psychological Association (APA), American Psychiatric Association (APA), and the International Association of Psychosocial Rehabilitation Services (IAPSR) have provided detailed guidelines for their members to promote culturally competent practice. The U.S. Department of Health and Human Services (DHHS, 2000) has issued a report on cultural competence standards. Samplings of recommended guidelines for culturally competent organizations include the following:

1. Have forms written in all verbal interchanges with the use of inclusive language.
2. Examine data derived from psychosocial histories and intake forms. Do questions provide room for sexual orientation? Rather than ask about marital status, ask about partner or significant other. Instead of next of kin, ask name of responsible party and that person's relationship to the client.
3. Encourage participation of partners in treatment.
4. Display pictures or posters of known lesbian/gay/bisexual/transgender (LGBT) figures in offices; post lists of LGBT-friendly AA or Narcotics Anonymous meetings.

5. Provide pamphlets on tables that show ethnic holidays, celebrations, reading materials in various languages, and diverse resource lists (e.g., gay pride groups).
6. Ensure that offices and programs display mission statement which has language that explicitly honors diversity and commitment to working with all individuals.
7. Display ads for programs that have health promotion, pro wellness, and health-oriented philosophies in waiting rooms. Have a kiosk that offers resources, including different languages, orientations, and community service agencies (e.g., a rainbow-colored flag that explicitly states openness to treating diverse clients).

Additionally, the New Freedom Commission on Mental Health (2003) report offers recommendations for leaders who are committed to addressing the work-force crisis in mental health services for racial and ethnic minority populations. These are:

- Recruiting and retaining racial and ethnic minority and bilingual professionals
- Engaging minority consumers and families in work-force development, training, and advocacy
- Developing training and research programs that target services to multicultural populations

Castro and colleagues (1999) describe five elements of successful, culturally competent health promotion programs. These are (1) ensuring the availability of health and mental health services in different languages when needed, (2) hiring bilingual/bicultural staff and providing them with cultural competence training, (3) integrating ethnic and diverse cultural aspects of interpersonal relations into the programs services (e.g., *la familia Latina, personalismo, respeto, simpatica*), (4) adjusting the services offered to the levels of acculturation that exist within the targeted population, and (5) being sensitive to other aspects of the local culture that would make the program culturally operative in the local community. The key to effective cultural competence training is the extent to which it generates positive outcomes for clients, not merely increased awareness, knowledge and skills of trainees.

As a consequence of these issues and recommendations, leaders/administrators will increasingly be expected to create organizational environments that provide culturally competent programs and staff. In turn, staff will be working with an increasingly diverse group of people and their capacity to do this will depend on the acquisition of culturally competent skills. Clients, for their part, value providers who have the ability to empathize, communicate, connect cross-culturally, and incorporate cultural aspects into their program designs. The result will be more effective and targeted health promotion interventions and services for diverse audiences (Castro *et al.*, 1999).

Character

Character refers to the values and behaviors exhibited by leaders who generate trust and commitment (Lewis *et al.*, 2004). Character in a leader also means having the courage to make bold decisions and stand up for issues that may prove unpopular. One way of determining the values of a leader is by the principles from which she or he operates.

Principles. As discussed in Chapters 5 and 6, health promotion principles are useful guideposts for staying focused on the values and direction of one's work. Using meta-analyses of leadership literature, Terry (2003) identifies three core principles of effective leadership: authenticity, service to others, and shared power—all of which speak to the character of a leader. In other words, health promotion practice requires leaders whose intent is to affect positive, sweeping, measurable, and memorable improvements in mental health care (Terry, 2003). There are two additional health promotion principles that seem particularly applicable: principle of relevance (starting where the people are) and the principle of participation (eliciting participation of staff, community, clients, and family members). These are important because they involve a multistaged process that mobilizes people and resources for a common purpose. These principles also have excellent relevance to management because they help promote ownership in the organization while also fostering active learning through participation (Wheatley, 1999).

Community

Although typically described in geographic terms (e.g., neighborhoods), the term *community* refers to the shared characteristics of a group of individuals, such as beliefs (e.g., faith community), religion (e.g., Muslim community), situation (e.g., refugee community), and sexual orientation (e.g., lesbian, gay, bisexual, transgender—LGBT community). These four communities represent "shared characteristics" and are described in Box 11.1.

Box 11.1. ***Key Communities with Whom Mental Health Leaders Work***

■ The Faith Community

Background. For many ethnic peoples, the church or temple may be their first stop when it comes to seeking answers for psychological or emotional distress. Often individuals with mental illness and their family may trust religious organizations and their leaders far more than community mental health centers. Clemens (2005) points out that faith-based agencies (e.g., Catholic Charities, Lutheran Family Services) and religious settings (e.g., churches, temple, synagogues and mosques) often serve as surrogate families and community centers for a significant part of a population. As Cnaan (2002) summarizes the role of congregations in social welfare, it is "the invisible caring hand."

Faith-based providers are the only source of care for some persons with mental illness. Dossett and colleagues (2005) review the pros and cons of providing mental

(continued)

health services within religious organizations. On the benefit side, implementing mental health services within religious organizations could benefit some high-risk populations, such as recent immigrants, because they have limited access to medical services but high rates of participation in religious organizations. Additionally, religious organizations possess tangible resources, such as meeting space and staff members as well as intangible resources such as values of hope, healing and community, Some faith based communities also have health screening and education programs that could be extended to include mental health services.

On the obstacle side, at least in the United States, the constitutionally of faith-based community initiatives has been questioned because of laws regarding church-state separation. Also, dispute over the appropriate roles of clergy members and health professionals and over moral and health related interpretations of behavior raise ethical questions.

In an effort to understand the perspectives toward mental health services of staff employed at faith-based agencies, Dossett and colleagues (2005) conducted a community survey of attitudes toward mental health services and barriers to providing these services. The survey was distributed to 56 member organizations of the Queens Care Health and Faith Partnership, a nonprofit, public charity that provides health care for low-income uninsured residents of the city of Los Angeles. Approximately 42 agencies responded. Results found that while 69% felt that referrals to nonreligious counselors were appropriate, 50% were reluctant to collaborate with formal governmental agencies. Barriers to providing mental health services included limited professional training, reluctance to partner with government programs, and financial and staffing limitations. Staff had various ranges of perspectives of mental illness, with some viewing mental illness as a spiritual or moral problem while others viewed mental illness along a medical model of interventions. Still others considered the importance of faith healing or exorcism as useful interventions.

Additional research has found that, in minority communities in particular, the clergy often serve as first-line providers of mental health care to community members and liaisons to assist members in accessing formal mental health services (Young et al., 2003). Further, the National Comorbidity Survey (Elhai & Ford, 2007) reported that clergy provide more mental health care than psychiatrists. Finally, from a health promotion standpoint, these faith-based leaders also may be critical in helping the mental health system and providers better understand the community.

Recommendations. Considering the importance of faith-based organizations and leaders in the lives of so many people of color and diverse ethnic background, the Mental Health Freedom Commission Report (2003) recommends enlisting their support and partnership in mental health care. This effort would involve leaders in mental health agencies working with faith communities and leaders to help:

1. Increase understanding of mental and physical health in their communities
2. Reduce stigma associated with mental disorders and problems
3. Encourage individuals and families to seek help
4. Collaborate with mental health providers
5. And when necessary, link people with appropriate services

■ The Muslim Community

Background. In the United States, the Muslim community, with an estimated population of 6 to 9 million, is considered one of the most rapidly growing minority communities. Muslims place great value on the integrity and functioning of the family and consider Islam to be central to their daily way of life (Ali et al., 2005). Thus, when there are family problems, Muslims will naturally consult with their Islamic clergy, referred to as *imams*. Guidance is generally derived from references and interpretations of the holy scriptures of Islam, *The Qur'an* and *The Hadith*.

In one unique study, Ali and colleagues (2005) examined the roles of imams in meeting the counseling needs of their communities. Using an anonymous, 79-item, self-report questionnaire, surveys were sent to 730 mosques across the country. Sixty-two responses (or an 8% rate of response) were returned. Respondents represented Arab Americans, South Asian Americans, and African Americans. The principal finding of this study is that congregants came to their imams with issues beyond spiritual or religious concerns. These issues were: family problems, experiences with discrimination since September 11, 2001, social service needs and psychiatric symptoms.

The authors conclude that despite little formal training in counseling, imams dealt with extensive mental health and social service issues. The authors noted that imams are less likely than other clergy to have formal comprehensive counseling training that might help them to effectively address their community's multidimensional needs.

Recommendations. From these limited data, it is recommended that leaders in the mental health community offer their professional services, such as technical assistance or consultation, to imams. This gesture has the potential to play a role in improving access to services for minority Muslim communities in which there currently appear to be unmet psychosocial and mental health needs (Ali, et al., 2005).

(continued)

■ The Refugee Community

Background. Mounting evidence points to the overwhelming effects of war trauma on the mental health of affected individuals, families, and communities in many regions of the world (Musisi et al., 2005). These effects may span generations with significant negative impacts on the public health and socioeconomic development of affected societies. The World Health Organization (WHO, 2004b) raises the call for concern with its review of the status of refugees. They note that

> considerable psychiatric disability exists in exiled refugees, massively traumatized communities who stayed behind in their countries of war, physically or sexually tortured war victims and combat veterans. The most common diagnoses are post traumatic stress disorder (PTSD, depression and anxiety—all of which are frequently associated with comorbid disorders such as substance abuse, personality changes, traumatic brain injury, dissociation, psychotic decompensation and suicidal behavior. In addition, ample evidence points at the transgenerational effects of such traumas. War, in general, has a severe impact on the post-war societies and their capacity to cope with the social, health and mental health consequences (p. 34).

Recommendations. While the most desirable strategy is to prevent war-related trauma through local, national, and international peacekeeping and diplomacy efforts, prevention efforts are not always available to individuals whose nations are the victims of preemptive strikes by dominant nations. However, much can be done to promote the health of individuals and communities when peacekeeping has failed. Leaders in the mental health field can support the use of health promotion strategies to assist individuals and communities to rebuild themselves—whether in their home country or host country. Musisi and colleagues (2005) offer several health promotion strategies for dealing with refugees and communities who have experienced war. Examples are family reconciliation, providing funding and personnel to rebuild a country's physical and mental health services and social infrastructures, mental health education, restoring human rights, and offering emotional, social, and economic support to refugees.

These are all macro–health promotion strategies that require the support of international agencies and local mental health organizations. As the authors point out, apart from PTSD, few of these strategies have been evaluated in rigorous outcome studies. The Freedom Commission Report (2003) offers three recommendations that local mental health leaders can implement in partnership with federal agencies (e.g., National Institute of Health and Substance Abuse Mental Health Services Administration) to address the multiple effects of trauma on refugees. These are (1) undertake a sustained program of research on the impact of trauma on the mental health of specific populations, such as women, children and victims of violent crime and terrorism; (2) enhance the evidence base of trauma with refugees; and (3) evaluate service models for treating post-traumatic stress disorder and other trauma related disorders in public mental health settings (p. 77).

■ The Lesbian, Gay, Bisexual, Transgender Community

Background. Unlike other diverse communities, the size of the lesbian, gay, bisexual, transgender (LGBT) community is difficult to determine. Simply getting a sense of the incidence and prevalence of health and mental health issues in the LGBT community is made difficult by the fact that reliable information on the size of the LGBT population is not available, epidemiologic studies on alcohol and drug abuse rarely ask about sexual orientation and research studies cannot be compared because of inconsistent methodologies (U.S. Department of Health & Human Services, 2001b). These numbers are even more elusive for ethnic minority group members. However, of the few existing prevalence studies of homosexuality in the United States, Michaels (1996) estimated that 10% of men and 5% of women report same-gender sexual behavior since puberty; 8.0% of men and 7.5% of women report a homosexual or bisexual identity. The data on the number of transgender people are more limited. Some psychiatric literature estimates that one percent of the population may have had a transgender experience but this is based on people who have sought mental health services (Seil, 1996).

If understood as a community, one must understand that marginalization is a serious experience for LGBT individuals. LGBT people, unlike other ethnic groups who can return to supportive family or neighborhoods, may not always escape discrimination. Isolation, then, is a common experience and one that health promotion can directly impact.

Health Issues. LGBT clients have similar concerns and face many of the same physical and mental health crises as other mental health clients in treatment. In general, studies indicate that

- When compared with the general population, LGBT people are more like to use alcohol and drugs, have higher rates of substance abuse, are less likely to abstain from use, and are more likely to continue heavy drinking into later life

(continued)

- Some evidence suggests that approximately 30% of all lesbians have an alcohol abuse problem (U.S. DHHS, 2001b; IASWR, 2005)

Further, LGBT clients who abuse substances are also more likely to have co-occurring mental and physical disorders. If they have experienced hate crimes or domestic violence, they may be at greater risk for experiencing posttraumatic stress disorder. Due to fear of discrimination or marginalization in accessing health care, some LGBT may have been reluctant to seek health care. This hesitation may result in late diagnosis or poor treatment outcomes. Additionally, transgender individuals may encounter risks related to taking hormones.

Another health concern is for gay and bisexual men who are sexually active with multiple partners and are at risk for contracting STDs, HIV/AIDS, and hepatitis A and hepatitis B. Hepatitis C may also be spread by sexual contact but is more likely to be contracted through intravenous drug use. The convergence of HIV, hepatitis, and substance abuse is a major public health concern that has not been adequately addressed in the LGBT communities, especially regarding the vaccines for hepatitis A and hepatitis B.

Recommendations. LGBT individuals have unique difficulties that require sensitivity on the part of mental health organizations. Counselors need to be sensitive to the issues and needs of LGBT clients which can be easily overlooked. In terms of assessment, clinicians need to focus on family dynamics. LGBT may have close connection to what is called a family of choice—a legal spouse or unrelated individuals who support and care about the client.

Also, heterosexism can affect LGBT people by causing internalized homophobia, shame and negative self-concept (U.S., DHHS, 2001b) and just anger at the oppression which may resort in substance use. Many LGBT individuals in therapy report feeling isolated, fearful, anxious, depressed, and angry and report difficulty trusting others.

Substance abuse treatment for an LGBT individual is the same as that for other types of clients and focuses primarily on stopping the substance abuses that interferes with well-being of the client. It differs from mainstream practices in that the client and counselor address the client's feelings about his or her sexual identity and impact of homophobia and heterosexism. Even if the client is secure in their identity, he or she may harbor the effects of society's negative attitudes, which can result in feelings of doubt, confusion, fear, and sorrow (ISAWR, 2005).

Treatment options consist of referral to a support group that works with families of origin known as PFLAG (Parents, Families and Friends of Lesbians and Gays). While many issues are similar across the clinical and interpersonal spectrum, providers must recognize that other issues are unique experiences for the LGBT clients and their families. LGBT have many issues to contend with: antigay violence, hate crimes, physical attacks, and discrimination—all of which contribute to the role of substance use and abuse. Growing up in a society that says they should not exist and certainly should not act on their sexual feelings clearly has distressing consequences in later life.

In order to provide outreach to the LGBT community, mental health leaders in organizations must do what has been recommended for other individuals from diverse communities: hire staff that are trained in these dual issues, develop workplace awareness training to decrease potential for sexist or homophobic behaviors and develop programming that is issue specific to concerns that LGBT communities feel is important.

Community has also been defined as having distinctive units: functional spatial units that meet basic needs for sustenance (e.g., housing), units of patterned social interaction (e.g., associations) and/or symbolic units of collective identity (e.g., pink ribbons symbolizing solidarity with cancer survivors) and as social units in which people come together to act politically to make changes (e.g., consumer rights groups) (Minkler & Wallerstein, 1997). Regardless of the definition, administrators of mental health organizations are increasingly recognizing that community involvement, commitment, and engagement are necessary prerequisites for addressing social (e.g., discrimination) and environmental (e.g., housing) problems that affect individuals with mental illness and their families.

Good leaders are also known to be committed to these various aspects of community and have an understanding of what it takes to have a healthy and vibrant community, both within and beyond their organizations. One example of a "healthy community" endeavor is the Healthy People 2010—Healthy Communities Project (U.S. Department of Health & Human Services, 2001). This project is part of a national policy initiative and serves as the framework for mental health leaders who are involved in health promotion efforts at the community level. This initiative defines a "healthy community" as one that

> embraces the belief that health is more than merely the absence of disease; a healthy community is a safe community that includes those elements that enable people to maintain a high quality of life and productivity—local jobs, housing, religious institutions, grocery, shopping. It offers access to health care services that focus on treatment, prevention and wellness for members of the community (U.S. DHHS, 2000).

Mental health leaders who subscribe to this concept can play an important role in the political life of their communities by working with local businesses, law enforcement, transportation services, and housing boards to achieve these aspects of quality community life and the pursuit of wellness—which is recognized as a core health promotion value. See Box 11.2 for a review of this health initiative.

Box 11.2. United States: Healthy People 2010

Background. *Healthy People* 2010 was developed by citizens in a multiyear process coordinated by the U.S. Department of Health and Human Services (USDHHS, 2000). First developed in 1979 (U.S. Department of Health, Education and Welfare, 1979), this project was designed to improve the health of the American people by targeting key health indicators that were known to contribute to a healthy life. Now in its third edition, *Healthy People* 2010 is a comprehensive guide that encourages local and state leaders to develop community- and statewide efforts to promote healthy behaviors. It is based on the assumption that individual and community health are often inseparable and that it is critical for both individuals and the community do their parts to increase life expectancy and improve quality of life.

Description. *Healthy People* 2010 is designed to achieve two goals: (1) to increase the quality and years of healthy life and (2) to eliminate health disparities—defined as an inequality or gap that exists between two or more groups. Health disparities are believed to be the result of the complex interaction of personal, societal, and environmental factors. To achieve these goals, *Healthy People* 2010 identifies 10 leading health indicators and 28 focus areas that reflect major public health issues in the United States. These indicators and focus areas highlight a combination of individual behaviors, physical and social environmental factors, and important health system issues that are known to impact the health and mental health of individuals and communities. Recommendations for action are listed for each health indicator. It is noteworthy that over half of the recommendations call for health promotion activities and virtually all 10 indicators and 28 focus areas are persistent issues for individuals with mental illness. They account for most of the illness and disability that various community providers see in their settings.

■ Health Indicators and Recommendations

- Physical Activity: Promote regular physical activity
- Overweight and Obesity: Promote healthier weight and good nutrition
- Tobacco Use: Prevent and or promote reduction in tobacco use
- Substance Abuse: Prevent and or promote reduction in substance abuse
- Responsible Sexual Behavior: Promote responsible sexual behavior
- Mental Health: Promote mental health and well-being
- Injury and Violence: Promote safety and reduce violence
- Environmental Quality: Promote healthy environments
- Immunization: Prevent infectious disease through immunization
- Access to Health Care: Increase access to quality health care

■ Focus Areas

Focus areas include access to quality health services for arthritis, osteoporosis, and chronic back conditions; cancer; chronic kidney disease; diabetes; disability and secondary conditions; educational and community-based programs; environmental health; family planning; food safety; health communication; heart disease and stroke, HIV; immunization and infectious diseases; injury and violence prevention; maternal, infant, and child health; medical product safety; mental health and mental disorders; nutrition and overweight; occupational safety and health; oral health; physical activity and fitness; public health infrastructure; respiratory diseases; sexually transmitted diseases; substance abuse; tobacco use; and vision and hearing.

Adapted from Office of Disease Prevention and Health Promotion, Office of Public Health and Science, Department of Health and Human Services, (February 2001) Healthy People in Healthy Communities. Washington, DC: Government Printing Office. p. 4.

In essence, before mental health clinicians are to be successful with clients, agency leaders must first be successful with the community. The field of health promotion has long recognized the power of communities to aid in the healing, health, and mental health of individuals and their families. Leaders within the mental health field are only now beginning to embrace the benefits of broad community involvement.

Castro and colleagues (1999) remind us that mental health organizations which serve minority or diverse populations must establish strong relations with the communities they serve. This includes outreach to those communities and typically requires that administrators must personally go into the community, at least periodically, to communicate and demonstrate commitment and support "from the top." These efforts can help fortify a health promotion program, in part, by grounding it in the true needs of the local community.

Leadership and Health Promotion

Terry (2003) summarizes that leadership is about engagement and modeling bold action. The following five strategies are modified versions of leadership actions identified by Terry (2003, pp. 162–167) as necessary for achieving a vision of health promotion.

1. *Leaders lead by fiscal example.* They commit at least 5% of mental health program budgets into research and evaluation of health promotion initiatives.
2. *Leaders welcome scrutiny.* Invite outside reviewers or evaluators to evaluate existing clinical and organizational practices to see if mental health policies and programs support health promotion practices.

3. *Leaders are active, not passive.* Acknowledge and support mental health programs that demonstrate effectiveness using health promotion strategies.
4. *Leaders are teachers.* Offer to speak to local health and mental health care organizations, business clubs and fraternal organizations about the value of health promotion as a community strategy for addressing health, social, and environmental issues.
5. *Leaders are collaborators for community change.* Commit to working outside the mental health profession to bring together politicians, business, and community leaders for the purpose of creating partnerships that promote community change for health and mental health using the principles and strategies of health promotion.

Two examples of community collaboration are offered; one represents local community leadership; the second represents national leadership and vision. These are described in Boxes 11.3 and 11.4.

Box 11.3. Leaders in Action at the Community Level: Cascadia Behavioral Healthcare, Inc.

Project: "The Commons"—Promoting Individual and Community Health Through Better Housing

The sign in the mental health clinic's waiting room reads "Write in a core value." All staff, managers, and clients are guided by these core values and most clinical and organizational decisions, such as housing needs, are influenced by these words. These core values permeate the entire organization and may explain in part how one CEO and her organization came to receive a prestigious housing award.

The winner of the 11th Annual 2005 Charles L. Edson Tax Credit Excellence Award for Special Needs Housing went to Cascadia Midland Commons Apartments, a housing program of Cascadia Behavioral Healthcare, Inc., a community-based mental organization located in Portland, Oregon. Described by officials as "breathtaking, a major flagship in efforts to end homelessness and a prime example of successful collaboration," this award went to "the most outstanding low-income-housing tax-credit project." This prestigious national honor was bestowed by the Charles L. Edson Foundation of Washington, D.C., to programs that "encourage tenant self-sufficiency, unique design features and exemplify community involvement and support."

Leading the innovation for this program is Leslie Ford, MSW, Cascadia's President and CEO, and Neal Beroz, Vice President of Housing. Ford noted how federal, state, and county officials as well as the private sector, including neighbors, joined with nonprofit Cascadia Behavioral Healthcare, Inc. to create this program. Recognizing that safe, affordable housing is one of the most essential needs in the lives of individuals with mental and physical illness who have had histories of homelessness, Ford and Beroz, along with a dynamic management team, core housing specialists and intensive case management teams have made "quality housing" a priority of the agencies mission and goals. The Commons represents the end product of this commitment. The Commons is a 46 -unit apartment complex designated for individuals who have been chronically homeless and for special populations including families and individuals with a serious chronic physical or mental illness. Located on a 1.38-acre site and designed by award-winning architect William Wilson, the program was designed to maximize access to the natural outdoor environment and indoor opportunities for socialization. The site is landscaped with native vegetation and designed to provide a variety of large and small outdoor spaces. The two buildings, totaling 39,500 square feet, include amenities such as high-speed Internet access, a gas fireplace, a large community room with kitchen, several smaller lounges, and large balconies. A spacious main hallway and atrium displays framed consumer artwork.

This organization illustrates the positive impact of innovative, collaborative, team-oriented, community-centered leadership. Ford and her team have long heralded the benefits of community partnerships as a means to create healthy living environments that are health-promoting and contribute to individual and community health and wellness.

Source: Adapted from M.Schorr (2004),*Cascadia Newsletter*, V01.3, Issue 6, 2004, Portland, OR.

Box 11.4. ***Leaders and Government in Action: The New Zealand Approach to Health Promotion: Building on Strengths and Mental Health Promotion Project Background***

The government of New Zealand, as documented in its constitution and national policies, has made a commitment to reduce the inequalities in health and mental health experienced by some groups. The Treaty of Waitangi is New Zealand's constitutional document which recognizes the Maori as both a social group and as tangata whenuam, the indigenous people of New Zealand. The treaty is based on health promotion principles of partnership, participation and protection.

■ Leaders and Government in Action

As a consequence of the governments commitment to equality, New Zealand is embarking on a national effort to enhance mental wellbeing and to reduce

(continued)

inequalities in mental wellbeing by improving the social, economic, cultural, political and physical environments in which citizens live. This effort has received local, regional and national recognition in part because of the effort of Ministry Health officials, Matheson and Wilson, to step forward and endorse this initiative. *Building on Strengths* (Ministry of Health, 2002) is the name of the five year national plan for mental health promotion established by the Ministry of Health of New Zealand. Although the product is of many hands and organizations, this initiative owes much of its enthusiasm to two leaders: Don Matheson, Deputy–Director General of Public Health and Janice Wilson, Deputy Director, Mental Health of New Zealand.

Project: Building on Strengths

The document is a result of a two year project sponsored by the Public and Mental Health Directorates of the Ministry of Health of New Zealand and supported by the efforts of numerous health service providers, academics, policy analysts, clinicians, mental health administrators and mental health consumers. The document is based on the premise that the health sector is not alone in having a role to play in promoting mental health and it is therefore crucial that other sectors—government agencies, local government and local communities—step forward to coordinate mental health promotion activities, strengthen communities and build the capacity of individuals to cope. Guided by the New Zealand Health Strategy—which sets the strategic direction for all health services in New Zealand—and the New Zealand Disability Strategy—which aims to improve the ability of people experiencing disability to participate in community life, *Building on Strengths* is designed to achieve three aims:

1. build the case for increased mental health promotion activity; i.e., activity that keeps people mentally well
2. outline planned priority actions that will begin to lay a foundation for mental health promotion now and in the future and
3. provide guidance for the health sector and other sectors on what they can do to contribute to mental health and well being and see a role for themselves in promoting positive mental health for New Zealanders (Ministry of Health, 2002, p. 7).

Building on Strengths is a new approach to mental health in that it builds a case for investment in mental health promotion and a place of higher priority on the public health and health promotion agenda of the government. As a policy guide, it aims to provide the necessary leadership to remove the potentially negative consequences of inequalities for the community's well being.

Mental Health Promotion

Building on Strengths is a policy framework built around the concept of mental health promotion, defined as "the process of enhancing the capacity of individuals and communities to take control over their lives and improve their mental health. Mental health promotion uses strategies that foster supportive environments and individual resilience, while showing respect for culture, equity, social justice and personal dignity." (Ministry of Health, 2002, p.19).

The framework is based on the three central notions:

1. mental health is more than the absence of mental illness
2. mental health is distinguishable but inseparable from general health
3. integrating mental health promotion and general health promotion strategies offers the best prospect of achieving a healthy mind in a healthy body in a healthy society

Why Mental Health Promotion? The World Health Report (2001) reminds us that mental health problems are not exclusive to any special group and are found in people of all regions, all countries and all societies. Epidemiological studies have found that more than one in four individuals will develop one or more mental health problems during their lifetime (WHO, 2001). Further, mental health problems are seen not only in poor social and emotional well being but strain health and lead to lower quality of life. Hosman & Jané-Llopis (1999) point to research indicating that mental health promotion programs have proven to be cost-effective and bring about health, social and economic development to society.

Jane-Llopis and colleagues (2003) emphasize that mental health promotion strategies focus on five main goals: (1) enable people to improve their mental health by developing personal skills and resilience, (2) create supportive environments, (3) empower people and communities, and (4) protect, support and sustain emotional and social well-being by promoting the factors that enhance and protect mental health, and (5) show respect for culture, personal dignity while fostering equity and social justice. The importance of mental health promotion has been recognized by a number of international organizations: Global Program on Health Promotion Effectiveness (GPHPE), a multi-partner program coordinated by the International Union for Health Promotion and Education (IUHPE) in collaboration with the World Health Organization. Among these partners has emerged an official project entitled "*Mental Health Promotion Project*" whose aims are to develop as sustainable approach for mental health promotion which is evidence based and facilitates adaptation and implementation suitable to different regional needs.

(continued)

■ Mental Health Promotion Project

Description. The unique aspect of this project is that it is heavily value and principle driven and as such, cannot have a distinct boiler plate approach. Starting with the determinants of mental health, *Building Strengths* describes the fundamental notions of what constitutes or determines mental health: participation in society, valuing diversity and safe, cohesive communities. From this starting point, the project presents a broad picture of who the framework targets. The targeted population for the project is adults, disadvantaged groups, people affected by mental illness, Maori, Pacific peoples, older adults and children and youth. The settings for the project are diverse and may include home, childcare and early education, schools, churches, cultural centers, Maria, Iwi aor Hapu and whanau centres, health sector, primary health care settings, neighborhoods, social and recreational settings, sporting facilities and organizations, local government, work place, housing services, correctional services. The project utilizes an array of culturally and population appropriate theoretical models which include a population health model, community development model, primary health care model, strengths model, recovery model, Te Pae Mahutonga and Fonofale model (Samoan holistic health model).

The program aims to:

1. focus on links between positive mental health and the determinants of health
2. provide information and data on factors that influence the mental health status of New Zealanders
3. emphasize the need for intersectoral and multidisciplinary approaches to planning, implementation and evaluation of mental health promotion activities
4. identify the structures and resources needed at a national and district level to support and sustain mental health promotion development.

■ Summary

Building on Strengths and the *Mental Health Promotion Project* has all of the key elements of a strategic plan discussed in this chapter: vision statement, values, principles, goals, priority action goals and outcomes. Leaders in mental health promotion can easily bring this document to various stakeholders—employees, families, consumers, business and community groups, and professionals—for dialogue, discussion and endorsement. Selected examples of the framework are provided in Table 11.3. Mental health leaders would do well to follow this crisp and succinct strategic plan format knowing that it was developed through extensive participation by the very participants who have a stake in the outcomes.

■ The Art of Strategic Planning: Strategies for Incorporating Health Promotion into Mental Health Practice Settings

Strategic thinking and planning is an essential skill in today's mental health care business world. Success in these organizations doesn't just happen. They plan, develop, diversify, and implement strategies that are designed to ensure their success. This section begins by reviewing the definition, concepts (e.g., timelines, role of leaders and management team) and stages of strategic planning.

Overview

Strategic planning is defined as "the process by which an organization makes decisions and takes actions to enhance its long-term performance. The purpose of a strategic plan is to provide the direction for the organization by identifying the markets in which an organization competes, as well as ways in which it competes in those markets" (Lewis *et al.*, 2004, p. 149). It involves the use of timelines and an understanding of the role of leaders and management team.

Time Lines. In previous generations, organizations may have devised 3- and 5-year strategic plans. However, given the fluctuating mental health care industry, changing federal reimbursement plans, new funding initiatives, and legislative mandates, most progressive mental health organizations now design flexible strategic plans with open-ended time lines.

Role of Leader. A central responsibility of a leader is to help the organization and/or community develop its vision and then assist in developing a flexible strategic plan for how to get there. The key to developing a flexible strategic plan is having a leader who is a strategist and uses participatory management as the main decision-making style. Decisions then are the result of a group decision-making process (Wheatley, 1999). Leaders are really also about building healthy organizational communities—both inside the organization and externally to the larger community (Lewis *et al.*, 2004, p. 414).

Role of Management Team. The role of the management team is to initiate the actions necessary to get the organization from where it is to where it's going; keeping its operations transparent and its attitude nimble so that it can be poised to respond to current market opportunities—such as new funding initiatives.

Stages of Strategic Planning

The following strategic planning model is taken from management literature and is applicable to a wide variety of organizational situations. The model has four stages: strategic analysis, formulation, implementation, and control. For purposes of this chapter, the model is discussed in its relationship to incorporating health promotion into the mental health workplace. For a summary of the model, see Table 11.2.

Stage 1: Strategic Analysis. The purpose of a strategic analysis is to assess the current condition or climate of the organization. The first step in this process is to ask the ques-

TABLE 11.2. ***Four Stages of Strategic Planning for Incorporating Health Promotion into the Mental Health Workplace: Stages, Purpose, and Questions***

	Stages	Purpose	Question
Stage 1	Strategic Analysis: . Mission Statement . Internal Analysis . External Environment	Assess current condition or climate of organization	"What is the current position of our organization?"
Stage 2	Strategic Formulation: . Vision Statement . Strategic Goals . Alternative Strategies . Grand Strategy (e.g., stability, growth, & portfolio assessment models)	Develop business strategy	"Where do we want to be?"
Stage 3	Strategic Implementation: . Functional . Institutional	Develop a *functional* strategy for personnel, services and marketing, and an *institutional* strategy for recognizing organizational structure (e.g., organizational chart), agency culture (e.g., beliefs) and leadership development	"What is our market and how can we enhance in-house leadership opportunities?"
Stage 4	Strategic Control: . Feed Forward . Feedback	Identify problems and offer remedies, monitor implementation of strategic plan and evaluate quality and effectiveness of organizational performance	"What were the changes in our internal and external environments and how did we perform according to our goals?"

Adapted from Lewis, P., Goodman, S. & Fandt, P.(2004). *Management Challenges for Tommorrow's Leaders.* Mason, OH: Thomson Publishing.

tion: What is the current position of our organization? The rationale underlying this question is based on the notion that in order to determine where the organization could and should be, one has to understand where it is in its development or maturity. In order to answer the question, there are three key areas and activities to perform in this stage:

1. *Mission Statement:* Assess the mission of the organization via mission statement. Some would argue that *mission statements* are just empty words or phrases but most agree that an organizational mission statement helps keep people focused on common goals and helps define the identity of the organization. In fact, research has found that mission driven organizations outperformed rivals by an average of 30% in key financial measures (see Lewis *et al.*, 2004, p. 152). The mission statement describes the services, target markets, or strategies for growth of an organization.
2. *Internal Analysis:* Conduct an internal analysis of the organization listing the strengths and weaknesses. An internal analysis encourages an assessment of the strengths, also referred to as competencies, and unique qualities and candid appraisal of organizations weaknesses, meaning areas that need improvement.
3. *External Environment:* Examine the external environment, listing the opportunities and threats. The environmental analysis encourages an examination of opportunities or environmental trends or markets that an organization can capitalize on or use to improve its competitive position (p. 153). Similarly, the organization also needs to examine environmental threats or conditions that jeopardize the ability of the organization to survive.

Stage 2: Strategic Formulation. After the analysis is complete and people have a good sense of where the organization is, the next natural step is to formulate a business strategy. This step begins by asking the question: Where does the organization want to be? This question is answered by identifying the following areas and then conducting corresponding activities:

1. *Vision Statement:* Creating a vision statement for the organization. The vision statement describes what the organization wants to be as well as how it wants to be perceived by others as doing.
2. *Strategic Goals:* Setting strategic goals. Strategic goals are very broad, prospective statements describing what the organization wants to achieve in the long run. The key to having useful strategic goals is for them to be specific, measurable, time-linked, and realistic but hopeful.
3. *Alternative Strategies:* Identifying alternative strategies. Alternative strategies are different approaches to achieving the strategic goals of the organization.
4. *Grand Strategy:* Evaluating and choosing the grand strategy that propels the agency toward its vision and goals. Lewis and colleagues (2004) note that most organizations have what is called a "grand strategy"—one that is a

comprehensive, all-encompassing general approach. The grand strategy uses two broad categories: *stability* and *growth.*

Stability strategy refers to an organizations continuation of offering the same kind of services as in the past and is usually associated with start up organizations. Using market penetration, in which the organization enters a specific geographic market with a given set a services, stability is usually the preferred strategy at this stage. Generally speaking, once the market is penetrated, the organization moves to a growth strategy.

Growth strategies are designed to increase profits of an organization and involve developing new services or markets and to reposition the organization as a market leader with its industry.

Choosing the right strategy to implement the strategic plan is critical and some organizations use what is called *portfolio assessment models.* These are documents that classify the organizations holdings or activities into categories based on important criteria: competitive position, variety of programs, and revenue sources. It is assessed or evaluated on its mix of business units—programs and services. An excellent example of steps one and two of a strategic plan is illustrated in Table 11.3. This example illustrates how one government made explicit the vision, values, principles, and goals of their country's mental health promotion initiative.

Practice Example: Focus Group. An example of a beginning step toward developing a new vision is for administrators to start with a review of current clinical and administrative mental health activities that occur in their programs. The format for this review can occur as a focus group consisting of staff, consumers and managers listing the activities that the organization does to meet its philosophical, clinical, and administrative goals. Table 11.4 illustrates what the final product of a focus group might look like. The original concept for this strategic planning leadership model is borrowed from the work of Paul Terry of the Park Nicollet Institute in Minneapolis, Minnesota (Terry, 2003). He identified nine examples of how leadership is moving the health promotion field from "one way of being" to "another" (p. 165). The first question is: *What are we doing now?;* this is listed under *present.* The next step would be to identify specific activities that reflect future or emerging practices, best practices, and evidence-based practices for mental health populations. The question for the future is: *What should we be doing?*

For example, participants are asked to describe the common model of the organization, the agency focus, what strategy it uses to follow that focus, the target of intended change, kinds of professional relationships, the interpersonal style or approach used by those professionals, what design or framework the organization uses, what kinds of outreach are in place, and, finally, what kind of fiscal policy is used. Then participants, using these same categories, are asked to list the features they would like to see in the future. By illustrating these two categories side by side, administrators and staff alike can see what they have been doing and compare that to what they are moving toward—which is hopefully an integration of health promotion concepts into mental health

TABLE 11.3. *Mental Health Promotion Strategic Plan: The New Zealand Model*

TITLE: Building Strengths: Toward Mental Health and Well-Being

VISION: The Vision of Building on Strengths Is to "achieve maximum levels of positive health and well-being."

VALUES

- Community Participation
  Every community and its members—regardless of disability, ethnicity, gender, age, economic and social status, or sexual orientation—have the right to fully participate in society generally and in their own particular society.

TITLE: Building Strengths: Toward Mental Health and Well-Being

VISION: The Vision of Building on Strengths Is to "achieve maximum levels of positive health and well-being."

VALUES

- Community Participation
  Every community and its members—regardless of disability, ethnicity, gender, age, economic and social status, or sexual orientation—have the right to fully participate in society generally and in their own particular society.

- Passion
  The combination of wisdom and scientific knowledge are valuable in promoting resilience and supportive environments.
- Empowerment
  People are able to exercise more control over, and take responsibility for, making a positive difference to their mental health and well-being.
- Cooperation and Trust
  Alliances across the health and other sectors are essential to the achievement of mental health for all.
- Understanding
  Diversity and differences are celebrated and it is acknowledged that people with mental illness can recover and live healthy productive lives.

PRINCIPLES
The first principles are from the New Zealand Health Strategy

- Collaboration
  National strategies, across multiple sectors, can contribute to improved mental health and well-being.
- Strengthen Communities
  All action will be consistent to the Treaty of Waitangi (New Zealand Constitution), contribute to a social climate that values contributions of a culturally diverse society, and promote human potential and social justice.
- Integration
  Mental health is a component of all health-advancing systems and activities and it is important to share knowledge about ways to reduce inequalities in mental health.

(continued)

TABLE 11.3. ***Mental Health Promotion Strategic Plan: The New Zealand Model (continued)***

- People-Centered
  It is important, in reducing mental health problems, to put people first, and people have the right to be involved in determining their future.

GOALS

The goals of *Building on Strengths* aim to:

1. Reduce the inequalities in mental health that are experienced by some groups
2. Create environments that are supportive of positive mental health
3. Improve individual and community resiliency skills

PRIORITY ACTIONS TO ACHIEVE GOALS

1. Reorient health services ... to reduce inequalities between socioeconomic groups.
2. Strengthen community action ... in mental health promotion activity and create opportunities for improved access to mental health promotion services.
3. Create safe and supportive environments ... through alliances that foster health promoting, supportive environments in cities, communities, workplaces, schools, and homes.
4. Develop personal skills ... by emphasizing mental health protective factors (e.g., individual – adequate nutrition; family/social – family harmony; school context – sense of belonging; life events and situations – availability of opportunities at critical turning points or major life transitions and community/cultural factors – attachments to networks within the community) such as resiliency, social support and life skills development.
5. Build healthy public policy ... through improved research and evaluation to identify and address mental health promotion needs.

OUTCOMES

- Individual: increased resiliency and life skills development (e.g., self-esteem, mastery, sense of coherence)
- Community: improved access to mental health–promotion services, safe environments, increased social networks, social support, and cohesive communities
- Sectoral: mental health–promoting policies, partnerships, and programs to reduce structural barriers to mental health

Adapted from Ministry of Health (2002). Building on strengths: A new approach to promoting mental health in New Zealand. Wellington, New Zealand: Ministry of Health. Also available at http://www.moh.govt.nz

practice. Terry's examples are similar to the current issues in the mental heath field and thus are adapted as a useful heuristic guide for helping leaders direct models of change.

Stage 3: Strategic Implementation

Once the organization has formulated its strategic plan, it's time for implementation. Up to this point, the organization has engaged in conceptual planning. There are two ways to proceed: (1) functional strategy and (2) institutional strategy.

TABLE 11.4. ***Moving from Present to Future: Using Focus Group Strategies to Develop a Vision of Health Promotion for Mental Health Organizations***

	Present ⟶	**Future**
Focus Group Questions	"What are we doing now?"	"What should we be doing?"
Categories:	Examples:	Examples:
▪ Model	Psychodynamic & case management	Health promotion, wellness, & recovery
▪ Focus	Primary focus on individuals	Individuals, families, & communities
▪ Strategy	Teaching risk reduction	Creating learning environments
▪ Target	Individual behavior change	Social learning and networks
▪ Professional Relationships	Discrete disciplines compete	Collaboration via interdisciplinary teams
▪ Approach	Isolated problems	Integrated practices
▪ Design	Risk-based disease management	Assets based community development
▪ Outreach	Market-based programming	Evidence-based education
▪ Fiscal Approach	Cost containment	Combination public–private funding and business ventures

Adapted from Terry P. (2003). Leadership and achieving a vision: How does a profession lead a nation? *American Journal of Health Promotion,* 18(2), 162–167

Formulating a functional strategy involves several work groups who can address issues like marketing, service planning, and personnel. An institutional strategy requires a broader view. A key step in the overall institutional strategic plan is looking at the *organizational structure*, *agency culture*, and *leadership*—especially if the plan and its actions are to be accepted. These are described below.

- *Organizational structure* is typically presented as the organizational chart which shows the relationships of people and or services.
- *Agency culture* refers to the shared beliefs, values and norms that link people together and set the climate for the organization.
- *Leadership* in the ranks is critical to fulfilling the mission of the organization. Strong organizations are those that tend to have opportunities for autonomy, rewards for good work, and transparent and supportive management systems. At the top of the organization, the leader must be a visionary who, in turn, is able to transmit, share and nurture that vision to other leaders and managers in the ranks. Successful organizations can often trace their successes throughout all

ranks—from case managers to therapists, to management team members to office staff. In this respect, the tenets of health promotion can be embraced as a management style.

Stage 4: Strategic Control

The last stage of the strategic planning process involves monitoring the implementation of the strategic plan and evaluating quality and effectiveness of organizational performance. Referred to as *strategic control*, this refers to the ability to identify problems and offer remedies or solutions. Two techniques for managing control include (1) feed-forward and (2) feedback controls.

Feed forward is one mechanism designed to identify potential changes in external or internal environments that may effect the operations of the organization. For example, proposed federal cuts in external NIH funding could affect programs that are federally funded, which could, in turn, have internal effects by eliminating staff assigned to these programs. The idea of feed-forward control allows organizations to keep abreast of potential market changes and therefore stay in control of certain aspects of operations.

Feedback controls refers to the comparison of actual performance to planned performance of the organization. Using retrospective data, the organization can look back to see what it planned to do—(strategic goals) and compare it to current status of goals. Examples of data would be financial results, number of housing units built, and the number of new programs related to health promotion instituted.

Four Action Plans to Integrate Health Promotion into Mental Health Practice Settings

Following the lead of Preventive Medicine (Dibble, 2003), administrators of mental health programs can apply the strategic model used by the Office of Behavioral and Social Sciences, National Institutes of Health Working Group on the Integration of Effective Behavioral Treatments into Clinical Care (Gruman & Follick, 1998). The model offers four action plans that are relevant to integrating health promotion into mental health practice settings. These are (1) health promotion advocacy, (2) health promotion research (3), public communication, and (4) protocol dissemination and implementation.

- *Advocacy*. Health promotion advocacy is two pronged: *clinical* and *economic advocacy*. In *clinical advocacy*, providers support and assist in change efforts for individuals, family and communities. *Economic advocacy* refers to the need for mental health administrators to advocate for increased coverage and reimbursement for brief health promotion interventions (e.g., fitness program) that are based on clinically preventable burden (e.g., obesity due to medication-induced weight gain) and cost-effectiveness (reduced hospital stays due to cardiovascular complications) as opposed to only medical diagnosis.

Other suggestions include lowered insurance premiums for sustainable healthy behaviors by clients (and employees) and incentive rewards or bonuses to mental health teams that accomplish health promotion goals.

- *Research.* Health promotion research is another action item that requires advocacy. Dibble (2003) argues that in order to design safe, multisite behavioral interventions, mental health administrators must advocate for long-term funding for an interdisciplinary research network that has a coordinated research agenda. This includes the dissemination of results and the need for social marketing research. The goal of the research network would be to facilitate understanding of various components of health promotion such as understanding client's readiness to change and cues to action, maintenance of healthy behaviors, and specific individual, family, community, clinician, cultural, ethnic and practice factors that affect intervention effectiveness. A coordinated and funded research network could also address key social factors (e.g., poverty) that contribute to health risks. In order to achieve the vision of integrating health promotion into culturally competent mental health practice, Terry (2003) suggests that mental health organizations must abandon practices with marginal or no scientific evidence and instead mobilize passionate, dedicated new leadership and staff who will advocate, study and implement evidence-based health promotion practices in a manner that is culturally compatible to the clients, families and community served.
- *Communication.* Public communication advocacy refers to action involving the use of the media to increase public awareness about approaches to deal with stigma and building healthy communities through health promotion activities. People with psychiatric disabilities have a lengthy history of being negatively stereotyped in the media. A 1990 Robert Wood Johnson Foundation report found that people received most of their impressions of individuals with mental illness through the media and that most of these impressions were negative. Maio (2003) pleads the case that mental health professionals have an ethical obligation to address the media's presentation of people with psychiatric disabilities. One U.S. organization, International Association of Psychiatric Rehabilitation Services (IAPSRS), has recently adopted language guidelines to help practitioners appreciate the power of the written and spoken word. These guidelines can be located at www.iapsrs.org. They are typical of health promotion approaches to empowerment by offering a positive portrayal of people in recovery and who are experiencing mental illness. Mental health professionals can effectively utilize health promotion campaigns to teach the public via the media—like Photovoice, discussed in earlier chapters.
- *Dissemination and implementation.* Protocol dissemination and implementation advocacy refers to the need for administrators to request, as needed, technical assistance funding in order to deliver evidence-based health promotion practice guidelines to all staff. According to research by Rosen (1995), fewer than 1% of social workers use research or guidelines to inform their mental health practice.

Most mental health staff are not trained in procuring evidence-based documents or websites much less documents related to health promotion. Further, left to their own limited time, they will most likely not plough through some of the more cumbersome protocols. Without technical assistance to support training and implementation of evidence-based health promotion protocols in mental health settings, administrators run the risk of clinicians delivering services that may not have the empirical support necessary for achieving the minimum standard of care.

■ Moving Forward: Helping an Organization Change

Reasons for Change. In recent years, health and mental health systems have focused on the necessity for change and the change process. The need for organizational change for mental health systems has emerged out of several conditions:

1. Changing funding patterns (e.g., changes in state/provincial or national reimbursement plans for mental health and health services)
2. New research evidence recommending more integrated and efficacious treatment approaches (e.g., psychoeducation with substance use treatment)
3. Changing practice models (e.g., moving from a disability and pathology focused model of care to a health promotion, wellness and recovery model)

While change is a constant state, administrators must help their organizations work with and not against change. The change process is complex and not always welcomed or embraced by employees and or clients. It is a part of an administrator's job to help the organization and its member's understand the need and movement toward change and to overcome reluctance to change. Doing this requires an understanding of both the organization as it currently exists and its vision for what it wants to become.

The Challenges of Organizational Change

Change is essential to any mental health organization's growth and survival. Similar to the discussion of readiness to change for individual growth, readiness to change must also be considered for organizations. As in personal change, organizations must recognize the need to change and learn to manage the change process efficiently.

Organizational change is defined as "any alteration of activities in an organization that involve the structure of the organization (e.g., creating a more horizontal integration of management), the transfer of work tasks (e.g., nurse practitioners teaching mental health counselors how to conduct health education groups), the introduction of new techniques (e.g., health promotion coaching), systems (e.g., new community based partnerships between health clinics and mental health services), technologies (e.g., web-based communication technologies), or behavior among and between providers, consumers, and family members (e.g., consumer and family-friendly mental health agencies) (Lewis *et al.*, 2004, p. 23).

Resisting Change. People resist change for a number of reasons: change is not in their best interests, fear of the unknown, insecurity, lack of abilities or skills to cope with new job requirements, and loss of vested interests such as power, responsibility, authority, control, or prestige (Argyris, 1993; Lewis et a;., 2004). It would seem that, at best, people want things to be different in terms of antecedents and consequence, but they don't want to change their behaviors. In other words, change can be threatening and some individuals may assess the consequences of imposed change in a totally different way from those who are initiating the change. For example, in health promotion language, a "psychotherapist" may be reclassified as a "life coach." While this change in title reflects the new language and relationship favored by the health promotion orientation, it may not be as "sexy" a title as "psychotherapist" and certainly represents a different image and perhaps one that the clinician does not understand or appreciate.

Beyond a title change, resistance can be encountered when agencies embrace entire new practice models. For example, health promotion may be a new concept to staff (and some administrators) of traditional behavioral health or mental health organizations. If a mental health administrator were to take a top-down approach and direct clinicians to change or upgrade their practice methods to incorporate health promotion concepts, principles, and related strategies, staff will most likely "resist" the directive and maintain the status quo. When change is made unilaterally or without those affected perceiving the need for change, sabotage of changes imposed by management may occur (Drucker, 1993).

A Case of "We Didn't Like It." One example of subtle sabotage is be found in a federally funded evaluation report of at-risk teen moms who were receiving home-based support for parenting skills and substance use prevention (Sussex & Corcoran, 2005). Although the counselors had received extensive training in motivational interviewing and the readiness-to-change model, study results, manipulation check, and chart reviews of the exposure to the intervention indicated that after 18 months, motivational interviewing tasks occurred at a remarkably low rate. In fact, the only activity/intervention that did occur was "counseling-talk therapy"—a loosely defined clinical approach that was provided with no clear-cut goals, outcomes, or structure, and then the number of hours of the intervention was less than half an hour every other week or so. When counselors were asked at the end of the study why they did not apply the motivational interviewing techniques, their response was: "We didn't like it." Clearly, the counselors had not been brought on board with the vision of the agency or the goals of the grant. As a footnote to this story, the agency did not receive subsequent funding; additionally, most of the counselors who "did not like" the intervention and therefore did not implement it were laid off when the funding ran out.

Lewis and colleagues (2003) note that too many managers install changes, undertake training or research programs and redesign structures with the mistaken belief that simply because the change was made, it will be successful. The above story is a splendid example of such false assumptions.

Five Steps for Organizational Change

Change Theory. One long-standing framework for understanding organizational change is *force-field analysis.* Originally developed by organizational researcher Kurt Lewin in the 1950s, this framework has continuing relevance for mental health administrators. It is defined as "a systematic, step-by-step process for examining pressures that support or resist a proposed change." This framework is based on the following assumption: just because you introduce a change does not guarantee that the change will be successful. Force-field analysis is one way for administrators to understand the steps necessary to introduce and gather support for change. These steps include (1) creating a shared vision, (2) communicating and sharing of information, (3) empowering others to act on the vision, (4) institutionalizing the new approaches, and (5) evaluating the results (Lewis *et al.,* 2004, pp. 357–358).

Step One: Create a Shared Vision. Articulating the "vision" or goals of the mental health organization is the first step that administrators, staff and consumers can use to jump start the change process. Leaders seeking to implement a new vision need to determine what approaches are sustainable and teach others to focus on what works—like evidence-based practice (EBP) (Terry, 2003) The very act of developing a vision helps bring awareness for the need for change and prompts discussion about forces supporting and resisting change efforts—what Lewis and colleagues (2004) refer to as "unfreezing." They suggest that many organizations are "frozen" into safe and predictable ways of functioning or performing.

When all stakeholders can be involved in setting a new vision, participants are more likely to work toward successful change and thus unfreeze themselves from the old way. For example, one behavioral health care agency sent its CEO and management team to visit every clinic and program for the purpose of meeting with staff and consumers to get input and ideas about proposed changes and the need for a new vision of themselves. Candid discussions were held regarding budget restraints and changes in fields of practice—moving from long-term psychotherapy models to brief treatment, evidence based practice approaches with an emphasis on health promotion. From these meetings emerged a new vision and values statement that was staff and consumer-owned.

Step Two: Communication. Sharing information is a key strategy that helps gain staff support, while also helping them learn. Based on the notion that new behaviors are learned more readily from verbal, written and nonverbal messages, a manager needs to discuss changes with staff, continually circulate minutes and memos and role model the desired goals. Of organizations undertaking a change process, Lewis and colleagues (2004) identifies four of the most commonly expressed concerns and related questions of employees:

1. Need for information—"What's going to happen? What does the change look like?"
2. Personal involvement—"How will I fit in and will I survive the change?
3. Implementation—"How do I get started on the change?"
4. Impact—"How will the change benefit us and the organization and what will be different?" (p. 360).

Agency administrators can utilize agency based workshops to communicate planned changes, interagency technologies—such as email—can keep personnel posted of updates and perhaps most importantly, administrators can role model the new behaviors that support the vision.

Step Three: Empower Employees. Thought to be the most important step in any health promotion approach is the notion of empowerment. From a management perspective, empowerment is defined as "the interaction of the leader giving away or sharing power with those who use it to become involved and committed to high quality performance" (Lewis *et al.*, 2004, p. 599).

Successful organizational change can often be credited to employees who have felt empowered and strengthened by the process of change. Their development is encouraged at two levels: individual and organizational. Individual development includes "anything that helps an individual learn how to adapt and change" (p. 360). Examples are participation in training or classes at educational institutions, mentoring from supervisors and observational learning. Organizational development refers to "teaching people to interact successfully with others in the organization" (p. 360). Examples include group and team training and setting goals that match with program or organizational goals. Thus, by improving the lives of employees, the organization is improved.

Step Four: Institutionalize and Rewarding New Approaches. This step refers to the notion that goals, structures, and behaviors must be institutionalized and rewarded if the changes are to be the new status quo. Just like we want to unfreeze the old way of thinking and doing, as discussed in Step One, this step intends to institutionalize or refreeze the new approaches and behaviors. The way to refreeze new approaches is to reinforce new behaviors by showing the positive results of change, usually through feelings of accomplishment or rewards from others. We know from behavioral therapy principles that behaviors that are positively reinforced tend to be repeated. Consequently, administrators need to plan how to reward employees who have embraced the vision and engaged in new behaviors that support that vision. Reward systems should be designed carefully, reevaluated often and compatible with employee expectations or the change will likely fail (Lewis*et al.*, 2004).

Step Five: Evaluate. Similar to outcome measures for client change, managers also need to measure and evaluate whether the change has had the intended effects.

Evaluation methods can be designed by both managers and employees and in some cases, consumers. Managers who are making the change can establish the criteria for judging its success before the change is instituted. Employees can be asked what criteria for success the changes should be evaluated and consumers can provide information on what they consider to be successful outcomes. When an agency begins to move to incorporating a health promotion orientation to service delivery, managers, employees and consumers can each identify what outcomes they consider to be good under this integrated model. By having a three-tier approach to evaluation, the entire organization can benefit from this multilevel feedback system.

Targets of Change

There are a variety of elements that a mental health organization can change in its commitment to embrace a health promotion focus. These elements may be determined by a number of sources: results of staff and consumer satisfaction surveys, consumer and family demands, community focus group feedback, funding priorities, trends in best practice approaches, and/or legislative mandates. Mental health organizations can target change at four levels: *individual*, *group*, *organizational*, and *environmental.*

Individual. At the *individual* level, the targets of change are usually in the general category of human resource changes and involve looking at ways of improving levels of employees motivation and performance, new staffing strategies, employee training or development programs. Let's take motivation and employee training as examples. To achieve an environment in which health promotion is a key philosophy of the staff, an organization will need to understand what motivates employees to provide innovative approaches to care and treatment. This could be done by using motivational interviewing techniques (discussed in Chapter 7). For example, employees could individually and as a group (or team) be asked the question: What do you know about health promotion and what are the pros and cons of integrating this approach into your practice approaches? Based on these responses, the human resource department could create a training session entitled: Innovative Models of Practice: Health Promotion.

Group. At the *group* level, managers may consider changing the relationships within programs. This might include a redirection from an individual psychotherapy model that works with clients one on one, isolates staff, and is office-bound to an interdisciplinary team approach that utilizes group meeting/staff conference areas and links clients to community health and recreational programs (e.g., yoga classes at the downtown YWCA).

Organizational. At the organization level, Lewis and colleagues (2004) describe six ways that managers may change their organizations. Managers can influence change in: (1) basic goals and strategies of the organization, (2) quality and variety of services offered; (3) organizational structure; (4) the composition of staff teams; (5) organizational processes such as reward, communication, or information processing systems; and (6) culture.

For example, a manager of a mental health organization or a program can identify the agency's central goals (e.g., to serve all Medicaid eligible adults diagnosed with persistent and severe mental illness), delineate the strategies to get there (e.g., community outreach), create services that are evidence-based and wraparound in design for these populations (e.g., psychoeducation and illness management curriculums), build an organizational infrastructure (e.g., speedy intake process, clinicians trained in evidence-based and health promotion approaches), hire, (re)train and support staff to do their jobs (e.g., specific trainings on psychopharmacology); build in monetary and nonmonetary incentives for employee growth and development (e.g., ski packages for a team's timely billing) and, last, foster an agency culture through role modeling that is empowering for staff and clients alike (e.g., actions speak louder than words).

Environmental. Last, at the *environmental* level (also referred to as community), an organization can also work to change sectors of its environment. As stated earlier, effective mental health leaders and organizations are those that work with the community to affect change. Nicola and Hatcher (2000) consider that the best way to advocate for the integration of health promotion and mental health in the community is through building community based constituencies among various health and mental health providers and organizations. They define constituencies as a "body of votes or group of supporters or patrons and or a group served by an organization or institution or clientele" (p. 2). For example, research has shown that when mental health organizations and county housing departments work together, clients lives are enhanced, homelessness is reduced and housing values can actually be improved. This is illustrated in the example Box 11.3.

One technique that mental health leaders can use to begin the process of change through community dialogue is MAP-IT, short for *m*obilize, *a*ssess, *p*lan, *i*mplement and *t*rack. Developed as a model for community participation through the federal policy initiative *Healthy People* 2010 (U.S. DHHS, 2000), MAP-IT is a strategy that helps community leaders by providing a step by step approach to community involvement and change. The five key steps are described below and illustrated in Figure 11.1

The first step is to mobilize people of like mind around a community issue. It is important to understand why people participate in community coalitions. Nicola and Hatcher (2000) offer insight on the motivations that move people to act: people participate when they feel a sense of community, see their involvement and the issues as relevant and worthy of their time, believe that the benefits of participation outweigh the costs, and view the process and climate of participation as open and supportive of their right to have a voice in the process (p. 3).

The second step is to have these same people assess and prioritize key issues and resources. Using the 10 health indicators as a guide (listed in Box 11.2), survey coalition members to get a sense of the issues and then prioritize. Just as important as identifying the issues is looking at the "gifts" or assets that the coalition members bring to the table. McKnight and Kretzman (2005) offer an excellent model for mapping and assessing community assets. Based on the assumption that every community has a wealth of

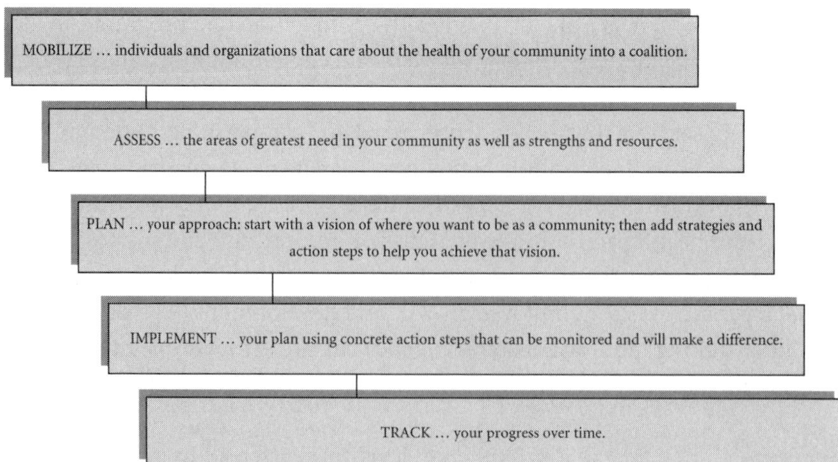

FIGURE 11.1. Strategy for change using community dialogue: MAP-IT (mobilize, assess, plan, implement and track). Reprinted from U.S. Department of Health and Human Services (2001). *Healthy people in healthy communities: A community planning guide using healthy people* 2010, p. 7. Washington, DC: USDHHS.

strengths and resources both monetary and nonmonetary, they encourage community leaders to look broadly at local businesses, faith communities, medical associations, and neighborhood associations as potential assets.

The third step is to create an action plan with concrete steps once resources and assets have been identified and priorities set. The plan of action should include action steps, assignment of responsibility, information and data collection and a timeline. While *Healthy People* 2010's time line is a decade, mental health leaders may not have that much time to devote to a community action effort. The recommendation is to be realistic about time lines rather than over optimistic which can result in feelings of failure for coalition members.

The fourth step is for coalition members to begin to implement strategies and action steps that were identified in the planning stage. By this stage, each coalition member will have his or her own areas of responsibility and can report on their progress. Other aspects of this step is monitoring or tracking all aspects of the process. This may be done with notes, filling in time lines of activities, or keeping a running poster board of events so members can check in. Some activities may even utilize on-line postings to keep members informed.

The fifth step involves analyzing and/or evaluating data collected and then providing a report. Documentation of events is critical if coalition members are to stay involved and feel that their efforts have been valued. Wallack (IOM, 2000b) recommends that this could be a good stage for media advocacy—which could include a combination of the "old" media (e.g., television, radio) and "new" media techniques—posting report on web. Whichever approach you use, simply be aware that this last stage is critical and goes a long way in publicly supporting the groups efforts.

In other words, building healthy communities requires problem solving by people engaged in addressing health and mental health issues that matter to them. When people work together to effect change, long-term health improvements are achieved (Nicola & Hatcher, 2000). The benefit of this model is that it places the responsibility for achieving change and the goal of health on a larger domain, the community, rather than using an individual orientation which can be limited. Overall, leaders must understand what motivates and moves people to action on other mental health issues. For details of this report, see www.health.gov/healthypeople/document/tableofcontents.htm

■ Final Challenge: Readiness to Change: Is Your Organization or Community Ready to Change to a Health Promotion Model of Care?

As we have discussed in this chapter and throughout this text, change is not easy. As O'Donnel (2003) notes, in the clinical field, we know that roughly 20% of people who have a health risk (e.g., hypertension) are ready to make a change and the remaining 80% are probably not. The age old question remains: How do we reach these (80%) people? The same issue can be said for mental health organizations that are undergoing change.

A small percentage of staff may be ready for a change, but most likely the rest will not be as eager. How do we reach those staff? The dilemma becomes more complicated when community involvement is needed in order to facilitate systems change. For example, how does a mental health organization improve the coordination of health and mental health services with the local health clinics without the cooperation of neighborhood pharmacies? How do we reach these community members?

Nicola and Hatcher (2003) note that people are motivated to work for change when conditions are no longer acceptable to them. In other words, leaders have to recognize the readiness of individuals—be it clients, staff, or community members—to take action. This can be determined by understanding their perception of the issue(s). They offer seven questions that mental health leaders should ask in order to determine organizational or community "readiness to change" to a health promotion model of practice.

Now, think of a "community" (i.e., organization, agency, neighborhood) that you are involved with that is struggling with an issue or topic. Ask yourself the following questions:

1. Are there perceptions that a problem or issue even exists that threatens the health or mental health of their clients or the solvency of the organization?
2. Is the issue perceived to be important, achievable, and deserving of community action?
3. Is there a science base to resolve the problem?
4. Is community collaboration likely to happen—due to political and public interest and will as well as history of leadership and collaboration?
5. Are resources available for action?

6. Is the political and social climate supportive of the goals of the organization?
7. Is there a community infrastructure to sustain interest and community action? (p. 3)

Based on these answers, leaders (or interested participants) will understand the readiness of the organization or community to change and the level of action that may be possible. Now, based on your answers, how would you assess your communities "readiness to change?"

■ Conclusion

Mental health administrators can look to the field of health promotion for strategies on how to best balance individual, organizational and social responsibility for health and mental health. Health promotion is certainly not without its limitations or detractors—as discussed in earlier chapters. For example, there are respectable differences of opinion regarding the appropriateness of some mental health interventions that incorporate health promotion components based on modifiable risks (e.g., Family Psychoeducation for high intensity mental health system users) with some viewing these interventions as cost shifting the responsibility of care to the family and not the system. Policy makers will not always understand the downstream value of advocating and endorsing public policy that supports health promotion and wellness models of care, not always seeing the immediate economic benefits, or understanding the scientific support and client preference for certain interventions. Providers/clinicians will require extensive workforce (re)training in order to learn and then embrace health promotion approaches to care, which is arguably not a reimbursable service in some public settings and therefore not a priority training need. And most importantly, health promotion approaches may be a hard sell to clients, their families and communities who are unfamiliar with the concepts of wellness, empowerment, strengths, hope and recovery—all tenets of the health promotion model.

These are good debates and help keep stakeholders sensitive to the impact of any approach that touches the lives of people. However, the evidence seems to keep coming in: health promotion can reduce the burden of health care costs (O'Donnel, 2003; Terry, 2003) and enhance the quality of life of clients and the community. This book has attempted to build on an approach that is already actively embraced by governments, policy makers, providers, communities, and clients across the globe. In this respect, health promotion is for all of us, if we have the common sense to promote it.

In conclusion, perhaps the wisest commentary on the subject of integrated health promotion into mental health care comes not from contemporary management and health literature but from the classic Daoist writings of He Shang Gong, as quoted and translated in *The Bamboo Bridge*. Although originally written as a guide for understanding behavior, the passage sums up the philosophy and practice of health promotion.

> To manage the body, take good care of the breath (qi), then the body will be whole and integrated. To manage the kingdom, take good care of the people, then the kingdom will be at peace. Managing the body is inhaling and exhaling essential breath (qi) without letting the ear hear. Managing the kingdom is a distribution of gentle power (de) without allowing those below (the people) to know it as such (Cleary, 1991).

Health promotion is like the essential breath, quiet but necessary; mental health resembles the kingdom of people for which the essential breath is necessary for all in order to become one.

In Our Own Words . . . Family and Consumer Perspectives on Mental Health Treatment Services: Service System Improvement

Topic: Feedback for Agency Directors and Providers about Ways to Improve Mental Health Services

Summary

As Chapter 11 illustrates, feedback, as a core health promotion principle, is a key strategy that any organization and provider can use to improve performance. As noted early in the chapter, if the field of health promotion and its accompanying philosophy, principles, and practice strategies is to move forward and be fully integrated into mainstream mental health organizations and practice, it will require a fundamental shift in the way mental health organizations provide leadership, develop strategic plans, and plan for organizational change. Staying with this theme, consumers and family members were asked to provide recommendations to agency directors and providers on ways to improve mental health services. As noted below, both consumer and family groups acknowledged the importance of education and training, at all levels—ranging from agency providers and administrators to law enforcement (e.g., police and probation officers) and the general public. Both also reiterated the importance of family- and consumer-centered services that incorporated holistic approaches and real participation on the part of consumers and family members. Also, family members recommended that agencies invest in staff salaries as a means to retaining good caseworkers.

What Can We Learn?

Based on these recommendations (and those listed throughout this book), it's evident that consumers and family members want and value education, want to provide education to others, and value choice and respect as "first-line" approaches to participating in mental health services. If agencies and providers are to move forward with incorporating health promotion principles, strategies, and approaches into their organizations, administrators already have a ready and willing group of "instructors"—namely, consumers, family members, providers, administrators, and policy makers. Good leadership is about embracing existing resources (e.g., stakeholders), building new ones, and honoring the experiences of all involved. This is not rocket science . . . but it *is* health promotion science.

Let's now turn to our final focus group conversation as reported by family members and consumers.

Focus Group Question: *"If you could make recommendations for improved mental health services for yourself or your family member, what would you want the agency director and providers to know?"*

Family Perspectives

Core Themes	Summary of Experiences	Comments
(Ranked in order of priority)		
First—Invest in caseworkers through salary and training	High caseworker turnover could be impacted by paying better wages to hard working front line workers and ensuring they get top of the line training—particularly training that sensitized workers to family's experience.	"Continuity of services is very important; starting over is so counterproductive." (J., *parent*)
Second—Involve family	Importance of having a paid family advocate on staff as resource for staff, families, and clients.	"We are the best resource for an agency—if they would let us." (M., *parent*)
Third—Increase public awareness and work with criminal justice system	Families felt that agencies could do a better job of having an active campaign of changing public attitudes about mental illness by working with politicians and media and entertainment industry to create positive messages. A crucial part of public awareness needs to be done with criminal justice systems to rid notion that mental illness is a crime.	"When probation officer doesn't know about mental illness yet has several clients with severe mental illness, then someone needs to do some big time education."

Consumer Perspectives

Core Themes	Summary of Experiences	Comments
(Ranked in order of priority)		
First—Education & Training in Holistic Care	Consumers felt that agencies could improve care by requiring providers to be trained in alternative and state of the art treatments (e.g., homeopathy, use of personal care assistants—PCA's, dialectical	"Older meds are crap; this population is fragile and you just can't leave a client without a therapist for four months; we need skills and options to help

(continued)

Focus Group Question: ***"If you could make recommendations for improved mental health services for yourself or your family member, what would you want the agency director and providers to know?"*** *(continued)*

	behavior therapy, cognitive therapy and new medication); consumers valued agencies that provided them with a menu of treatment options.	us cope while agency personnel changes." (R., *consumer*)
Second—Address Stigma of Diagnoses	Agency directors need to understand the stigma that is perpetuated by negative use of diagnostic labels for some consumers. Directors have to first understand that stigma exists and then proceed with a plan to address it.	"It is important for agency directors and providers to realize that labels, although the important for mental health providers, can have devastating effects due to the stigma attached to the diagnosis." (J., *consumer*)

EPILOGUE

■ Final Thoughts

As noted throughout this book, health promotion is a concept that is advancing worldwide, providing us with lessons to practice and common ground from which to grow. Gone—or perhaps more accurately going—are the days when providers attributed poor health and mental illness to primarily individual actions. Norms for community health have now been established, confirming that the determinants of health and mental health are largely influenced by social, political, environmental, and economic factors. This is not to suggest that individuals bear no responsibility for their ill health or for the consequences of lifestyle choices, but the locus of responsibility now is viewed as a shared phenomenon. Consequently, strategies aimed at promoting health and wellness for mental health populations should be multi-level, intersectoral, culturally sensitive, community based, and meaningful to the targeted members.

■ Lessons Learned

This book has defined and illustrated many strategies for integrating health promotion into the field of mental health practice. The task is complex and the rewards are increasingly less distant. Although mental health reform involves more than just teaching individuals and community partners about a new approach (i.e., health promotion), there are lessons to be learned and applied in the present that can make this task successful. Two core lessons drawn from this book are summarized below.

1. ***Mental health consumers and family members are valuable resources for mental health providers, administrators, and policy makers.*** The data from the consumer and family focus groups reported in this book support three core conclusions:

- families are a resource to mental health agencies and providers
- consumers are sophisticated users of services who desire education, comprehensive care and collaborative relationships with providers
- communication needs to improve between city and county agencies that work with mental health populations.

So, what does this information mean for family members who have a loved one with a mental illness and to the consumers themselves? In terms of family, the data suggest that the majority of family concerns were associated with larger systems issues. Family expressed repeatedly that they wanted the "system" to help educate them about mental illness, and that they needed the mental health system to support their efforts at caring for a relative with mental illness. Additionally, the data emphasized that the mental health system(s) lacked an integrated care approach that addressed the consumer's physical and mental health/illness, and perhaps most poignantly, the crisis and legal "systems" could be a lethal option for their relative with mental illness. All too often, family members reported that the existing systems were set up in a manner that excluded family involvement and, at times, seemed to be more of an impediment than an aid to promote their family member's mental and physical health. As one family member said, "Police are not always trained to deal with a mental health crisis. If you have a broken leg and call 911 you get help. If you have a mental illness and call 911, there's a good chance that you or your family member can get shot or killed. What kind of crisis help is that?"

Consumers, on the other hand, were very clear that they wanted services that were first and foremost oriented toward a holistic, wellness approach to care that promoted the integration of physical, mental, and spiritual well-being. These services need to include education and be delivered by providers who offered a more interpersonal approach to the clinical relationship; in addition, consumer participation is a key component within all of these relationships and services. Overall, consumers want a wellness oriented approach to recovery, education in order to understand things better, meaningful relationships with their caseworkers, and opportunities to be involved in the change process. As one consumer said, "Our spirits are broken and we need healing. We need more options that embrace our spiritual, mental, and physical well being."

So how can this information be used to increase public and professional awareness of the needs of families and consumers who participate in the public mental health system? Two recommendations are offered: (1) community mental health agencies infuse their programs, policies, and procedures with a philosophy of family-friendly, wellness-oriented care that is based on the principles and practice of health promotion, citizen participation, social justice, and recovery and (2) mental health centers, public health clinics, law enforcement agencies, family and consumer organizations (e.g., NAMI) can benefit the community by working collaboratively on behalf of mental health consumers and their family members to co-educate each other and the general public about mental illness and mental health.

2. ***Successful mental health reform calls for the integration of health promotion at three levels: individual, interpersonal, and intergroup.*** One report, in particular, entitled Promoting Health: Intervention Strategies from Social and Behavioral Research and published by the Institute of Medicine (2000) summarizes the very best of key social and behavioral research and concluded that interventions need to:

1. Use multiple approaches (e.g., education, social support, laws, incentives, behavior change programs) and address multiple levels of influence simultaneously (i.e., individuals, families, communities, nations).
2. Take account of the special needs of target groups (e.g., women, children, families of children and adults with mental illness).
3. Take the long view of health outcomes, as changes often take many years to become established.

4. Involve a variety of sectors in our society that have not traditionally been associated with health promotion efforts, including law, business, education, social services, and the media. (IOM, 2000b, p. 6)

More than ever, it is now clear that mental health interventions that incorporate a health promotion component can mediate physiological processes and do not merely correlate with positive health outcomes due to improvements in health behavior or knowledge (IOM, 2000b). If individuals with mental health conditions and their families are to gain access to health promoting resources (e.g., education, income, health, and social supports), then providers, administrators, researchers, and policy makers must forge collaborations among various disciplines—biological, behavioral, social, economic, and public health sciences. This move requires what is now referred to as vertical systems integration and is the focus of the new report issued by the National Institutes of Health, Office of Behavioral and Social Sciences Research. Their latest report, *The Contributions of Behavioral and Social Sciences Research to Improving the Health of the Nation: A Prospectus for the Future* (2007) highlights the need for understanding the interaction of individual vulnerability with human-created environments. This report can be accessed at http://www.thehillgroup.com/OBSSR_Prospectus.pdf.

■ Strengthening the Bonds Between Health Promotion and Mental Health

Health promotion and mental health have much to offer each other. For example, both fields are concerned with educating clients about risks associated with certain individual and/or life style choices (e.g., substance abuse and needle sharing). Mental health has led the way on addressing these issues and thus can enrich the health promotion field about client risk factors. On the other hand, health promotion can view these same risks from the perspective of what constitutes protective factors and healthy lifestyles, and can influence the mental health field in this respect.

Both fields are concerned with supporting clients in their recovery from mental illness. While mental health systems and providers have only recently begun to integrate the concept of recovery into the design and delivery of services, health promotion is all about focusing on wellness, quality of life, and hope—all of which are components of recovery-based services. Health promotion can help to make the concepts of recovery relevant to people in their everyday lives and activities.

Some disciplines within mental health (e.g., social work) have a tradition of using a person and/or family-centered approach and may use their collective expertise in client-centeredness at the individual level or analysis and application. On the other hand, the interdisciplinary nature of health promotion lends itself to a tradition of using a variety of providers to provide population-centered, community-organizing approaches to address health and mental health issues. The field of health promotion has long recognized the power of community to aid in the healing, health, and mental health of individuals and their families. In combination, both fields provide the full range of professional expertise needed to address the needs of multiple stakeholders and communities.

Health promotion and mental health share similar goals of providing interventions with demonstrated effectiveness. Health promotion will benefit from the theoretical and methodological developments within mental health. As this book has illustrated, there are an increasing number of evidence-based mental health interventions (e.g., illness management and recovery) that are derived from solidly established theoretical concepts, like cognitive behavioral theory and have undergone rigorous evaluation. As health promotion strives to demonstrate effectiveness of its approaches, much can be shared in the form of evaluation strategies. For example, health promotion, with its emphasis on holistic and community-based strategies, should influence the design of traditional mental health research to include more macro elements of assessment (e.g., social networks, healthy communities). Both have the benefit of drawing on the research of an effective international network of researchers, practitioners, and organizations.

In partnership, health promotion and mental health can address the full spectrum of interests, issues, needs, and goals of individual, family, and community stakeholders. Separately, these two fields can do little more than continue to compete for scarce resources while providing disjointed care. A final quote of ancient wisdom is drawn from an old Chinese proverb: *Go in search of people. Begin with what they know. Build on what they have.* Integrating health promotion into the field of mental health starts with working with our clients and their families and communities, respecting what they know, and building on the foundation of their strengths. In this way, we are better prepared for the challenges ahead in promoting the mental health and wellness of all peoples.

References

Abrams, D. B., Emmons, K.M., Linnan, L., & Biener, L. (1994). Smoking cessation at the workplace: Conceptual and practical considerations. In R. Richmond (Ed.), *International Perspective on Smoking: An International Perspective,Baltimore, MD: Williams & Wilkins,* pp. 137–169.

Ali, O, Milstein, G., & Marzuk, P. (2005). The imam's role in meeting the counseling needs of the Muslim community in the U.S. *Psychiatric Services*, 56, 702–705.

Allison, D., Mentore, J., Heo, M. (1999). Antipsychotic-induced weight gain: A comprehensive research synthesis. *American Journal of Psychiatry*, 156, 1686–1696.

Allison, D. B., Mentore, J. L., Heo, M., Chandler, L. P., Appalleri, J. C., Infante, M. C., et al. (1999). Antipsychotic induced weight gain: A comprehensive research synthesis. *American Journal of Psychiatry*, 156, 1686–1696.

American Internet User Survey. (1999). Cyber dialogue study shows U.S. Internet audience growth slowing. Cyberdialogue, Internet report: www.cyberdialogue.com

American Psychiatric Association (1994). Guideline for the treatment of patients with bipolar disorder. *American Journal of Psychiatry*, 151(December supplement), 1–36.

American Psychiatric Association (2000). *Diagnostic and Statistical Manual of Mental Disorders* (4th ed.), Text Revision. Washington DC: Author.

Anderson, D. (2004). Understanding the relationship between health risks and health-related costs. *American Journal of Health Promotion*, 18(3), 261–263.

Anderson, L.A., DeVellis, R.F., Boyles, B., & Feussner, J.R. (1989). Patients' perception of their clinical interactions: Development of the multidimensional Desire for Control Scales, *Health Education Research*, 4, 383–397.

Angels, R., & Williams, K. (2000). Cultural models of health and illness. In I. Cuéllar & F. Paniagua (Eds), *Handbook of Multicultural Mental Health*. p. 34. San Diego, CA: Academic Press.

Angermeyer, M.C. (2003). The stigma of mental illness from the patients point of view – an overview. Psychiatric Praxis, 30(7), 358–366.

Ali, O., Milstein, G., & Marzuk, P. (2005). The Imam's role in meeting the counseling needs of Muslim communities in the United States. *Psychiatric Services*, 56(2), 202–205.

Anthony, W., & Blanch, A. (1987). Supported employment for persons who are psychiatrically disabled: A historical and conceptual perspective. *Psychosocial Rehabilitation Journal*, 11(2), 5–23.

Anthony, W. (2000). A recovery-oriented service system: Setting some systems level standards. *Psychiatric Rehabilitation Journal*, 24(2), 159–168.

Anthony, W. (2003a). At issue: Studying evidence-based processes, not practices. *Psychiatric Services*, 54(1), 7.

Anthony, W. (2003b). Letter: Process, not practice. *Psychiatric Services*, 54, 402.

Anthony, W, (2003c). Expanding the evidence base in an era of recovery. *Psychiatric Rehabilitation Journal*, 27, 1–2.

Argyris, C. (1993). *Knowledge for action: A guide to overcoming barriers to organizational change*. San Francisco, CA: Jossey-Bass.

Ashton, J. (1992). *Healthy cities*. Philadelphia: Open University Press.

Bandura, A. (1977). *Social learning theory*. Englewood Cliffs, NJ: Prentice Hall.

Barkley, R. (1998). *Treatment of childhood disorders*. pp. 249–337. New York: Guilford Press.

Barrios, B.A., & O'Dell, S. L. (1998). Fears and anxieties. In E. J. Mash & R. A.

Bartels, S., Dums, A., & Oxman, T. (2002). Evidence-based practices in geriatric mental health care. *Psychiatric Services*, 53, 1419–1431.

Baum, F. (1998). *The new public health: An Australian perspective*. Melbourne: Oxford University Press.

Beattie, A. (1991). Knowledge and control in health promotion: A test case for social policy and social theory. In J. Gabe, M. Calnan, & M. Bury (Eds.) *The Sociology of the Health Service.* pp. 162–202. London: Routledge.

Becker, D., & Drake, R. (2003). *A working life for people with severe mental illness.* New York: Oxford University Press.

Becker, D., Drake, R., & Naughton, W. (2005). Supported employment for people with co-occurring disorders. *Psychiatric Rehabilitation Journal*, 28(4), 332–338.

Bell, C. Pimping the African-American community. (1996). *Psychiatric Services*, 47, 1025.

Bell, M., Lysaker, P., & Bryson, G. (2003). A behavioral intervention to improve work performance in schizophrenia: Work behavior Inventory feedback. *Journal of Vocational Rehabilitation*, 18, 43–50.

Bennett, T., & Cross, A. (1997). Maternal and child health. In F. D. Scutchfield & C. W. Keck (Eds.), *Principles of public health practice* pp. 327–336. Albany, NY: Delmar Publishers.

Bentley, K., & Walsh, J. (2001). *The social worker and psychotropic medication: Toward effective collaboration with mental health clients, families and providers* (2nd edition). Belmont, CA: Wadsworth.

Berren, M., Santiago, J. Zent, M., & Carbone, C. (1999). Health care utilization by persons with severe and persistent mental illness. *Psychiatric Services*, 50(4), 559–561.

Biegel, D., Swanson, S., & Kola, L. (2007). The Ohio Supported Employment Coordinating Center of Excellence. *Research on Social Work Practice*, 17(4), 504–512.

Black, H. (1979). *Black's law dictionary*. St. Paul, MN: West Publishing.

Blank, M., Mandell, D., Aiken, L., & Hadley, T. (2002). Co-occurrence of HIV and serious mental illness among Medicaid recipients. *Psychiatric Services*, 53, 868–873.

Bloom, M. (1996). *Primary prevention practices.* Thousand Oaks, CA: Sage.

Bond, G. (2004). Supported employment: Evidence for an evidence-based practice. *Psychiatric Rehabilitation Journal*, 27(4), 345–359.

Bond, G., Becker, D., Drake, R., Rapp, C., Meisler, N., Lehman, A., Bell, M., & Blyler, C. (2001). Implementing supported employment as an evidence-based practice. *Psychiatric Services*, 52, 313–322.

Bond, G. R., Becker, D. R., Drake, R. E., Rapp, C. A., Meisler, N., Lehman, A. F., Bell, M.D., & Blyer, C.R. (2003). Implementing supported employment as an evidence-based practice. In R. E. Drake & H. H. Goldman (Eds.), *Evidence-based practice in mental health care* (pp. 29–38). Washington, DC: American Psychiatric Association.

Bond, G., Drake, R., Mueser, K., & Latimer, E. (2001). Assertive community treatment for people with severe mental illness: Critical ingredients and impact on patients. *Disease Management & Health Outcomes*, 9, 141–159.

Borchardt, C. M., & Bernstein, G. A. (1995). Comorbid disorders in hospitalized bipolar adolescents compared with unipolar depressed adolescents. *Child Psychiatry and Human Development*, 26, 11–18.

Bordick, P. Graap, K., & Vonk, E. (2004). Post-traumatic stress disorder and trauma assessment scales. In A. Roberts & K. Yeager (Eds.), *Evidence-based practice manual: Research and outcome measures in health and human services.* pp. 517–523. New York: Oxford University Press.

Bowen, N. K., Bowen, G. L., & Woolley, M. E. (2004). Constructing and validating assessment tools for school-based practitioners: The elementary school success profile. In A. Roberts & K. Yeager (Eds.) *Evidence-based practice manual: Research and outcome measures in health and human services.* pp. 509–517. New York: Oxford University Press.

Bracht, N., Kingsbury, L., & Rissel, C. (1999). A five-stage community organization model for health promotion: Empowerment and partnership strategies. In N. Bracht (Ed.) *Health promotion at the community level: New advances* (2nd ed.). pp. 83–104. Thousand Oaks, CA: Sage.

Brady, K (1989). Weight gain associated with psychotropic drugs. *Southern Medical Journal*, 82, 611–617.

Brain Injury Association of America (2004). Web-page www.biausa.org

Breucker, G., & Schroer, A. (2000). *Settings 1: The evidence of health promotion effectiveness: Shaping public health in a new Europe,* Part Two. Paris: Jouve.

Bride, B., & Real, E. (2003). Project Assist: A modified therapeutic community for homeless women living with HIV/AIDS and chemical dependency. *Health & Social Work,* 28(2), 166–168.

Brody, E. Mental health. In C.E. Koop, C.E. Pearson, & M.R. Schwarz (Eds.). *Critical Issues in Global Health* pp.127–134, San Francisco, CA: Jossey-Bass.

Brown, S. (1997). Excess mortality of schizophrenia: A meta-analysis. *British Journal of Psychiatry,* 171, 502–508.

Brown, I., Renwick, R., & Nagler (1996). The centrality of quality of life in health promotion and rehabilitation. In R. Renwick, I. Brown, & M. Nagler (Eds.). *Quality of life in health promotion and rehabilitation: Conceptual approaches, issues and applications.* pp. 3–13. Thousand Oaks, CA: Sage.

Brown, S., Birtwistle, J., Roe, L., & Thompson, C. (1999). *Psychological Medicine,* 29(3), 697–701.

Brown, E., & Jemmott, L. (2000). HIV among people with mental illness: Contributing factors, prevention, needs, barriers and strategies. *Journal of Psychosocial Nursing and Mental Health Services,* 38(4), 14–19.

Browne, C., & Mills, C. (2001). Theoretical frameworks: Ecological model, strengths perspective and empowerment theory. In R. Fong & S. Furuto (eds.), *Culturally competent practice: Skills, interventions and evaluations.* pp. 10–32. Needham Heights, MA: Allyn & Bacon.

Bureau of the Census (2001). *Profiles of General Demographic Characteristics 2000: Census of Population and Housing: United States.* Washington, DC: U.S. Department of Commerce.

CDC Diabetes Surveillance System (2004). Available at www.cdc.gov/diabetes/statistics/prev/national/fig2.htm

Callicutt, J. (1997). Overview of the field of mental health. In T. Watkins & J. W. Callicutt (Eds.) *Mental health policy and practice today,* pp. 3–17. Thousand Oaks, CA: Sage.

Campell, T. L. (2002). Physical disorders. In Sprenkle, D. H., *Effectiveness research in marriage and family therapy.* Chapter 11 Alexandria, VA: American Association of Marriage and Family Therapists (AAMFT).

Casiano, M., & Hawkins, D. (1987). Major mental illness and childbearing: A role for the consultation-liaison psychiatrists in obstetrics. *Psychiatric Clinics of North America,* 10, 35–51.

Castro, F., Cota, M., Vega, S. (1999). Health promotion in Latino populations: A sociocultural model for program planning, development and evaluation. In R. Huff & M. Kline (Eds.), *Promoting Health in Multicultural Populations: A handbook for practitioners.* pp 137–167. Thousand Oaks, CA: Sage.

Catford, J. (2004). Health promotions record card: How principled are we 20 years so? *Health Promotion International,* 19(1), 1–4.

Centers for Disease Control (2002). Vaccines to prevent hepatitis A and hepatitis B. *IDU-HIV Prevention Report.* Atlanta: Academy for Educational Development.

Center for Substance Abuse Treatment. (1999). Enhancing motivation for change in substance abuse treatment. *Treatment approved protocol (TIP) Series* 35. DHHS Publication No. (SMA) 99–3354. Rockville, MD: Substance Abuse and Mental Health Services.

Center for Substance Abuse Treatment. (2005). Substance Abuse Treatment for persons with co-occurring disorders. *Treatment approved protocol (TIP) Series* 42. DHHS Publication No. (SMA) 05–3992, Rockville, MD: Substance Abuse and Mental Health Services Administration.

Chafetz, L., White, M., Collins-Bride, G., & Nickens, J. (2005). The poor general health of the severely mentally ill: Impact of schizophrenic diagnosis. *Community Mental Health Journal* 41(2), 169–184.

Clark, G., Herinckx, H., Kinney, R., Paulson, R., Cutler, D., & Oxman, E. (2000). Psychiatric hospitalizations, arrests, emergency room visits and homelessness of clients with serious and persistent mental illness; Findings from a randomized trial of two ACT programs vs usual care. *Mental Health Services Research,* 2, 155–164.

Cleary, J. (1991) Worldly wisdom: Confucian teachings in the Ming dynasty. Boston: Shambhala Publications.

Clemens, N. (2005). The faith community and mental health care. *Psychiatric Services*, 56, 133.
Cnaan, R. (2002). *The invisible caring hand: American congregations and the provision of welfare.* New York: Columbia University Press.
Cohen, S., & Williamson, G.M. (1988). Perceived stress in a probability sample of the United States. In S. Spacepan, & S. Oskamp (Eds.), *The Social Psychology of Health*, pp. 31–67. Thousand Oaks, CA: Sage.
Consensus Report (2004). Antipsychotic drugs, obesity and diabetes: Consensus Development. *Diabetes Care*, 27, 596–601.
Cook, J. (2005). Mental illness self-management through wellness recovery action planning. *Mental Health Recovery and WRAP Newsletter*. Retrieved at http://www.mentalhealthrecovery.com/art_selfmanagement.html Sept. 8, 2005.
Cook, J. A. (1998). Independent community living among women with severe mental illness: A comparison with outcomes among men. In B. L. Levine, A. K. Blanch, & A. Jennings (Eds.), *Women's mental health services: A public health perspective*, pp. 99–129. Thousand Oaks, CA: Sage.
Coombe, C. (1999). Using empowerment evaluation in community organizing and community-based health initiatives. In M. Minkler (Ed.), *Community organizing and community building for health*, pp. 291–307 New Brunswick, NJ: Rutgers University Press.
Coombe, C. (1999). Using empowerment evaluation in community organizing and community-based health initiatives. In M. Minkler (ed.), *Community organizing and community building for health*, pp. 291–307. New Brunswick, NJ: Rutgers University Press.
Coorigan, P. W., McCraken, S. G., & Holmes, E. P. (2001). Motivational interviews as goal assessment for persons with psychiatric disability. *Community Mental Health Journal*, 37(2), 113–122.
Copeland, M. E. (1997) *Wellness recovery action plan*. Dummerston, VT: Peach Press.
Copeland, M. E. (2002). *Developing a recovery and wellness lifestyle: A self-help guide*. Retrieved November 2006 from www.mentalhealth.samhsa.gov/publications/allpubs/government/default.asp
Copeland, J. Hall, W., Didcott, P., & Biggs, V. (1993). A comparison of a specialty women's alcohol and other drug treatment service with traditional mixed-sex services: Client characteristics and treatment outcomes. *Drug and Alcohol Dependence*, 32, 81–92.
Corcoran, K. (1998). Clients without a cause: Is there a legal right to effective treatment? *Research on Social Work Practice*, 8, 589–596.
Corcoran, K. & Fischer, J. (2000). *Measures for clinical practice: A sourcebook*. Volume 2: *Adults*. New York: Free Press.
Corcoran, K., & Roberts, A. (2005). Adolescents growing up in stressful environments, dual diagnosis and sources of success. *Brief Treatment and Crisis Intervention*, 5(1), 1–8.
Corcoran, K., & Vandiver, V. (1996). *Maneuvering the maze of managed care: Skills for mental health practitioners*. New York: Free Press.
Corcoran, K., & Vandiver, V. (2004). Implementing evidence-based practice. In A. R. Roberts & K. Yeager, (eds.), *Handbook of practice-focused research and evaluation*. pp. 15–19. New York: Oxford University Press.
Corrigan, P., Steiner, L., McCracken, S. (2001). Strategies for disseminating evidence-based practices to staff who treat people with serious mental illness. *Psychiatric Services*, 52, 1598–1606.
Corringan, P., & Watson, A., (2003). Factors that explain how policy makers distribute resources to mental health services. *Psychiatric Services*, 54, 501–507.
Corrigan, P., Watson, A., Warpinski, A., Gracia, G. (2004). Implications of educating the public on mental illness, violence and stigma. *Psychiatric Services*, 55(5), 577–580.
Corrigan, P., Watson, A., Gracia, G., Slopen, N., Rasinski, K., & Hall, L. (2005). Newspaper stories as measures of structural stigma. *Psychiatric Services*, 56(5), 551–556.
Coverdale, J., McCullough, L., Chervenak, F., Bayer, T., & Weeks, S. (1997). Clinical implications of respect for autonomy in the psychiatric treatment of pregnant patients with depression. *Psychiatric Services*, 48(2), 209–212.

Cox, E., & Parsons R. (1994). *Empowerment-oriented social work practice with the elderly*. Belmont, CA: Brooks-Cole.

Creer, T. L., Holroyd, K. A., Glasgow, R. E., & Smith, T. W. (2004). Health psychology. In M. Lambert (Ed.), *Bergin and Garfield's handbook of behavior change* (5th ed.). New York: Wiley.

Crismon, M. L., Trivedi, M., Pigott, T. A. (1999). The Texas Medication Algorithm Project: Report of the Texas consensus conference panel on medication treatment of major depressive disorder. *Journal of Clinical Psychiatry*, 60, 142–156.

Crnic, K. S. (1998). Mental retardation. In Mash, E.J. & Barkley, R. A. (Eds.), *Treatment of childhood disorders*, Chapter 6. New York: Guilford Press.

Cruz, C., & Spence, J. (2005). *Oregon tribal evidence-based and cultural best practices*. Portland, OR: Oregon Department of Humans Services/Office of Mental Health and Addiction Services.

Czajkowski, S. (2003). Effects of treating depression and low perceived social support onclinical events after myocardial infarction. *Journal of American Medical Association*, 289, 3106–3110.

Dana, R. H. (1993). *Multicultural assessment perspectives for professional psychology*. Needham Heights, MA: Allyn & Bacon.

Dandoy, S. (1997). The state health department. In F.D. Scutchfield & C.W. Keck (eds.), *Priniciples of public health practice*, pp. 68–86. Albany, NY: Delmar Publishers.

Davidson, L., Haglund, K., Stayner, D., Rakfeldt, J. Stayner, D., & Tebes, J. (1999). Peer support among individuals with severe mental illness: A review of the evidence. *Clinical Psychology: Science and Practice*, 6, 165–187.

Davis, A. F. (1973). *American Heroine: The life and legend of Jane Addams*. Chicago: Ivan R. Dee.

Davis, K. (1997). *Exploring the intersection between cultural competency and managed behavioral health care policy.* Alexandria, VA: National Technical Assistance Center for States Mental Health Planning.

Delbecq, A., Van de Ven, A. H., & Gustafason, D. H. (1975). *Group techniques for program planning: A guide to nominal group and Delphi processes*. Glenview, IL: Scott, Foresman.

Denning, P. (2000). *Practicing harm reduction psychotherapy: An alternative approach to addictions.* New York: Guilford Press.

Department of Health and Human Services (1999a). *Mental Health: A Report of the Surgeon General. United States Public Health Service Office of the Surgeon General*. Rockville, MD: Department of Health and Human Services, U.S Public Health Service.

Department of Health and Human Services (1999b). *Mental Health: Culture, Race, and Ethnicity: A Supplement to Mental Health: A Report of the Surgeon General*. Rockville, MD: U.S. Department of Health and Human Services Administration, Center for Mental Health Services, National Institutes of Health, National Institute of Mental Health.

Department of Health and Human Services (2005). *Substance abuse treatment for persons with co-occurring disorders*. Center for Substance Abuse Treatment. Treatment Improvement Protocol (TIP) Series 42, DHHS Publication No. (SMA) 05–3992. Rockville, MD: Substance Abuse and Mental Health Services Administration.

Dewar, T. (1997). *A guide to evaluating asset-based community development: Lessons, challenges and opportunities*. Chicago: ACTA Publications.

Dhooper, S. (1997). *Social work in illness prevention and health promotion. Social Work in the 21st Century*. Thousand Oaks, CA: Sage.

Dibble, R. (2003). Eliminating disparities: Empowering health promotion within preventive medicine. *American Journal of Health Promotion*, 18(2), 195–199.

Dickerson, F., Pater, A., & Origoni, A. (2002). Health behaviors and health status of older women with schizophrenia. *Psychiatric Services*, 53, 882–884.

Dickey, B., Normand, S., Weiss, R, Drake, R & Azeni, H. (2002). Medical morbidity, mental illness and substance use disorders. *Psychiatric Services*, 53, 861–867.

DiMatteo, M. R., , Hays, R.D., Gritz, E.R., Bastani, R., Crane, L., Elashoff, R., Ganz, P. et al. (1993). Patient adherence to cancer control regimens: Scale development and initial validation. *Psychological Assessment*, 5, 102–112.

DiNitto, D. (2000). *Social welfare: Politics and public policy* (5th ed.). Needham Heights, MA: Allyn & Bacon.

DiNitto, D. (2007). *Social welfare: Politics and public policy* (6th ed). Needham Heights, MA: Allyn & Bacon.

Dixon, J., Sindall, C., & Banswell, C. (2004). Exploring the intersectoral partnerships guiding Australia's dietary advice. *Health Promotion International*, 19(1), 5–14.

Dixon, L., Kreyenbuhl, J., Dickerson, F., Donner, T. W., Brown, C.H., Wolheiter, K., et al. (2004). A comparison of type 2 diabetes outcomes among persons with and without severe mental illnesses. *Psychiatric Services*, 55(8), 892–900.

Dixon, L., McFarlane, W.R., Lefley, H., Lucksted, A., Cohen, M., Falloon, I., et al. (2003). Evidence-based practices for services to families of people with psychiatric disabilities. In R. E. Drake & H. H. Goldman (Eds.), *Evidence-based practice in mental health care*, pp. 57–64. Washington, DC: American Psychiatric Association.

Dixon, L, Postrado, L., Delahanty, J., Fischer, P., & Lehman, A. (1999). The association of medical comorbidity in schizophrenia with poor physical and mental health. *Journal of Nervous and Mental Disease*, 187, 496–502.

Dossett, E., Fuentes, S., Klap, R., & Wells, K. (2005). Obstacles and opportunities in providing mental health services through a faith-based network in Los Angeles. *Psychiatric Services*, 56 (2), 206–208.

Doyle, J., Waters, E., & Jackson, N. (2003). New developments for effectiveness systematic reviews in health promotion: Cochrane Health Promotion and Public Health Field. *Journal of Promotion and Education*, 10(3), 118–119.

Drake, R., Essock, S., Shaner, A., Carey, K., Minkoff, K., Kola, L., et al. (2003a). Implementing dual diagnosis services for clients with severe mental illness. In R. E. Drake & H. H. Goldman (Eds.), *Evidence-based practice in mental health care*, pp. 39–46. Washington, DC: American Psychiatric Association.

Drake, R., McHugo, G., Bebout, R, Becker, D., Harris, M., Bond, G., et al. (1999). A randomized clinical trial of supported employment for inner city patients with severe mental illness. *Archives of General Psychiatry*, 56, 627–633.

Drake, R. E., Becker, D. R., Clark, R. E., & Mueser, K. T. (1999). Research on the individual placement and support model of supported employment. *Psychiatric Quarterly*, 70, 627–633.

Drake, R. E., Goldman, H. H., Leff, H. S., Lehman, A F., Dixon, L., Mueser, K. T., et al. (2003). Implementing evidence-based practices in routine mental health service settings. In R. E. Drake & H. H. Goldman (Eds.), *Evidence-based practice in mental health care*, pp. 1–5. Washington, DC: American Psychiatric Association.

Drucker, P. (1993). *Managing for the future: The* 1990'*sand beyond*. New York: Plume Books.

Dulmus, C., & Wodarski, J. (2002). Parameters of social work treatment plans. In A. Roberts & G. Greene (Eds.). *Social Work Desk Reference*, pp. 314–319. New York: Oxford University Press.

Dziegielewski, S. & Roberts, A. (2004. Health care evidence-based practice: A product of political and cultural times. In A. Roberts & K. Yeager (eds.). *Evidence-based practice manual: Research and outcome* measures in health and human services, pp. 200–205. New York: Oxford University Press.

Elhai, J. & Ford, J. (2007). Correlates of mental health service use intensity in the National Comorbidity Survey and National Comorbidity Survey Replication. *Psychiatric Services*, 58, 1108–1115.

Elmslie, J., Mann, J., Silverstone, J. T., Williams, S. M., & Romans, S. E. (2001). Determinants of overweight and obesity in patients with bipolar disorder. *Journal of Clinical Psychiatry*, 62, 486–491.

Emmons, K. (2000). Behavioral and social science contributions to the health of adults in the United States. In B. Smedley & S. Syme (Eds.), *Promoting health: Intervention strategies for social and behavioral research*. Institute of Medicine Report. Washington, DC: National Academy Press.

Epstein, N. B., Baldwin, L. M., & Bishop, D. S. (1983). The McMaster family assessment device. *Journal of Marital and Family Therapy*, 9, 171–180.

Eulau, H., & Prewitt, K. (1973). *Labyrinths of democracy*, p. 465. Indianpolis, IN: Bobbs-Merrill.

Evans, C., & Degutis, L. (2003). What it takes for congress to act. *American Journal of Health Promotion*, 18(2), 177–181.

Expert Consensus Guideline Series (1999). Treatment of post-traumatic stress disorder: The expert consensus panels for PTSD. *Journal of Clinical Psychiatry*, 60 (Supplement 16), 3–76.

Fallot, R. & Harris, M.(2002). The trauma recovery and empowerment model (TREM): Conceptual and practical issues in a group intervention for women. Community Mental Health Journal, 38: 475–485.

Fawcett, S., Paine-Andrews, A., Francisco, V., et al. (1996). Empowering community health initiatives through evaluation. In D. Fetterman, S. Kaftarian, & A. Wandersman (Eds.), *Empowerment evaluation: Knowledge and tools for self-assessment and accountability*. Thousand Oaks, CA: Sage. pp.161–187

Felker, R., Yazel, J., & Short, D. (1996). Mortality and medical comorbidity among psychiatric patients: A review. *Psychiatric Services*, 47, 1356–1363.

Felkner, B., Barnes, R., Greenberg, D., Chaney, E., Shores, M., Gillespie-Gateley, L., et al. (2004). Preliminary outcomes from an integrated mental health primary care team. *Psychiatric Services*, 55(4), 442–444.

Fellin, P. (1996). *Mental health and mental illness: Policies, programs and services*. Itasca, IL: Peacock.

Fellin, P. (2001). *The community and the social worker*. Itasca, IL: Peacock.

Fellin, P. (2001). Understanding american communities. In J. Rothman, J. Erlich, & J. Tropman (Eds.), *Strategies of community intervention*, pp. 118–132. Itasca, IL: Peacock.

Finch-Guthrie, P. (2000) Care planning for older adults in health care settings. In R.L. Kane & R.A. Kane (Eds.) Assessing older persons, pp.406–437. New York: Oxford University Press.

Fischer, J., & Corcoran, K. (2007a). *Measures for clinical practice and research: A sourcebook, Volume* 1, *Couple, families, and children*. New York: Oxford University Press.

Fischer, J. & Corcoran, K. (2007b). *Measures for clinical practice and research: A sourcebook*. Volume 2: *Adults*. New York: Oxford University Press.

Fleishman, M. (2003). Economic grand rounds: Psychopharmacosocioeconomics and the global burden of disease. *Psychiatric Services*, 54(2), 142–144.

Fletcher, J. M., & Taylor, H. G. (1997). Children with brain injury. In E. J. Mash & L. G. Terdal (Eds.), *Assessment of childhood disorders* (3rd ed.), pp. 453–480. NY: Guilford Press.

Foreyt, J. P., Poston, W. S., Winebarger, A. A., & McGavin, J. K. (1998). Anorexia nervosa and bulimia nervosa. In E. J. Mash & R. A. Barkley (1998). *Treatment of childhood disorders*. pp. 647—691. New York: Guilford Press.

Frankish, C., Lovato, C., & Shannon, W. (1999). Models, theories and principles of health promotion with multicultural populations. In R. Huff & M. Kline (eds.), *Promoting health in multicultural populations: A handbook for practitioners*, pp. 41–72. Thousand Oaks, CA: Sage.

Frese, F., & Davis, W. (1997). The consumer-survivor movement, recovery, and consumer professional. *Professional Psychology: Research and Practice*, 28, 243–245.

Fristad, M., & Arnold, J. (2204). *Raising a moody child: How to cope with depression and bipolar disorder*. New York: Guilford Press.

Frytak, J. (2000). Assessment of quality of life in older adults. In R. Kane & R. Kane (Eds.) *Assessing older persons: Measures, meaning and practical applications*, pp. 200–236. New York: Oxford University Press.

Furlong, M., McCoy, M., Dincin, J., Clay, R., McClory, K., & Pavick, D. (2002). Jobs for people with the most severe psychiatric disorders: Thresholds Bridge North Pilot. *Psychiatric Rehabilitation Journal*, 26(1), 13–22.

Galan, F. (2001). Intervention with Mexican American families. In R. Fong & S. Furuto (eds). *Culturally competent practice: Skills, interventions and evaluations*, pp. 255–268. Needham Heights, MA: Allyn & Bacon.

Gambrill, E. (1999). Evidence-based practice: An alternative to authority-based practice. *Families in Society*, 80, 341–350.

Gambrill, E. (1995). Less marketing and more scholarship. *Social Work Research*, 19, 38–47.

Ganju, V. (2003). Implementation of evidence-based practices in state mental health systems: Implications for research and effectiveness studies. *Schizophrenia Bulletin*, 29(1), 125–128.

Garvin, C. D., & Tropman, J. E. (1992). *Social work in contemporary society*. Englewood Cliffs, NJ: Prentice Hall.

Geffner, J., & R. Falconer (Eds.). *The cost of child maltreatment: Who pays? We all do*, pp. 15–37. San Diego, CA: Family Violence and Sexual Assault Institute.

Geller, B., Craney, J. L., Bolhofner, K. (2002). Two year prospective follow-up of children with a prepubertal and early adolescent bipolar disorder phenotype. *American Journal of Psychiatry*, 159, 927–933.

George, T. (2002). Care meanings, expressions and experiences of those with chronic mental illness. *Archives of Psychiatric Nursing*, 15(1), 25–31.

Germain, C. B., & Gitterman, A. (1995). Ecological perspective. In R. I. Edwards & J. G. Hopps (Eds.), *Encyclopedia of social work*, Volume 1 (19th ed.). Washington, DC: NASW Press.

Gingerich, S., & Mueser, K. T. (2005). Illness management and recovery. In R. Drake, M. Merrens, & D. Lynde (Eds.), *Evidence-based mental health care practice*, pp. 395–424. New York: Norton.

Glazer, W. (1988). Defining best practices: A prescription for greater autonomy. *Psychiatric Services*, 49, 1013–1016.

Goldberg, R., Seybolt, D., & Lehman, A. (2002). Reliable self-report of health service use by individuals with serious mental illness. *Psychiatric Services*, 53(7), 879–881.

Goldman, K. (1999). Medical illness in patients with schizophrenia. *Journal of Clinical Psychiatry*, 60 (Supplement 21), 10–15.

Goldman, K. (2000). Comorbid medical illnesses in psychiatric patients. *Current Psychiatric Reports*, 2, 256–263.

Goodman, S. H. & Gottlieb, G. L. (2002). *Children of depressed parents*. Washington, DC: American Psychological Association.

Gorman-Smith, D., & Tolan, P. (1998). The role of exposure to community violence and developmental problems among inner-city youth. *Development and Psychopathology*, 10, 101–116.

Gostin, L. (2000). Legal and public policy interventions to advance the population's health. In B. Smedley & L. Syme (Eds.), *Promoting health: Intervention strategies from social science and behavioral research*, pp. 390–416. Washington, DC: Institute of Medicine–National Academy Press.

Gould, R. A., & Clum, G. A. (1993). A meta-analysis of self-help treatment approaches. *Clinical Psychology Review*, 13, 169–186.

Green, L., & Kreuter, M. (1999). *Health promotion planning: An educational and Ecological approach* (3rd ed.). Mountain View, CA: Mayfield.

Green, L., & Kreuter, M. (2005). *Health program planning: An educational and ecological approach* (4th ed.). New York: McGraw-Hill.

Green, L. & Kreuter, M. (1991). *Health promotion planning: An educational and environmental approach* (2nd ed.). Mountain View, CA: Mayfield Publishing.

Greenburg, J. S., Kim, H. W., & Greenley, J. R. (1997). Factors associated with subjective burden in siblings of adults with severe mental illness. *American Journal of Orthopsychiatry*, 67(2), 231–241.

Greenburg, J. S., Seltzer, M. M., Krauss, M. W., & Kim, H. (1999). Siblings of adults with mental illness or mental retardation: Current involvement and expectation of future caregiving. *Psychiatric Services*, 50(9), 1214–1219.

Gruman, J., & Follick, M. (1998). *Putting evidence into practice: The OBSSR Report of the Working Group on the Integration of Effective Behavioral Treatments into Clinical Care*. Bethesda, MD: Office of Behavioral and Social Science Research, NIH.

Gutierrez, L. (1992). Empowering ethnic minorities in the twenty-first century. In Y. Hasenfield (Ed.), *Human services as complex organizations*, pp.320–338. Thousand Oaks, CA: Sage.

Gutierrez, L. (1991). Empowering women of color: A feminist model. In M. Bricker-Jenkins, N. Hooyman, & N. Gottlieb (Eds.). *Feminist social work practice in clinical settings*. Thousand Oaks, CA: Sage.

Hammen, C., & Brennan, P.A. (2003). Severity, chronicity and timing of maternal depression and risk for adolescent offspring diagnoses in a community sample. *Archives of General Psychiatry*, 60, 253–258.

Hancock, T., & Minkler, M. (2005). Community health assessment or healthy community assessment: Whose community? Whose health? Whose assessment? In M. Minkler (Ed.) Community organizing and community building for health, (2nd ed.), pp. 138–157. New Brunswick, NJ: Rutgers University Press.

Handen, B. (1997). Mental retardation. In E. J. Mash & L. G. Terdal (Eds.), *Assessment of childhood disorders* (3rd ed.), pp. 369–407. New York: Guilford Press.

Harman, J. S., Childs, G. E., & Kelleher, K. J. (2000). Mental health utilization and expenditures by children in foster care. *Archives of Pediatrics and Adolescent Medicine*. 154, 1114–1117.

Hawkins, D., Catalano, R., Arthur, M. (2002). Promoting science-based prevention in communities. *Addictive Behaviors*, 27(6), 951–976.

Hawkins, J. D., Catalano, R. F., & Miller, Y. (1992). Risk and protective factors for alcohol and other drug problems in adolescence and early adulthood: Implications for substance abuse prevention. *Psychological Bulletin*, 112, 64–105.

Herbeck, D., West, J., Ruditis, I., Duffy, F., Fitek, D., Bell, C., et al. (2004). Variations in use of second generation antipsychotic medication by race among adult psychiatric patients. *Psychiatric Services*, 55(6), 677–684.

Herman, H., Saxena, S., & Moodie, R. (2004). *Promoting mental health: Concepts, emerging evidence and practice*. Geneva: World Health Organization.

Hodges, V., Burwell, Y., & Ortega, D. (1998). Empowering families. In L. M. Gutierrez, R. J. Parsons, & E. Cox (Eds.), *Empowerment in social work practice: A source book*, pp.146–162. Pacific Grove, CA: Brooks Cole.

Hogarty, G. (2002). *Personal therapy for schizophrenia and related disorders: A guide to individualized treatment*. New York: Guilford Press.

Hollingsworth, S. (2006). Taking the first step: Overcoming stigma. *National Alliance of Mentally Ill: Voice Newsletter*, October, Issue 9, pp. 1–6. Arlington, VA: NAMI Publications.

Holmberg, S. & Kane, C. (1999) Health and self-care practices of persons with schizophrenia. *Psychiatric Services*, 50(6), 827–829.

Horton, M. (1990). *The long haul: An Autobiography*. New York: Doubleday.

Horwitz, A.V., & Scheid, T. L. (Eds.) (1999). *A handbook for the study of mental health: Social context, theory and systems*. New York: Cambridge University Press.

Horwitz, A., & Scheid, T. (1999). Approaches to mental health and illness: Conflicting definitions and emphases. In A. V. Horwitz & T. L. Scheid (Eds.) *A handbook for the study of mental health: Social contexts, theories and systems*, pp. 1–11. NY: Cambridge University Press.

Hosman, C., & Jane-Lopis, E. (1999). Political challenges 2: Mental health. In *International Union for Health Promotion and Education. The evidence of health promotion effectiveness: Shaping public health in a new Europe*, pp. 29–41. Brussels: ECSC-EC-EAEC.

Hosman, C., & Jane-Llopis, E. (2005). Effectiveness and evidence: Levels and perspectives. In C. Hosman, E. Jane-Llopis, & S.Saxena (Eds.). *Prevention of mental disorders: Effective interventions and policy options*. Oxford, UK: Oxford University Press.

Hughes, R. (1994). Introduction. In L. Spaniol, M. Brown & L. Blankertz (Eds.), *An introduction to psychiatric rehabilitation*. Columbia, MD: International Association of Psychosocial Rehabilitation Services.

Hutchinson, D. (2005). Structured exercise for persons with serious psychiatric disabilities. *Psychiatric Services*, 56(3), 353–354.

Hutchinson, D., & Hamilton, K. (2002). Rehabilitation and recovery services: Instructor Orientation Packet. Boston: Center for Psychiatric Rehabilitation, Boston University.

Ingram, R. E., Price, J. M. (2000). *Handbook of vulnerability to psychopathology: Risk across the lifespan*. New York: Guilford Press.

Institute for the Advancement of Social Work Research. (2005). *Symposium Report: Enhancing the health and well-being of LGBT individuals, families, and communities: Building a social work agenda*. Washington, DC: NASW Press.

Institute of Medicine (1988). *The Future of Public Health*. Washington, DC: National Academy Press.

Institute of Medicine (1994). *Reducing risks for mental disorders: Frontiers for preventive intervention research*. P. J. Mzarel & R. J. Hagarty (Eds.). Washington, DC: National Academy Press.

Institute of Medicine (1999). *Marijuana and medicine: Assessing the science base*. Washington, DC: National Academy Press.

Institute of Medicine (2000a). *Marijuana as medicine: The science beyond the controversy*. Washington, DC: National Academy Press.

Institute of Medicine (2000b). The role of mass media in creating social capital: A new direction for public health. Paper contribution, L. Wallach. In *Promoting health: Intervention strategies from social and behavioral research*, pp. 337–365. Washington, DC: National Academy Press.

Institute of Medicine (2000c). Behavioral and social science contributions to the health of adults in the United States. Paper contribution, F. K. Emmons. In *Promoting health: Intervention strategies from social and behavioral research*, pp. 254–336. Washington, DC: National Academy Press.

Institute of Medicine (2001). *Clearing the smoke: Assessing the science base for tobacco harm reduction*. Washington, DC: National Academy Press.

Institute of Medicine (2000). *The healthy development of young children*. Paper contribution, A. S. Fuligini & J. Brooks-Gunn, *Promoting Health: Intervention strategies from social and behavioral research*, 170–216. Washington, D.C: National Academy Press.

Institute of Medicine (2000). Understanding and reducing socioeconomic and racial/ethnic disparities in health. Paper contribution, B. J. House & D. Williams, *Promoting health: Intervention strategies from social and behavioral research*, pp. 81–124. Washington, D.C: National Academy Press.

Institute of Medicine (2003). *The future of the public's health in the 21st century*. Washington, DC: National Academy Press.

Institute of Medicine (2001). *Crossing the quality chasm: A new health system for the 21st century*. Washington, DC: National Academy Press.

Institute of Medicine (2002). *Speaking of health: Assessing health communication strategies for diverse populations*. Washington, DC: National Academy Press.

Israel, B., Checkoway, B., Schulz, A., & Zimmerman, M. (1994). Health education and community empowerment: Conceptualizing and measuring perceptions of individual, organizational and community control. *Health Education Quarterly*, 21(2), 149–170.

International Union for Health Promotion and Education (2000). *The evidence of health promotion effectiveness: Shaping public health in a new Europe. Part One*. Paris, France: Jouve.

Jaffee, K., Liu, G., Canty-Mitchell, J., Qi, R.A., Austin, J. & Swigonski, N. (2005). Race, urban community stressors, and behavioral and emotional problems of children with special health care needs. *Psychiatric Services*, 56, 63–69.

Jané-Llopis, E., Barry, M., Hosman, C., Patel, V., & Mittlemark, M. (2003). Mental health promotion within the International Union for Health Promotion and Education (IUHPE). *International Journal of Promotion and Education*, 10(3), 130–131.

Janzen, C., Harris, O., Jordan, C., & Franklin, C. (2005). *Family treatment in social work: Evidence-based practice for myriad challenges* (4th ed.). Pacific Grove, CA: Brooks Cole.

Jeste, D., Gladsjo, J., & Lindamer, L. (1996). Medical comorbidity in schizophrenia. *Schizophrenia Bulletin*, 22, 413–430.

Jones, B., Barnes, B.,Elton, P. Davies, L., Dunn,. G., Lloyd, H. et al., (2006). Randomized controlled trial of the effect on quality of life on second vs. first generation antipsychotic drugs in schizophrenia. *Archives General Psychiatry*, 63, 1079–1087.

Jordan, C. & Franklin, C. (2003). *Clinical assessment for social workers: Qualitative and quantitative methods* (2nd ed.). Chicago: Lyceum Books.

Jorge, M., Robinson, R., Moser, D., Tateno, A., Crespo-Facorro, B., & Arndt, S. (2004). Major depression following traumatic brain injury. *Archives of General Psychiatry*, 61, 42–50.

Katz, M. F., & Kreuter, M. W. (1997). Community assessment and empowerment. In F. D. Scutchfield & C. W. Keck (Eds.), *Principles of public health practice*, pp. 147–156. Albany, NY: Delmar Publishers.

Kawachi, I. (1999). Health consequences of weight gain. *Therapeutic Advances in Psychoses* 7, 1–3.

Kaye, D. L., & Pataki, C. S. (2002). Somatic disorders and functional syndromes. In Kaye, D. L., Montgomery, M. E., & Munson, S. W. (Eds.). *Child and Adolescent Mental Health*, pp. 350–370. Philadelphia: Lippincott, Williams & Wilkins.

Kaza, M., & Kreuter, M. (1997). Community assessment and empowerment. In F. D. Scutchfield & C. W. Keck (Eds.), *Principles of public health practice*, pp. 147–157. Albany, NY: Delmar Publishers.

Kazdin, A. (2004). Psychotherapy for children and adolescents. Chapter 12 in Lambert, M. (Ed.), *Bergin and Garfield's handbook of psychotherapy and behavior change* (5th ed.). New York: Wiley.

Kazdin A. E., & Marciano, P. L. (1998). Childhood and adolescent depression. In E. J. Mash & R. A. Barkley (Eds.), *Treatment of childhood disorders*, pp. 211–248. New York: Guilford Press.

Keene, J., Galasko, G., & Land, M. (2003). Adverse dental implications from antidepressant dry mouth. *Journal of American Dental Association*, 134(1), 71–80.

Kendall-Tackett, K. (2003). *Treating the lifetime health effects of childhood victimization*. Kingston, NY: Civic Research Institute.

Kessler, R., Nelson, C., McKonagle, K., Edlund, M., Frank, R., & Leaf, P. (1996). The epidemiology of co-occurring addictive and mental disorders: Implications for prevention and service utilization. *American Journal of Orthopsychiatry*, 66, 17–31.

Kiesler, C.A. & Sibulkin, A. (1987). *Mental hospitalization: Myths and facts about a national crisis.* Thousand Oaks, CA: Sage.

Kingsbury, L. (1999). Emerging public and private health sector partnerships: Selected U.S. enterprises. In N. Bracht (Ed.), *Health promotion at the community level: New Advances* (2nd ed.), pp. 219–228. Thousand Oaks, CA: Sage.

Kirmayer, L. (1993). Is the concept of mental disorder culturally relative? In S. Kirk & L. Einbinder (Eds.), *Controversial issues in mental health*, pp. 1–9. Needham Heights, MA: Allyn & Bacon.

Kitzman, H., Olds, D., Sidora, K., Henderson, C., Hanks, C., & Cole, R. (2000). Enduring effects of nurse home visitation on children's criminal and antisocial behavior: 15 year follow-up of a randomized trial. *Journal of the American Medical Association*, 278, 637–643.

Klein, A., Cnaan, R., & Whitecraft, J. (1998). Significance of peer social support for dually diagnosed clients: Findings from a pilot study. *Research on Social Work Practice*, 8, 529–551.

Kohn, L. (2000). The Recovery Center. In L. Anspacher & K. Furlong-Norman (Eds.). Recovery & Rehabilitation, *Center for Psychiatric Rehabilitation Newsletter, Vol.1*(2) p.1,

Kopelowicz, A., & Liberman, P. (2003). Integrating treatment with rehabilitation for persons with major mental illnesses. *Psychiatric Services*, 54, 1491–1498.

Kramer, T., & Glazer, W. (2001). Our quest for excellence in behavioral health care. *Psychiatric Services*, 52, 157–159.

Kruger, R. A., & Casey, M. A. (2000). *Focus groups: A practical guide for applied research.* (3rd ed.). Thousand Oaks, CA: Sage.

Labonté, R. (1994). Health promotion and empowerment: Reflections on professional practice. *Health Education Quarterly*, 21, 253–268.

Labonte, R. (1996). Measurement and practice: Power issues in quality of life, health promotion and empowerment. In R. Renwick, I. Brown, & M. Nagler (Eds). *Quality of life in health promotion and rehabilitation*, pp. 132–145. Thousand Oaks, CA: Sage.

Lalonde, M. A. (1974). *New perspectives on the health of Canadians.* Ottawa: Ministry of National Health and Welfare.

Lawson, W. (1996). The art and science of the psychopharmocotherapy of African-Americans. *Mt. Sinai Journal of Medicine.* 63, 301–305.

Leahy, R., & Holland, S. (2000). *Treatment plans and interventions for depression and anxiety disorders.* New York: Guilford Press.

Lees, J., Manning, N., & Rawlings, B. (2004). A culture of inquiry: research evidence and the therapeutic community. Psychiatric Quarterly, 75: 279–294.

Leff, H.S. (2005). Evidence in intervention science. In R. Drake, M. Merrens, & D. Lynde (Eds.), *Evidence-based mental health care practice*, pp. 189–216. New York: Norton.

Lefley, H. P. (1996). *Family caregiving in mental illness.* Thousand Oaks, CA:Sage.

Lehman, A. F., Kreyenbuhl, J., & Buchanan, R. W. (2004). The schizophrenia Patient Outcomes Research Team (PORT): Updated treatment recommendations. *Schizophrenia Bulletin*, 30, 193–217.

Leviton, L. (1989). Can organizations benefit from worksite health promotion? *Health Services Research*, 24(2), 159–189.

Lewinson, P. M., Klein, D. N., & Seeley, J. R. (2000). Bipolar disorder during adolescence and young adulthood in a community sample. *Bipolar Disorder*, 2, 281–293.

Lewis, P., Goodman, S., & Fandt, P. (2004). *Management: Challenges for tomorrow's leaders,* (4th ed.). Mason, OH: Thomson–Southwestern.

Lin, N., & Peek, K. (1999). Social networks and mental health. In A. V. Horwitz & T. L. Scheid (Eds.). *A handbook for the study of mental health: Social contexts, theories and systems*, pp. 241–258. New York: Cambridge University Press.

Link, B. G., Mirotznik, J., & Cullen, F. T. (1991). The effectiveness of stigma coping orientations: Can negative consequences of mental illness labeling be avoided? *Journal of Health & Social Behavior*, 32, 302–320.

Link, B., & Phelan, J.C. (1999). The labeling theory of mental disorder (II): The consequences of labeling. In A. V. Horwitz & T. L. Scheid (Eds.), *A handbook for the study of mental health: Social contexts, theories and systems.* pp. 361–377. New York: Cambridge University Press.

Link, B. G., Phelan, J. C., Bresnahan, M., Stueve, A., & Pescosolido, B. (1999). Public conceptions of mental illness: Labels, causes, dangerousness, and social distance. *American Journal of Public Health*, 89(9), 1328–1333.

Linnan, L., Bowling, M., Childress, J., Lindsay, G., Blakey, C., Pronk, S.et al (2007). Results of the 2004 National Worksite Health Promotion Survey, *American Journal of Public Health*, Vol.97, 11, Accessible http://www.ajph.org/cgi/external_ref?link_type+ARTICLEWORKS&action=cart

Lukens, E. & McFarlane, W. (2004). Psychoeducation as evidence-based practice: Considerations for practice, research and policy. *Brief Treatment and Crisis Intervention*, 4(3), 205–225.

Lupton, D. (1995). *The imperative of health: Public health and the regulated body.* Thousand Oaks, CA: Sage.

MacDonald, G., & O'Hara, K. (1997). *Ten elements of mental health, its promotion and demotion: Implications for Practice.* Lanarkshire, Scotland: Society of Health Education and Health Promotion Specialists.

Magana, S., Greenburg, J., Seltzer, M. (2004). The health and well-being of black mothers who care for their adult children with schizophrenia. *Psychiatric Services*, 55, 711–713.

Magana, S., Ramirez Garcia, J., Hernandez, M. & Cortez, R (2007). Psychological distress among Latino family caregivers of adults with schizophrenia: The roles of burden and stigma. *Psychiatric Services*, 58 (3): 378–384.

Maio, H. (2003). Responsibility for word. *Psychiatric Rehabilitation*, 27(3), 100–101.

Manderscheid, R., Brown, D., Milazzo-Sayre, L., & Henderson, M. (2002). Crossing the quality chasm of racial disparities. *Family Therapy,* 1 *(2)*, 18–24.

Mann, C., & Himelein, M. (2004). Factors associated with stigmatization of persons with mental illness. *Psychiatric Services*, 55(2), 185–187.

Manning, M. (2001). Culturally competent assessments of African American communities and organizations. In R. Fong & S. Furuto (Eds.). *Culturally competent practice: Skills, interventions and evaluations*, pp. 119–131. Needham Heights, MA: Allyn & Bacon.

Marlowe, D., & DeMatteo, D. (2003). Drug policy by analogy: Well, it's like this . . . *Psychiatric Services*, 54(11), 1455–1456.

Marsh, D. T., Dickens, R. M., Koeske, R. D., Yackovich, N. S., Wilson, J. M., Leichliter, J., et al. (1993). Troubled journey: Siblings and children of people with mental illness. *Innovations and Research*, 2(2), 13–23.

Marti-Costra, S., & Serrano-Garcia, I. (1983). Needs assessment and community development: An ideological perspective. *Prevention in Human Services*, 2(4), 75–88.

Martin, C. S., Kaczynski, N. A., Maisto, S. A., Bukstein, O. M., & Moss, H. B. (1995). Patterns of DSM-IV alcohol abuse and dependence symptoms in adolescent drinkers. *Journal of Studies on Alcohol*, 56, 672—680.

Martinsen, E., & Stanghelle, J. (1997). Drug therapy and physical activity. In W. P. Morgan (Ed.), Physical activity and mental health, pp. 81–92. Washington, DC: Taylor and Francis.

Mash, E. J., & Terdal, L. G. (1988). Behavioral assessment of childhood disturbance. In E. J. Mash & L. G. Terdal (Eds.), *Behavioral assessment of childhood disorders* (2nd ed.), pp. 3–65. New York: Guilford Press.

Mathews, C., Glidden, D., Murray, S., Forster, P., & Hargreaves, W. (2002). The effect of treatment outcomes of assigning patients to ethnically focused inpatient psychiatric units. *Psychiatric Services*, 53(7), 830–835.

Mattaini, M. (2005). Mapping practice: Assessment, context and social justice. In S. Kirk (Ed.) *Mental Disorders in the Social Environment*, pp. 63–82. New York: Columbia University Press.

McClay, W. (2004). Impact of a health coaching technique on quality of life in a worksite wellness setting. Unpublished thesis, Master of Science in Health Studies. Portland, OR: Portland State University.

McCubbin, H. I., & Thompson, A. I. (Eds.) (1991). *Family assessment inventories for research and practice.* Madison, WI: University of Wisconsin.

McCubbin, H. I., Thompson, A. I., & Elver, K. M. (1996). Family Attachment and Changeability Index 8 (FACI8). In H. I. McCubbin, A. I. Thompson, & M. A. McCubbin (Eds.). *Family assessment resiliency, coping and adaptation inventories for research and practice*, pp. 725–751. Madison, WI: University of Wisconsin.

McCubbin, M., LaBonte, R., & Dallaire, B. (2001). Advocacy for healthy public policy as a health promotion technology. *Center for Health Promotion*. Available athttp://www.utoronto.ca/chp/symposium.htm

McDaniel, S., Hepworth, J., & Doherty, W. (1992). *Medical family therapy: A biopsychosocial approach to families with health problems.* New York: Basic Books.

McDermott, B. E. (1995). Development of an instrument for assessing self-efficacy in schizophrenic spectrum disorders. *Journal of Clinical Psychology*, 51, 320–331.

McDiarmid, E., Rapp, C., & Ratzlaff, S. (2005). Design and initial results from a supported educated initiative: The Kansas consumer as provider program. *Psychiatric Rehabilitation*, 29(1), 3–9.

McEvoy, J.P., Scheifler, P.L. & Frances, A. (1999). The expert consensus guideline series: Treatment of schizophrenia. *Journal of Clinical Psychiatry*, 60 (Supplement, 11), 1–80.

McGinnis, J. M., & Maiese, D. R. (1997). Defining mission, goals and objectives. In F. D. Scutchfield & C. W. Keck (Eds.), *Principles of public health practice*, pp. 131–146. Albany, NY: Delmar Publishers.

McGurk, S., & Mueser, K. (2003). Cognitive functioning and employment in severe mental illness. *Journal of Nervous & Mental Disorder*, 191, 789–798.

McHenry, E. (2000). *New recovery center offers holistic approach. Boston University Bridge Newsletter*, Feb. 11, 3 (23), p.1. Retrieved July 19, 2007. Available at www.bu.edu/cpr/newsletter/recovery/rr-recoverycenter.html

McKnight, J. & Kretzman, J. (2005). Mapping community capacity. In M. Minkler (Ed.), *Community organizing and community building for health*, pp. 158–172. New Brunswick, NJ: Rutgers University Press.

McKnight, J., & Kretzman, J. (1990). *Mapping community capacity*. Evanston, IL: Northwestern University, Center for Urban Affairs and Policy Research.

McLellan, A., Lewis, D., O'Brien, C. (2000). Drug dependence, a chronic medical illness: Implications for treatment insurance and outcome evaluation. *Journal of American Medical Association*, 284, 1689–1695.

McPherson, T., & Cook, R. (2004). Prevention connection: Substance abuse prevention training for health promotion practitioners. *NIDA Notes*, 19 (3). Bethesda, MD: NIDA Publications. See www.drugabuse.gov/NIDAnotes/NNV0119N3/Tearoff.html

Mechanic, D. (2001). Mental health policy at the millennium: Challenges and opportunities. In R. W. Manderscheid, & M. J. Henderson (Eds), *Mental health, United States* – 2000. *Substance Abuse and Mental Health Services, Center for Mental Health Services*, pp. 53–63. DHHS Publication No. SMA 01–3537. Washington, DC: U.S. Government Printing Office.

Mechanic, D. (1999). Mental health and mental illness: Definitions and perspectives. In A. V. Horwitz & T. L. Scheid (Eds.) *A handbook for the study of mental health: Social contexts, theories and systems*, pp. 12–28. New York: Cambridge University Press.

Melfi, C., Croghan, T., Hanna, M., & Robinson, R. (2000). Racial variation in antidepressant treatment in a Medicaid population. *Journal of Clinical Psychiatry*, 61, 16–21.

Mellan, T., Miller, A., Weissman, E., Crismon, M., Essock, S., & Marder, S. (2003). Evidence-based pharmacologic treatment for people with severe mental illness: A focus on guidelines and algorithms. In R. E. Drake & H. Goldman (Eds.), *Evidence-based practices in mental health care*, pp. 65–71. Arlington, VA: American Psychiatric Association.

Mellman, T. A., Miller, A. L., Weisman, E. M., Crismon, M. L., Essock, S. M., & Marder, S. R. (2003). Evidence-based pharmacologic treatment for people with severe mental illness: A focus on guidelines and algorithms. In R. E. Drake & H. H. Goldman (Eds.), *Evidence-based practice in mental health care*, pp. 65–72, Washington, DC: American Psychiatric Association.

Menz, F.E., Hansen, G., Smith, H., Brown, C., Ford, M., & McCrowery, G. (1989). Gender equity in access, services and benefits from vocational rehabilitation. *Journal of Rehabilitation*, 55(1), 31–40.

Meyer, J. M., & Nasrallah, H.A. (2003). *Medical illness and schizophrenia*. Washington, DC: American Psychiatric Publishing (this is correct; I verified the book.

Michaels, S. (1996). The prevalence of homosexuality in the United States. In R. P. Cabaj & T. S. Stein (Eds). *Textbook of homosexuality and mental health*, pp. 43–63. Washington, DC: American Psychiatric Press.

Miller, C., & Martinez, R. (2003). Shifting physical health care responsibilities at a community mental health center. *Issues in Mental Health Nursing*, 24, 441–456

Miller, C.L., Druss, B., & Rohrbaugh, R. (2003). Using qualitative methods to distill the active ingredients of a multifaceted intervention. *Psychiatric Services*, 54(4), 568–571.

Miller, L. (1997). Sexuality, reproduction, and family planning in women with schizophrenia. *Schizophrenia Bulletin*, 23(4), 623–635.

Miller, L., & Finnerty, M. (1996). Sexuality, pregnancy, and childbearing among women with schizophrenia-spectrum disorders. *Psychiatric Services*, 47, 502–505.

Miller, W. (2004). Motivational interviewing in service to health promotion. *The Art of Health Promotion*. Newsletter published bi-monthly as part of the American Journal of Health Promotion. *Jan/Feb*, 1–10.

Miller, W., & Rollnick, S. (2002). *Motivational interviewing: Preparing people for change* (2nd ed.). New York: Guilford Press.

Milner, K., & Valenstein, M. (2002). A comparison of guidelines in the treatment of schizophrenia. *Psychiatric Services*, 53(7), 888–890.

Min, S. Y., Whitecraft, J., Rothbard, A. B., & Salzer, M. S. (2007). Peer support for persons with co-occurring disorders and community tenure: A survival analysis. *Psychiatric Rehabilitation Journal*, 30(3), 207–213.

Ministry of Health (2002). *Building on Strengths: A new approach to promoting mental health in New Zealand/Aotearoa*. Wellington, New Zealand: Ministry of Health. Also available at http://www.moh.govt.nz

Ministry of Health (2003). *Like Minds, Like Mine—National Plan: 2003–2005: Project to counter stigma and discrimination associated with mental illness*. Wellington, New Zealand: Ministry of Health. Also available at http://www.moh.govt.nz

Minkler, M. (1999). Measuring community empowerment. In M. Minkler (ed.) *Community Organizing and Community Building for Health*, p. 289. Brunswick, NJ: Rutgers.

Minkler, M., & Wallerstein, N. (1997). Improving health through community organization and community building: A health education perspective. In M. Minkler (Ed), *Community organizing and community building for health*, pp. 30–52. New Brunswick, NJ: Rutgers University Press.

Mittlemark, M. (1999) Health promotion at the community level: Lessons from diverse perspectives. In N. Bracht (Ed.), *Health promotion at the community level: New advances* (2nd ed.), pp. 3–27. Thousand Oaks, CA: Sage.

Moniz, C., & Gorin, S. (2007). *Health and mental health policy: A biopsychosocial perspective* (2nd ed.). Needham Heights, MA: Allyn & Bacon.

Morriss, P. (1987). *Power: A philosophical analysis*. Manchester, UK: Manchester University Press.

Mowbray, C., Nicholson, J., Bellamy, C. (2003). Psychosocial rehabilitation service needs of women. *Psychosocial Rehabilitation*, 27(2), 104–112.

Moynihan, R., Heath, I., & Henry, D. (2002). Selling sickness: The pharmaceutical industry and disease mongering. *British Medical Journal*, 324, 886–891.

Mueser, K. T., Corrigan, P. W., Hilton, D. W., Tanzman, B., Schaub, A., & Gingerich, S. (2002). Illness management and recovery: A review of the research. *Psychiatric Services*, 53, 1272–1284.

Mueser, K. T., Noordsy, D. L., Drake, R. E., & Fox, L. (2003). *Integrated treatment for dual disorders: A guide to effective practice*. New York: Guilford Press.

Muir-Gray, J. (1997). *Evidence-based healthcare: How to make health policy and management decisions*. London: Churchill Livingstone.

Murray, C., & Lopez, A. (Eds.) (1996). *The global burden of disease: A comprehensive assessment of mortality and disability from disease, injuries and risk factors in 1990 and projected to 2020*. Cambridge, MA: Harvard University Press.

Musisi, S., Millica, R., & Weiss, M. (2005). Supporting refugees and victims of war. In C. Hosman, E. Jané-Lopis, & S. Saxena, (Eds.), *Prevention of mental disorders: Effective interventions and policy options*. Oxford, UK: Oxford University Press.

Myers, M. G., Brown, S. A., & Vik, P. W. (1998). Adolescent substance use problems. In E. J. Mash, & R. A. Barkley (1998). *Treatment of childhood disorders*, pp. 692–729. New York: Guilford Press.

Nasar, S. (1998). *A beautiful mind: The life of mathematical genius and Nobel laureate John Nash*. New York: Simon & Schuster.

National Cancer Institute (2003). *Theory at a glance: A guide for health promotion*. Retrieved 7/11/2005. Available at http://www.nci.nih.gov/aboutnci/oc/theory-at-a-glance/page2/print?page=&keyword

National Institute on Alcohol Abuse and Alcoholism (2000). *Health risks and benefits of alcohol consumption*, 29(1). Washington, DC: NIAAA. Available at http://pubs.niaaa.nih.gov/publications/arh24–1/05–11

Navarro, V. (2003). Equity: A challenge for the future in a multi-cultural world. *International Journal of Health Promotion and Education*, 18(3), 114–117.

Nelson-Becker, H. (2006). Development of a spiritual support scale for use with older adults. In W. Nugent (Ed.), *Approaches to measuring human behavior in the social environment*. Binghamton, NY: Haworth Press.

Nelson-Gardell, D., & Harris, D. (2003). Childhood abuse history, secondary traumatic stress, and child welfare workers. *Child Welfare*, 82, 5–26.

Netski, A., Welsh, C., & Meyer, J. (2003). Substance use disorders in schizophrenia. In J. Meyer & H. Nasrallah (Eds.), *Medical illness and schizophrenia*, pp. 163–183. Arlington, VA: American Psychiatric Association.

New Freedom Commission on Mental Health (2003). *Achieving the promise: Transforming mental health care in America. Final report.* DHHS Publication No. SMA -03–3832. Rockville, MD: Department of Health and Human Services.

Nicola, R., & Hatcher, M. (2000). A framework for building effective public health constituencies. *Journal of Public Health Management Practice*, 6(2), 1–10.

Nicholson, J., & Henry, A. (2003). Achieving the goal of evidence-based psychiatric rehabilitation practices for mothers with mental illnesses. *Psychiatric Rehabilitation Journal*, 27(2), 122–130.

NIDA Publications—NIDA Notes, V01.19, No. 3 Tearoff, retrieved 3/31/2006. Web-based program to train practioners to add prevention messages to wellness programs. Available at http://www.drugabuse.gov/NIDA_notes/NNV0119N3/Tearoff.html

Nikkel, R. (1994). Areas of skill training for persons with mental illness and substance use disorders: Building skills for successful community living. *Community Mental Health Journal*, 30, 61–72.

North Cumbria Health Department—NCHD (2002). *North Cumbria Mental Health Promotion Strategy*. Carlisle, Cumbria, UK: Author.

Nugent, W. R., & Thomas, J. W. (1993). Validation of the self-esteem rating scale. *Research on Social Work Practice*, 3, 191–207.

Nutbeam, D. (1998). Evaluating health promotion: Progress, problems and solutions. *Health Promotion International*, 13, 27–44.

Nutbeam, D. (2000). *Health promotion effectiveness: The questions to be answered. The evidence of health promotion effectiveness: Shaping public health in a new Europe* (2nd ed.), pp. 1–11. Brussels-Luxembourg: European Commission, International Union for Health Promotion and Education.

O'Donnell, M. (1989). Definition of health promotion. *American Journal of Health Promotion*, 3(3), 5.

O'Donnell, M. (2003). A new vision, a new plan. *American Journal of Health Promotion*, 18(2), iv–v.

O'Hagan, M. (2003). *National plan: 2003–2005: Project to counter stigma and discrimination associated with mental illness*. Wellington, New Zealand: Ministry of Health

O'Hare, T. (2005). *Evidence-based practices for social workers*. Chicago: Lyceum Books.

Okazawa-Rey, M. (1998). Empowering poor communities of color: A self-help model. In L. Gutierrez, R. Parsons, & E.O. Cox (Eds). *Empowerment in social work practice: A sourcebook*, pp. 52–64. Pacific Grove, CA: Brooks Cole.

O'Neill, M. (2003). The consequences of a new form of empowerment on health promotion interventions. *International Journal of Health Promotion and Education*, 18(3), 126.

Olds, D., Robinson, J., O'Brien, R., Luckey., D., Pettitt, L., & Henderson, C. (2002). Home visiting by paraprofessionals and by nurses: A randomized, controlled trial. *Pediatrics*, 110, 486–496.

Olfson, M., Sing, M., & Schlesinger, H. (1999). Mental health/medical care cost offsets: Opportunities for managed care. *Health Affairs*, 18(2), 79–90..

Olson, D. H. (1986). Circumplex Model VII Validation studies and FACES-III. *Family Process*, 25, 337–351.

Oregon Department of Health and Human Services (2005). *Evidence-based practice guidelines*. Oregon Office of Addiction and Mental Health Services. Retrieved from website..www.oregon.gov/DHS/mentalhealth/ebp/main.shtml.

Patterson, R.E., Kristal, A.R., Glanz, K., McLerran, D., Hebert, J., Heimendinger,J. et al (1997). Components of the working well trial intervention associated with adoption of healthful diets. American Journal of Preventative Medicine, 13 (4), 271–276,

Payne, M. (1997). *Modern social work theory* (2nd ed). Chicago: Lyceum Books.

Pederson, A., O'Neill, M., & Rootman, I. (Eds.) (1994). *Health promotion in Canada: Provincial, national and international perspectives*. Toronto: Saunders.

Peele, P., Axelson, D., Xu, Y., & Malley, E. (2004). Use of medical and behavioral health services by adolescents with bipolar disorder. *Psychiatric Services*, 55, 1392–1396.

Peltier, L. G., Tuson, K. M., & Haddad, N.K. (1997). Client motivation for therapy scale: A measure for intrinsic motivation, extrinsic motivation, and amotivation for therapy. *Journal of Personality Assessment*, 68, 414–435.

Perese, E., & Perese, K. (2003). Health problems of women with severe mental illness. *Journal of American Academy of Nurse Practitioners*, 15(5), 212–219.

Perrin, B. (1998). Effective use and misuse of performance measurement. *American Journal of Evaluation*, 19(3), 367–379.

Perron, B. (2002). Online support for caregivers of people with a mental illness. *Psychiatric Rehabilitation*, 26, 70–77.

Perry, A., Tarrier, N., Morriss, R. et al. (1999). Randomized controlled trial of efficacy of teaching patients with bipolar disorder to identify early symptoms of relapse and obtain treatment. *British Medical Journal*, 318, 149–153.

Perry, B.D. (2001). The neuroarcheology of childhood maltreatment: The neurodevelopmental costs of adverse childhood events. Cited in K. Franey, B. D. Perry, R. Pollard. Homeostasis stress, trauma, and adaptation: A neurodevelopmental view of childhood trauma. *Child and Adolescent Psychiatric Clinics of North American*, 7, 33–51.

Perry, B. D., Pollard, R., Blakley, T. L., Baker, W. L., & Vigilante, D. (1995). Childhood trauma, the neurobiology of adaptation, and "use-dependent" development of the brain: How "states" become "traits." *Infant Mental Health Journal*, 16, 271–291.

Peterson, B., West, J., Tanielian, T., & Pincus, H. (1998). Mental health practitioners and trainees. In R. Manderscheid & M. Henderson (Eds.), *Mental Health United States* 1998, pp.214–246. Rockville, MD: Substance Abuse and Mental Health Services Administration.

Phelan, E. A., Cheadle, A., Schwartz, S. J., Snyder, S., Williams, B., Wagner, E. H., et al. (2003). Promoting health and preventing disability in older adults: Lessons from intervention studies carried out through an academic-community partnership. *Family and Community Health*, 26(3), 214–220.

Phelan, J. C., & Link, B. G. (1999). The labeling theory of mental disorder (1): The role of social contingencies in the application of psychiatric labels. In A. V. Horwitz & T.L. Scheid (Eds.), *A handbook for the study of mental health: Social contexts, theories and systems*, pp.139–150. New York: Cambridge University Press.

Phillips, E., Barrio, C., & Brekke, J. (2001). The impact of ethnicity on prospective functional outcomes from community-based psychosocial rehabilitation for persons with schizophrenia. *Journal of Community Psychology*, 29(6), 657–673.

Pi, E., & Simpson, G. (2005). Cross-cultural psychopharmacology: A current clinical perspective. *Psychiatric Services*, 56(1), 31–33.

Pickett-Schenk, S. (2003). Family education and support: Just for women only? *Psychiatric Rehabilitation Journal*, 27(2), 131–139.

Pilisuk, M., McAllister, J., & Rothman, J. (1999). Social change professionals and grassroots organizing: Functions and dilemmas. In M. Minkler (Ed.), *Community organizing and community building for health*, pp. 103–119. New Brunswick, NJ: Rutgers University Press.

Poland, B., Green, L., & Rootman, I. (2000) Reflections on settings for health promotion. In B. Poland, L. Green, & I. Rootman (Eds.). *Settings for health promotion: Linking, theory and practice*, pp. 341–351. Thousand Oaks, CA: Sage.

Prochaska, J. O., & DiClemente, C. C. (1983). Stages and processes of self-change of smoking: Toward an integrative model of change. *Journal of Consulting and Clinical Psychology*, 51, 390–395.

Prochaska, J. O., & DiClemente, C. C. (1984). *The transtheoretical approach: Crossing the traditional boundaries of therapy*. Homewood, IL: Irwin.

Procidano, M.E., & Keller, K. (1983). Measures of perceived social support from friends and family: Three validation studies. *American Journal of Community Psychology*, 11, 1–24.

Raeburn, J., & Rootman, I. (1996). Quality of life and health promotion. In R. Renwick, I. Brown, & M. Nagler (Eds.). *Quality of life in health promotion and rehabilitation: Conceptual approaches, issues and applications*, pp. 14–26. Thousand Oaks, CA: Sage.

Ramasubbu, R., & Patten, S. (2003). Effect of depression on stroke morbidity and mortality. *Canadian Journal of Psychiatry*, 48(4), 250–257.

Reid, R., & Berger, L. (2002). A national syringe exchange program: Estimating its value and impact. Paper presentation delivered at 4th International Conference on Evaluation and Practice, Tampere, Finland.

Renwick, R., & Friefeld, S. (1996) Quality of life and rehabilitation. In R. Renwick, I. Brown, & M. Nagler (Eds). *Quality of Life in health promotion and rehabilitation*, p. 30. Thousand Oaks, CA: Sage.

Rey, T. (1999). *CODAC Family health promotion Program status report*. Tucson, AZ: CODA Behavior Health Services, Inc. Available at http://www.codac.org

Richardson, C., Faulkner, G., McDevitt, J., Skrinar, G., Hutchinson, D., & Piette, J. (2005). Integrating physical activity into mental health services for persons with serious mental illness. *Psychiatric Services*, 56(3), 324–331.

Rissel, C., & Bracht, N. (1999). Assessing community needs, resources, and readiness. In N. Bracht (Ed). *Health promotion at the community level: new advances* (2nd ed,), pp. 59–71. Thousand Oaks, CA: Sage.

Robbins, S., Chatterjee, P., & Canda, E. (1998). Contemporary human behavior theory: A critical perspective for social work. Needham Heights, MA: Allyn & Bacon.

Roberts, A., & Yeager, K. (2004). Systematic reviews of evidence-based studies and practice-based research: How to search for, develop and use them. In A. Roberts & K. Yeager (Eds.), *Evidence-based practice manual: Research and outcome measures in health and human services*, pp. 3–14. New York: Oxford University Press.

Robertson, A., & Minkler, M. (1994). New health promotion movement. *Health Education Quarterly*, 21, 295–312.

Robinson, T., Patrick, K., Eng, T., & Gustafson, D. (1998). An evidence-based approach to interactive health communication: A challenge to medicine in the information age. *Journal of American Medical Association*, 280, 1264–1269.

Roe, D., Rudnick, A., & Gill, K. (2007). The concept of "being in recovery." *Psychiatric Rehabilitation Journal*, 30(3), 171–173.

Roper, W., & Mays, G. (2000). Performance measurement in public health: Conceptual and Methodological issues in building the science base. *Journal of Public Health Management Practice*, 6(5), 66–77.

Rosen, A., & Proctor, E. (2002). Standards for evidence-based social work practice: The role of replicable and appropriate interventions, outcomes and practice guidelines. In A. Roberts & G. Greene (Eds.). *Social workers' desk reference*, pp. 743–747. New York: Oxford University Press.

Rosenstock, I., Strecher, V., & Becker, M. (1988). Social learning theory and the health belief model. *Health Education Quarterly*, 15, 175–183.

Rosenthal, R. (2006). Overview of evidence-based practice. In A. Roberts & K. Yeager (Eds.), *Foundations of evidence-based social work practice*, pp. 67–80. New York: Oxford University Press.

Saari, K. (2004). Serum lipids in schizophrenia and other functional psychoses. *Acta Psychiatr Scand*, 110, 279–285.

Sackett, D. (1996). Evidence based medicine: What it is and what it isn't. *British Medical Journal*, 312, 71–72.

Sacks, S., & Ries, R. (2005). *Substance abuse treatment for persons with co-occurring disorders: A treatment improvement protocol (TIP) Series* 42. DHHS Publication No (SMA) 05–3992. Center for Substance Abuse and Treatment. Rockville, MD: Substance Abuse and Mental Health Services Administration.

Sadock, B. J., & Sadock, V. A. (2007). *Synopsis of psychiatry* (10th ed.). Philadelphia: Lippincott, Williams & Wilkins.

Saleebey, D. (1999). Introduction: Power in the people. In D. Saleebey (Ed.), *The strengths perspective in social work practice* (2nd ed.), pp. 3–18. White Plains, NY: Longman Publishers.

Samaan, R. A. (2000). The influences of race, ethnicity and poverty on the mental health of children. *Journal of Health Care for the Poor and Underserved*, 11, 100–110.

Sanchez, E. (2003). Meeting public health needs in a new era. *Health Law News*, February, 16(2), 6.

Sands, R. (2001). *Clinical social work practice in behavioral mental health: A post-modern approach to practice with adults* (2nd ed.). Needham Heights, MA: Allyn & Bacon.

Santos, C. W., & Barratt, M. S. (2002). Anxiety disorders in children and adolescents. In D. L. Kaye, M. E. Montgomery, & S. W. Munson (Eds.). *Child and Adolescent Mental Health*, pp. 166–183. Philadelphia: Lippincott Williams & Wilkins.

Sarason, I. G., & Sarason, B. R. (1999). *Abnormal psychology: The problem of maladaptive behavior* (9th ed.). Englewood Cliffs, NJ: Prentice Hall.

Sattler, J. (1992). *Assessment of children*. San Diego, CA: Sattler.

Sattler, J. M. (1998). *Clinical and forensic interviewing of children and families: Guidelines for mental health, education, pediatric, and child maltreatment fields*. San Diego, CA: Sattler.

Schorr, M (2004). Midlands Commons Grand Opening. Cascadia Newsletter, Vol.3, Issue 6, Nov. Dec., p.1, Portland, Oregon

Schroeder, C. S., & Gordon, B. N. (2002). *Assessment and treatment of childhood problems: A clinical guide* (2nd ed.). New York: Guilford Press.

Schwartz, A., Bradley, R., Sexton, M., Sherry, A., & Ressler, K. (2005). Posttraumatic stress disorder among African Americans in and inner city mental health clinic. *Psychiatric Services*, 56(2), 212–215.

Scottish Health Education Authority (1997). Effectiveness of mental health promotion interventions: A review. *Health Promotion Effectiveness Reviews: Summary Bulletin*, no. 4.

Scully, J. (2004). A great leap backwards. *Psychiatric Services*, 55, 1424.

Segal, S., Bola, J., & Watson, M. (1996). Race, quality of care, and antipsychotic prescribing practices in psychiatric emergency services. *Psychiatric Services*, 47, 282–286.

Segal, S., Silverman, C., & Temkin, T. (1995). Measuring empowerment in client-run self-help agencies. *Community Mental Health Journal*, 31, 215–227.

Seil, D. (1996). Transexuals: The boundaries of sexual identity and gender. In R. P. Cabaj & T. S. Stein (Eds). *Textbook of homosexuality and mental health*, pp. 743–762. Washington, DC: American Psychiatric Press.

Sheldon, B. (1995). *Cognitive-behavioral therapy: Research, practice and philosophy*. London, UK: Routledge.

Sherer, M., Maddox, J. E., Mercandante, B., Prentice-Dunn, S., Jacobs, B., & Rogers, R. W. (1982). The self-efficacy scale: Construction and validation. *Psychological Reports*, 51, 663–671.

Sheridan, C., & Radmacher, S. (2003). Significance of psychsocial factors to health and disease. In C. Sheridan & S. Radmacher (Eds.), *Psychosocial treatment for medical conditions*, pp. 3–26. New York, NY: Brunner-Routledge.

Shumway, M., Saunders, T., Shern, D., Pines, E., Downs, A., Burbine, T., et al. (2003). Preferences for schizophrenia treatment outcomes among public policy makers, consumers, families and providers. *Psychiatric Services*, 54, 1124–1128.

Siegel, C., Haugland, G., & Schore, R. (2005). The interface of cultural competency and evidence-based practices. In R. Drake, M. Merrens, & D. Lynde (Eds.) *Evidence-based mental health practice* pp. 273–299. New York: Norton.

Signorelli, N. (1989). The stigma of mental illness on television. *Journal Broadcasting & Electronic Media*, 33, 325–331.

Simon, G., VonKorff, M., & Barlow, W. (1995). Health care costs of primary care patients with recognized depression. *Archives of General Psychiatry*, 52, 850–856.

Social Health Reference Group (2003). Consultation paper for the development of the Aboriginal and Torres Strait Islander National Strategic Framework for Mental and Social and Emotional Well Being, 2004–2009. Canberra: Commonwealth Department of Aging.

Solomon, P. (2004). Peer support/peer provided services underlying processes, benefits and critical ingredients. *Psychiatric Rehabilitation Journal*, 27(4), 392–401.

Solomon, P., & Draine, J. (2001). The state of knowledge of the effectiveness of consumer provided services. *Psychiatric Rehabilitation Journal*, 25, 20–27.

Solomon, P., & Stanhope, V. (2006). Recovery: Expanding the vision of evidence-based practice. In A. Roberts & K. Yeager (Eds.), *Foundations of evidence-based social work practice*, pp. 336–348. New York: Oxford University Press.

Spaniol, L., Koehler, M., & Hutchinson, D. (1994). *The recovery workbook: Practical coping and empowerment strategies for people with psychiatric disability*. Boston: Center for Psychiatric Rehabilitation, Boston University.

Spears, L. (1999). Picturing Concerns. *Contra Costa Times*, April 11, A1, A32.

Spector, R. (2000). *Cultural diversity in health and illness* (5th ed.). Englewood Cliffs, NJ: Prentice Hall.

Spoth, R. L., & Dush, D. M. N. (1988). The adult health concerns questionnaire: A psychiatric symptoms checklist. *Innovations in Clinical Practice: A Sourcebook*, 7, 289–297.Sarasota, FL: Professional Resource Exchange, Inc.,

Stanhope, V., Solomon, P., Pernell-Arnold, A., Sands, R., & Bourjolly, J. (2005). Evaluating cultural competence among behavioral health professionals. *Psychiatric Rehabilitation Journal*, 28(3), 225–233.

Starr, P. (1982). *The social transformation of American medicine*. New York: Basic Books.

Sue, S., Fujino, D., Hu, L., & Takeuchi, D. (1991) Community mental health services for ethnic minority groups: A test of cultural responsiveness hypothesis. *Journal of Consulting and Clinical Psychology*, 59, 533–540.

Substance Abuse and Mental Health Services Administration (2001). *A provider's introduction to substance abuse treatment for lesbian, gay, bisexual and transgender individuals*. U.S. Department of Health and Human Services, Center for Substance Abuse Treatment. Rockville, MD: DHS Publication No. (SMA) 01–3498.

Substance Abuse and Mental Health Services Administration (2005). United States Department of Health and Human Services. *Transforming mental health care in America: Federal action agenda: First steps*. DHS Pub. N. SMA-05–4060. Rockville, MD: SAMHSA. Available at www.samhsa.gov

Sussex, B., & Corcoran, K. (2005). *STAGES (strong teens achieving goals: efficacy and sufficiency): Final report*. Washington, DC: Center for Substance Abuse & Prevention. (Available from K. Corcoran, PSU, Portland OR, 97207.)

Sviridoff, M., & Ryan, W. (1996). *Prospects and strategies for community-centered family service*. Milwaukee, WI: Family Service America.

Tang, K. C., Ehsani, J. McQueen, D. (2003). Evidence-based health promotion: Recollections, reflections and reconsiderations. *Journal of Epidemiology and Community Health*, 57, 841–843.

Teasdale, C., & Jennett, B. (1974). Assessment of coma and impaired consciousness. A practical scale. *Lancet*, 2, 81–84.

Terry, P. (2003) Leadership and achieving a vision: How does a profession lead a nation? *American Journal of Health Promotion*, 18(2), 162–167.

Thoits, P. (1999). Sociological approaches to mental illness. In A. V. Horwitz & T. L. Scheid (eds.) *A handbook for the study of mental health: Social contexts, theories and systems*, pp. 121–139. New York: Cambridge University Press.

Thomas, A., Lavrentzou, E., Karouzos, C., & Kontis, C. (1996). Factors which influence the oral condition of chronic schizophrenic patients. *Special Care in Dentistry*, 16(2), 84–86.

Thomlison, B., & Corcoran, K. (2008). *Evidence-based internship: A field manual*. NewYork: Oxford University Press.

Thompson, A. I., & McCubbin, H. I. (1996). Organizational climate scale (OCS). In H. I. McCubbin, A. I. Thompson, & M. A. McCubbin (Eds.), *Family assessment: Resiliency,* coping *and adaptation: Inventories for research and practice*, pp. 791–821. Madison, WI: University Wisconsin.

Thompson, B., & Kinne, S. (1999). Social change theory: Applications to community health. In N. Bracht (Ed.) *Health promotion at the community level: New advances* (2nd ed.), pp. 29–46. Thousand Oaks, CA: Sage.

Thyer, B. (2007). Evidence-based social work: An overview. In B. Thyer & J. Wodarski (Eds). *Social work in mental health: An evidence-based approach*. New York: Wiley.

Thyer, B. A. & Myers, L. L. (2003). Linking assessment to outcome evaluation using single system and group research designs. In C. Jordan & C.Franklin (Eds.), *Clinical assessment for social workers: Qualitative and quantitative methods* (2nd ed.), pp.385–405. Chicago: Lyceum Books.

Torrey, W. C., Drake, R. E., Dixon, L., Burns, B. J., Flynn, L., Rush, A. J., et al. (2003). Implementing evidence-based practices for persons with severe mental illnesses. In R. E. Drake & H. H. Goldman (Eds.), *Evidence-based practice in mental health care*, pp. 5–10. Washington, DC: American Psychiatric Association.

Trattner, W. (1999). *From poor law to welfare state*. New York: Free Press.

Tripodi, S., Springer, D., & Corcoran, K. (2007). Determinants of substance abuse among incarcerated adolescents: Implications for brief treatment and crisis intervention. *Brief Treatment and Crisis Intervention*, 7, 34–39.

Turkat, I.D., & Pettegrew, L.S. (1983). Development and validation of the Illness Behavior Inventory. *Journal of Behavioral Assessment*, 5, 35–45.

Umbricht, D., & Kane, J. (1996). Medical complications of new antipsychotic drugs. *Schizophrenia Bulletin*, 22, 475–483.

Unger, J. (1996). Stages of change of smoking cessation: Relationships with other health behaviors. *American Journal of Preventive Medicine*, 12, 134–138.

Universal Health Care, HealthPartners Medical Group, Rocky Mountain HMO (2002). *Connecting the dots: Health plans' pivotal role in chronic illness improvement. Accelerating change today for America's Health.* Institute for Healthcare Improvement, National Coalition on Health Care. Washington, DC: National Coalition on Health Care, pp. 23–27. Accessible through website: www.improvingchroniccare.org

U.S. Department of Health, Education and Welfare (1979). *Healthy people: The surgeon general's report on health promotion and disease prevention*. Washington, DC: U.S. Department of Health, Education and Welfare.

U.S. Department of Health & Human Services (1999). *Mental Health: A Report of the Surgeon General*. Rockville, MD: U.S. Department of Health and Human Services, Substance Abuse and Mental Health Services Administration, Center for Mental Health Services, National Institute of Mental Health.

U.S. Department of Health & Human Services (2000a). *Cultural competence for evaluators*. Public Health Service, Alcohol, Drug Abuse, and Mental Health Administration, Office for Substance Abuse Prevention, Rockville, MD: Department of Health and Human Services.

U.S. Department of Health and Human Services (2000). *Healthy People* 2010 (2nd ed.). *With understanding and improving health and objectives for improving health*. 2 vols. Washington, DC: U.S. Government Printing Office.

U.S. Department of Health and Human Services (2000). *Understanding and improving health and Objectives for improving health: Healthy people* 2010 (2nd ed., vol. 1). Washington, D.C.: U.S. Government Printing Office

U.S. Department of Health and Human Services (2001). *Healthy people in healthy communities: A community planning guide using healthy people* 2010. Washington, DC: U.S. Government Printing Office

U.S. Department of Health and Human Services (2001b). *A provider's introduction to substance abuse treatment for lesbian, gay, bisexual and transgender individuals*. Substance Abuse and Mental Health Services Administration, Center for Substance Abuse Treatment. Publication No. (SMA) 01–3498. Washington, DC: U.S. Government Printing Office.

U.S. Department of Health and Human Services (2005). *Surgeon general's call to action to improve the health and wellness of persons with disability: calling you to action*. U.S. Department of Health and Human Services. Rockville, MD: U.S Department of Health and Human Services, Office of the Surgeon General.

U.S. Department of Health and Human Services (2006). *New definitions*. Address Discrimination and Stigma Center, Substance Abuse and Mental Health Services Administration, Center for Mental Health Services. Accessible through http://oas.samhsa.gov/nsduh/2k6nsduh/AppC.htm

U. S. Public Health Service Office of the Surgeon General (2001). *Mental health: Culture, race, and ethnicity: A supplement to mental health: A report of the surgeon genera*l. Rockville, MD: Department of Health and Human Services, U.S. Public Health Service.

U.S. Public Health Service Office of the Surgeon General (2001). *Mental health: Culture, race and ethnicity: A supplement to mental health: A report of the surgeon general*. Rockville, MD: Department of Health and Human Services, U.S. Public Health Service.

Van Ryn, M., & Heaney, C. (1997). Developing effective helping relationships in health education practice. *Health Education & Behavior*, 24(6), 683–702.

Vandiver, V. (2007). Health promotion as brief treatment: Strategies for women with co-morbid health and mental health conditions. *Brief treatment and crisis intervention*, 7(3), 161–175.

Vandiver, V. (2008). Managed care. In T. Mizrahi & L. Davis (Eds), The *Encyclopedia of Social Work, 20th Edition*. Washington, DC: Oxford University Press.

Vandiver, V. (2002). Step-by-step practice guidelines for using evidence-based practice and expert consensus in mental health settings. In A. Roberts & G. Greene (Eds.), *Social workers' desk reference*, pp. 731–738. New York: Oxford University Press.

Vandiver, V., & Corcoran, K. (2002). Guidelines for establishing effective treatment goals and treatment plans for axis I disorders. In A. Roberts & G. Greene (Eds.), *Social Work Desk Reference*, pp. 297–304. New York: Oxford University Press.

Vandiver, V., Johnson, J., & Christofero-Snider, C. (2003). Supporting employment for adults with acquired brain injury. *Journal of Head Trauma Rehabilitation*, 18(5), 457–463.

Vandiver, V., Jordan, C., Keopreseuth, K., Yu, M. (1995). Family empowerment and service satisfaction: An exploratory study of Laotian families who care for a family member with mental illness. *Psychiatric Rehabilitation*, 19(1), 47–54.

Vanina, Y., Podolskaya, A., Sedky, K., Shahab, H., Siddiqui, A. Munshi, M., et al. (2002). Body weight changes associated with psychopharmacology. *Psychiatric Services*, 53(7), 842–847.

Vaux, A., Riedel, S., & Stewart, D. (1987). Modes of social support: The social support behaviors (SSB) scale, *American Journal of Community Psychiatry*, 15, 209–237.

Velasquez, M., Maurer, G., Crouch, C., & DiClemente, C. (2001). *Group treatment for substance abuse: A stages-of-change therapy manual*. New York: Guilford Press.

Vonk, E., & Early, T. (2000). Cognitive-behavioral therapy. In A. Roberts & G. Greene (eds.), *Social workers' desk reference*, pp. 116–120. New York: Oxford University Press.

Wagner, E. (2002). *The changing face of chronic disease care. Accelerating change today for america's health, institute for healthcare improvement*, pp. 2–5. Washington, DC: National Coalition on Health Care. Accessible through website: www.improvingchroniccare.org

Wahl, O. (1995). *Media madness: Public images of mental illness*. New Brunswick, NJ: Rutgers University Press.

Wainberg, M., Cournos, F., McKinnon, K., & BErkman, A. (2003). HIV and hepatitis C in patients with schizophrenia. In J. Meyer & H. Nasrallah, (Eds.), *Medical illness and schizophrenia* (pp.115–140). Washington, DC: American Psychiatric Publishing.

Walkup, J., McAlpine, D., Olfson, M. (2000). Patients with schizophrenia at risk for excessive antipsychotic dosing. *Journal of Clinical Psychiatry*, 61, 344–348.

Wallerstein, N. & Bernstein, E. (1994). Introduction to community empowerment, participatory education, and health. *Health Education Quarterly*, 21, 141–148.

Wallston, K. A., Wallston, B. S., & DeVellis, R. (1978). Development of the multidimensional health locus of control (MHLC) scales. *Health Education Monographs*, 6, 160–170.

Walsh, J. (2000). *Clinical case management with persons having mental illness: A relationship -based perspective*. Belmont, CA: Brooks Cole.
Wang, C., Cash, J., & Powers, L. (2000) *Who knows the streets as well as the homeless?* Health Promotion Practice Vol.1, No.1, pp.81–89.
Ware, J. E., Kosinski, M., & Keller, S. D. (1994). *SF-36 physical and mental health Summary Scales: A user's manual*. Boston: Medical Outcomes Trust.
Warner, R. (2005). Local projects of the world psychiatric association program to reduce stigma and discrimination. *Psychiatric Services*, 56, 570–575.
Webster-Stratton, C. (1997). From parent training to community building. Families in society: *The Journal of Contemporary Human Services*, 78, 156–171.
Weeghel, J., Audenhove, C. V., Colucci, M., Garanis-Papadatos, A., Muijen, M., Norcio, B., et al. (2005) The components of good community care for people with severe mental illnesses: Views of stakeholders in five European countries. *Psychiatric Rehabilitation Journal*, 28(3), 274–281.
Weiden, P. J., Kozma, C., Grogg, A., & Locklear, J. (2004). Partial compliance and risk of rehospitalization among California Medicaid patients with schizophrenia, *Psychiatric Services*, 55(8), 886–891.
Weiden, P. J., (1997). Pharmacological management of non-compliance. *Journal of Practical Psychiatry and Behavioral Health*, Vol.4, 239–245.
Westbrooks, K. L., & Starks, S.H. (2001). Strengths perspective inherent in cultural empowerment: A tool for assessment with African American individuals and families. In R. Fong & S. Furuto (Eds), *Culturally competent practice: Skills, interventions and evaluations*, pp. 101–118. Needham Heights, MA: Allyn & Bacon.
Wheatley, M. (1999). *Leadership and the new science: Discovering order in the chaotic world*. San Francisco, CA: Berrett-Koehler.
Whitley, R., Harris, M., Fallot, R., Berley, R. (2007). The active ingredients of intentional recovery communities: Focus group evaluation. Journal of Mental Health. Accessed 12/30/07 http://www.informaworld.com/smpp/content~content=a784122244~db=all
Wilkinson, W. (2002). Implementing *Olmstead*. *Health Law News*, 15(2), 1–14.
Wirshing, D., & Meyer, J. (2003). Obesity in patients with schizophrenia. In J. Meyer & H. Nasrallah (Eds.), *Medical illness and schizophrenia*, pp. 35–52. Arlington, VA: American Psychiatric Publishing.
Wolfe, V. V. (1998). Child sexual abuse. In E. J. Mash & R. A. Barkley (1998). *Treatment of childhood disorders*, pp. 545—597. New York: Guilford Press.
Woollard, J., Beilin, L., Lord, T., Puddey, I., MacAdam, D., & Rouse, I. (1995). A controlled trial of nurse counseling on lifestyle change for hypertensives treated in general practice: Preliminary results. *Clinical and Experimental Pharmacology and Physiology*, 22, 466–468.
World Federation for Mental Health (2007). Making mental health a global priority: Promotion and prevention. Retrieved August, 2007. Available at http://www.e-logosetc.com/oowfmh/oopolicyrights.htm
World Health Organization (1986). A discussion document on the concepts and principles of health promotion. *Health Promotion Journal International*, 1, 73–76.
World Health Organization (1986). *The Ottawa charter: Principles for health promotion*. Copenhagen: WHO Regional Office for Europe.
World Health Organization (1978). *Declaration of Alma-Ata*. International Conference on Primary Health Care, Alma-Ata, U.S.S.R., Sept.6–12. Geneva, Switzerland: World Health Organization.
World Health Organization (1983). *New approaches to health education in primary health care: Report of a WHO expert committee*. Technical Report Series 690. Geneva: World Health Organization.
World Heath Organization (1986).*Ottawa charter for health promotion*. Ottawa: Canadian Public Health Association.
World Health Organization (1992). *The ICD-10 classification of mental and behavioral disorders: Clinical descriptions and diagnostic guidelines*. Geneva: World Health Organization.

World Health Organization (2001). *The World Health Report* 2001. *Mental Health: New understanding, new hope*. Geneva: World Health Organization.

World Health Organization (2002). *Atlas: Mental health resources in the world*. Geneva: World Health Organization. Available at www.cvdinfobase.ca/mh-atlas/

World Health Organization (2004a). *Promoting mental health: Concepts, emerging evidence, and practice: Summary report*. Geneva: WHO Library Cataloguing-in-Publication Data.

World Health Organization (2004b). *Prevention of mental disorders: Effective interventions and policy options: Summary report*. Geneva: World Health Organization.

World Health Organization (2005a). *The Bangkok charter for health promotion in a globalized world*. Retrieved 7/8/2007, http://www.who.int.healthpromotion/conferences/6gchp/Bangkok_charter/en/print.html

World Health Organization (2005b). *New Bangkok charter for health promotion adopted to address rapidly changing global health issues. Press release*. Retrieved 7/8/2007. http://www.who.int/mediscentre/news/releases/2005/pr34/en/print.html

World Health Report (2001). *Mental health: New understanding. New hope*. Geneva: World Health Organization.

Yeich, S. (1994). *The politics of ending homelessness*. Ladham, MD: University Press of America.

Yelena, V., Podolskaya, A., Sedky, K., Shahab, H., Siddiqui, A., Munshi, F. et al. (2002). Body weight changes associated with psychopharmacology. *Psychiatric Services*, 53(7), 842–847.

Young, J., Griffith, E., Williams, D. (2003). The integral role of pastoral counseling by African-American clergy in community mental health. *Psychiatric Services*, 54, 688–692.

Zahniser, J., Sanchez, M., & McGuirk, F. (1993). *The journey of Native American people with serious mental illness*. Executive Summary. Boulder, CO: WICHE Publications.

Zuvekas, S. Rupp, A., & Norquist, G. (2007). Cost shifting under managed behavioral health care. *Psychiatric Services*, 58(1), 100–108.

INDEX